PIAF

Piaf

A BIOGRAPHY BY

Simone Berteaut

HARPER & ROW, PUBLISHERS

New York

Evanston

San Francisco

London

My thanks to Marcelle Routier, who was good
enough to lend me her valuable collaboration.

SIMONE BERTEAUT

The publisher wishes to acknowledge the enormous
contribution made by June Guicharnaud in the preparation
of the translation from the French.

First published in France under the title *Piaf*. © Opera Mundi, Paris, 1969.

PIAF. *English translation Copyright © 1972 by Harper & Row, Publishers, Inc. All
rights reserved. Printed in the United States of America. No part of this book may
be used or reproduced in any manner whatsoever without written permission
except in the case of brief quotations embodied in critical articles and reviews.
For information address Harper & Row, Publishers, Inc., 10 East 53rd Street, New
York, N.Y. 10022. Published simultaneously in Canada by Fitzhenry & Whiteside
Limited, Toronto.*

FIRST EDITION

STANDARD BOOK NUMBER: 06-010313-2

LIBRARY OF CONGRESS CATALOG CARD NUMBER: 75-138706

This book is for you, Edith. I wrote it truthfully; I haven't faked any-thing. It's your voice in it—laughing and crying. Your last words still ring in my ears: "Don't do anything stupid, Momone."

Ever since, I've waited to hold your hand again, but, my God, how long this "tour" has been.

Contents

Illustrations follow page 152.

PART ONE

✻

Her life was so sad it seems almost too beautiful to be true.

SACHA GUITRY

Chapter 1

From the Sidewalks of Belleville to the "House" in Bernay

My sister Edith . . . anyway, we had the same father: Louis Gassion. He wasn't a bad guy. Liked to screw around a lot and was good in bed. He never was quite sure exactly which kids were his—but then his breeders weren't always sure who the father was either. He had kids on his hands that weren't his and some he didn't even know about. He had more than nineteen he knew of, but try and keep the record straight! In his world you don't tell city hall before you make a baby, or afterward either.

Another man gave me his name on my birth certificate, even though he wasn't my real father: Jean-Baptiste Berteaut.

My mother, who was married at fifteen and divorced at seventeen, already had three daughters whose fathers were anybody's guess. She was living on her own at the time in the same hotel as Gassion, in the cité Falguière. He'd been called up, so I was conceived during an agreeable furlough in 1917. This was no one-night stand though; the two of them had liked each other for a long time and proved it whenever they got together.

But that didn't stop Mother. Men were hard to come by in those days, so once Papa had gone back to the front, she latched onto an eighteen-year-old kid straight off the train from Autun, Jean-Baptiste Berteaut, who had no second thoughts about saddling himself with a twenty-year-old woman with three daughters, plus the one in the making: me.

And when good old Jean-Baptiste left for his regiment on his twentieth birthday, he had five kids to support. Even before I reached the age of reason there were nine of us at home and not all of us Papa Berteaut's, as we called him. It was a funny thing, but my mother and he adored each other, though that never stopped her from carousing around with a purseful of money, and coming home with the purse empty but another kid in her belly.

I was born by accident in Lyons and was taken back to Paris when I was eleven days old. My mother sold flowers on the sidewalk in the rue de la Mare, up toward the rue des Pyrénées, opposite the Belleville church.

I hardly ever went to school. Nobody in our family seemed to think it was really necessary. I did go now and then though—especially when classes started in the fall, to get the special payment for electricity, and on January first, to get shoes. This was the only good my mother could see in school. As far as the rest of it went, she would say, "An education's like money; got to have a lot of it, or else people think you're crummy." And since in those days school wasn't that compulsory, I went to the school of hard knocks. You don't learn fancy manners there, but you soon learn about life.

I often went to see Papa Gassion at his hotel in the cité Falguière; I liked visiting him, because I knew I was loved there. He thought I looked like him, skinny, limber as rubber, big dark eyes—I was the spitting image of him! He made me do exercises, treated me to big glasses of straight grenadine over ice and slipped me a few pennies now and then. I liked my father.

He called me just plain Simone—none of those nicknames parents usually give their kids. He was happy when he saw me, and thought I was growing like a weed. That probably was enough to make him think my mother was feeding me all right and bringing me up decently. The whole business of shooting up in the world must have stopped one day though, because I'm still only four feet eleven.

He was an acrobat, free lance—not in carnivals, circuses or vaudeville shows. His stage was the sidewalk. He knew every street, every square of pavement that would bring in the cash. He didn't set his show up just anywhere. He was known in the business as a guy with a sharp eye for the good corners. A professional. His name was a reference. If you said, "I'm Gassion's little girl," you were more or less respected.

On an avenue or a boulevard, anything wide enough for people to stop and hang around, Papa would spread out "the carpet"—his little square of threadbare rug. People passing by knew this was serious business; there was going to be a show.

He'd start his act by gulping some wine out of a bottle—a crowd pleaser, because if a guy takes a drink before he does his turn, it means he's really going to sweat. Then he'd make his pitch. Edith, who tagged along with him for six years of her life—until she was fourteen—imitated him very well. She adored doing imitations of people. She'd clear her throat like Papa, her voice would get hoarse and she'd be off on her spiel:

"Step right up, ladies and gents. No big ads, nothing flashy, the performer will work right in front of you; no net, no sawdust, nothing fancy. We'll start for a hundred sous."

At this point some pal of his would toss ten sous on the carpet, and another one twenty.

"I can see you're real enthusiasts, connoisseurs. For my honor and your pleasure I'm going to do right before your very eyes a balancing act on my thumbs, the only one of its kind in the world. The great Barnum himself, king of the circus, offered me fabulous sums. But I told him, 'A guy from Paree can't be bought.' Right, ladies and gents? 'Keep your gold; I'll keep my freedom!'

"Just a few more contributions and we'll begin the show that has flabbergasted the crowned heads of every country and other places as well. Even Edward, King of the English, and his son, the Prince of Wales, came down into the street from their palace to see me, just like everybody else. Everyone's equal in the presence of Art! Just another kind little gesture on your part, my princes, and we'll get on with it!"

And our old man would give them a show for their money; he was a good acrobat.

I was barely able to walk when he began to loosen up my joints. He told my mother, who didn't give a damn, "Got to teach Simone a trade; it'll help her out in life. . . ."

My whole life was lived in the street. My mother came home late at night or not at all. I don't know what she was up to; I was too little. Sometimes she took me to a cheap joint and danced while I slept on a chair. There were times when she forgot all about me and I ended up at the state orphanage, and later in a house of correction. The state always took me under its wing.

Later, I remember, she was a concierge in Ménilmontant, at 49 rue des Panoyaux. I was five.

I'd see Papa Gassion, but I didn't know Edith. I was two and a half years younger, and she was in Bernay, in the Eure. I heard about her, but that was all.

Papa loved her more than he loved me. "It's only natural," he'd say. "You have a mother and she doesn't."

I had one, if you want to put it that way. I thought for a long time, though, that all mothers were like that. The other kids in Ménilmontant didn't seem to be any better off, and we thought the kids who bragged about their mamas doing this and that were stuck-up. We didn't hang around with them. They didn't belong to *our* world.

I was born in a hospital. But Edith was born in the street, right on the pavement.

"Edith wasn't born the way everybody else is," my father told me. "It was right in the middle of the war, after the taxis of the Marne. I was in the infantry, one of those *poilus* who were supposed to march or croak—it's always the poor who get the good jobs because there are so many more of them. Edith's ma, Line Marsa—Anita Maillard was her real name—was a chanteuse. She was born in a circus, and was a real sawdust kid. She wrote me, 'I'm going to be having the baby soon; ask for a leave.'

"I was lucky—I got one and made it home.

"See, that business about flowers on our rifles, that had been over and done with for a year. And that nice, clean, joyous war, nobody believed in it any more. Berlin was a long way to hoof it.

I went straight to our dump. No coal, black bread full of straw, no coffee, no wine.

"I found the neighbors' wives yakking around my better half! 'This rotten war, and her man at the front. . . .'

" 'Beat it, ladies,' I said. 'I'll take care of everything.' It was the nineteenth of December, 1915."

When Edith told how she was born, she'd add, "Three o'clock on a December morning's no time to pop out of your mother's belly to see if it's better outside than in. . . ."

"It happened in a flash," my father went on. "I hardly had time to say hello, drop my pack, buy a bite to eat and hit the sack, when Line started to shake me and yell.

" 'Louis, this is it! The pains have started. It hurts like hell! The kid's coming!'

"Looking so pale, her face all gaunt, it sure was no time to ask her to marry me.

"Ready for anything, I'd gone to bed in my underpants. So I jumped into my duds, grabbed Line by the arm, and down we went into the street. There wasn't a damn cab in sight—they'd either already gone home or else weren't out yet. It was cold enough to freeze your balls off. We started down the rue de Belleville. Line was nagging and bawling.

" 'Don't let it be a boy—he'd have to go to war!'

"We staggered down the sidewalk like we were loaded. Line was holding her belly with both hands. And right there at the foot of a lamppost, she stopped and flopped down on some steps.

" 'Leave me here and quick get the cops to call an ambulance.'

"The rue Ramponeau police station was a few feet away. I ran into their den yelling, 'My wife's having a baby on the sidewalk!'

" 'Goddamn!' the sergeant said, a guy with a mustache and graying hair. And there were the cops, grabbing their capes off the hooks and rushing to the scene as if they were all licensed midwives.

"My daughter was born on a cop's cape under a lamppost in front of number 72 rue de Belleville."

There was no better way to "arrive" in the world. For putting over realistic songs later in life, Edith was branded the day she was born.

"Her mother wanted to name her Edith in memory of an English girl, Edith Cavell, a heroic spy who'd been shot by the Krauts just a few days before, on the twelfth of December. 'The name Edith sounds refined,' she said, 'and with a first name like that she sure won't go unnoticed.'

"After two months, Line, who was an artiste but had a heart of stone, handed Edith over to her mother, who lived on the rue Rébeval," Gassion explained.

Edith's family on her mother's side (sounds pretty classy, said like that) wasn't a bit like a family in a picture book or in proper stories for children. The grandmother and her old man were trash, two sponges soaked in red wine. "Alcohol kills 'the worm' and keeps you going," the grandmother used to say. So she'd add a little red wine to the milk in Edith's bottle. Edith called her Mena. She never knew her name, and since she didn't know any other sort of life, she thought this was what a home was like.

All this time, Private Gassion scratched his lice and hunted for his crabs in the muck of the trenches, along with other "heroes" like himself. Line had long since stopped writing to him. She had given him the kiss-off without any fancy phrases.

"Louis, we're all washed up. I've sent the baby to my mother's. There's no use coming to see me when you get back."

But that was no reason for him to abandon his kid. When he got a leave at the end of 1917—his last—he went to visit Edith and saw how awful she looked. She was all skin and bones, with a head like a balloon perched on four matchsticks. The breastbone of a chicken on the prow of a barge. So dirty you wouldn't have touched her without tongs. Still, he wasn't very snobbish about things like that. He said to himself, "Gotta do something about it. Gotta put the child in a safe, decent place. When this bitch of a war is over, I'll be doing my act again. The streets aren't any kind of a place for a little kid to grow up. What'll I do?"

At this time there weren't all the ways to get help that there are now. Anyway, it would never have occurred to our old man to ask anybody to help them. He might have been poor and living from hand to mouth, but he would never have dropped his daughter off at the state orphanage the way you leave a puppy at the dog pound.

So Papa Gassion, in his washed-out sky-blue uniform, sat down in a bistro and ordered a "mominette"—absinthe. When he had the dough he drank the "green stuff," even though he never got soused on anything but red wine, which was cheaper and not as bad for your health. But that day he needed something really strong. He'd decided he'd write a letter to his mother, who was a cook for one of her cousins, once removed, in Normandy. The cousin was a decent sort who could have been a farmer's wife, but instead ran a "house," a brothel, in Bernay.

Like a shot, Gassion's mother and "Madame" wrote back: "Don't worry, Louis, we'll come get your kid."

The "commandos" charged then and there. Louise, the grandmother, and "Madame" Marie, the cousin, came to snatch Edith from her mother's mother, who kept saying over and over, "But the little one liked it here with us, she liked it. . . ."

They took her away, and the "ladies" of the house clapped their hands and said, "A kid in a brothel's a good sign; it brings luck."

They immediately set to work scouring Edith. Two, three, four washings: she was scaly with dirt. They scraped away, she cried and struggled. Later Edith still talked about it.

"Grandma Louise had bought me new clothes; when she threw my old rags in the trash I cried, but when she tried to take my shoes off, I yelled for all I was worth, 'They're my Sunday ones!' My toes were sticking clear through them."

As they were cleaning her up, they noticed her eyes had sores and were all covered with sticky stuff. They chalked it up to the fact that she was so filthy.

It was only two months later that one of Madame's girls noticed Edith kept bumping into everything and didn't seem to see the light or the sun. She was blind. Edith remembered those days very well. She spoke of them with a kind of terror that never really left her.

The girls adored her and spoiled her.

"They were really great to me. I was their mascot. I couldn't see anything, but I could hear everything. They were good girls—not at all like streetwalkers. The two are worlds apart and . . .

"I had got used to walking with my hands in front of me to protect myself. I bumped into everything. My fingers, my hands had become sensitive; I recognized different materials by touch, and people's skins too. I could say, 'That's Carmen, this is Rose.' Most of all, I lived in a world of sounds and words; the ones I didn't understand I kept turning over and over in my head.

"What I really liked was the player piano; I liked it lots more than the regular piano—there was one of those too, but it wasn't used except on Saturday nights when the piano player came. I thought the other one, the old music box, had a fuller sound.

"I lived in the dark, the world of night, so I was very sensitive. And there's one sentence I never forgot. It was about the dolls people tried to give me. I never got them. When anyone wanted to give me one, Grandma would say, 'Don't bother, she can't see. She breaks everything.'

"So these 'ladies,' these good girls who thought of me as the kid they'd had or dreamed of having, made me rag dolls. I spent whole days at a time sitting on a little bench with dolls I couldn't see on my knees, trying to 'see' them with my hands.

"The greatest time of the day was the noon meal. We all talked and laughed. I told stories. They weren't very long, but they were mine, things that had happened to me.

"My other grandmother, the one on my mother's side, had taught me to drink red wine. I howled when they made me drink water instead in the brothel. 'Don't want any water. Mena says it's not good for you, it makes you sick. I don't want to be sick.'

"As I sat on my little bench in my darkness, I used to try to sing. I could listen to myself for hours, and when someone asked me, 'Where did you learn that?' I'd puff up with pride and answer, 'Rue Ramponeau.' Mena used to hang out in a bistro there.

"She used to drag me to dance halls, cabarets, places with accordion bands, to drink other people's health. She'd say in her voice of the Paris streets, 'Sing, darling, sing "She Was the Swallow of Our Block." '

> *On l'appelait l'hirondelle du faubourg,*
> *Ce n'était qu'une pauvre fille d'amour . . .*

"That used to make the others laugh and they'd buy her a drink."

Edith remembered living in the brothel and that the "ladies" were nice, that they danced the "java" in the evenings, that it was gay, that the place had atmosphere. It smelled of smoke and liquor, and champagne corks popped. She could catch distant echoes, but that was all. Her grandmother thought Edith had no business being with the grownups, so Edith's ear caught what it could on the fly.

Some of the customers knew her. There were two sorts for Edith: those with cultivated voices and laps of soft fabric, and others who were coarser and felt prickly.

The ladies, as Edith called them, were all soft and smelled good. Edith never saw them again after she left, until Father died; some of them came to his funeral.

"I didn't know Papa. I'd hardly ever heard of him, let alone seen him, until I was about four, I think, and was taken to the seashore. For me, the sea was a music I didn't understand at all, with smells I'd never smelled before. I sat right in the sand; it wasn't like the dirt people told me not to touch because it was filthy. They filled my hands with sand, and it slid and slid. . . . It was like water you could hold on to.

"I heard a man's voice I didn't know. 'They told me you had a little girl here called Edith.'

"So I stretched out my hands and arms to touch, and said, 'Who is it?'

" 'Guess.'

" 'It's Papa!'

"I didn't see him till two years later.

"I always thought my days spent in darkness gave me a very

special sensitivity. Much later, when I really wanted to hear, really 'see' a song, I'd close my eyes, and when I wanted to bring it out of the very depths of myself, out of my guts, out of my belly, when the song had to come from far away, I'd close my eyes."

I was still just a little kid when I heard about Edith. When my mother chatted with her pals, she said, "Yes, Simone has a sister Edith; she's blind."

So I had a blind sister—a blind half sister. She was in some little burg with my father's mother and it didn't interest me much to hear about her, because I had a whole raft of half brothers and half sisters right there at home. I didn't find her any more interesting than the others.

A little while after she was born, she got cataracts. She was blind for more than three years before anyone even noticed! Finally, Grandma Louise took her to Lisieux. Then she could see. For Edith it was a miracle, and she always believed in it. From that day on she was truly devoted to Saint Theresa of the Infant Jesus. She not only wore a medal for a long time, but always kept a little image of the saint on her night table.

The "miracle" that gave Edith back her sight happened in a rather funny way, I must say. I don't know who told Edith about it; I think it was Papa. Of course, at seven she could remember a lot. Edith remembered everything very well.

Bernay wasn't like the rue Rébeval. Their thinking there was more up-to-date. In a brothel you see people, high-class people, educated gentlemen. You don't think of a little blind girl as a bit of bad luck; you take care of her. Even if it costs money. And these houses took in piles of money, even in Bernay, in the Eure.

A miracle happened, if you like. The doctor in Bernay had told Edith's grandmother there wasn't much chance Edith could be cured. But Grandma Louise regularly took Edith to be treated with silver nitrate anyway. She didn't complain, but it burned. In her darkness she dreamed of light and sunshine. She tried to remember the rue Rébeval in Paris and the way it was when she could see. But she'd been very small then and had never seen very well. Light to her was all haze.

The whole town and the house were devoted to the little saint of Lisieux. One day Carmen said, "Maybe the little Carmelite with her shower of roses could work a miracle for our little girl." The whole bordello started praying, even the ladies who didn't have much reason to believe in miracles.

Grandma Louise and Madame thought it was a good idea, and between customers the girls made novenas.

Prayer is like money—it has no smell—and Madame made a vow: if Edith recovered her sight, she would donate ten thousand francs to the church—in 1921 that was a pile of dough. To seal the bargain they'd go shake the little saint's hand, the way bargains are made in Normandy.

The date was set: August 19, 1921. The fifteenth was a holiday, and they couldn't shut up shop. At the house things were at fever pitch. Madame had said, "Girls, we're all going to go. We'll close the place. That way you'll get a breath of fresh air."

Edith was rigged up in brand-new clothes. The ladies were tricked out like respectable middle-class women, real ladies on a mission of charity. Hats and gloves, but no makeup.

That morning in the parlor, Madame clapped her hands out of habit and made the girls pass inspection. The shoes weren't quite right—too many patent-leather ankle boots and high heels. The girls went out so seldom that all they had were work shoes.

As they paraded through town, curtains moved at the windows in Bernay. Call in your roosters—the chicks are loose! They missed the point. The ladies were off on a pilgrimage.

On the local choo-choo they relaxed a little. They ate snacks and laughed, but didn't answer any of the men. They damn well knew what a man's made like, and men in the street didn't have anything other men don't. Besides, one didn't speak to strangers.

That day Lisieux was treated to the sight of an unbelievable procession—all the girls trooping along practically on each other's heels. They walked with their eyes lowered; you'd have sworn it was a convent on the march. They went to the basilica with Edith, and all day long, more or less, they burned candles and told their beads. They also grabbed the chance to ask a favor for themselves. They heaved sighs. They choked back tears. They bathed, they wallowed in purity. As they left the basilica, they felt clean as could be except for their feet.

"God, my dogs are numb! Can't wait to get these clodhoppers off! Can't wait to get into my slippers!"

Dead beat, fagged out, the ladies went home that night and had an enormous feast with no men around; they even tossed off some champagne. They slid between the sheets with the good feeling of having really done their duty.

They awaited the miracle patiently. It was set for the twenty-fifth of August, Saint Louis's day, Papa Gassion's saint's day. Grandma Louise had prayed, "Saint Theresa of the Infant Jesus, let the little one see for Saint Louis's day."

The miracle was that it really happened, that very day.

At the stroke of noon on August 25, the ladies got up, one by one, dragging around the kitchen in their negligees, mingling their heavy perfume with the warm smells of the sauces, yawning, eyelids puffy, watching Edith. They looked at her eyes and asked her one question after the other.

"Can you tell it's sunny?"

The kid held out her hand.

"Yes, I can feel it; it's hot."

At seven that night, the whole house was down in the dumps. The miracle certainly was taking its time. They didn't dare believe in it any more.

"We have to put her to bed; it's time. Maybe tomorrow," said Grandma Louise.

But no Edith. They finally found her in the parlor, playing "*Au clair de la lune*" on the piano with one finger. This didn't surprise any of them—she liked doing that.

"Time for bed."

"No! What I see is too pretty."

They were stunned. They'd been waiting for the miracle, they believed in it. But now they didn't dare to.

Grandmother trembled.

"What is it that's pretty, darling?"

"This!"

"You can see?"

She could see. And the very first thing she saw were the piano keys. They all fell on their knees, crossed themselves, and the house was closed. Too bad for the customers; business and miracles don't mix!

Edith was almost seven years old.

Then Papa Gassion showed up, and was very happy. Edith was like other kids—she could see! He had a normal child.

Edith went to school for about a year. She had everything to learn. But the "nice" people in Bernay were scandalized. When Edith's father got into town, the young village priest gave him a lecture.

"You've got to take this child away. You must understand that her presence here is shocking. While she was blind, it was all right to let your little girl be raised in a 'house' like that, but now that she can see, sir, what an example for a pure little soul! Such a situation cannot be tolerated."

And so Edith, the "pure little soul," landed on the sidewalk next to Papa.

Those few years weren't good ones. She often spoke to me about them, but she was bitter. Father, though, considered them pretty funny and was quite willing to talk about them.

From about the age of eight to fourteen, Edith was dragged from dance halls to cheap bars, from sidewalks to public squares, from cities to villages. Later, when she told me the story of this period of her life, Edith said:

"I walked so much with Papa I really shouldn't have any feet left. My legs ought to be worn away up to the knees. My job was to pass the hat. 'Smile,' Papa used to say. 'That makes people give.'

"To get a few pennies to pay for an 'amourette' [absinthe] he had some odd tricks up his sleeve. We'd go into a café, he'd spot some dame who didn't look too bitchy and he'd tell me, 'If you sing something for the lady, you can pass the hat and buy yourself some candy.'

"I'd sing and he'd push me toward the woman. That made others feel they should give too.

"He'd take my winnings away from me, in a very fatherly sort of way.

" 'Give me your pennies, I'll keep 'em for you.'

"We had to live somehow.

"He never told me so, but I knew he loved me. And I didn't tell him so either.

"One night, I was singing in a café in a little mining town—Bruay-les-Mines, I think. A middle-class couple was listening to me, with reproachful, wooden faces. The woman blurted out:

" 'She is going to ruin her voice.'

"Even in those days I really belted out a song at the top of my lungs.

" 'Where's your mama?' the lady went on.

" 'She doesn't have a mother,' Papa said to her.

"And all sorts of tender nothings and advice came pouring out. After an hour, having paid for Papa's drink and 'a grenadine for the little girl,' they told Papa they wanted to take care of me: I'd go to a boarding school, I'd learn to sing, they'd adopt me. They offered Papa lots of money, and he got hopping mad.

" 'Are you crazy? My kid's not for sale. Maybe my daughter doesn't have a mama any more, but she has mothers.'

"It was true I didn't lack for mothers. He took up with different dames all the time.

"Papa had plenty of nerve. He'd discovered a trick that worked every time. When he was through with his act, he'd pick his handkerchief up off the carpet, wipe his hands with it and announce:

" 'And now my little girl's going to pass among you to take up a collection, then she'll do three dangerous front somersaults and three backward somersaults to thank you!'

"I'd go around the circle of onlookers and come back to Papa, who at that point turned into a real genius. He'd stroke my forehead with his hand and say:

" 'Ladies and gentlemen, would you have the heart to let this little girl do dangerous somersaults with a fever of 104? She's sick. Your money's going to be used to take her to the doctor. I'm an honorable man though—if I make a promise, I keep it. If there's anybody that still wants her to do the somersaults, she'll do 'em.'

"Then he'd slowly go around the circle again, saying, 'Anybody that wants her to do 'em, raise their hand.'

"No one dared raise his hand at the sight of that poor, pale, skinny kid with the bulging forehead and feverish eyes burning in her face like two holes.

"There was only one time when things threatened to go wrong. 'I paid, and I want to see it. What kind of a con job is this?' some grouch complained.

"Papa didn't turn a hair.

" 'The kid'll sing you "*J'suis vache*." ' "

> *Trois semaines après qu'il était parti,*
> *Je couchais avec tous ses amis.*
> *Ah, j'mériterais des coups de cravache,*
> *J'suis vache.*

"I was nine years old. . . ."

That was the first time Edith sang in the streets. It wasn't the last. Papa had dreamed of making an acrobat out of her. He used to say, "This kid's got everything in her throat and nothing in her hands and legs."

No, he wasn't a bad father. He did everything he could and more.

He may have done a bad job. Edith always had a lot of step-mothers. Maybe having just one would have been better, but there were some good ones in the lot, and when she was a kid she had enough to eat more often than I did.

I would have liked being with Papa like she was, instead of being with my mother. He would have let me, the poor man, only he couldn't saddle himself with a kid like me. What in hell could he have done with me? What a pain in the ass it was just having little Edith on his hands!

Chapter 2

❧
❧
❧

The Street, My Conservatory

During the time she was "working" with Papa Gassion, I didn't know very much about Edith. I knew she'd lived in a whorehouse. I knew what whores were—I saw them every day, I gabbed with them—but I didn't know what a "house" was. My mother said, "It's a hotel whores are shut up in." I decided they were numskulls to shut themselves up like that when one's so free and happy in the street, but I didn't think any more about it; I didn't give a damn. At twelve I had other problems besides thinking about my fifteen-year-old half sister.

I knew Edith had lived with Papa and had beat it. "Your sister takes after her mother—she flew the coop," Mama said. That didn't tell me very much, but I sort of admired Edith for leaving.

I used to go to see Papa, who continued to loosen me up and had me take lessons from his pal Camille Ribon, a man everybody called Alverne, who specialized in standing on his thumbs. Every time I did a stunt, Papa'd say to me, "Your sister doesn't know how to do that," which made me rather proud, but that's as far as it went.

Alverne used to see Edith all the time, and he made her work. Even though she'd left him, Papa forced her to go have lessons. It fitted in with his ideas about how he should bring his daughter up. He also taught her the history of France. When he didn't know a

18

date or made a whopper, he'd say, "All that's so long ago, it doesn't matter if you're a hundred years off."

As the rue des Panoyaux was right near the rue des Amandiers, I often used to go to Alverne's. Papa had told my mother, "Simone ought to come and see her sister some night after work."

Because that's what I was doing—working. I was twelve and a half. I had a job at the Wonder Company assembling automobile headlights, which were much more complicated than batteries. I earned eighty-four francs a week, for ten hours' work a day. I was on a machine called a crimper. Working conditions were criminal in those days. Other kids in the neighborhood, my pals, went to work at Luxor and Traizet, companies that supplied parts to Wonder. That was the way things were; that was our life.

It was right about then that Mama said to me, "Listen, your half sister Edith's at Alverne's today. We'll go over and see how she looks."

I liked the idea. Alverne had a lousy-looking place, but the food was good and he often invited us to a meal. That's all I was interested in. I didn't give a damn about Edith.

It was a very shabby little room, pretty cruddy. There were some rings in a doorframe, and hanging from them was a shapeless thing in boy's Jockey shorts going through all sorts of contortions. It wouldn't have occurred to me that this was my sister if I hadn't noticed two little white hands.

"You Edith?"

"Yes," she said.

"Well, you're my sister."

We began to talk a little, in a kind of forced way, being all sugary to each other. Then she said to me:

"Can *you* do this?"

Since I'd already done acrobatics with Papa, I did some then and there, much better than she could. Edith always needed to admire people. She had to admire them to love them. So now her goddamn eyes popped out. She was really happy—and amazed. I was her sister and I could do things she couldn't. She thought that was great. Later on she was the one who flabbergasted me.

"What do you do?" she asked me.

"Nothing very exciting. I work in a factory and earn eighty-four francs a week."

I envied her. I thought she was quite well dressed. She had on a sweater and skirt that fit and looked like they'd been bought specially for her.

Since Edith couldn't get interested in people without wanting to take care of them, she immediately said to me:

"You can't go on doing that. You're coming with me."

"What do *you* do?" I asked.

"I sing in the streets."

Now *my* eyes popped out.

"Does that bring in the dough?" I asked.

"It sure does! I don't have a boss, I'm free, I work when I feel like it. If you want, I'll hire you!"

I was bowled over. I thought she was terrific. I'd have followed her to the ends of the earth.

Edith had got the idea of singing in the streets because she'd sung with Papa in army barracks and on public squares. Papa would rather she'd done acrobatic dancing. A little kid who's got rubber bones gets to people more than a singer. But Edith really had no talent in that direction. When Gassion wasn't in Paris, he used to do his contortionist act in cafés, preferably out toward Versailles. He liked the place. This made quite an impression on Edith, and it gave her a real taste for soldiers, especially those in the Colonial Forces and in the Foreign Legion.

There was a little bench at Alverne's. We sat down and Edith told me all about what she was up to.

"I learned to sing with Papa, see. I know the good spots. I know how to go about things."

"But you aren't with him any more."

"No. We got a little fed up with each other. He swiped all my dough. I'd also had a bellyful of stepmothers—the last one especially. She used to smack me in the face, and I'm too old for that. What's more, she once knocked me around because a guy kissed me.

"When I left Papa I felt like getting some sort of steady work.

I'd had my fill of living from hand to mouth, and besides, I couldn't just stake myself out on the pavement and start singing; there's got to be two of you and you've got to have music, otherwise you look silly. People don't take you seriously. You don't look like you're working, you look like you're begging. Get what I mean?"

"So what did you do?"

"I read the ads in *L'Ami du peuple*. I chose that sheet because of the name. It set me back fifteen centimes. I got me a job in a dairy store on the avenue Victor Hugo. Some job! I got up at four in the morning, delivered the milk, washed up the store. It's a real snazzy neighborhood, but the tips were nil. All you ever see are the damn maids, and they keep the tips for themselves, the little sluts!

"I couldn't help singing. But the boss didn't like my voice, so he canned me. I worked at another dairy store, but it wasn't for me."

"How did you happen to start singing?"

"It was because of a little guy called Raymond. He liked my voice. He had a pal, Rosalie, and we worked as a group: Zizi, Zozette and Zozou. We sang in public squares and in barracks. I'm not with them any more, but I went on singing and it's going all right. I accompany myself on the banjo. I know how to play one— I learned how."

Night had fallen. We had to say good-bye to each other and it was nice out. I remember Edith said to my mother:

"Listen, if you want, she can come and work with me. You'll see—singing in the streets brings in the dough."

My mother couldn't care less. I could just as well have been a streetwalker, as long as she got some money out of it.

So Edith and I went out together. We worked our first street— the rue Vivienne. We must have hauled in a hundred francs or so that night. When my mother tumbled to the fact that singing paid better than working at the Wonder factory, she was in seventh heaven.

Edith said, "We'll divide things half and half."

We went dancing with my mother in the Temple section of town; she liked it there. Don't get the idea that the dance halls we went to were real dance halls. It was all pretty lousy—hoods and pimps. There were two or three guys who could just about play the accordion and the banjo. In those days you shelled out the money and you danced in sawdust.

> *Ça sentait la suer et l'alcool,*
> *Ils portaient pas de faux cols*
> *Mais de douteux foulards de soie.*

My mother had blown all the dough Edith had given her: fifty francs. All the way home she kept giving me the "Momone dearie" business. She even kissed me, though I knew she couldn't stand me.

That night, sleeping four in a bed at home, on a folding cot without sheets or blankets, I thought about Edith. *She* was free. There was another way of living! I thought about it so much I couldn't get to sleep.

Finally I did, of course. But I woke with a start. I was going to miss Edith! I jumped out of bed (I slept with all my clothes on), put on my shoes and ran till I was out of breath.

Edith had told me to meet her around ten that day. I was late. Maybe I'd missed her and blown the whole thing. I'd have missed the most important meeting of my whole life. Edith was my one chance.

I got there just as she was coming out of Alverne's; luckily we bumped into each other. A few seconds later and I'd have loused up everything. I might have met her again, but it wouldn't have been the same. I'd have gone back to the factory and lived with my family—that drunken, good-for-nothing, whoring bunch.

To them I was already a money machine. Anyway, I'd had the feeling Edith loved me. Being loved: that really meant something to a kid from my neighborhood. When she saw me, her expression changed. I saw that smile people only give you once in a great while, and felt those few seconds of happiness you feel all over. We kissed each other as though we'd been separated for ten years.

I put my hand in hers and we went out and sang in the streets. My job was to pass the hat, and we got quite a bit this time too. That evening we went to my mother's and I again gave her part of our takings. A few days went by, and things were still going fine. It was only later Edith kicked up a fuss.

"I didn't clear out of the old man's to live the way I want only to fall under your mother's thumb and have to report to her and account for myself. I'm sick of your mother; we're not going to bring her dough every night. Got to be free to work. We're going to live together."

I couldn't say a word—I was too happy.

We hunted up my mother. Edith had the cheek to say, "I'm hiring your daughter for good; she'll be my responsibility. She's going to come and live with me—I've got a room."

My mother, a practical sort, answered, "That's all right with me, but you'll have to sign a paper for me."

Edith didn't back down. She gave me a contract—the first one she ever signed. It was pretty funny because my mother hardly knew how to read and Edith hardly knew how to write. But she gave her the paper:

I, Edith Giovanna Gassion, born December 19, 1915, in Paris, residing at 105 rue Orfila, a performer by profession, do declare that I am hiring Simone Berteaut for an unlimited length of time, for a salary of fifteen francs per day, plus room and board. Signed, sealed and delivered in Paris, on . . . , 1930.

My mother kept this scrap of paper in the drawer of the cupboard for a long time and showed it to everybody.

I couldn't have been dizzier if I'd been hit over the head. I couldn't get over it. Fifteen francs a day was lots of money, much more than I got at the Wonder Company, especially since they didn't pay for Sundays and my new job did.

We took off together. What were we? Two kids without a thing to our names. Two little bits of things four feet ten, weighing ninety pounds.

Every day Edith handed fifteen francs over to my mother, in coins she counted out one by one into her hand. Then after a while we only went to my mother's every other day, then every three days, then not at all. That's how I left my mother for good at the age of twelve and a half. As for her, she really didn't give a damn.

Don't get the idea that life with Edith wasn't organized. Edith always was a good organizer. She had a way of getting other people to do what she wanted. She could ask them whatever she pleased, the wildest sort of thing, and I never saw a man or woman who said no. You didn't say no to Edith—it wasn't possible.

I was the one who sang the first songs when we started out in the morning. I was a lousy singer. It's only lately, though, that I've realized I sing badly. I'd always thought Edith kept me from singing out of jealousy. You sometimes get the silliest notions. . . . But it didn't matter much; what counted for me wasn't singing, but living with Edith.

I was home alone not long ago. The tape recorder was sitting there, so I had myself a little music festival. I listened to myself sing some of my favorite songs. What a comedown! I couldn't believe my ears. I knew my voice wasn't anything compared to Edith's—she was unique. But singing that badly! It was godawful. In a sense it pleased me. The only little cloud inside me had just blown away.

I used to sing the first songs because Edith had trouble singing in the morning. She had to wait for her voice to come back, even when she was fifteen. When she woke up she had absolutely no voice at all. She had to drink coffee and gargle with something, and to do that we had to earn ten francs. So I was the one who hauled in the first ten francs. It took so long!

As soon as she'd swallowed the coffee and gargled, that was the end of that; we could work any part of town. She could have sung all day and all night. We didn't, but she could have. The amazing thing is that she always had that same voice—the voice everybody got to know. The voice worth millions later on.

She sang so loud her voice drowned out the noises in the street, even the honking horns. She used to say, "You see, Momone, I'm going to sing, and people on the fifth floor, the sixth floor and even the top of the Eiffel Tower will take a look."

It was true—people threw us pennies that seemed to fall from heaven. She drew big crowds in the street. In fact, one day a cop in civvies said to her, "Listen, this is my beat. I can't let you do this. Go across the street and sing 'The Barge' for me. It's my favorite song, and no one sings it the way you do."

We went across the street. Edith sang for him and he handed her five francs. She kept them and that night we showed them to our pals.

"A cop paid me to sing. That's what I call fame, right?"

We didn't work courtyards yet. We did much later when we worked nights in cabarets. She'd be dead tired in the mornings and would sit down on the garbage cans. Damned if she didn't go to sleep on them!

Audiences in courtyards are lousy. They won't go out of their way to come and listen to you; you have to force them to. So some like it and others don't. . . .

There were concierges who didn't take to you either; you had to parley with them, and it didn't always work out. Since Edith didn't have much patience, she'd tell them to go fuck off. People would yell and open their windows, but not to throw pennies out. As soon as it got a little cold, all the dames stayed inside where it was warm. They were bigger tightwads than men. For every one who was sentimental and dreamy, who got tears in her eyes when she heard a love song, there was a whole raft of housewives with hearts of stone, hearts covered with calluses—and with mugs like the ones *they* had, love songs didn't set them to dreaming, didn't even make them feel sorry for themselves. They'd forgotten!

It was different in the streets. People went out of their way to come see if they liked us—and they stayed. Edith never held out her hand. That was my job. I looked them straight in the eye and zeroed in on them. Edith used to say:

"With the orbs you've got, stick right with 'em. Don't let a single one get away."

So I'd stare at them till they put their hands in their pockets. Men were a softer touch than women. A man's got less nerve—he doesn't dare pass two kids by without coughing up something.

We didn't have any special neighborhood. We changed often— it gave us a chance to sightsee. When we got to a new part of town, our first job was to hunt up a policeman and ask him where the station was, then go sing as far away from it as possible. Singing in the streets together wasn't allowed—the law called it "collective begging."

We got hauled off to the station more than once, but they always let us go. They were always nice to us, because we were very young, just kids really. The cops thought it was just some crazy notion of ours. They didn't take us seriously, and what's more, we made up stories to tell them. We said we lived with our papa and mama, who didn't have much money and were pretty stingy, so we fooled around and sang to buy ourselves dresses, shoes, tickets to the movies—anything. And it worked. The only thing you couldn't tell them was the truth. I was a minor and so was Edith. That was enough to send us to the Bon Pasteur shelter, or some other joint like it. Two kids dragging around the streets all day long looked a little immoral. And hobnail boots were the keepers of virtue!

We didn't dress like hobos, but we weren't far from it. I had a beret I used for taking up the collection. We both had bangs—we cut them ourselves—because Edith thought it was better if people could see right off the bat that I was her sister.

"You see, it's better if you look like me when I tell the cops you're my sister. We don't have any papers and that way they believe us."

I didn't mind, I had nothing against it; it pleased me to look like Edith. I loved her from the very first, not because she was my sister—blood doesn't speak very loudly when you're only half sisters —but because she was Edith.

We lived at the Hotel de l'Avenir, at 105 rue Orfila. It's still there. Every time I pass by, I stop and look at the window on the fourth floor, ours, the window of our room. There was just the one room, with no running water—a bed, a table with a basin, a sort of dilapidated closet, maybe a little night table, but nothing else. The name of the hotel—the Hotel of the Future—seemed a bit ironic to me, and I told myself that, indeed, the only thing we had to look forward to was the future. But as we'd be coming home very early in the morning on the métro, so sleepy we'd be staggering, Edith would open one eye and say:

"Never mind, Momone. We'll be rich. Filthy rich. I'll have a white car and a black chauffeur. We'll both dress exactly alike."

She was convinced that's how it would be. That she was bound
to become a star. But to make sure, she'd go to church to pray to
little Sister Theresa of the Infant Jesus. She used to say to me, "Give
me twenty cents. I'm going to light a candle to her." Edith never
had a sou on her. Even later, I was always the one who kept the
money.

Meanwhile we sang in the streets. When we had enough money,
we went to a restaurant and gobbled up everything in sight. Then
we went out and sang again so we could go to the movies. We never
thought about the ten francs we'd need the next morning; we'd end
up the day without a cent to our names. We simply had to spend
everything we made. And it was that way the rest of Edith's life.
We sometimes had days when we earned three hundred francs; that
was lots of money back in 1930.

When I met Edith, she'd already slept with men; at fifteen that
was already past history. She didn't remember the first one. He left
her with nothing—no memories, not a blessed thing. She'd met the
second one at Alverne's—a sidewalk performer who played the
banjo and the mandolin. He sang "When the White Lilacs Bloom
Again" and passed the hat. He'd taught her three notes of "Boys
in the Navy." She always started with that on her banjo. She played
it badly, but she did have one. It was like the guitar is now—everybody could play a little.

Our usual repertoire was made up of three songs: "The Barge,"
"The Rogue" and "My Beautiful Pine Tree." But for the rich
neighborhoods it had to be better, so we also sang them all of Tino
Rossi's songs because *they* had class! And we knew "The Vagabond
Kids":

> *C'est nous les mômes, les mômes de la cloche,*
> *Clochards qui s'en vont sans un rond en poche . . .*

That wasn't for the classy sixteenth arrondissement, but it was our
national anthem. You had to know how to choose your repertoire
for each neighborhood. Basically it's like in vaudeville shows. The
street's a good school. That's where you get your diploma in singing. You see the audience—it's there in front of you, touching you.

You hear its heart beating and it says what it thinks. You know what pleases it, what it doesn't like. And if it cries now and then, the take'll be good.

In certain neighborhoods we used to go barefoot, but in others we had to wear rope sandals, because going barefoot shocked people. If we didn't wear the sandals, we took in less money. To save wear and tear on them, we tied them together by the laces and hung them around our necks. Now that I think of it, we were the first hippies, with banjo instead of guitar, and like them, we weren't very clean. . . . It's no different; what it all comes down to is: poetry, hope and wanting to live your own life while you're young.

I don't remember being either hungry or cold. My memories tell me it was never winter that year. It must have been cold sometimes, but I just don't remember. There was never any rain either!

We worked all of Paris, from Passy to the Porte de Montreuil. On Saturdays we stayed away from the ritzy neighborhoods. People there do their shopping on Saturdays; they're in a hurry and have a hell of a lot of other things to do besides listen to you.

During the week you could work the Champs Élysées. Passy and the sixteenth arrondissement were good in the morning; the women were still around. If they saw two kids singing in the street, they felt like opening the window and giving money, but they shut the windows right away because of the cold. It was a charitable audience, not an audience of music lovers.

Saturdays we'd hit the working districts; people there gave less at a time but gave more often. Then, too, they gave for pleasure, because they were happy, not just to be charitable. For them Edith would sing "Titania":

> *Mon maître Satan m'envoie faire la ronde;*
> *J'ai des provisions de joie et de plaisir.*
> *J'ai de quoi flatter tous les vices du monde,*
> *Et mon coeur est prêt pour le moindre désir.*

We made a good living. We had enough money to buy clothes, but we dressed badly—a skirt and sweater, that's all we ever wore.

From time to time we'd buy new ones because the old ones had got too dirty even for us. We never washed anything.

There already was a whole raft of young guys and older men flocking around Edith. She made a hit with them. I was still very young; I couldn't go over as well with them. But we were so mangy, it did put them off a little. No doubt about it: when it didn't work, even later on, it was because we were dirty.

When Edith was seventeen and I was fourteen and a half, we also started to work army barracks. But we did that mostly in the middle of winter; it gave us somewhere warm to hang out. Edith already had a soft spot for soldiers. There was a whole rigmarole to go through. You had to ask the colonel's permission, and that took time. For a while we worked different barracks with a pal called Zoé. I don't know what became of her. She was a big help to us. You can't be prudish with soldiers—they don't go for that. Zoé took up with any of the guys. If there was one nobody wanted, she'd take him.

All this took place in mess halls and canteens. Edith sang and I did my acrobatic number. When we were through, the guys would make dates to meet us in cafés. That's how Edith got to know all the bistros where legionnaires, soldiers in the Colonial Forces and sailors hung out.

A soldier isn't much. A soldier's a uniform. You don't owe them anything and they don't ask for anything. Hanging out with them, we got the feeling they liked us—anyway, that we were alive. . . . Even when we didn't work barracks any more, we still went to their bistros. You aren't a nobody if a guy looks at you; you're alive. And then you can joke and fool around as much as you please. Soldiers aren't hard to get along with.

Chapter 3

Four in One Bed

One evening we met Louis Dupont in a bistro near the Romainville fort. He'd come to buy some wine to take home. He lived in Romainville, where his mother had a shack. He took to Edith. It was love at first sight, and that very night he came to live with us.

He was a little blond kid. He was eighteen and Edith was seventeen. I didn't think he was anything to get excited about; he seemed rather ordinary, insignificant. She'd had guys from the Colonial Forces who were a damn sight better built. But that one sat down at our table, just like that, put his mother's red wine down on the marble top, looked at her, and said:

"You from around here?"

"No," she said, "I'm from Ménilmontant."

"That's why I've never seen you before."

"That's right."

"Will you be back?"

"I don't know. It depends."

"On what?"

"On whether I feel like it."

"Won't you feel like it?"

"I've no way of knowing."

"Can I buy you a drink?"

"How about my sister? Can't she have one?"

"Three Pernods," he ordered.

"What do you do for a living?" P'tit Louis asked.

"I sing. I'm a performer."

"Ah!" he said, dumfounded. "And does it pay?"

"A little. How about you?"

"I'm a bricklayer. That's my trade, my real one. But right now I don't have a job so I'm working as a delivery boy. I have a bike. I like pedaling around, and then there's the tips, so I make around a hundred and sixty a week."

Edith and I laughed. He was peeved.

"Come on, that's not bad—I'm only eighteen."

"Listen, on good days we make three hundred in a day. But so what? I like you, and money can't buy that."

They went on talking about themselves as if their lives depended on it. I'd tuned out—they made me tired—and besides, that kind of conversation, all that playacting, was old hat to me. But this time things didn't end the way they usually did.

He left to take the wine to his mother; he wasn't a bad guy. Edith was worried stiff while he was gone.

"Listen, Momone, do you think he'll be back?"

"Of course. He's hooked."

"You think he likes me?"

She patted her hair the way they do in the movies. And went off to put new lipstick on, a terrific red, bloody as a hunk of beef. She tugged at her sweater, which for once was fairly clean. There was a worried look in her eyes, the kind that comes from love.

I was to see and hear those gestures and words repeated so many times during our life together that I ought to have found them worn and threadbare. Edith was eighteen every time she fell in love. It was always her first and last love, the kind that only comes along once and lasts a whole lifetime. Edith believed it and I believed it.

When Edith was in love, she went wild. She ate her heart out, she was jealous and possessive, she had doubts, she howled, she locked her guys up. She was demanding, she was unbearable; they slapped her around and she cheated on them. She was impossible.

That was what love meant to her. She blossomed in the midst of shouts and scenes—they made her happy.

"When love gets lukewarm, Momone, you either have to heat it up again or chuck it. Love doesn't keep on ice!"

Whether she was in love for a year or a day, it was always the same story; she didn't see any difference.

"Love isn't a question of time, it's a question of quantity. I couldn't do any more loving in ten years than I can in a day. It's all right for the middle class to keep feeling the same old thing. People like that are thrifty, they're stingy; that's why they're rich: they don't burn all their kindling at once. That may be a good system when it comes to dough, but it's no good at all for love."

In the Romainville joint she was only seventeen, she'd just met P'tit Louis and she was already on tenterhooks waiting for him. I was only fourteen and a half and I had to follow her lead. So I did.

"If the bastard doesn't come back, I may do something assy," she said.

It wouldn't have been the first time. To forget, she'd drink or hunt up another guy.

The two of us sat there at our table, our arms crossed, staring at the door, waiting.

P'tit Louis came in. No, it couldn't be—it had to be his brother or somebody else in his family! When we'd first met him, he was wearing blue overalls and his hair was a mess. Now he had on a jacket and tie, and his hair was plastered down with cooking oil, with a neat part on the side.

"My name's Louis Dupont," he said. "They call me P'tit Louis. How about getting together?"

"All right," said Edith ecstatically.

It was as simple as that. Of course, lots of stories went around: that he'd heard her sing, that he admired her. As a matter of fact, he hated her singing; it sent him off his rocker. He thought it was no way to make a living. He was jealous because when she sang, men ogled her, and deep down he was scared she'd forget him. Like all the others, he wanted to keep her all for himself.

There they were, sitting across from each other in the bistro and looking at each other. It was mostly Edith's face that changed. Her eyes got huge, and suddenly looked both warm and gentle. This was love, and her whole body was trembling with it.

All three of us went back to the Hotel de l'Avenir on the rue Orfila. The thought that I should sleep somewhere else would never have occurred to any of us. For us to have had separate rooms, we'd have had to have the kind of money we didn't have. Anyway, we didn't see anything wrong about it. There was a deep purity in Edith that nothing ever spoiled. Three in a bed may not be right, of course, but at seventeen and as poor as we were, love is so marvelous, it's made silently. It lulled me, and I dropped off to sleep like a little kid.

If Edith shacked up with P'tit Louis, it was because he was the first one who'd ever thought to ask her to. She daydreamed about it.

"You see," she said, "this is it—I've settled down. That's not bad at seventeen. Do you think he'll ask me to marry him?"

"Would you say yes?"

"I guess so."

P'tit Louis didn't dare. His mother needed his paycheck and she would never have let him.

Things happened fast. Two months later Edith was pregnant.

"I'm going to have a baby! We're going to have a baby. Are you pleased?"

I didn't quite know what to make of it. I told myself it wasn't going to make our life any simpler. But neither of us really realized that. We didn't understand any of it. We didn't have a thing ready. We didn't have any idea what was needed for a newborn baby.

For a few days Edith felt important. "I'm going to have a kid," she told her pals with a serious look on her face. They had mixed feelings about it. Not Edith. She was living with P'tit Louis, she was going to have a baby and that was fine; it was the way things were. P'tit Louis was pretty happy, but he didn't know any more about it than we did.

Edith may have come close to becoming the wife of a bricklayer, a good little mother who at the beginning would have sung as she cooked and then wouldn't have sung at all any more. Maybe she'd have become a drunk and yelled and screamed if there'd been too many kids.

Nothing was changed for us. P'tit Louis went on with his work, and Edith with hers. He wanted her to stay home and drove us nuts harping on the subject.

"Your job's miserable. First of all, being a performer isn't a trade; it's not real work. You're going to be a mother. There's no such thing as a mother who sings in the streets!"

Poor guy! His dream was Edith in two rooms with a toilet on the landing and a good job as a skilled factory worker. And his dream almost came true.

Edith couldn't really sing in the streets now that she was pregnant—a big belly was godawful. We didn't look like performers any more—we looked like beggars. So we worked making pearl funeral wreaths. They were signing people on for the job near the rue Orfila. We did the backgrounds, painting the pearls black with a spray gun. Then some other women—real artistic—made the flowers on the wreaths with colored pearls. Edith sang while she worked, and her friends thought it was great.

Louis Dupont kept saying, "See? It's terrific. You're paid every week, it's steady work, and you're inside where it's warm. You sing. Isn't all that a nice change for you?"

It didn't change very much. We were still eating out of cans in our little room, with all of us sitting on the bed because there weren't any chairs. P'tit Louis had set us up in housekeeping. He'd swiped three knives, three forks and three glasses from his old woman's. Edith didn't want any plates.

"I'm never going to do dishes," she announced.

And she never did.

"Anyway, I'd rather eat in restaurants," she said. Working in the streets, we could afford restaurants, but not when we worked on wreaths.

It got Louis nowhere to say, "Making wreaths is a good job. There'll always be corpses." He plagued her, but Edith didn't want to make wreaths, she wanted to be in the streets, she wanted her freedom. The street's magical, it's wonderful. Singing in the streets in those days was almost a fairy-tale world for us.

P'tit Louis was jealous. The two of them argued and fought. More than once they ended up at the Gambetta police station close by. It just couldn't work. He was a little workman, and she was already Edith Piaf. She didn't know it, you couldn't see it, but that's who she was.

He was jealous and he had every reason to be. She cheated on him, time and time again, even though she was fond of him. She kept him around. I don't know if she still loved him. . . .

She always needed to have a man around the house. For her it was something to lean on. Edith acted with P'tit Louis the way she was to act with all her men; it never varied.

It was simple. Edith was a healthy girl. P'tit Louis had made her a baby. He was the father. This was something real, not a lot of crap.

She had an easy pregnancy. If she hadn't gotten bigger, she wouldn't have felt a thing. On the day we'd been told to, we went to Tenon Hospital. She stayed and I went back to the wreath place.

"When's it going to be?" the girls at the factory asked me.

"Right away."

"Does your sis have everything she needs for the kid?"

"She doesn't have anything. What does she need?"

"Well . . . diapers, belly bands, shirts. It's not Baby Jesus! The kid can't go around with a bare ass."

We hadn't thought of that. The girls couldn't get over it. They were amazed that anybody could be that dumb.

"You aren't going to wrap him in newspapers. Get going—you got to take all those things to your sister."

"What'll I buy 'em with?"

This stumped them. It stumped me too.

"Don't you worry," Big Angela said to me. "We'll take care of things." The girls gave us everything, a layette and the whole works. They were terrific.

Edith was happy to have her baby—a little girl. She named it Marcelle. She liked that name. It's one that crops up several times in her life. Take the people she loved best: Marcelle, her daughter; Marcel Cerdan; Marcel, my son and her godchild. The name Louis also meant a lot in her life: Louis Gassion, our father, P'tit Louis, Louis Leplée, Louis Barrier.

Cécelle, as we called her, was a fine-looking baby, and Louis was happy. He immediately recognized her as his legal daughter, but he didn't offer to marry Edith. He was wise not to, because it was all over between them; Edith would have said no.

Now that there was the baby, Louis imagined he could hold on to Edith and lay down the law. At first Edith said:

"I'm going back on the streets. Cécelle needs money; I'm going to earn some. You know where you can shove that wreath job."

There were four of us in the room now and once again I slept four in the same bed. There was no heat; Edith warmed herself in P'tit Louis's arms. I was lucky enough to have Cécelle; I went to bed wearing a heavy sweater and under it I put her warm little body next to mine.

We didn't know the baby's milk had to be boiled, so she drank it unboiled. We rinsed the bottle because it seemed right, and then gave it to her just like that. We did warm it, and we put sugar in it, because Edith said sugar was nourishing and made babies strong.

We wrapped the kid up and took her with us when we went out singing. She always went with us. Edith wouldn't have left the baby behind for anything in the world. It was her way of loving her. She wouldn't have dreamed of leaving her alone all day at the hotel. When we went from one end of Paris to the other, we took the métro, never the bus, because of the drafts.

When the baby's clothes were dirty, we worked a street and bought her new ones. Until she was two and half she wore only new clothes. We never washed anything. It's a good method. Anyway, we didn't know how to do laundry. Edith knew how to sing, all right, but she didn't know how to wash!

It wasn't a bad way to live. We lived from day to day, but it wasn't bad. Things weren't so hot when it came to living with P'tit Louis though. He made a few deliveries on his bike, and Edith sang in the streets. Louis stayed with Cécelle in the hotel. When we'd get home late at night, he'd be snoozing. Sometimes Edith woke him up, and other times she'd leave him alone, but we always made a row when we came in, and this made the kid cry. Some nights we didn't go home at all. The knocking around Edith got for it didn't change her; she did whatever she pleased.

And anyway, something new was about to happen. Edith was beginning to have ideas about her profession; the whole thing was still vague, but it was already on her mind.

She knew the streets. She knew her work. She'd learned. She hadn't really made progress; she didn't sing any better, but she'd gotten together a kind of repertoire, made up of popular songs—songs from the working districts, sidewalk refrains. There was something better in the offing.

Edith used to stop and daydream in front of the posters advertising "real" performers, the ones who sang in vaudeville shows, at Pacra, at L'Européen, at A.B.C., at Bobino, at Wagram: Marie Dubas, Fréhel, Yvonne Georges, Damia—the "great stars." On the boulevards people would go into bistros and bars to hear them on the jukebox. They were real artists, and Edith's ears ate them up.

"It's as if I could see them," she'd say. "No kidding, I see them when I hear them. That's what comes from having been blind. Sounds have shapes, faces, gestures; voices are like the lines on the palm of your hand—everybody's are different."

That's what was new. Edith was beginning to realize that singing is a profession.

I took her up to the place du Tertre. It was when we began going up to Montmartre that Edith started making progress. It gave her self-confidence. She could see people at the place du Tertre who were serious about their work, yet not earning much of anything, just small change. Edith arrived on the scene and sang; the others watched her and were jealous; she made money right off the bat. She raked in more than the professionals. That made her think. Singing wasn't just the streets; there were songs to be sung other places, where the "great stars" were.

One night as Edith and I were walking down the rue Pigalle, we went by a nightclub, the Juan-les-Pins. Charlie, the doorman and barker, who worked on the dawdlers and loiterers to get them to come in, was standing outside. He talked with us. He saw we were just kids, and not much to look at. As usual, we were hardly well groomed. But Charlie thought we were fun to talk to; we weren't like the customers he was used to. He asked us what we did.

"I sing," Edith said.

All of a sudden Lulu, the owner of the place, popped out of her nightclub like a devil—the only word for it—looking pretty unfriendly, standing there with her hands on her hips, and dressed like a man from head to foot. I've always thought that underneath she must have worn men's Jockey shorts too, to look more like a man.

"What are you doing?" she called to Charlie.

"I'm talking with these kids here. This one sings and wants to become a pro," he said, pointing to Edith.

"Oh, you sing, do you?" Lulu said. "Well, come on inside and show me what you can do."

Once she'd heard Edith, she said:

"You're all right. You know how to sing. What about her?"

"She's my kid sister."

"So what?"

"She dances. She's an acrobat."

"Have her get undressed."

So Lulu stripped me then and there and said, "She'll do." She wasn't hard to please! Once I got my sweater and skirt and panties off, there was nothing left of me. One puff of breath and I'd have been airborne. Lulu slipped me a balloon and got some music playing. When I faced the audience, I hid my privates with the balloon, and when I faced away from them, I let the balloon go up in the air. I uncovered everything, but there was no one to see—that was what was perverted about it. I was bare-ass naked, doing a striptease. It was O.K. though, because I'd grown a lot and was slim. I didn't particularly want to be padded out everywhere. As a matter of fact, I didn't have any bosom or any behind. I didn't have anything. Flat as an ironing board.

"You look sort of sexless, like a kid. Everybody likes that—all my customers go for it. They get a kick out of minors. How old are you?"

"She's fifteen. She's my sister. I answer for her."

I wasn't quite fifteen, but we all knew the laws about minors. There wasn't a kid on the streets who didn't know them. Information like that gets around fast. Us girls stuck together.

Lulu's was Edith's first engagement. Straight off the streets. But don't get the idea it was a revolution. Edith sang, people liked her, but that was all it amounted to—there weren't all that many toasts to her. Nobody realized it meant something. Lulu didn't do anybody any favors; she wasn't the philanthropic type, or a patroness ready to hand out dough for art. If she hired Edith, it was because she'd pay off.

One person didn't hang out the flags—P'tit Louis. It was no national holiday for him; he looked more like it was All Souls' Day.

"It's a joint where whores hang out. I'll never see you again. What I'm saying is, we're all washed up."

Edith didn't go along with that. She wanted someone to sit with Cécelle at night. But it didn't last long. We cleared out and took the kid with us to the Au Clair de la Lune. It was handy for our jobs. Anyway, Edith liked the neighborhood. Blanche, Pigalle, Anvers were all right in her book. We got along very well without Louis as a nursemaid. The kid was about a year and a half old, it seems to me, and wasn't hard to take care of.

We didn't take Cécelle to Lulu's. We carted her around with us during the day, but not at night. At night we left her sleeping in a room, but she made our life a lot tougher.

There were times when we were so dead tired we slept under the seats at Lulu's. The B girls were good kids; they'd sit there with their legs hiding us so Lulu wouldn't see us. One of the waiters there was also a pal of ours. When he cleared a table and found a plate hardly even nibbled at, he'd look at us and say, as he passed, "Go to it, it's all yours." We'd rush down to the basement, he'd sneak us the plate and we'd eat. That was the good part about the place. But there was another side too. Lulu supposedly paid Edith fifteen francs a night. That was the agreement, but Lulu never coughed up. She kept fining us. We'd been hired to arrive at 9 P.M., but if we got there at 9:05 we were fined. She slapped us with a five-franc fine almost every night; and since there were two of us, that made ten francs. In the morning we'd leave the joint with a hundred sous in our pockets. It's not easy to arrive bang on time without a watch, especially when you don't have any notion of time. And Edith was never in a hurry when she was horsing around. Besides that, Lulu used to wallop us, me especially. I never knew why—she must have liked it.

What would have paid off was "collecting corks." You sat with the customer, gabbed with him and above all made him drink some "bubbly." You kept the corks, and when the joint closed, you lined them up the way a cat lines up its mice. They're counted and you get your dough. You have to be a real glamour girl to do that though. It's hard to make it when you don't have either an ass or big tits. Boy, did the girls at Lulu's look great without any clothes on! And were they well groomed! In those days girls wore lots of makeup, terrific eyelashes, blood-red lipstick, dizzying hairdos and platinum dye jobs. No man would have dreamed of inviting us two grubby little kids to sit with him. We kept our stage costumes on the whole time. Edith sang in a sailor suit because of the name of the joint—Juan-les-Pins. Her pants were sky-blue satin and her middy was dark blue with a little sailor collar. The costume was furnished by the house and wasn't even Edith's size.

I can still feel the atmosphere in the place—heavy, smoky, and so sad you could die! We stayed there from nine o'clock at night till the last customer had collapsed over his bottle. The piano player would bang out any old thing, sitting there with all the drooping girls sick and tired of having nothing to wait for. I don't think any of them are around any more, or anyway very few.

The piano player would play a song for Edith, who sang it in an undertone:

> *C'était un musicien qui jouait*
> *Dans les boîtes de nuit*
> *Jusqu'aux lueurs de l'aube*
> *Il berçait les amours d'autrui.*

Dawn would finally come, and it was out with the last customer! Out with the girls! Out with the pianist! And especially, out with the two of us. . . . Edith would breathe the pure air of the rue Pigalle, take me by the hand and say:

"Come on, Momone, let's sing."

All she wanted to do was work a street. She needed to feel clean, and street audiences were the only ones who gave her that feeling.

She needed to see windows open—windows where women looked out. They, at least, had had a night's sleep. They'd toss us the few coins we needed for coffee, gargling and breakfast, and as soon as we'd picked up enough money we could go back and sleep.

Edith was very strict with me at Lulu's—very, very strict indeed. She was watching over my virginity. I didn't have it long; six months later it was gone, but she continued to keep a sharp eye on me. I was fifteen years and three months old, I think, when I lost it. And I hardly even noticed: it didn't disturb anybody.

Not a soul could touch Momone. Momone was sacred. Momone was Edith's kid sister. Even when Edith slept with some guy she didn't leave me behind; she took me with her. I was so bushed, it didn't bother me or keep me from sleeping.

Since we'd got rid of P'tit Louis, we didn't have a man around any more, and there was no need to rent a room by the day. So we'd keep changing hotels. We were at the Eden, which was next to L'Eléphant, a restaurant that served meals for four francs fifty, wine and tip included, and every tenth meal was free. It was practical and saved us money. We stayed at quite a lot of hotels in the rue Pigalle, because we'd rent a room for twelve hours—it cost less that way. The twelve hours gave the baby a chance to sleep. Then we'd drag her around with us in the streets. Once, though, when we didn't have a cent to our names, we went seven days without sleeping, and then dozed off on a bench with the kid near the square d'Anvers.

Cécelle was healthy, she was pretty, and she had a nice disposition. She laughed all the time. P'tit Louis didn't approve of the way we lived. He'd come prowling around our hotels; he was terrifically clever at sniffing us out. Edith had broken up with him, but when she talked about him she used to say, "My baby's father is in business!"

She had lots of men hanging around her. Though she didn't go over big at Lulu's, she did at other places, and me too. It was the tough guys who liked us. One of our hangouts was Le Rat Mort, which isn't there any more. It wasn't any place for virtuous types, who wouldn't have stayed that way for long.

The people who hung out in Pigalle at night weren't exactly first class. They were the kind of guys who took to us. We weren't very particular, and they weren't either. Besides, we were very close to them, almost the same breed, working-class kids. We gave them a laugh. We were a change from their girls, all fresh from Brittany, whom they put straight to work in the streets. They'd say, "These two kids are great; they're a riot." Besides, this gave them a chance to relax between the fun and games with their girls.

Burglars, pimps, con men and fences were our friends—and so were their girls, their steadies. It was the underworld—the real one. That's what we liked. Those guys didn't make a big to-do about things. You came in, they said hello; you left, they said good-bye. They never asked where you came from. Or if they did, it was because they were pimping for you—although not for us.

Edith always hated being asked questions, to have to give an account of herself. In the streets we were free, and that's why she liked it so much. It was quite enough being cooped up in Lulu's place at night. But we didn't rake in a pile every time, and it wasn't always fun.

One morning we went back to the hotel and found Mme Jézéquel, our landlady, waiting for us. I wonder when that woman slept. She was always around, collecting for the rooms.

"I've got news for you," she announced.

"Bad?"

"That depends; you're the one to say. Your husband's come and taken the baby away. I couldn't do anything about it. He had his delivery bike outside—he put her in it and took off. What could I say? She's his daughter."

"Fine. He was supposed to." Edith always said the right thing at the right time.

P'tit Louis had said, "I'm taking my daughter back because this is a lousy life for a child. If her mother wants her, tell her to come get her." It was clear: he hoped this would make Edith come back to the rue Orfila hotel to live with him again. To him she was the mother of his child, his wife; she had to come back. But that wasn't the way to handle Edith. As a matter of fact, there weren't any right ways, once it was all over.

Edith didn't say a word. To be honest, the kid had been a bother when she was working.

P'tit Louis kept Cécelle. He couldn't take care of her, so she stayed by herself in the hotel. She was better off with us, because when all was said and done we hadn't taken such bad care of her. She got fresh air and was healthy.

We missed her at first. We didn't say so to each other, but there was an emptiness. We'd often worked for her. Edith used to say in a stern voice that the baby needed this or that. "Momone, we've got to get going. Cécelle mustn't lack for anything." And we'd get going.

From the day P'tit Louis took Cécelle away from us, Edith never spoke of him again—no reproaches, no memories, no nothing; blackout. Then one evening when we were so down in the dumps we could have puked, P'tit Louis came—he always knew how to find us. He didn't mince words.

"The baby's in the hospital; she's very sick," he said.

We raced to the children's hospital. Cécelle was tossing her head from side to side on the pillow. Edith murmured, "She recognizes me; I'm sure she does. You can see she does."

I didn't want to disillusion her, but Marcelle was only two and a half years old and had meningitis. She was already in a world that had nothing to do with us.

Edith tried to meet the doctor in charge of the ward. He refused to see us. . . . It wouldn't have changed anything, but I've often thought that if she'd been Edith Piaf then, he'd have seen her.

When we got to the hospital the next morning, we went upstairs and the nurse asked Edith where she was going.

"To see Marcelle Dupont."

"She died at six forty-five."

Not another word; not a single unnecessary word.

Edith wanted to see Marcelle one last time. They sent us to the morgue. Since she wanted a lock of Marcelle's hair and there was nothing to cut it off with, the morgue attendant lent her a nail file. It was hard to cut, and the baby's head kept wobbling. . . . These are memories you can't forget.

We had to dig up money for the burial. P'tit Louis said he didn't have any. He wasn't bad; he was just young. He was maybe twenty when the baby died, and Edith nineteen. No one actually realized what had happened. We were only kids.

Edith and I had to take care of everything. Her solution was to get soused on straight Pernod. I really thought that was the end of her. I found a hotel room near a joint where we used to hang out. With the help of some guys, I got her upstairs and even got her to sleep. The next morning things were better and we went back to Lulu's. Somebody'd told Lulu Edith had lost her baby, and she'd taken up a collection among the girls. But we needed ten francs more to bury Marcelle—eighty-four francs in all. Edith went out for a walk on the boulevard, saying, "What the hell . . . I'll do it."

It was the first time. She'd never done it before, never. She walked along the boulevard de la Chapelle and met a man who suggested going to a hotel room. She went with him, and when up in the room he asked her why she was doing it, Edith told him she needed the money to bury her little girl and was ten francs short. The guy gave her even more and left. All that for an undertaker to carry the little box to the cemetery under his arm like a package!

It was a very dark moment in our lives. One of the rottenest times we ever went through, maybe *the* rottenest, but to tell the truth, it didn't last long. Only a few days later we'd forgotten Marcelle had died. It was terrible. We just stopped thinking about her. We didn't go to the cemetery. Not ever. We were only kids, and we didn't give it another thought.

Chapter 4

※
※ ※
※

Papa Leplee

The streets during the day, Lulu's at night—our life went on as before. We'd already been in the nightclub more than a year, but the impresario Edith dreamed of still hadn't shown.

This was a rather unusual period for Edith. All her life she had waited for love; now she wasn't waiting for it any more. She didn't even think about it. She was waiting to become a real pro. And her chance still hadn't come along.

At Lulu's, Edith sang the best she could. We'd gone to a publisher to buy sheet music for the words. She couldn't read a note and didn't know the melodies had to be transposed in her key, but, not knowing this, she wasn't bothered by it. She had somebody play her the melody two or three times and by then she knew it. She had an extraordinary memory for music. The pianist who accompanied her played however he felt like playing, and Edith would sing without paying much attention to him. The surprising thing is that it worked out anyway.

Edith's following had grown a little because of her being at Lulu's. There was a demand for her, and she appeared in different places: at Le Tourbillon and Le Sirocco, and as an added attraction here and there. None of it amounted to much, but that didn't matter; we were quite happy. People have the wrong idea about Edith. She wasn't sad. She loved to laugh. She used to split her sides all the time, and what's more, she was sure she'd make it. She'd put her hand on my shoulder and say:

"Don't worry. Our day'll come; we'll get out of this stinking poorhouse, all this filth."

We were up to our necks in it.

But common sense told me that all these more or less crummy joints, these little dance halls in the gray streets and suburbs of Paris, weren't springboards for somersaulting to the moon. As for love, that part wasn't any too hot either—just passing affairs. Edith didn't give a damn. She took anything. It was all pretty lousy.

Edith really liked the underworld. She liked tough guys. Real he-men, not small fry who didn't know the score, punks who tried to look like hoodlums but didn't make it. We became good friends with quite a few of the pimps, and they never dropped us, never forgot us.

As far as their business went, they stayed off our backs. They were too professional to ask Edith to whore for them. But two of them damn well lived off us anyway, and at the same time: Henri Valette and Pierrot. It was Edith who had them in bed, but I used to give them money. They had us work the streets, but not as whores. The idea would never have occurred to them. They protected us. In the underworld, having a protector who was really a tough guy gave you an in, and our two were great.

Edith took them to "sing" with us in the street. They'd stake out the corner and watch for cops. They were our shills—tossing in a fiver or a tenner to get the others to give. They didn't risk losing anything because we gave it back to them, slipping in their cut. It didn't last very long. They got fed up with it and so did we! They couldn't gad around all the streets of Paris—it got to be work and it didn't do their reputations any good, because pimps who got up at eight in the morning to stand on a corner looking out for pennies and cops, they lacked class. Henri and his chum Pierrot wore beautiful felt hats as light as feathers, Borsalinos or mouse-colored velours. We thought we looked pretty nifty when we showed up at Le Rat Mort with them. After all, we had taste—a taste for them—and they were the only ones who didn't slap Edith around. They just didn't take us seriously as broads.

We stopped working for them, but we didn't leave the under-world. It had become our world.

One day, for no reason, we decided to go to the Champs Élysées. We'd worked several streets, but we'd had bad luck. Edith kept saying, "If things go on like this, I'm quitting. This isn't our lucky day."

But it turned out to be just that.

We were on the rue Troyon—and there Louis Leplée came into Edith's life. He was a very well dressed, very elegant gentle-man. Not our sort of customer. He had silver-blond hair, and his getup was a bit foppish. Well, that gentleman with his gloves, a little too well groomed, a little too well turned out, kept staring at Edith. He looked at her so intently I thought, "It can't be true. As soon as she stops singing he's going to propose to her; he's all set—he's already got the gloves!"

He walked over to her and said, "I have a cabaret on the rue Pierre Charron—Gerny's. If you want to sing at my place, come see me tomorrow." As he said this, he gave us a ten-franc note.

Edith didn't understand what was going on. He'd written his address on a corner of his newspaper. She gave it to me and said, "For God's sake don't lose it. It may be worth a fortune." Every five minutes she'd stop singing and say, "You still got it?"

Going home that night, Edith was beside herself with joy. We'd gone to take a look at the entrance of this cabaret. It wasn't any-thing like Lulu's joint.

"This guy's got a snazzy cabaret. He's going to take care of me. I know I'll find an impresario in a place like that—one's bound to turn up. It's on the Champs Élysées? You haven't lost the paper?"

And it was that little bit of torn newspaper that determined Edith's future. That very night, we went out drinking to celebrate. We drank a lot and told the story to everybody in Pigalle. . . .

We bumped into Fréhel, the singer. She hung out at the Pigalle Bar too. The first time we'd met her we were so impressed, our mouths hung open. Her name was often on posters, and she'd been to Russia. To us she was a real lady. But that didn't keep her from hanging around with pimps. And would she get stinko! Then she had no class, really, but what a singer! She sang songs like *"Tel qu'il est il me plaît"* and *"Mon Homme."*

Fréhel said to Edith, "Don't go to Gerny's. He'll inveigle you into something. White slavery still exists. You mustn't go. You don't get hired like that, especially not for the Champs Élysées."

Fréhel used to say she didn't believe in Edith. She did everything possible to spoil her act. She wanted her to wear flat heels onstage, or show her arms, the ugliest things about her. But we didn't know anything—we believed her. "You'll look smaller. It'll be more touching that way. Your little arms will melt the audience. Dress in red, in green . . . anything!" she'd say.

But we'd stopped seeing her. Edith had finally caught on. That night, the night Leplée came along, we were really happy. We had a lot of drinks to celebrate, sure, but we weren't blind drunk.

The next morning we went out singing in the streets as usual, with the black coffee and the gargling. . . . Nothing had changed. Edith had put on her black skirt to go see Leplée. It was the only one she had, but she'd brushed it. Not with a brush—we didn't have one. We took newspapers and wet them and then rubbed the spots. She'd plastered down the ends of her bangs with soap, and the rest of her hair went every which way. We'd bought her a lipstick, a nice dark garnet-red color, so she'd look O.K., and we even splurged on two pairs of rope sandals. We couldn't go to Leplée's barefoot. They were navy blue, practical: you didn't have to clean them. And navy blue's respectable. The idea was to look proper.

Legend has it that Edith was late for her appointment with Louis Leplée. It isn't true. We arrived at La Belle Ferronnière—he had asked us to wait for him there—half an hour ahead of time. Don't forget that a woman like Edith, with only one idea in her head from the very beginning—singing—realized it was a unique opportunity, a miracle, to meet a cabaret owner with dough, who was well dressed, who spoke to us politely. It was sensational.

We got there ahead of time and were scared stiff he'd make asses of us. We were so petrified we couldn't talk. Leplée took Edith to his cabaret. There was nobody there. It was in the afternoon, around four o'clock. He had Edith sing all her songs. No accompaniment. He let her sing the way he'd first heard her, and then said in a calm voice:

"Fine. You come across better here than you do in the street. What's your name?"

"Gassion. Edith Giovanna."

"It's no good. In your profession . . ."

He talked to her about her "profession." He spoke to her as if she were a singer, a real one. Here was a well-dressed gentleman, who smelled good and whose tone of voice and words weren't what we were used to, saying all this. Edith wondered if he was serious. She looked at him with those huge eyes of hers that devoured her whole face. She seemed to be looking at God Himself.

I often saw that expression on Edith's face—the expression she had when she was working, when she was listening, when she wanted to understand completely, to retain everything, to let nothing get by her.

"A name's very important. What's your name again?"

"Edith Gassion. But I sing under the name Huguette Elias."

He swept these names aside with an elegant gesture. I was fascinated by his fingernails—they were so clean, so shiny. Edith and I had never thought about a man getting his nails done. The pimps we hung around with were too small-time for that.

"I think I've got a name for you, dear: Piaf."

"Piaf, like a street sparrow?"

"Sure. Somebody else is called 'Sparrow,' but what do you think of 'la môme Piaf'?" *

We weren't too crazy about Piaf. It didn't sound enough like a performer to us. That night Edith said to me:

"D'you like Piaf?"

"Not much."

She began to think it over.

"You know, Momone, 'la môme Piaf' doesn't sound all that bad. I think Piaf's got style. A little sparrow's cute—it sings! It's gay, it's spring, it's us! That guy's not so stupid."

Edith looked up to M. Leplée right from the start. She was fond

* Literally, "Kid Sparrow."

of him. There was real affection between them. She called him "Papa Leplée," and he called her his adopted daughter.

Beginning the next day and for at least a week after that, maybe more—anyway, it seemed a long time to us—Edith rehearsed with a pianist. At the beginning there was friction. Edith had a hard time following the music. It was up to the pianist to follow her, not the other way around, to her way of thinking.

"I'm the one that's singing, not him; he can damn well figure it out."

She sang the way she wanted to.

Leplée put out a lot of publicity to get her started. Everywhere you went there were posters and newspaper ads: "At Gerny's, straight from the streets—La Môme Piaf."

"That's me! Get a load of my name! Pinch me, Momone, I can't believe it."

That wasn't true. She believed it, all right. But that was her favorite kind of playacting. She couldn't talk about anything else. And I was puffed up with pride at being her sister.

Edith, who sang the way other people down a glass of water, who had no sense of responsibility, began wondering about all sorts of things. During that week she didn't touch the bottle, she didn't sleep around—nothing. She was getting back her virginity!

All she could talk about was her good luck, and she was worrying.

"You know, I'll be all alone in the cabaret opening night. I'll be the star. Papa Leplée's sure got a lot of cheek. If it doesn't go off all right, it'll damn well break him. And what if I don't make it? What if they all boo?"

Gerny's dazzled us; it was the top of the heap. The only night-clubs we knew were the ones in Pigalle and the rue Blanche, and not the most elegant ones. So when Edith looked in our little piece of mirror and fiddled with her hair, saying, "I'm going to Gerny's on the Champs Élysées," it staggered us.

Actually, Louis Leplée's cabaret wasn't terribly elegant, but it was fashionable and it was Parisian. You didn't go there to see a show. You went there to have dinner, to hear singers who weren't necessarily famous but who were amusing. The place had atmosphere. You went there most of all to have fun, *à la française*.

Louis Leplée said to Edith, "I'm not Polin's nephew for nothing. You're too young to know, but around 1900 he was the king of the café concerts. Thanks to him I've got singing in my blood. You can trust me, dear. You're not like the rest of them, and the public likes that."

She believed him. She knew he was right.

He hadn't taken any risks with her. He was experimenting because he loved singing, real singing, and was fed up with smutty songs and dirty jokes. His street singer would either tickle Paris society between its heart and its belly, or she would make it split with laughter. Either way it would say, "That Leplée, has he got ideas! Always something new! What a guy; a genius!" He couldn't lose. If Edith was a fiasco, even though it wouldn't reflect on his place, he'd have been upset, because he believed in her the minute he met her. We'd never known a nice man like Leplée. We didn't even know people like that existed.

He was the one who began to teach Edith her profession. She didn't know the first thing about it. At Lulu's she got by just belting 'em out. The lights, the music, the setting for a song, the songs themselves, the gestures—she didn't know anything about that. She planted herself there, her hands against her skirt, and sang.

He didn't dare tell her too many things. He was afraid he'd spoil her naturalness. Even so, he had her learn new songs: *"Nini peau d'chien," "La Valse brune," "Je me fais si petite."* He'd thought of everything but her dress. He didn't have the slightest idea how poor we were.

"Do you have a dress for tomorrow night?"

Edith didn't hestitate. "Sure, a terrific black one."

It wasn't true. She didn't have a dress. Leplée was skeptical.

"What's it like? Long? Short?"

"Short."

"Wait—it mustn't look like a Sunday dress."

"It's as simple as can be."

"Bring it tomorrow."

When we left, Edith said to me:

"We don't have time to work a street and we've got to have some dough. What a jerk I am—I hadn't thought of a dress. Let's go ask our pimp Henri. He can't turn us down."

He certainly couldn't; we'd worked for him for a week once. It hadn't brought in much cash, but even so . . . He liked us—he thought we were funny kids. Henri didn't have enough dough for a dress, but he did give us enough for yarn and needles. We started to knit.

Edith knitted very well, she adored it, and later all her men benefited—each one got a handmade sweater. As we knitted, she laughed and joked.

"Papa Leplée said all the swells would be there, and me, the star, I'll be wearing a plain black knit dress. What a shock! I come straight off the streets, right? Well, you don't trail around in the streets in a dress with a train."

We knitted like mad all night long, with needles as big as fenceposts to make it go faster. Every hour she'd try it on and ask me, "Do you think it's going to fit?"

She'd chosen black as her color. Not that she liked black all that much, but she always wore black onstage.

The skirt was easy—it was straight. The sweater too, but we had trouble with the sleeves. We had to start them all over again, and the dress ended up with only one sleeve.

Edith had a solution for everything. "I'll sing with bare arms like Fréhel. It'll look dressier."

The next night, the night of the premiere, we got to Gerny's almost two hours ahead of time. Edith put my hand on her chest and said:

"Feel my heart racing? Well, it'll just have to get used to it. This won't be the last time I'll make it pound!" How right she was! She drove it hard to the very end.

Leplée arrived.

"Go get dressed—I want to see," he said.

We rushed to the lavatory, our dressing room. When he came down and saw the dress, he nearly fainted. That very polite guy began to shout:

"You're out of your mind! Shit, I don't believe it! Bare arms! Good Christ, you must think you're Damia or Fréhel. They've got arms, but look at you, just take a look at yourself, with those matchsticks. . . ."

He had taken poor Edith by the arm and was shaking her like a rag in front of the mirror.

"It just isn't true. You've ruined everything; girls like you can't be trusted. And that other idiot"—me—"she couldn't tell you how lousy you looked. I could weep. You blew it!"

As far as weeping went, we were the ones doing that. Everything down the drain because we had no money. And believe me, Louis Leplée hadn't given us a cent.

Luckily, Maurice Chevalier's wife, Yvonne Vallée, was there. When she heard Leplée shouting, she came to see what was the matter.

"Louis, you're losing your head; you're driving this little girl crazy. She won't be able to sing."

"And you think she can sing in that getup?"

"Aren't there any sleeves?"

"I only have one," Edith said. "We didn't have time to knit the other one. I can't sing with just one sleeve?"

"Haven't you got a scarf?"

That was the fashion with the "realistic" singers. They all wore scarves. We didn't know that.

Edith, who never had very much color in her cheeks, was as white as the sink.

"That won't help. Everything's ruined; I won't sing."

Yvonne said to her, "Here—here's your other sleeve." She handed her her scarf, a large square of purple silk. Edith always liked purple after that. It was sacred to her; it was her lucky color.

Down in the toilets, a half hour before Edith was to go on, we weren't in very good shape. She was green with stage fright. I was shaking so hard I couldn't open my mouth to say anything without sounding like a pair of castanets. The place was full of beautiful clothes, the last word in elegance.

People came down to report a few of the names: Maurice Chevalier, Yvonne Vallée, Jean Tranchant, Jean Mermoz, Mistinguett, Maud Loti and Henri Letellier, the director of *Le Journal*, one of the biggest dailies at the time. All those names hit us right in the kisser and made us gasp. Edith, who loathed water, swallowed glass after glass of it.

"My saliva's so thick I could spit ten-franc pieces, Momone."

Out in the club people were laughing and singing. Everybody was joining in on the choruses. We'd never once been there in the evening, so we didn't understand. We were upset. It just couldn't be; they were never going to shut up long enough to listen.

Around eleven o'clock—as happened every night—Louis Leplée went around the cabaret with his musicians getting everybody to sing "*Les Moines de Saint-Bernardin*." After that came the evening's main attraction: the new one.

Laure Jarny, the manageress of Gerny's, came to Edith and said:

"You're on."

Edith looked at me. "Momone, I've got to be a success tonight. Luck like this only comes along once."

She quick made the sign of the cross—the first time she'd ever done it before singing. After that she never went onstage without crossing herself.

It wasn't like Lulu's. Monsieur Leplée didn't want me out in the club. I didn't have any business out there, I was such a sorry sight. He'd stationed me in the lavatory. But the job of being queen of the can they could keep. So I sneaked out and fell in behind Edith. I wanted to be in the audience that night.

It was hot. The women had bare shoulders and backs, or were wearing "little nothing" furs that weren't rabbit, rocks that weren't fake, and the guys were in tails and tuxedos. They were terribly noisy. The lighting was tango orange, the "in" color. When the floor was plunged in darkness, there were *ohs* and *ahs* and a lot of laughs from the broads.

Leplée stepped out in the single spotlight. He'd planned everything himself. He said a few words about how he'd discovered Edith on the corner of the rue Troyon, and said she was the genuine article, a revelation.

She came on, and Louis introduced her with a wave of his hand:

"Straight from the streets to Gerny's: la môme Piaf!"

There was a murmur, and then, when the spotlight picked her out and they saw her, they shut up. They didn't understand; they were waiting. Would they laugh or cry?

Isolated, in the cruel light, her hair limp, her face white, her mouth scarlet, her hands hanging down along the black knit dress that sagged a little, she looked pathetically lost. She began to sing:

> *C'est nous les mômes, les mômes de la cloche,*
> *Clochardes qui s'en vont sans un rond en poche . . .*

People kept talking as if she weren't there. With despair in her heart, her eyes full of tears, Edith kept on. She was suffering inside, but she kept singing, and kept telling herself, "I'll make it, I'll make it!"

And she did by the end of the first verse. She'd caught their attention. No one was talking now, but at the end of the song nobody budged. No applause—not a single sound, nothing but silence.

It was painful. I don't know how long it lasted, maybe twenty seconds . . . but that's a long time. The silence was strange. It got unbearable; it gave you a lump in your throat. But just then everybody began applauding like crazy—like a thundershower on a drum. I was weeping with happiness in my corner without realizing it.

I heard Leplée's voice saying to me:

"She's done it! She's got 'em in her pocket!"

It never even crossed his mind to send me back to my lavatory.

They were surprised—bowled over, in fact. They were thunderstruck to see a kid singing about being poor, singing the truth to them. It wasn't so much the words as Edith's voice that reminded them of all that. For Edith this was the toughest moment in her whole career, but to the very end of her life it was her finest hour. She was drunk without drinking a drop.

Once her act was over, she was invited to Jean Mermoz's table, and Mermoz called her "mademoiselle." She couldn't get over it. Edith, who never was embarrassed by anything, who had real nerve, couldn't say a word.

Maurice Chevalier, Yvonne Vallée and other elegant people

whose names I never knew were at the table. This success, this excitement went straight to our heads. We were so carried away we thought we heard bells ringing and birds chirping.

It's been said that Maurice Chevalier shouted, "This one really has it!" That's one of the legends, and there have been plenty of them, but this one isn't true. He'd already heard Edith sing—he'd been at a rehearsal with Yvonne. He hadn't said much of anything; what he'd said was more like, "Try her out, the public might like her. She's so natural!"

He was right. No one there had ever heard a voice like that one. She didn't force herself to be "realistic." She was born on the street, that's where she came from. Nobody had ever seen anybody like her onstage—a poor skinny little dame who didn't make any gestures, pitifully rigged out. Singers like Annette Lajon, Damia and Fréhel were big deals—literally. They filled up a stage just by coming on it.

The people had taken to Edith because she'd surprised them; because her songs hit them right where they lived! But she wasn't anything like what she became later. It took years of work before she developed into the one and only Piaf.

When we left the café, dawn was just beginning to break. It was marvelous weather, glorious weather. Edith, in her little black knit dress that looked positively seedy in the daylight, walked along like a queen. She took my hand.

"Come on, Momone, I have to be in the streets. That's what I owe all this to. We're going to go and sing; to say thanks. It'll do me good." She didn't sing the way she usually did. It was like a hymn; she was thanking Heaven. Edith's life had just changed. She said:

"It can't be. I saw those people in the papers yesterday morning, and I've just spent the night with them, sitting at their table; I can't get over it!

"They were great, honest-to-God nice. They could just have offered me a drink. I'd never drunk any champagne like theirs. Boy, is it good! The moneybags' lemonade—it sure doesn't taste like our sparkling stuff. I'll see to it you taste it someday. They took up a collection for me: I never would have dared. It was Mermoz who lent them his hat. Ah, think of how many girls that guy's got dreaming of him. He's so handsome, Momone! It wouldn't have cost him much, I can tell you that!"

She let go of my hand—she'd been holding it as we walked— and heaved a sigh.

"That's not for me yet . . . but the day'll come. Do you hear, Momone? Love is important to me. I'll have all the guys I want . . . and lots of money."

Back in our room, she was still talking about Mermoz. It went on for days and days. If she stopped dead in her tracks, I knew what she was going to say next.

"Look at me. I've seen Jean Mermoz! I was at Mermoz's table; I've drunk champagne with him. And do you know what he said to me?"

"Yes, I know: 'Mademoiselle, allow me to offer you a glass of champagne. . . .'"

I was a good audience. I was only seventeen, and I began to dream right along with her.

You've got to understand what we were: nobodies. Even the night before, we were scared stiff of the cops, who could put their big mitts on us and throw us in the clink. Our men were hoodlums. They could knock us around as much as they damn well felt like it. We had practically no family. If we'd gotten sick, we could have croaked in some corner or in the poorhouse. Our family tomb was the morgue, the potter's field at Pantin. The whole world could have fallen in on us and we'd have had to accept it. We weren't so dumb we didn't know it. And suddenly everything had changed. It was more than a dream, because in a dream you know it's some tall story you tell yourself just to keep going. This—this was real.

Edith had talked to Mermoz and the others; she'd sung for them, she'd drunk with them. The day before they wouldn't have turned around in the street to look at her. It was a startling change. Edith never stopped.

"Mermoz isn't just good looking. The way he talks! I could sit and listen to him for hours. Maurice Chevalier's a great performer, but he's nothing at all compared to Mermoz. He disappears. Mermoz dwarfs him. There are lots of men like Maurice in Ménilmontant, in Belleville. He's no better than me; he sings, so what? There's only one man like Mermoz in the whole sky of France."

And so it went, on and on. Our chums, Fréhel and the other broads, made fun of her. They called her "Mme Mermoz" and "Princess Piaf." It didn't impress Edith; she went on talking and made the story even better. Edith improved on any story she ever told; she always was inclined to lay it on thick. As time went by, the story got better and better: she was going to be a star; she was going to tour the United States; she'd refuse contracts. . . .

Fréhel threw cold water on her.

"Calm down, baby. Santa Claus comes only once a year and not for everybody. As long as people don't write songs for you, you'll never get anywhere. Your repertory is nothing but a heap of old songs. It's pitiful."

She didn't tell Edith this out of love for her. But it did us good. When it had to do with her profession, Edith caught on very fast; she did everything spontaneously when she was inspired. I watched her. I could see it all from the outside; I had time to mull it over.

I listened and gave her advice, because it seemed to me I had more taste than she had. That's why I took Edith to the rue du faubourg Saint-Martin and finally to the Casino Saint-Martin, where there was an accordionist, Freddo Gardoni, who was a fat cat, very fat. We explained to him that we were looking for songs, and he introduced us to music publishers in the rue Saint-Denis and the Petit Passage, and we went there to choose songs for Edith. It wasn't easy.

As far as song publishers were concerned, Edith didn't have a name. They had no reason to trust her to introduce a new song. So we had to fall back on old stuff. There was never anything for us. Edith would go into the most godawful rages, and Leplée would try to console her.

"What are you complaining about? I hired you for a week, and you've already been here a long time! Don't worry, the day will come when there'll be lots of people saying that without them, without their confidence in you, you'd never have made it. Be a little patient." But patience was never Edith's strong point.

We got into the habit of making the rounds of song publishers. We'd slouch down in a corner and listen to name singers try out the new songs the publishers offered them.

"Just seeing them work, just hearing them, I learn something," Edith used to say.

We were tiny, and still not very much to look at. We were rigged out a little better, but not much, and mostly our taste hadn't improved. We didn't make people suspicious, and that's how one day Edith met Annette Lajon, a singer who was very popular at the time. It was at the song publisher Maurice Decruck's. Maurice was fond of Edith. We were plunked down there as usual when a tall blonde woman came in. She was a woman who took up a lot of space—pretty, well dressed and very sure of herself.

She began singing *"L'Etranger":*

> *Il avait un air très doux,*
> *Des yeux rêveurs, un peu fous,*
> *Aux lueurs étranges . . .*
> *Comme tous les gars du Nord*
> *Dans les cheveux un peu d'or,*
> *Un sourire d'ange.*

> He looked very gentle,
> With dreamy eyes, a little mad,
> Strange lights in them . . .
> Like all guys from the North
> Gold in his hair, and
> An angel's smile.

"Momone, I've got to have that song," Edith whispered to me. "It's made for me. Listen to it, it's Mermoz. That's what I'd like to have happen with him. I'd sing that song with all my heart."

Edith sang about love during her whole career, and each song fit the guy in her life at the moment.

We sat there in our corner all through the rehearsal. Annette Lajon apparently didn't go for this. But she was a courteous woman, and she came over and said to Edith:

"What's your name?"

"Edith Gassion."

"Rehearsals are private, you know."

"Oh, but, madame, it's so nice to hear you. You sing so well." Edith was sincere, and Lajon let her alone.

When she left, Edith told Maurice Decruck she wanted *"L'Etranger."*

"You can't have it, dear. Annette's just introduced it. It's only right she should be the only one to sing it. You can have it later on," he replied.

In the street Edith burst out laughing.

"You saw me get around her with that admiration business. And I'll sing her song tonight," she said.

"How are you going to go about learning it?"

"I know it already."

It was true. But we didn't have the music. The piano player at Gerny's, Jean Uremer, was really good. Edith hummed the song for him several times. And that same night she made a hit with it. Leplée was delighted, and the two of us laughed over it like kids.

Four days later, we were in our lavatory when, in the mirror, I saw Annette Lajon come in. I yelled, "Edith!" She turned around and got smacked in the face hard enough to make her head swim. She had it coming.

"If you didn't have talent, I'd have slapped you right onstage."

Edith didn't say a word. There was nothing to say.

A few weeks later, Annette Lajon won the Grand Prix du Disque, with *"L'Etranger."*

There were gangs of elegant people at Leplée's every night. Ministers, industrialists, performers, society people, princes, the top of the heap. Edith thought she was a pro. But she was still only a ten-day wonder. That's why she was invited one day to an elegant dinner party, a real one, at Jean de Rovera's. We didn't know what that meant. Maurice Chevalier told Edith:

"You've got to go. He's the publisher of a big paper, *Comoedia*. I got you invited; I told him you were a riot. You'll see: you'll have a lot of fun. I'll be there, my dear."

"O.K.," Edith said, "but I won't go without Sis."

"All right. You'll see what real society is like. There'll be a minister there."

Edith wore her black knit dress—the same one, only it was finished now, because we'd finally knitted the sleeve. It was the only dress she had. I wore black too. Edith had learned that black is always dressy.

And there we were, sitting in the midst of these people in evening dresses and tails. The women wore jewels that shone like the crystal and silver on the table. I could never have imagined it, and neither could Edith.

There was a flunky behind each chair. Neither of us thought such things existed except in the movies. It's embarrassing to have some guy watch every move you make, and we were uncomfortable. Besides, we weren't next to each other—I was seated far away from her. I wasn't anything, just Edith's sister. The two guys on either side of me never said a single word to me, not even, "Would you like the salt? Some bread?" or "Everything O.K.?" Not a word. They were talking to their other table partners and listening to Edith. She was the one who interested them. They'd invited her because she was "natural."

These "nice" people were making fun of Edith. Since the beginning of the meal they'd got her to talk and were laughing at her. At first Edith thought maybe she was wittier than she'd ever supposed, or that it didn't take much to give these people a good time. And that was true—it didn't take much. They kept saying, "Oh, she's so amusing. She's really killing." And they'd egg her on. "How do you say *that?*" they'd ask. I thought she'd answer, "Oh shit," but she didn't. She couldn't get it through her head that they'd invited her just to make an ass of her. Since I was left out of it all, I began to realize what was happening. And I suffered for her.

They were such bastards they'd served only things that were hard to eat. Fish, for example. You've no idea how hard fish is to eat when you haven't learned how. You can't imagine what it was like for us to be at the table face to face with a sole.

After one course they brought us finger bowls. We'd never seen one. They all kept watching, waiting to see what Edith was going to do. I was waiting too.

Edith couldn't lose face, and as nobody did anything with those diabolical bowls, she decided to show them she knew what to do. She picked up the bowl and drank. It was logical enough: in France a bowl is made to drink out of. That's what they were waiting for. Everyone burst out laughing, and I can still hear their laughter ringing in my ears. Then they nonchalantly rinsed their fingers, and the meal went on. They were having fun giving Edith trouble. She didn't have any bread or anything to drink. There was always something she was missing. The flunkies in their white gloves joined in the fun. They'd become accomplices.

"I'd like some bread," Edith said.

"Give Mlle Piaf some bread."

"I'm thirsty, please," Edith said.

"Some water for Mlle Piaf, or I suppose you'd prefer wine?"

Finally Edith stopped asking for things. She'd caught on.

They took away her plate before she was finished.

They also served game. Nobody used his fingers. They stripped the bones with their forks and the tips of their knives. That's easy to do when you've been taught how, when you've never eaten any other way.

Seeing Edith's white, wooden face, I knew that she was going to do something, that she was thinking, "I can't just sit here like an idiot watching all their rotten mugs."

She grabbed hold of a drumstick and looked them all in the face.

"I eat with my fingers. It tastes better," she said.

Nobody laughed. When she'd finished, she wiped her hands on her napkin and got up.

"It's lots of fun here, but I can't stay. I've got work to do. Come on, Momone, M. Leplée is waiting for us."

I could have danced for joy. You should have seen the looks on their faces. They hadn't thought of that. They sat there like idiots.

Edith had coolly deprived them of their pleasure. They'd hoped she'd really disgrace herself and give them something to laugh about right to the end.

Edith wept on the sidewalk that night. She was so upset that when she got to Gerny's she told Leplée the whole story. She had big tears running down her cheeks; I was sick.

"Papa, I'm a nobody. I don't know anything. You should have left me where you found me—on the sidewalk."

"But they're the ones to be pitied, the imbeciles; they're the ones with bad manners," Papa Leplée exclaimed, stroking her hair. "Right, Jacques?"

Jacques Bourgeat was a friend of Leplée's. He seemed old to us—at least forty. He was nice. Sometimes he'd talk to us a little or give us a smile. And Bourgeat replied:

"You've just proved you're a great little dame. When you know what you don't have, it's not hard to get it, and you'll get it."

Edith and I noticed he spoke awfully good French, but that was all we thought about him. Then that night when we were going home, Edith said:

"Don't turn around, but somebody's following us. Don't worry, we'll fix him."

We took off, but he stayed right behind.

"Damn! We've had enough trouble tonight. Let's wait for him; we'll see what he wants. No mere man can frighten us!"

He was tall and well dressed, with a hat pulled down over his eyes and all bundled up in a silk scarf. "I know that profile," I said to myself. It was Jacques.

Edith couldn't stop laughing.

"I thought you were an old lecher!"

"You were so brave tonight, I wanted to talk to you. And help you a little. . . ."

She had just found a friend, a real one. He was the sort of man we'd never met up with before, the kind we couldn't find in the bistros we hung out in. Jacquot was something of a woman chaser, a bottom pincher, but not with girls like us. What could he have pinched?

He was a writer and a historian. And such a simple man! He was so good, Edith used to say to him:

"You're not good, Jacquot, you're stupid. You can't see evil even when it's right there under your nose."

"I don't like what's ugly, so I don't look at it," he'd answer. "I look at you, though, because you're beautiful inside."

It was Jacques Bourgeat, our Jacquot, who began to teach Edith piles of things. He wrote a poem for her in his book *Paroles sans histoire:*

> *La vie te fut dure;*
> *Va, ne pleure pas,*
> *Ton ami est là.*
> *La vie t'a blessée,*
> *Petite poupée;*
> *Va, reviens à moi . . .*
> *Je suis près de toi . . .*

> Life's been hard on you;
> Come on, don't cry,
> Your friend is here.
> Life has wounded you,
> Little doll;
> Come back to me . . .
> I am near you . . .

"Beautiful!" Edith used to say. "And he wrote it for me!"

He often used to see us home at dawn. Edith listened to him fervently. But there were times when she was ready to give up. It was too complicated for her. There were things she didn't understand, words she didn't know, and it bugged her to have to keep asking, "What does that mean?" Jacques guessed as much and patiently began teaching her French. He was the first one to write a song for her, *"Chand d'habits"*:

> *Chand' d'habits, parmi les défroques*
> *Que je te vendis, ce matin,*
> *N'as-tu pas, tel un orphelin,*
> *Trouvé un pauvre coeur en loques?*

Ragpicker, among the old clothes
I sold you this morning,
Didn't you, like an orphan,
Find a poor heart in rags?

Things were going off like skyrockets for Edith. There was her
first gala performance at the Médrano circus on February 17, 1936
—a benefit for the widow of Antonet, a great clown. Because the
list was arranged alphabetically, Edith's name was between Charles
Pélissier's and Harry Pilcer's.

"Look, Momone—my name's in big letters just like Maurice
Chevalier's, Mistinguett's, Préjean's, Fernandel's, Marie Dubas's. It's
a dream, Momone, a dream!"

How tiny she looked in the circus ring with the spotlight on
her in "our" knit dress! She was as pale as a clown, standing there
in the sawdust. But how huge my Edith really was!

After the gala performance she made her first record at Polydor:
"*L'Etranger.*" That made us laugh, but not spitefully, because we
thought old Lajon had been pretty decent to us, and she really had
been.

Afterward, Canetti put her on the Radio-Cité program. At the
end of the broadcast the switchboard was jammed by people wanting to know who la môme Piaf was, and wanting to hear more of
her. A six-week contract for Radio-Cité was signed with her on the
corner of a table. That night Papa Leplée said to Edith:

"Would you like to go to Cannes?"

"The Riviera!"

"Yes. You're going to the great charity ball and appear with all
the stars on the Silver Bridge."

"Oh, Papa, you don't mean it!"

For Edith the Silver Bridge—the great charity ball—just wasn't
true! It couldn't be!

We never bought newspapers, except to shine our shoes with,
but we did read paragraphs here and there, especially since Edith
had been at Leplée's, because her name was sometimes mentioned.
We knew there was such a thing as *the* charity ball and that it was
no place for us. Edith's feet no longer touched the ground. She was

flying through the air, and me too. We didn't know we were going to need a weird kind of parachute to come down.

Edith's love life was never simple. And at this point it was really nuts. Her work was going well, she was learning her profession and working hard. To keep her hand in, and because it was her vice, she used to work the streets now and then. As far as friendships went, she had Papa Leplée, whom she loved with all her sparrow's heart, and Jacques Bourgeat, who helped her understand lots of things and stayed our lifelong friend. During her life Edith wrote him more than two hundred letters—the only man she ever did that for. But as for love, she was really on the wrong track—fooling around with nothing but sailors, legionnaires and would-be hoodlums. It was a kind of madness with her. None of these guys came to hear her sing. They wouldn't have been allowed in. They waited for her at the stage door of Gerny's and at La Belle Ferronnière. They were patient enough. Never before had so many guys come down from Pigalle to the Champs Élysées. All night long they sat twiddling their thumbs waiting for her to come out. Maybe not fifty of them—no use exaggerating—but some came for her, and others came to help their buddies pass the time while they waited. It was quite a bunch.

Any performer, any star, who made fifty francs a day—a lot of money for those guys—was a gold mine! They drank and Edith paid. All her life she was the one who insisted on picking up the tab.

Leplée used to come out, cross the street and gab with Edith's men. He was a little too fond of those sailors, those wise guys, those petty hoodlums! Some of them really had handsome mugs. Leplée was generous. Between Edith and her boss the guys were able to wet their whistles in a big way and even get a bite to eat.

Louis Leplée hadn't waited for Edith to come along to get acquainted with the underworld, sailors and the Colonial Forces, and to hang out with them, but Edith had brought a whole bunch of them almost to his doorstep. And that was how she got herself locked up by the cops.

For seven months Edith was happy in her own particular way, and so what if it didn't suit other people? But on April 6, 1936, the roof caved in. Louis Leplée was murdered.

Il a roulé sous la banquette
Avec un p'tit trou dans la tête;
Browning, Browning . . .
Oh! ça n'a pas claqué bien fort,
Mais tout de même, il en est mort;
Browning, Browning . . .
On appuie là, et qu'est-ce qui sort
Par le p'tit trou? Madame la Mort.

He rolled under the seat,
A little hole in his head;
Browning, Browning . . .
Oh, it didn't make much noise,
But it killed him anyway;
Browning, Browning . . .
You press the trigger and what comes out
Of the little hole? Madame Death.

Edith sang "Browning" several years later, but it hurt her every time. It was always her Papa Leplée whom somebody knocked off in the dark.

"You know, kiddie"—Leplée often used to call her that—"in three weeks you'll be in Cannes on the Silver Bridge. Everything's coming along fine. But I want you to know it's not a sure thing for you yet."

"I know, Papa; I've got lots to learn."

"You've got to work."

"I know. But why pick tonight to tell me? What's wrong? You feel bad?"

"You said it. I had a bad dream last night, and I can't stop thinking about it. Mama was standing there next to me, saying, 'Poor Louis, prepare yourself. We'll see each other again soon. I'm waiting for you.'"

"Get off it! Dreams lie," Edith replied.

But clearly her heart wasn't in it. He'd suddenly made my blood run cold too. I just wanted to take off. Death scared the hell out of me.

"I don't believe in dreams, dear girl, but this one . . ."

The three of us stood there like fools. We didn't say anything; we didn't move.

"I wouldn't want to leave you now, Edith. You still need me. Things are moving too fast for you, you may lose your bearings; you can't go on alone. Basically you're a kid, an innocent kid, and people in this profession are nasty, very nasty. It's not just a question of claws and nails; they hit below the belt too. Anyway, behave yourself tonight. You've got a recording session at nine in the morning and a performance at Pleyel tomorrow night. So get to bed. No playing around. Promise?"

"Yes, Papa."

"You swear you will?"

"Yes, Papa. Here." She held out her hand and spit on the ground.

When we left, Edith said, "It's still early." I knew what that meant. Nobly, without believing a word of it, I said:

"We'd better get some sleep. You've got to work tomorrow."

She haughtily told me off:

"I'll get my work done. If you're tired, cut out. I'm going to have a drink, or else I won't be able to sleep. Papa and his dream have depressed the hell out of me! I've got to get it out of my mind. Do you believe in dreams?"

I wasn't sure.

"Just one drink," I said.

"I swear."

Edith wasn't stingy with promises that night.

What a night! One of our chums was leaving for the army. Edith kept her promise: only one drink—in each bistro. It was the number of bistros and nightclubs that counted. It had been a long time since we'd horsed around that much. We needed it, because with Papa Leplée it wasn't always such fun.

The boy about to enter the service was going wild. He kept yelling:

"It's the end of my life as a free man, you guys. You gotta stand by me." He was blubbering, the poor jerk. He had no reason to complain—we stood by him; we even carried him all the way to the station. How we ever got him on his train, as loaded as he was, I'll never know; but at eight in the morning Edith had one of those hangovers you never forget. And this one we really remembered.

We lived on a dead-end at the corner of the place Pigalle, on the third floor, because we had money. When we got there we looked at the time. Eight o'clock! Edith ordered a very strong triple coffee, swallowed it and said:

"Momone, I can't swing it. You've got to put the appointment off; I can't sing. I've got to get an hour or two's sleep. I'm going to call up. Come with me."

When she was in a state like that, she couldn't bear being alone. I wasn't focusing very well either. Everything around me was hazy and things kept moving.

"Hello. Papa?"

"Yes?"

She looked at me. "Oh, the bawling out I'm going to get!" And she went into her spiel:

"Listen, I can't make it. I'm just getting home now. I'll explain later. Can't we put it off till noon?"

"Come right away. You hear? Right away."

"O.K., O.K., I'm on my way."

She hung up.

"We've got to go, Momone. He said *vous* to me. He's mad. Do you think my voice sounded the way it usually does?"

In the taxi we were so goddamn worried we began to sober up. "Momone, I'd swear it wasn't Papa I talked to on the phone. What's going on?"

A big crowd had gathered in front of Papa's house at 83 avenue de la Grande-Armée. There was a whole bunch of cops and police cars there. We didn't know what it was all about, but we were petrified. At the entrance to the building a cop asked us:

"Where are you going?"

"To M. Leplée's."

A cop with his hat on the back of his head said to Edith:

"You're la môme Piaf. Come on upstairs; we've been waiting for you."

I stayed on the sidewalk. I should have taken off then and there, but I couldn't. Edith had motioned for me to stay.

People around me were chattering away:

"Some guy's been murdered. Louis Leplée, a nightclub owner."

"Well, in that world anything can happen," some of the damn early birds were saying.

I listened to them, wondering what Edith was doing inside. The concierge was giving herself airs, making speeches.

"There were four of them, all young kids. They got him with one bullet. They gagged his cleaning lady, Mme Secci, a pal of mine, but I wasn't the one who found her. . . ."

She seemed to be put out by this. She'd have liked to get everywhere first.

". . . It was the lady across the way. She came out to go shopping around eight o'clock, and who should she see but Mme Secci. They'd tied up the poor old woman. My neighbor called me. I helped her untie Mme Secci, who said, 'They've killed my boss.' What a shock!"

I didn't give a damn about her shock. All I wanted was information. And still no Edith!

"And she told us Leplée was still alive when she got there," the concierge went on. "He was sleeping, the way he usually was at that hour—he got home late. Then there was a knock at the door, the way friends of his usually knocked. She opened the door. Leplée was a man who let young men in at all hours. They waved a revolver—the murder weapon—in her face. What could she do? They tied her up and gagged her. She couldn't hear everything; their voices were too low. But she did hear them say to Leplée, 'You've had it . . . you won't take us any more!' Poor guy, sleeping in his bed—what a way to wake up!"

I listened till my ears rang, but I couldn't believe it. I was cold and had a headache. I was waiting for Edith. She'd explain.

She finally came out, with two horrible dames on each side of her, built like men. I smelled them out right away: policewomen. They had an air about them that was unmistakable. They were followed by two inspectors.

Poor Edith was holding her felt beret in one hand while with the other she dabbed her eyes with a handkerchief. She had big tears running down her cheeks, and a peaked, ravaged face. The two dames were holding her by the arms. They forced her to stop so the photographers could do their job—all that just to get their pictures taken.

Since Edith didn't speak, I didn't either. Her eyes met mine, though. Her smile—nothing but a grimace—said, "Don't worry, Momone; wait for me and behave yourself."

I saw her get into the paddy wagon, followed by the two inspectors. I'd found out everything I could. The concierge continued to rave on and on; she was now telling the same story with all sorts of frills. Her remarks, she could shove 'em; they didn't mean a damn thing to me. All I could think of was Edith. Edith, Edith!

I went back to our hotel and waited—not for long, because some cops came to get me. They nabbed me right off. And though their conversation wasn't uninteresting, it sure didn't sparkle.

"You palled around with Edith Gassion, the singer, didn't you?" they asked.

"Yes, m'sieur."

"You holed up with her."

"Yes, m'sieur, but I work too."

"Show us your paycheck stub."

"Well, Edith and I don't need things like that. I help her; I'm her dresser."

"Did you pass the hat in the street?"

"Yes, m'sieur."

"You were vagrants. You begged on the street, and you're a minor. Come on, hop to it, get your clothes. We're taking you in to the station. Do you know what special vagrancy is?"

There was nothing I could say. This was in 1936. The bastards had me go for a physical. I was put in with the whores for forty-eight hours, and then, since I was a minor, they sent me to the Bon Pasteur shelter, at the Pont de Charenton. I stayed there two and a half months.

They asked me a few questions about Louis Leplée, but they
realized I didn't know anything. If Edith and I had known something, though, if we'd had any ideas on the subject, we'd have kept
our mouths shut. We were very young, but not too young to know
that in the underworld it's not like with the courts; there's no
statute of limitations, and people have long, long memories. In any
case, we weren't girls who squealed to the cops, and it wouldn't
have brought Louis Leplée back to life anyway.

I was sad at heart and kept imagining all sorts of things. I had
no idea what had happened to Edith. I had news of her finally in a
way that wasn't the slightest bit poetic, and was perhaps even more
painful because of the place I got it. In the shelter there were newspapers in the crappers, and that's how I saw Edith's picture. I
pinched all the pages that had anything to do with the case:
CABARET SINGER IMPLICATED IN LEPLÉE CASE. They'd stoop to anything!

I hid the bits of newspapers in my clothes. It wasn't the whole
story; parts were missing; but I did learn they'd kept Edith as long
as they could, turning her over and over on their grill.

The things she must have had to put up with! I was sick about
it, and blubbered all night in my blanket that stunk of other girl's
filth. The sort of company Edith kept wasn't in her favor. I got a
good idea of what had happened, but no details. Two and a half
months later, when I found Edith again, she told me everything.
She hadn't forgotten a thing.

"Oh, Momone, when the cops pushed me into Papa Leplée's
bedroom and I saw him lying across his bed, in his nice silk pajamas,
with his head hanging on one side, I started crying so hard I choked.
He was handsome, you know—too pale, of course, but it looked
like he was sleeping. They made me take a good look, and it wasn't
pretty. There was a revolting hole full of blood where his eye
should have been. Laure Jarny [Gerny's manageress] was collapsed
in an armchair in the bedroom, sniffling in her handkerchief. She
kept repeating, 'Poor Edith . . . my poor child . . .' and I kept
shouting, 'It's not true, Papa Leplée, it's not true!'

"Then a cop said, 'You've seen him now. Come with us.'

"They took me to the Quai des Orfèvres, to Homicide. Commissioner Guillaume was in charge, a gruff guy with a big graying mustache. Seeing him like that, you almost wouldn't mind having him for a papa; he was the kind of guy who'd say, 'I understand everything.'

" 'You don't look stupid, my dear, so let's not waste time,' he said to me. 'All you have to do is tell us the truth.'

" 'I don't know anything; I was out on a spree with some pals,' I answered."

He turned Edith over to some detectives—young ones. Sometimes they're tougher than the old ones. And they began to question her as a witness. It wasn't a formal statement; they just wanted information. That was even better: it left the door open for anything.

As the police saw it, Edith had known Henri Valette, a pimp and a veteran of the Colonial Infantry. When she went to work at Leplée's she dumped him and, to get even, Valette had done Leplée in. It was simple, but cops aren't out for anything really complicated. Their brains are depraved, but not all that big. Edith was lucky. Leplée's cleaning woman didn't recognize Valette when they showed her his photograph.

So the cops concocted another story, the one I'd read in the papers under the headline: LA MÔME PIAF HAS TWO LOVES. According to this, Edith's lover was "Jeannot the gob." She was also carrying on with "Georges the spahi." This was true. Unfortunately for Edith, she'd introduced Georges the spahi to Louis Leplée. He had often been at Gerny's or at La Belle Ferronnière waiting for Edith, along with Jeannot and Pierrot the scarface.

Edith knew them all, which was also unfortunate.

"They asked me the same questions over and over again for hours:

" 'Was Georges your lover?'

" 'Yes.'

" 'Did he get along well with Leplée?'

" 'They were pals.'

" 'Don't think we're dumber than you. Georges was his lover?'

" 'I wasn't there.'

" 'If you go on like this, we're going to get angry. That'll be it for you. Didn't Georges come and pick you up with two pals, two young kids and a gob?'

" 'Yes.'

" 'Were you with Georges at seven in the morning?'

" 'No, I was with some of my pals.'

" 'Did Georges join you?'

" 'No.'

" 'You're lying.'

"It went on and on, Momone; they never let up. My brain was bursting. They ate sandwiches and drank beer and smoked. I couldn't take any more.

"Old Guillaume came for me. He took me by the hand like a sweet papa. And I found myself right back where it all began, in his office.

" 'Tell the truth. It's clear we know about your life; you can't hide anything from us.'

"Luckily they didn't know the half of it."

Edith was released anyway, but the police asked her to remain at their disposal.

The case was closed officially several months later. But not for Edith.

Chapter 5

Fernand Lumbroso

As for me, I was snug and cozy, so to speak. Off the streets anyway, with food and a place to sleep. And I had company, though not the same as at Gerny's. I was depressed as hell at having fallen so low.

No news from Edith. It was probably better that way. It would have been a black mark against me, because I'd just barely missed being involved in the Leplée case.

I thought I'd been abandoned, but I was wrong. The guys we knew, our pimps and their pals, were really great. After I'd been in the shelter two and a half months, a guy called La Boitouille, with the help of our Henri, came to get me out. What a deal! He'd managed somehow to get my mother to testify in court that she'd take me back.

I headed straight for Chez Marius, on the rue des Vertus, where Henri had told me Edith was singing. It was as simple as that. When Edith saw me, she smiled her marvelous smile, the one she'd had for me at Alverne's.

"You're finally here! You sure took your time about it. We'll start over," she said to me.

We were really up against the wall. Worse, even. Everybody had dropped her. She could count her friends on the fingers of one hand: Jacques Bourgeat, Juel the accordionist, and M. Canetti from Radio-Cité, who'd been a real help to her for a long time.

"I didn't lose my nerve, you know," Edith said to me, first thing. "I went to Papa Leplée's funeral at Saint-Honoré-d'Eylau. I put flowers on his grave with a card reading 'From your little sparrow.' It was Jacquot who paid for the flowers. If only you could have seen the expressions on all their mugs! They were wearing their solemn faces for special occasions; I had on my everyday one, the one Papa Leplée liked, drenched with tears. I couldn't have been a very pretty sight. I was wearing my black dress for the funeral, the one we knitted. The women all had black furs on. Everybody looked as if they thought I didn't belong there. But I did, Momone. And there weren't many like me who were entitled to be there!

"That night I was dumb enough to stop in at Gerny's. It was closed. The only people there had come to say good-bye to Laure Jarny: employees, the florist, the maître d'. Well, you know—some artists too, and one of them said to me, 'Poor Piaf, what a shame you've lost your protector. He was the only one who believed in you. Now you'll have to go out on the sidewalks again.' I felt like throwing a paving stone at him."

Her whole life long Edith trusted a lot of guys and even some dames who weren't worth the trouble, who deceived her, who cheated her, even though she was suspicious of them and didn't like them all that much. She dragged a whole bunch of flatterers and frauds along behind her who sucked up her dough like aphids on a rosebush. They revolted me to such a degree that sometimes, when I was too fed up with them, I got the hell out and went to get some air for a few days.

We talked like that part of the night, and hardly drank at all. Edith told me everything that had happened while I'd been gone. It wasn't fun; it wasn't amusing to hear.

Some nights she'd drag around, and some nights she'd go home. For weeks she sobbed in bed like a kid, with her head in the pillow. She went on living in Pigalle for quite a while. But now she was in a hotel on the rue de Malte.

Though her "friends" had dropped Edith, the press hadn't forgotten her, or the cops either. They kept her under surveillance, discreetly, prowling around like jackals.

"Every time I opened a newspaper," she said, "I got the jitters. They talked about the Leplée case, and since I was the only woman they could sink their fangs into, they tore me apart. Their stupid gossip became a tragic, filthy novel in installments. As I had nothing more to say, they invented things, not exactly complimentary. They hinted I was an accomplice, or even better, that I was one who'd driven the others to crime. It was disgusting."

As far as work went, Edith thought she was lucky. All kinds of cabaret managers buzzed around her like big green horseflies. They didn't offer her very much, but she couldn't be choosy. To them she reeked of scandal and it was a way for them to get free publicity.

Edith was hired by a club on the place Pigalle called O'dett's, after the name of the guy who ran it. He did female impersonations, a very funny act, in fact. That was more or less the type of club it was, but in good taste. Lots of snobs went there, and the décor was nice. It was an "in" place.

"Poor Momone, if you only knew," said Edith. "I had stage fright. The silence was enough to freeze you solid. A cemetery in the dead of winter would have been more inviting than those ice-cold people sitting at their tables. I sang; not a murmur; they were polite, and their politeness got me right in the gut.

"I bowed and left the stage the same way I'd come in, but I could hear them in my head, drooling things they'd read in the newspaper. 'Where there's smoke there's fire . . .'; 'She pimped for him . . .'; 'When they're off the streets, you have to expect anything. . . .' It's hard to sing without anybody ever clapping. You've got to need the dough to buy eats.

"O'dett was happy. I was the star attraction. It wasn't the streets they came to hear; it was the gutter, the sewer!"

One night they seemed to have left their fine manners in the cloakroom. After the first song, somebody booed in the silence. Poor Edith. That was only the beginning; it was going to get worse. A decent-looking guy with gray hair got up and gave them a piece of his mind.

"You don't boo in a cabaret. That's just for hoodlums."

"Don't you read the papers?" another guy answered.

"Yes, but I'll let the police pass judgment. They let her go. And here she's just like any other singer. If you don't like what she's doing, be quiet. And if you do, applaud."

And he began to clap. A few other people followed suit.

Edith didn't renew her contract though; she just couldn't take it any more.

"That's when I began going downhill. Canetti was really great. He got me jobs in neighborhood movie theaters—I was quite an attraction! The first movie house I sang in was the Pathé, at the Porte d'Orléans. There, too, everyone came to see the girl who'd been mixed up in the Leplée case. It was the same all over. I couldn't even hear my first song, they were booing so. Sometimes they'd calm down and sometimes not. It was like being in a wrestling match, and not always being the right weight. But every time, I went on with my act right to the end.

"You can imagine, Momone, how I felt after it was over: depressed, discouraged, ready to bawl. I got soused, but it was sad without you—and you rotting in that jail. I felt like a poor wretch surrounded by seedy bums."

"What about guys?"

"Zero. I just slept around. Can't stand to be alone. I don't even feel like talking about it. But now we're together again and we'll start over, Momone. Things'll work out."

But she didn't believe it. She wanted to give the whole thing up, and either go back to the factory or go back to singing in the streets. The streets were a possibility, so that's what we did. But that wasn't what I wanted her to do. It was a last resort. We'd known a different kind of life. People who wash every day, and talk the way they do in novels, smell so good. And anyway, our feet had got used to carpets—really much pleasanter.

One day I dragged her to a church and we prayed for something to happen. Something did. Was it our prayers being answered or the two Cinzanos we gulped down that gave us the nerve? You never know if a miracle's really happened: you do so many things to make it happen!

We changed all our plans in a little bar. We remembered the

magic word *impresario*. We rushed to the telephone book and looked up the number of Fernand Lumbroso, Marianne Oswald's impresario (she was a well-known singer among the educated). The miracle was that we'd remembered his name! With a telephone token in one hand and Edith's tiny hand in the other, I found myself in a phone booth under the stairway in a little bar, near the john as usual.

After a few words over the phone, he gave us an appointment right away.

We had no idea how we looked; all we did was run combs through our hair in the washroom. And with hair smelling like the soap we'd used to plaster it down, we showed up at Lumbroso's.

What really bowled me over was that the contract was signed on the spot: two weeks in a movie house in Brest. She was to appear during intermissions: four songs at twenty francs a day. That's miraculous when you don't have a cent to your name!

I took one look at that important gentleman and was sure my eyes and my young body would get both us round-trip tickets— and in first class! I was wrong: he stuck us in second class.

Brest was as godawful as the way I'd paid for the trip. I told myself that next time we'd sign for more money—and maybe that way we'd get to Nice!

So there we were on tour. Edith's first one. Brest is an impossible dump, gray and wet. What they call drizzle makes the pavements shine, but not the people. It was dreary. But at least they didn't give a damn about the Leplée scandal there. It was really out in the sticks. Edith appeared along with the film *Lucretia Borgia*, starring one Edwige Feuillère.

There weren't many people in the place during the week. Edith took up with some sailors the very first night, in a café. There was no lack of bluejackets in Brest; you had as many as you needed. By the second day we had our own gobs, sitting there with their feet propped up, spitting peanuts. But they were sweet, and they were our very own. We even had ensigns. That gave us class, and Edith sang for them.

I had a part in her act. I was what in vaudeville they call a foil.

I was dressed exactly like Edith, in a skirt and black sweater, a white collar, and a little red bow. We both had the same hairdo and were almost exactly the same height. So there were no problems; we were sisters.

I'd introduce Edith. I came onstage and everybody clapped. I announced, "Slum romances, street songs of Paris, recaptured by la môme Piaf, one by one." I held my arms out toward the wings, and the audience saw exactly the same girl come out. This gave them a laugh. My part in the act ended there, but I didn't leave the wings. Even then Edith needed to have someone close by when she sang.

Her accordionist, Robert Juel, followed her onstage, pulling his chair behind him, and then she'd begin. With nothing but an accordion backing her. We couldn't afford anything else. But it suited Edith—plebeian, no pretensions, no frills.

When I think of it, Edith's act was funny. Songs that were a little coarse and vulgar, in Fréhel's style. She also sang *"La Fille et le chien"* and *"Entre Saint-Ouen et Clignancourt."* Except for those Leplée had taught her, the songs in her repertoire were pretty comical.

We'd meet our sailor friends at the stage door. We were never alone; things in that department were pretty good. The guys were nice, and they didn't ask questions. But Edith hadn't forgotten the Leplée case. I could tell from the way, some nights, she looked at her drink, swallowed it and then said, "I'll have another," as if out of bravado.

The manager of the movie house wasn't happy; he was always complaining. Edith took this job less seriously than the one at Leplée's. She was careless about her appearance and arrived late. The "nice" people in town didn't like the show. And above all, our sailor friends chased away the important customers—there weren't that many of them to begin with—by behaving badly, kicking up a row, making fun of the respectable people and leaving after the intermission, as the film began. They made a hell of a racket. It made Edith laugh, but not the boss. The last night, as he was paying her, he said:

"Well, are you proud of yourself? Are you pleased with the work you did?"

"Sure," said Edith.

"Well, you'll never sing in my theater again."

When we got back to Paris two weeks later, Lumbroso wasn't very cordial. The manager had made a great to-do.

We went back to working neighborhood theaters, and the first night we came up against the Leplée case again; you don't get rid of scandal as easy as that. When Edith came onstage with Robert Juel, the audience started yelling:

"Get her and her pimp off."

Juel put his squeezebox down on the chair, stepped forward and said, "If there are any pimps around, they're in the audience."

It was like that every night. Robert even had fist fights with guys waiting for us at the stage door. I was so mad, I cried. This didn't last as long as the memory of it did, but we came out of it feeling empty and as wrung out as two rags.

Edith would cry and hold her hands out to me. "It's not true! It's not true, Momone—I'll wake up soon!"

Thanks to Leplée, she'd met a lot of decent people who would have helped her: Canetti, for example, and Jacques Bourgeat, and Raymond Asso, whom she'd met by chance, and many others. But she kept saying:

"I'd rather croak in the gutter with my mouth hanging open than ask them for anything! They ought to realize we're starving!"

That's what she said. But it didn't help matters any. They never could have guessed how hard up we were.

"Momone, luck is like dough: it goes faster than it comes." Edith took anything that came along, miserable jobs in sordid theaters. We had to live. Things just dragged on and on. . . . It was miserable.

The first fairly decent man she met was Roméo Carlès. He was a chansonnier—a satirical entertainer and singer—and one night at a café on the boulevard de Strasbourg he bought us a drink. He didn't know Edith, but was touched by her: she looked unhappy.

"What do you do?" he asked her.

"I sing."

Roméo gave it to her straight. "You'll never pick up a good contract hanging around here. You're short, badly dressed and you haven't got a bosom. Who are you going to attract?"

"I know. But meanwhile . . . you see, I'm starving."

"Would you like to sing my songs?"

"Are you kidding?" Edith answered. She knew Carlès only by name.

"Well, come listen to me one of these nights. I'm at Le Coucou and Le Perchoir."

The next day she made up her mind.

"Let's go hear Roméo, Momone."

I was worried because Edith was a bit loaded and in that condition she often did some pretty damnfool things. But we started out for Le Perchoir, a chic club on the rue Montmartre featuring chansonniers. As she came in, Edith began laughing and horsing around. Roméo Carlès was onstage and, in the loudest voice she could muster, Edith shouted:

"I've come to see my Roméo. Hey, Roméo, your Juliette's here!"

Le Perchoir had rather elegant audiences, and people were complaining. They even began to demand, "Throw her out." I was feeling about *this* big, but I didn't dare say anything. That would only have made things worse. Like a good chansonnier, Roméo took it very well, and was even witty. He played along with her. The audience laughed. I even heard somebody say, "It's part of the act."

"Well," I thought, "as far as his songs go, she really blew it." Not at all. Before singing *"La Petite Boutique,"* Roméo yelled to Edith from the stage:

"It's yours, my Juliette. Now be good, and listen hard."

Edith may have been a little tight, but since it was a question of her profession, she listened. The joke was over.

> Je sais dans un quartier désert
> Un coin qui se donne des airs
> De promesses aristocratiques . . .

In a deserted part of town
I know a place that puts on
Aristocratic airs . . .

At intermission she rushed backstage and said to Roméo:
"It's true? You're really giving me '*La Petite Boutique*'?"
"You don't deserve it."
"Oh, yes I do! Come on, listen, I'll sing it like this. . . ."
And she began to sing parts of it. (Edith kept this song in her repertoire for a long time.) Roméo was walking on air.
"How are you going to pay me?" he teased her.
"With a kiss," she answered.

That's how it all began between them—as simple as that. They stayed together for a while—six months or so. Edith was a sort of sideline for Roméo. Jeanne Sourza, the comic singer, a very talented one, played the biggest part in his life.

Edith was good friends with her Roméo. Physically he was just ordinary. What little hair he had was neatly plastered down. He was a nice man and, most of all, intelligent. The "street urchin" side of Edith pleased and amused him. He was the first one to trust Edith during this sad and rotten period. And, at that point, it counted more than love as far as she was concerned.

He went even further and wrote a song especially for her. The two of us, Edith and I, had inspired it— "*Simple comme bonjour*."

> *C'est une histoire si banale,*
> *Vraiment si peu originale,*
> *Que je n' sais comment en vérité*
> *J' vais vous l'expliquer . . .*
>
> It's a story so banal,
> Really so unoriginal,
> That I don't know how at all
> I'm going to explain it to you . . .

What finally rescued her entirely was that Lumbroso, a nice guy, "dared" to get her a short contract in Brussels.

"You're leaving right away—tonight. And behave yourself this time. Be on time. Don't get plastered. Otherwise I'm finished with you. I won't get you anything else. You may not realize it, but your name isn't worth very much any more. Besides, if you act the way you did in Brest, you'll really ruin yourself. I wouldn't give *that* for your future"—and he cracked his thumbnail as if he were getting rid of a crushed flea.

Edith promised Lumbroso she'd do anything he asked.

"Anyway," she told him, "they'll lay off me about Leplée in Brussels."

She left that same night, and I stayed behind. I was still a minor and didn't have a passport. I had to have my mother's permission to get one.

Edith wrote me from Brussels: "Give your mother everything we've got so she'll let you get your passport, and head straight here."

Everything we had wasn't much—three colored cushions and some blue pots we'd bought one day when Edith had decided we'd save money if we did our own cooking. They hadn't been used much. There was also an alcohol stove, but I saved that.

Thanks to the cushions and the pots, old lady Berteaut agreed to go with me to the police station and give her permission. But it took time. By the time I got my papers, Edith was back. I was mad as hell. All that for nothing!

"Don't worry, Momone, we'll go back there someday."

In Brussels, Edith had met a guy named Jean M——, a Belgian who was a musician in the club where she worked, near the place de Brouckère. I could tell right away she was in love. When Edith loved somebody, it was as if a spotlight had landed on her face: she became absolutely luminous.

And she was off, telling her story.

"I met a great guy, Momone—a good-looking blond. You know, a real northern type with blue eyes." I was sure that was true. Blue eyes always got her. "I just have to get another contract. It won't be hard. I was a hit in Brussels. I didn't make an ass of myself...."

She got her second contract.

"We're leaving, Momone! Wait till you see what it's like abroad. It's great! Brussels is like a foreign country even though it's so close. Everything's different there. You don't see things—or people—the same way."

She'd chewed my ear off to such a degree with that Jean M——— I could actually see him! But on the train she began to pull back, and the closer we got to Brussels, the more she ran him down. When we got to the station, I saw a fat bald guy, awful looking, so ugly you wouldn't believe it, standing on the platform. Luckily she'd prepared me by then!

We had a Belgian snack together with lots of fried potatoes and beer. Then Jean said to Edith:

"See you tonight at the club."

Edith didn't like that at all. "Let's go to his house and surprise him," she said.

So we took off, looking pretty shabby with our brown cardboard suitcases in our hands. It was the wrong address. Edith looked at me. She was annoyed. A hard little glint came into her eyes that I knew very well.

"By God, he took me for a fool. He'll pay for that. Get the lead out, Momone; I have to know where he holes up."

That evening at the club I asked him a few apparently innocent questions and managed to find out where he lived. He was shacked up with a woman who wasn't his wife, but he'd lived with her so long everybody thought she was.

He'd tried to put one over on Edith, all right. When I gave her the news she was really furious.

"I don't mind saying he's handsome even though he's ugly as a fat flea, and that I adore him even though I don't give a damn for him. But I don't want him to take me for one of those fat-assed whores who believe everything he says. Come on, Momone, we're gonna serenade him."

Since we were mad as hell, we sang under his window. He opened it right away (he'd recognized her voice) and threw down a few sous, hoping we'd leave. We left, and had a couple of drinks. Then we came back and made even more of a racket. Again he threw down some dough. So off we went and drank some more. Edith still hadn't given up.

That night when they met at the club, Edith was really stinko.

She had to go down some stairs to get onstage. There were musicians sitting on each side of the stairway, and Edith came down the steps on her ass—all the way! The stage was above the dance floor, so Edith's clowning couldn't help but be noticed. She clung to Jean as he sat there playing the piano, and shouted:

"Jean, I love you. I can't live without you, I just can't. You're so handsome, I can't forget you."

It didn't work. He kept a straight face and pretended not to be involved in the whole thing.

Then we went to the market nearby, bought some Camembert cheese and came back. I was tight as a tick. We weaved through the dancers on the floor and gave Jean the cheese. Edith yelled:

"Here, Jean, here's my good-bye present."

All the Belgians laughed and slapped their thighs. They couldn't contain themselves. We weren't being nasty—they should have paid us for the show! But no such luck! And so the romance ended, with Camembert cheese. . . . And when we got back to Paris, Lumbroso didn't exactly compliment us.

"You crazy drunken idiots. I've had more than enough of you. It's no use coming back here. There won't be anything ever again for you." These were words he had reason to regret later on. But we'd put him through a lot.

So we'd had a ball in Belgium. But when we got back to Paris without a cent, it wasn't funny at all. The time we were really poor wasn't when she was singing in the streets; it was now. A few months out of a whole lifetime isn't much, but these were long and hard. We even had to sell our duds, the few decent ones we'd bought during the Leplée days.

To earn a little money, I invented a routine: I'd stroll down the street between Clichy and Barbès, meet a guy and go have a drink with him. We'd talk and tell each other our life stories. At that point I'd take out a photograph of one of my little brothers, a year-old baby with a little teddy bear in his arms. Depending on the guy,

I'd say, "This is my baby. His father ran out on me, and I don't have enough money to pay for the months while he's nursing . . ." or "I have to buy medicine . . ." or "I left him with the concierge and I need money to go get him back. . . ."

It never failed. The guy'd give me money with the understanding I'd meet him the next morning. I never showed up. I didn't sleep with any of them; there wasn't any point. I won't say I didn't kiss them—I had to sometimes. In that case I chose ones that weren't too dirty.

Chapter 6

Raymond Asso: A Star Is Born

One day Edith happened to run into Raymond Asso again, in an artists' bistro, La Nouvelle Athènes. She'd met him at Gerny's in the good old days, and at the publishing houses where he took his songs. He also made the rounds for Marie Dubas, whose secretary he was.

He was a funny guy, around thirty and a veteran of the Foreign Legion. He'd also been in the spahis. Now, there was a recommendation! To Edith's way of thinking, there was no more handsome uniform, with the big cape, the pants, the boots, the tarboosh. It set her to dreaming. And me too. Guys like that hit us right in the gizzard. We wanted to make love with all of them, wrapped up in the folds of their cape!

So when Raymond talked to Edith about his life as a spahi, she listened with a beating heart and dreamy eyes. She was passionately interested in all the details, even the seventy-two regulation pleats in his red pants. And the desert, the sand, the sun—it was all warm and colorful. She could see it as though she'd been there herself.

What with all that, she'd normally have fallen into his arms. But that's not what happened. It didn't occur to her. Besides, there was something curt, something distant, about him that made Edith shy away.

Their meeting went more or less this way:

"Edith! How are things?"

"O.K., I guess."

"Not too great?"

"No, not very."

"Tell me about it."

They began to talk. Then they saw each other again. She trusted him. He always looked like he knew everything. He was a man, a real man, with a solid look about him. He was slender, skinny almost, with long hair, long muscles and a flat belly—but not good looking. He hardly ever laughed, but he had presence.

They talked together about singing. She asked him lots of questions, especially about Marie Dubas. She had a real thing for her. The woman fascinated her. Edith wanted to know everything—how she worked, how she chose her songs, how she lived. She'd had this admiration for Marie Dubas, this curiosity about her, long before meeting Raymond. We were still singing in the streets when Edith said to me one day when we had a little money:

"We're going to the A.B.C. to hear Marie Dubas."

We'd bought two seats in the peanut gallery. And Marie Dubas belted out songs that went right to our gut.

"What a woman!" Edith kept saying as she leaned forward in her seat, her little white hands clutching my arm.

From one song to the next, people either laughed or cried. She held them in the palm of her hand. It wasn't that she looked like much. She was of average height, with smooth black hair, and not very pretty, but she had dark, burning, unforgettable eyes; and as for her voice, you didn't have to ask yourself whether it was beautiful or not—you couldn't get it out of your head. A simple, chic dress. Gestures . . . When you saw her imitate a woman in the métro, you were right there. And when she sang *"La Prière de la Charlotte"* she broke your heart with her gestures—all that beggar's misery in her hands and arms.

Edith, her eyes full of tears, prayed and wept with her. I cried for both of them. Edith kept saying, "If I could do that . . . oh, boy! If I could do that . . ."

After the performance she said, "I'm going to her dressing room. Come on, Momone."

We had the nerve to go there, with our sagging skirts, our old sweaters, our rope sandals. Marie was nice to us, as if we'd been old pals. She asked Edith:

"Do you like singing?"

"I sing myself," Edith answered.

"Where?"

"In the streets."

Marie Dubas, Marie "the Great," didn't laugh. She looked at Edith. It warmed your heart.

"You'll come back and see me," she said.

She didn't state it as a question. She knew.

As we left the A.B.C., Edith said, "Did you see how she talked to me? Marie Dubas! You'll see, Momone, when that woman stops singing, no one will replace her."

And when Marie Dubas left the stage, she *was* never replaced.

A large part of Edith's interest in Raymond had to do with her interest in Marie. She was sure he knew how you become a Marie Dubas.

Raymond hung back at first. It was as if he was afraid to get involved. He could have done something for her right away, but he didn't. He just gave her advice, a bit grudgingly, along the lines of: "That's what *I* think, but you do what you want." He thought she shouldn't accept just anything that came along.

"That's a good one! I've got to eat."

"You need somebody to look out for you," he said, "in every way. You've got lots to learn."

It was an offer, but not a direct one. Edith didn't understand, or refused to understand. She felt she'd have to take the guy as well, but she didn't go for him. So she answered:

"Yes. I need an impresario. But all this time I've been looking, and I never found one."

"You need more than that—you need somebody to take you over completely. You've got everything to learn."

Edith was like an animal that's tamed but not broken in, as

skittish as a horse when a piece of paper flies up in front of its nose. She didn't have any patience, probably because she was a thorough- bred. What Raymond said to her was only too true. But she re- fused to listen to him; it made her depressed as hell. And then she'd complain:

"Maybe he's right . . . but he's a pessimist. I don't give a damn— I'll make it without him."

Those words kept them from really getting together for several months. He was still hesitant. He didn't believe in her enough. Edith wasn't in love. It couldn't work.

One night Raymond came to La Nouvelle Athènes with a hard look on his face—the way he looked on bad days.

"Listen, I've got a contract for you. You'll sign it and you'll be wrong."

"You shouldn't have bothered then," Edith answered. "Where's it for?"

Having a contract pleased me. Besides, Asso was beginning to get on my nerves. I wasn't for him; I was more against him. His know-it-all attitude bugged me.

"Nice. A month."

"The Riviera . . . No one could turn that down. Where in Nice?"

"At La Boîte à Vitesses."

"Is it a good place?"

"It'll do."

"You don't have to look like you're going to a funeral. It's more like the kind of news you have a drink on."

"If you want to wait, we'll find you something better."

"I can't wait. Anyway, I don't want to. I want to put some space between Paris, the Leplée case and me. They let me alone in Brussels. It'll be the same down there. It's the provinces."

She sure had illusions! The provinces always lag behind Paris. And down there the dirty label of the Leplée case was still stuck on Edith's back. That's why they were offering her a contract.

I was barely eighteen and couldn't understand Raymond. He was something of a gentleman. It wasn't till several years later that

I realized what our leaving for Nice had meant to him. Probably he hadn't wanted to tell her, but he had a thing about her. He was as proud as a rooster perched on a manure pile; if a hen wouldn't climb up to him, he wouldn't stoop to make advances to her.

He'd already made a bet with himself about her leaving: "If she leaves, I'll drop her; if she stays, I'll take care of her." That was Raymond's way. He thought it was curtains for him, that Edith was getting away from him, especially when she said:

"Did you find anything for Momone in that nightclub?"

"No."

"Too bad, but we'll work it out. I'm taking her anyway."

You should have seen the look on his face. He didn't like me. He'd hoped the trip would separate us. I thought he probably was planning to join her. Raymond was jealous of the influence I had on Edith. He was jealous of everything. He wanted to have her all to himself even then. I was a bother, in more ways than one: I had my opinion of him, I told him he was wrong if I felt like it, and I didn't gave a damn about him.

Before we left, he gave me a lecture.

"Listen, you're able to influence Edith. Keep her from running after men, from sleeping with everybody that comes along, from drink."

"Do it yourself. She's happy that way, and so am I."

Clenching his teeth with rage, he spit out:

"You know, you're her evil genius."

I laughed when he told me that. I made fun of him. I thought about it again later on. Edith's evil genius! That gave me a laugh, but I was wrong. Edith could be influenced, and one day he managed to convince her that this was true.

He wasn't happy she was leaving, but he took care of everything anyway. He bought us two new suitcases: "You'll be more presentable!" He got us second-class train tickets: "That'll give you some class." (At this time there were three classes on the train.)

As he knew us both very well, he went with us to the station and settled us in our seats. You'd have thought he was a father seeing his daughters off. He gave us all sorts of advice.

The train took forever to get started. Raymond was still standing there on the platform. I looked at the big clock. The minute
hand seemed to be playing leapfrog with the minutes. Finally the
train got under way. Raymond held Edith's hand as long as he
could. Edith let him—she didn't give a damn. But I said to myself,
"You're hooked, old pal." He did smile at me though. And then he
yelled, "Be good!" as if we were a couple of kids. Poor Raymond;
he was still innocent.

At the first stop we thought we'd change to third class, which
was stuffed with soldiers, but we didn't, because sitting next to
Edith in our compartment was a handsome guy who was too well
dressed to travel third. And things didn't take long. Edith devoured
him with her eyes. She slid down in her seat and he took her hand.
Then she put her head on his shoulder in an absolutely natural way.
Her power over men was unbelievable! I looked at the two of
them, and I saw the kind of love you only see in the movies. The
trip was off to a good start!

At one point he got up and went out in the corridor to smoke
a cigarette. We quick gulped down some wine. Edith's mind was
no longer on the bottles she'd bought and mine wasn't either. She
said. "I don't know where this guy's going. He said he was getting
off somewhere near Nice. I'll find out where, because I'm never
going to leave him. I'm mad for him, Momone."

When we got to Marseilles, we saw the sun. I was half asleep,
but even so it was beautiful. Then we plunged into dirty shadows
at the Saint-Charles station.

The guy said to Edith:

"I'm getting off to stretch my legs. Wait for me."

"Kiss me."

He kissed her. Nothing new there—they'd been doing it all
night.

He got off. Edith was watching him and so was I. Two police-
men fell in beside him and quietly slipped handcuffs on him. He
was done for. He turned around and smiled at her one last time. I
looked at Edith. She was dead white, with her mouth open as if to
scream. I passed her the bottle and she took a big gulp. We didn't

say a word to each other. There was nothing to say. The train started off again.

Edith never spared Raymond's feelings. That was the first story she told him when she got back. I could see from the wooden expression on his face that he didn't appreciate it. I wouldn't have dared tell him if I'd been Edith. But she was right to, because he wrote a song about it, one of his great successes, *"Paris-Méditer-ranée."*

> *Un train dans la nuit vous emporte,*
> *Derrière soi, des amours mortes,*
> *Et dans mon coeur, un vague ennui . . .*
> *Alors sa main a pris la mienne,*
> *Et j'avais peur que le jour vienne.*
> *J'étais si bien contre lui.*

> A train takes you away in the night,
> Leaving dead loves behind,
> And in my heart a vague pain . . .
> Then his hand took mine,
> And I was afraid dawn would come.
> I was so happy close beside him.

Our arrival in Nice was less poetic. But the first thing we saw as we were leaving the station was a sandwich man. Edith shouted, "Momone, he's got my name on his back! Catch him—we'll buy him a drink."

We lit out after the poor bum. Luckily men in his line of work drag their feet. We caught up with him and read: DID LA MÔME PIAF COMMIT MURDER? WAS SHE THE ONE? YOU'LL KNOW TONIGHT IF YOU COME TO THE BOÎTE À VITESSES.

Edith broke down.

"Oh, no, they're not going to begin that again! Murder! The bastards! The shits! It'll never end!"

I wasn't pleased, but I saw it differently. "They're pigs, all right, but still it's publicity. People will come because of you." This was an argument Edith caught onto very fast. She thought it over for a while—not long.

"I can stand it, but the babe who manages the club hasn't done it right. I want lots of sandwich men, and not just one poor bum. To make money on a scandal, you've got to do it big. I'll tell her." And she did. By instinct Edith was already a pro. She always knew what had to be done. She may have made mistakes in her life, but never in her work.

She soon showed what she had in her. She'd been hired for a month at the Boîte à Vitesses, and she stayed three. The pay wasn't so hot: a hundred francs a day for her and her accompanist. After paying him his share, we had fifty francs a day left, which wasn't a whole lot. We'd never eaten so much spaghetti. "Fill yourself up," she'd say. "It's nourishing and it doesn't cost much."

"Give me fifteen francs more a day and my sister'll do her dance number," she said to the boss. "She works in the biggest nightclubs in Montmartre. I talked her into coming with me because she needs sunshine. See how pale she is. You'll have to hire her if you want me to stay."

I was all set! My acrobatic numbers came off pretty well; I hadn't forgotten Papa's lessons. But the classical dancing! My act was different every night. I didn't even dance in time to the music; I did just any old thing.

The American fleet was often in at Villefranche, and the sailors made it over to Nice. Then's when we really lived it up. Edith adored American sailors. "They're not complicated. And since I don't know what in hell they're saying, they don't wear me out. Even if they blow up at you, it sounds nice."

They were blond, rosy, and they washed. Edith made them laugh. She'd say to them in English, "You good boys," with an accent that cracked them up. She could also say, "Yes," "No," "Good-bye," "Good morning," "Kiss me." That was enough for them to get along together. But since she didn't trust them, she used to lock them in, one to a room—which they had paid for, of course —so as to be sure of finding them there when she got back. After locking them in, she'd go off to do her turn at the Boîte à Vitesses. I say "them" because she sometimes had three of them waiting for her. Once one of them broke the door of his room down at five in the morning. The fleet was sailing, and Edith had forgotten and gone off carousing with some of the others.

Edith used to have drinking contests with them. She drank cognac by the bottle. Even though they came from the United States, they'd never seen anything like that. The amount she could down was unbelievable. Five or six apéritifs, a good dinner with a nice bottle of wine, a liqueur. . . . After gulping all that down, she used to have a big cup of café au lait to digest it. And she was never sick. . . .

We met Roger Lucchesi, the orchestra leader, with a pal of his. They took us out near Théoule. We'd never seen the Riviera. Was it beautiful! The red rocks and that blue sea, and then all the little houses looking like pastel candy . . . We'd thought all that only existed on postcards, a publicity gimmick to attract tourists. We didn't want it to show, but we couldn't get over it.

Edith also sang in the streets in Nice. Not a lot. It didn't bring in very much in a town like that. Singers passing the hat staked out in front of the restaurants with terraces, along the Quai des États-Unis, on the water's edge. They mostly went in for local color, things like *"O Sole Mio"* or *"Santa Lucia."* Kids bumming around just didn't go with the surroundings. We also celebrated Edith's twenty-first birthday there. But don't think there was a birthday cake with candles. We didn't know about such things. No, all we did was get ourselves a good bottle of wine to celebrate having lived together six and a half years. Six years . . . When you talk about them, they go by fast, but it takes a long time to live them. . . . There are those three meals a day to eat, and you have to hustle for them!

When the Nice engagement was over, we took the train, third class. Not because of the soldiers or sailors, but because it was the only class we could afford. We didn't meet any guys, and there was no shoulder for Edith's head. We held hands because we felt depressed. Edith had no more illusions: Nice was zero, and nothing was waiting for her in Paris—no contract, not even any hope.

Our arrival at dawn at the Gare de Lyon was dark and bleak. It smelled good though—we were home. This was our town. It was "Paname," Paree, the Paris she sang of later:

Oh! mon Paname!
Que tu es loin d'ici . . .
Et que la Seine était jolie
Sous le soleil du mois de juin.

Oh, my Paree!
How far away you are . . .
And how pretty was the Seine
In the June sunshine.

We were a sorry sight on the station platform. Edith was half asleep and so was I. No one was waiting for us. Raymond? Edith hadn't even written to him, hadn't even answered his letters.

"What'll we do?" Edith asked.

I had no suggestions. I was bushed and had run out of ideas. She decided to phone Raymond.

"Listen, Raymond, you told me you were ready to take charge of me. Well, I'm all for it."

She listened and then hung up.

"He said, 'Come right away. Take a taxi!' "

I couldn't get over it.

"Why did you think of *him?*" I asked.

"Do you see anybody else around? After all, he didn't have to say, 'If you need me some day, call me.' Well, I've done it."

"You didn't tell me that."

"So?"

We came close to having a fight. But I was too exhausted. And anyway, whether it was him or someone else, somebody had to take care of Edith and me.

We got out in Pigalle, at the Hotel Piccadilly. Raymond was waiting for us. He was shacked up there with Madeleine. It had been going on for so long you would have thought they were married. Looking nastier than ever, he said to us:

"I've taken a room for you."

He looked a little damp around the eyes, with something like happiness. Because of the words "Come right away," Edith's real career was about to begin.

It was Leplée who discovered Edith, but Asso who made her.

It wasn't all that easy, but what a tremendous job he did! Raymond was somebody. He immediately laid down his conditions to Edith:

"I'll help you. I know the profession and the people in it. If you listen to me, I guarantee you'll never be poor again. But your days of having fun are over too. You're going to have to work hard and do what I tell you. Pimps and booze are out. Yes or no. If you say yes, I won't ever let you down. If you say no, you can go knock on somebody else's door. I'm not a sucker."

Edith was stunned. Nobody had ever talked to her like that. His words and the tone of his voice said everything.

Her answer was yes.

I honestly wanted her to say no. I don't know how much I'd have given for her to say no. But if she'd said no on my account that day, I really would have been her evil genius.

Edith didn't look on Raymond the way she did her other men, the ones she took to bed. He was the one who could write her good songs, find her contracts, take care of her. She believed everything he told her. She trusted him. Still, it wasn't enough. A man who said good night as she was about to climb into bed couldn't handle her.

Then one day everything changed. She opened the door of our room, laughing. She was laughing so hard she couldn't talk.

"Guess who I just met on the stairs, Momone. Raymond!"

"So what?" I answered. "You meet him twenty times a day—he lives upstairs."

"I'm crazy, Momone. I'm in love!"

"Oh, I see."

"No, not 'Oh, I see.' Guess who I'm in love with."

As if you could ever know with Edith!

"With Raymond Asso!" she shouted triumphantly.

There was a piece of news!

"I was coming upstairs and he was going down. I looked at him and it all clicked—why we've been fighting, why he's been getting on my nerves—everything. I've been in love with him! What a stupid idiot I've been for not realizing it! This is the first time that's ever happened to me. Usually I think of it right off the bat."

"What do you like about him?"

"Well, Momone, you have to be blind not to see that he's good looking. He has sensational eyes, they're so blue—there's no other blue like it."

Every time, their eyes were never the blue of anybody else's. Blue was the barometer. When Edith said of her man of the moment, "Do you think his eyes are really blue? They're gray, and not even a nice gray," the guy could pack his bags! The good days were over for him. We could have made a collection of blue eyes— we'd had every shade of them. And I'd heard her thoughts on the subject before:

"Blue eyes attract people, Momone. They're made of light. And what's more, people's eyes can't fool you. Everything else lies— words, gestures. You can fake anything, except the look in your eyes."

I thought she was right. She sometimes made mistakes though. But since Raymond had the right sort of eyes, he was 1-A, fit for service. I didn't find him all that handsome; I thought he was rather ordinary looking. To me he was a black, dry tree in winter, a perch for crows, not sparrows!

"Don't argue, Momone. I've got it bad."

When she "had it bad," there was nothing more to say.

He didn't mince any words with me.

"You'll see, Simone; now that things are going well between Edith and me, we'll do good work."

"You've still got a long way to go."

He told me off, in his usual superior way.

"Never mind. I've seen others like her. I'm no choirboy, and I'll put it to you straight: If you want us to be pals, you mustn't louse up the works. For once it's not you who's going to win. Got it?"

"Yes, sergeant!"

That made him laugh. But not me.

The first few days everything went along as smooth as silk. Edith kept bending my ear:

"He's so terrific, Momone! A real man. And he knows so many

things. I trust him—you know what I mean? For me Raymond's better than an impresario. He's the man I needed. Don't you think life's weird? There he was right within reach, and I didn't see him. Boy, am I lucky to have met him!"

She was so up in the clouds, she didn't even hold it against Madeleine for existing. But it made me think. I was sure it was going to make trouble. There's no such thing as a woman who lets go of a man easily. Even when they don't want them any more, they don't give them to another woman as a gift! In the beginning Edith was careful, and didn't make a big show of her relationship with Raymond. When she was alone with him, it was because they were working. She'd say to Madeleine and me:

"While you two do the shopping, I'm going to work with Raymond."

The work sessions took place in our room. I made the shopping last as long as I could. Edith had said:

"I'm counting on you, Momone. I need at least two hours!"

It wasn't easy when all you had to buy was bread, a can of sardines, wine and a Camembert. Besides, I didn't have a watch. I'd look at every clock I came across and go around to all the stores and compare the prices.

I could see Madeleine wasn't really taken in by all this. She'd probably been through the same thing before with Raymond. So she just waited for the whole thing to blow over and I did too. Now that I think of it, it was really funny: when we were together we looked like two wives whose husbands were cheating on them.

You have to give Raymond credit: turning "La Môme Piaf" into Edith Piaf was no easy job. She not only had everything to learn, but he had to keep tabs on her. As soon as Raymond wasn't there, she'd take off. She couldn't stand being alone, she was always ready to listen to everybody, and she couldn't resist the pleasure of inviting people to have a drink or have a little fun. She wasted time as easily as she wasted money. She had no more notion of the one than of the other.

Once the first "I love you"s and "I adore you"s were over, Raymond began to make her work. He had some surprises there

too. He didn't know us very well at all and couldn't imagine anyone could be as ignorant as we were.

We had some weird sessions in our room! Edith sprawled out on the bed, and Raymond straddling his chair with his pipe in his mouth. He'd be sitting there with his head bent a little to one side, puffing on his pipe . . . pull, puff. There were horns blowing in the street, and snatches of dance hall music in the distance. The carnival would be on in Pigalle. I'd say:

"There's a carnival in Pigalle, Edith. Want to go?"

Edith would get a happy look on her face, raise her head and smile.

"Now there's an idea," she'd say.

"No," Raymond would say, "no more of that."

I'd get an awful urge to bite him and shout:

"You can't tell us what to do!"

It was like a hunger pang. Suddenly I was eighteen and needed merry-go-rounds, lights, music.

"Yes I can," he'd answer.

Then he'd point at Edith with the stem of his pipe.

"Do you hear *your* Simone. A carnival! So what? Will going to a carnival help you sing? You've got other things to do. You don't even know how to read."

"You're exaggerating."

"Even in your songs there are words you don't understand— I've noticed. If you don't know what you're singing, how do you expect other people to understand?"

It took just a few minutes for Raymond to win. That bothered me, but I realized he was right. Edith didn't know anything; she barely knew how to read. She deciphered a text so slowly she was immediately bored by the whole thing. As for writing, the only people she wrote to were me and Jacques. She wasn't ashamed to write to him; it wasn't important. And I hardly knew any more than she did. . . .

At first, in order for her to sign autographs without making spelling mistakes, Raymond made her models she copied and learned by heart. Even when she was "the Great Piaf," she still used Asso's phrases: "With kind wishes from Edith Piaf . . ." "Cordially . . ." and so on.

Edith sat down on the bed with her legs hanging over the edge. She looked like such a little kid! She eyed me sternly.

"Listen, Momone, we've got to start learning. It's true—there's a whole bunch of words we don't know." In cases like that, it was always "we." I had to learn with her. But there was one thing she could never stand—the dictionary.

"The Larousse is a sucker's game. You look for a word, you find it, it refers you to another one, and you're right back where you started. . . . And all the grammar books are too complicated. I know the present, the past and the future. That's enough to get by on."

She'd shake the book under my nose.

"Just look. The conditional, the pluperfect, the imperfect . . . What good will they do me? Let's forget it."

But Edith was too smart not to realize there were lots of things she didn't know. It worried her.

"Do I look as idiotic as all that? It's true I don't know very much. Do you think all the stuff Raymond's teaching me is going to be of any use?"

I had to answer yes.

Raymond used me. When Edith would start to yawn or talk about something else or say to him, "I'm fed up!" he would answer dryly, "Simone caught on. She likes this. You're not any dumber! So prove it."

That annoyed Edith. If I could do it, she could too. You had to change the bait on her every so often. She didn't nibble on the same one for very long. The day Edith angrily answered him back, saying, "Simone can go to hell for all I care," Raymond shot back:

"And Marie Dubas too?"

"What the devil's she got to do with it?"

"You think all you have to do is open your mouth on a stage! You don't give two cents for what happens afterward. You go off on a drunk with gigolos you've picked up, and that's what you call living! You're dead wrong. I'm going to tell you what the devil

Marie Dubas's got to do with it, as you put it. If somebody mentions Baudelaire, she doesn't ask for his phone number so he can write her a song. If a man kisses her hand, she doesn't slap him in the puss. If she's served fish, she doesn't eat the bones or spit them out on her plate because she doesn't know what to do with them. If she's introduced to a minister, she doesn't ask him, 'Your job going O.K.?' "

"I come from the streets. Everybody knows it. So what? If they don't like me, they can leave me alone."

"That's just what they'll do. It's no disgrace to come from the lower class, but it *is* a disgrace to want to keep on being filthy and ignorant. Marie Dubas knows how to behave in life, at the table, with people. She knows how to receive guests. I'm sick of you and your whims and your damn foolery. . . ."

Edith was choking with anger and pale with rage. I thought she was going to smash everything in the room. She had a terrible temper tantrum. Suddenly she was quiet. There was dead silence. Then she became very humble. I pitied her—she looked so tiny, so lost.

"I'm going to learn, Raymond; don't give me up. I love you, you know, I really do. . . ."

So Raymond took her in his arms and called her "my little girl." He stroked her hair tenderly. After having made her swallow vinegar, he poured on the honey, the rose jam, the sweetness.

"If you help me, if you listen to me, little girl, you'll be the greatest of all."

Raymond was a leader. He knew just what to do. He called her "Didou," "Didi," "my Edith"—and we weren't used to that kind of thing. Words like that count with girls like us. So Edith melted.

"He's so intelligent! He knows so much, and the way he talks! It's really different to be treated like that. I really like him, you know. Do I ever! He can make me do anything he wants."

This wasn't completely true. There were ups and downs in their relationship. Edith would get tired of it all. It's not much fun at twenty-one to keep hearing: "Don't do that"; "Hold your fork like this, and don't put your knife down on the table"; "Don't fill your glass up to the brim"; "Don't make noise when you eat, don't talk, eat with your mouth closed."

It drove Edith nuts. She liked to loll all over the table when she ate—she felt more comfortable that way. She didn't give a damn about behaving properly. But she had such a need to learn that she got interested anyway. Raymond had got it across to her that it was indispensable. She was haunted by a cruel memory: the dinner at Rovera's with Maurice Chevalier. She had to erase that memory.

When she'd finished learning one thing, Raymond would attack in another area.

"You don't know how to dress."

That was true. Edith had terrible taste. She adored puffs and pleats and little flounces and loud reds. It didn't bother her to wear blue, purple, yellow and green at the same time—she thought it looked gay. I'd never made a fuss about it. When we went out together, I used to let her traipse around dressed in clothes straight out of a carnival. I myself wore very simple little dresses, a bit on the tight side so guys would notice me. I kept hoping I could take my pick that way. But it never worked; she always took off with the best ones. . . .

The day Raymond said that to Edith, they had a kind of scrap.

"Don't go butting into things you don't know anything about. Clothes are none of your business," Edith said.

"You look nice onstage in your little black dress."

"That's the main thing. I do what I want on the street."

"You should have the same style in the street as you do onstage; it's part of your image, part of your personality."

Having good table manners, learning not to sound like an ass, discovering nice ways to say things—all that had already bowled us over. But when we heard talk of "personality," it really floored us! Edith caught on right away though, because it had to do directly with her profession.

In order to get to know that "terrific personality," Raymond had Edith talk. She told him stories for hours at a time. She adored talking. I had a ball listening to her. From the very first second, she could guess what you had to say to a man to get him to like you.

She instinctively told him what he wanted to hear. She was never wrong. She didn't have to try. The truth was what pleased the man. And since she had to be seductive—she would have flirted with a chair rung if it wore pants—she'd change her life story to suit the guy, who'd swallow everything and ask for more.

"Momone, I don't lie; I improve on my life."

Raymond got the same treatment as the others, except that for him she trotted out the poetic parts, the romantic parts—the poor little dame from the streets, from the working-class districts, a little seedy, but so engaging. . . .

She touched things up, all right—her father the acrobat, her mother the unsuccessful singer, me, the half sister she protected. The men she picked up. The nights she felt bad. . . . Nothing was missing.

Raymond didn't give a damn if it was true or not. She helped him build and embellish her new image. It was by listening to her that he realized Edith couldn't sing other people's repertoires; she had to have one her own size. Nothing ready-made: she needed things made to measure, hand sewn. So he got to work and wrote songs for her.

Raymond would get out his packet of rough-cut tobacco. With his head lowered, he'd slowly fill his pipe, with gestures that were always the same. He would crush the tobacco with his broad, flat thumb, raise his head, take a deep breath, light his pipe and "tell" us his song.

He took notes on a laundry list pad with a blunt pencil. He didn't always need a complete story like the one on the train he used for "*Paris-Méditerranée.*" He needed only the tiniest hint to start him off. One day I said to him:

"You know, Edith used to hang out on the rue Pigalle and—"

He began writing. It was on its way. And the next day he read us "*Elle fréquentait la rue Pigalle.*"

> *Elle semblait tout' noir' de péchés,*
> *Avec un pauvr' visage tout pâle,*
> *Pourtant y' avait dans l' fond d' ses yeux,*
> *Comm' qu'èque chos' de miraculeux,*

Qui semblait mettr' un peu d' ciel bleu,
Dans celui tout sal' de Pigalle.

She seemed all black with sin,
Just a poor pale face,
But deep in her eyes
There was something miraculous,
That seemed to put a little bit of blue
Into the dirty sky of Pigalle.

It was so great when the three of us talked things over. How I
loved that! When we worked, Madeleine often came and brought
us coffee. As far as work was concerned, we were all one family,
all huddled together, keeping each other warm. It was those other
times, when Edith wanted to keep Raymond for the night, that
things went wrong. But it was mostly later on that there began to
be scenes. At this time we were busy "creating" Edith and we all
pitched in to help Raymond.

Once the words were written, it was Marguerite Monnot who
set them to music. That was Raymond Asso's genius—to have got
Marguerite in on the deal. The first time Edith and I saw Raymond
and Marguerite together, we couldn't imagine what the two of
them had in common.

Asso was something of a tough guy, the nervous sort. Marguerite had a sweet oval face, blond hair, a dreamy look about her,
and a constant little smile that slowly came across her mouth like
tenderness gone astray. The least little thing made Raymond explode, but she would just sit there, dreaming.

Raymond had said to Edith, "I'm going to introduce you to
Marguerite Monnot. She's the one who wrote the music for
'*L'Etranger.*'" That was quite a reference. It was a song we remem-
bered very well!

Marguerite turned up at some time or other—she was always
early or late. All three of us were there in the room waiting for her.
When she came in, she said:

"Hi, children. I like your place."

Raymond laughed.

"This is a hotel, you know."

"Oh, is it? It's nice anyway. . . ."

She couldn't have said that, really, if she'd taken a good look. The Piccadilly was no Ritz. It couldn't have been more ordinary, even a little crummy. There was more backing showing in the carpet than wool. But it didn't matter. Marguerite never saw anything.

Edith immediately got all excited about her. It was as if she were seeing through her. She put her hand trustingly in Marguerite's.

"I just know you're a great girl!" Edith said. "And boy, do you have talent!"

"Oh!" said Marguerite, in the tone of a lady who realizes she's just been raped.

Edith called her Guite right away. She loved her from the start.

The first time Edith went to Guite's, there was a moment so full of emotion we felt like bawling. Marguerite said to her:

"Touch the piano. Put your hands on it."

Edith placed her hands on the keys and closed her eyes.

"When I was five years old, this was my dream, Guite. I was blind."

Marguerite had beautiful virtuoso's hands. She placed her fingers over Edith's.

"Play, play with me."

Edith's face was radiant. She gave a big silent laugh like a kid overcome with happiness.

"Guite, you just made me feel the music from inside."

That's how Edith learned to strum on the piano. She adored it. She said she understood better when she read the music herself.

Marguerite and Raymond together were like Cinderella's glass slipper and a hobnailed boot. But when they worked on a song, everything changed; it was a love match. They rang Edith in on the act. Edith would read the text, and even at that time she read it as if she were singing it; Marguerite would dream; and Raymond would wait—he wasn't sure about a song until the music was written. After the reading was over, Marguerite would say, "Oh, children . . ." That didn't necessarily mean it was good. She'd listen again and then she'd be off.

"I think I feel it." And Marguerite played her piano. She was in her own world. As a matter of fact, she never left it.

"Guite's always completely at sea," Edith would say. But she loved her dearly. They were rarely apart till Marguerite died in 1961, a quiet death. She hadn't looked sick, and we didn't know— she never talked about herself. She just looked more and more like she was in another world, and died the way she'd lived, without a sound. She slipped into death as lightly as she'd gone through life.

Marguerite was as important to Edith as Raymond. She was the one who taught her what a song was, who showed her music wasn't just a melody, that according to the way you interpreted it, it could say as many things as the words, with as many nuances.

Edith always used to say, "The nicest present Raymond ever gave me was Guite. What an extraordinary woman! She doesn't live here on earth, she lives somewhere else, in a blue world full of clean and beautiful things. You know, the angels must be like Guite."

That didn't keep Edith from yelling at Guite:

"You haven't got your feet on the ground, Marguerite." (This meant that what was coming was serious, because Edith adored nicknames—Guite, Momone, Riri and so on; when she used your real name, she wasn't fooling.) "You're impossible! You're the greatest songwriter there is, but you don't push hard enough. You don't bother about publicity. You sign any contract that comes along. You ought to be put under court supervision so somebody could take care of your business affairs."

And Guite, off in the clouds, would politely reply:

"It's all so unimportant. . . . Listen. This'll calm you down." And she'd start improvising. It might last for hours. . . . There was nothing surprising about it. At the age of three and a half, at the Salle des Agriculteurs, Marguerite Monnot had played Mozart and gotten her first fee.

She should have had a concert career instead of writing songs:

she'd studied with Nadia Boulanger and Cortot. She composed her first song by accident. Tristan Bernard, the great humorist of the interwar years, had brought her a poem, "Ah, the Pretty Words of Love."

"Won't you write a little melody for it?"

"I don't have any idea how."

"Try."

The song was delightful. It was sung in a film by Claude Dauphin. She wrote *"L'Etranger"* just as simply. It was a huge success. After that she wrote *"Mon Légionnaire."* And from then on, success never abandoned Marguerite. She not only wrote the music for almost all of Edith's songs, but also *Irma la Douce*, starring Colette Renard, a mixture of tender poetry and the Paris working-class spirit, which was also a big success in the United States.

Music flowed from Marguerite's fingers; all she had to do was put her hands to the keys. She was real only when she was composing, and then she was the greatest of them all.

When you're telling a story, things sound easy. They flow along, and you can let yourself glide around your memories. But among the three of us—I should say the four of us, because Madeleine wasn't about to let herself be forgotten—the ballad often changed tone. It creaked, it lacked lubrication! There were brawls that made the windows slam shut. Edith gave up several times. If someone tells you, "You dress like a whore . . . you eat like a pig . . . a six-year-old kid reads better than you do . . ." all day long, it soon gets to be a pain in the ass.

Edith and I had never been kept on a leash. Even in the days with Leplée we'd lived in the streets; we were free. We didn't know what a master was, and mostly we didn't want one. When she'd had a bellyful of the guy, Edith would say to me:

"Your Raymond's bugging me. Come on, we're getting out of here."

I wasn't going to stop her. We were suffocating in that little room in the Hotel Piccadilly; we needed air. We went out on binges mostly at night, while Raymond was with Madeleine. He was still keeping up appearances. And that made Edith blow her top too.

"Either he's mine or he's hers. He'll have to decide if he wants this to go on."

Edith always did her living between eleven at night and six in the morning. And men who wanted to keep her had to be there at night, and not only in bed. She'd say:

"You can't live the same way at night as you do in the daytime. Nights are warm and full of lights. People aren't the same; they're easy to get along with. At night everybody's my pal, even if I don't know them. We don't look the same—we're all beautiful."

And so she'd drag around from bistro to nightclub to café. We'd meet our pimps, our pals, and drink with them. When she woke up, she'd have a hangover and wouldn't want to work. Raymond would make one hell of a row.

One morning there was a fight, a real battle. She was in bed, half asleep, and me next to her. Edith gave such a big yawn you could see her tonsils.

"Raymond, get off my back—out of my sight."

"You're going to listen to me."

"Don't shout. My head's falling apart."

"Simone, make her her coffee and get a move on."

"Fuck off," I answered.

"That's enough!" he screamed. "This has to stop. You've got to change, Edith, or I'm going to drop you. Do you hear?"

He was shaking her; and she kept falling asleep—a real free-for-all! He even smacked her. She finally listened to him; he wouldn't give up. He was determined to win that battle.

He was pacing up and down the room—he didn't have far to go —his jaw set, a tough look in his eye. I wasn't saying anything. I was handing coffee around and listening. He got the whole thing off his chest.

"You live like a whore without making the dough! You're going to drop your pimps and their floozies and your gang of pals that are no good for anything but leeching off you. You let yourself slide into that shit! You're going to drop them. You've got to for your career. Do you think you can have them trailing after you when you sing at the A.B.C.? The newspapermen will laugh themselves sick!"

"My pals came to Gerny's, didn't they?"

"You're damn right. And see where it got you!"

Then suddenly a word surfaced in the middle of all this. . . .

"I'm going to sing at the A.B.C.? You're kidding!"

"No, I'm working on it and I'll succeed."

That was all she'd taken in: the A.B.C.! We both looked at each other. Edith in a big vaudeville theater! We couldn't believe it. But Raymond wasn't bluffing.

He was brave enough to go look up all Edith's pimps. What a job to clean them out! They weren't all just spineless hoodlums or cute guys; some of them were really tough.

Edith and I had been pimped for. That hadn't lasted long, but they had a claim on us. It didn't bother Edith at all to give a man money. She felt more like it was the man who depended on her than the other way around. How did Raymond do it? He never told us. Since it annoyed him, Edith chose not to ask him anything. He was a veteran of the Foreign Legion though. He proved it by getting rid of the whole bunch of them. A real housecleaning! He got them all! He had some magic words. If a guy dared lift a hand against him, his blue eyes would narrow and he'd say curtly, "I loathe physical contact." The words dumfounded me. They must have had the same effect on the others. He always got away with it.

Edith wasn't passionately in love with Raymond. She trusted him, and she couldn't get along without him. She had an animal instinct, and she felt he was the only one who could get her off the streets. Asso was the first contact Edith had ever had with a man who thought of anything besides drinking, having fun and making love. Just seeing him, you felt he had brains. He wasn't very handsome, and not very young, but what he had was better. Edith wasn't wrong to trust him.

I felt that cleaning out the pimps was a sign of other things to come, that it wouldn't stop there. I was afraid for me and for Madeleine. I knew my Edith; she believed in give-and-take. And she was true to form. Edith had to do something with her evenings, her nights. If she wasn't going to live it up any more, she had to have Raymond at home. . . .

So Madeleine began making scenes. And Edith didn't mince words. "Raymond, tell your woman you're fed up with her."

"Be patient, Edith."

"You got rid of my pals, you made a vacuum, you chose me. So leave Madeleine or else I'm gonna give it all up. And you first of all."

Raymond was deeply in love with Edith. He loved her three times over: as his woman, as his creation and as his child. He also knew nothing could hold Edith back. He hadn't won his victory yet, but he could feel it nice and warm in the hollow of his hand, like the bowl of his pipe. He wouldn't let her go.

He had an old score to settle with me. I was a bother to him and had to go. I meant too many inconveniences for him. Anyway, it's hard for guys to sleep three in a bed. It's funny—they never get used to it. In the beginning it was always like that. We had only one room, so there was no other solution. During the day I cleared out, but at night I was there.

We had squabbles even when it came to songs. Since it seemed to me that I'd told him a story, given him an idea, like the one about the rue Pigalle, I didn't make any bones about saying to him, "Well, I don't want that in there. I'd do such-and-such instead." He didn't like that. It didn't go over very well.

He was also very demanding. He always had something to say about the way I was dressed. I was his special target. I was still a filthy kid, only eighteen and a half. If I say exactly how old I was, it's because half a year counts at that age! And to get back at him, because he'd said to me, "Look at you; you're setting a bad example for Edith," I'd run him down when I talked to Edith. I didn't let him get away with a thing. Edith listened to me. It was easy—I made her laugh and he didn't.

I realized this couldn't last; that it was unbearable. I took a hard line and so did he. We weren't about to back down—especially me!

Raymond was a clever one. He was smart—smarter than I. He'd been scheming for a long time, lovingly lingering over the details.

He decided first off to leave Madeleine and live with Edith. He couldn't do this, naturally, if they stayed at the Piccadilly and kept meeting on the stairs.

He picked the Hotel Alsina, on the avenue Junot. A completely different sort of place: a room with a bath, a telephone, carpeting, a decent lobby. It was in another class! The contract with the A.B.C. was in the wind; you could feel it. There must have been something to it, because the Hotel Alsina cost dough and Raymond wasn't well heeled and Edith wasn't working much. He'd decided I'd be the last step in his "housecleaning." All he had to do now was dump me.

Edith had gone out. He was waiting for me in the room. Skinny as he was, it seemed to me he took up lots of room in our digs. I looked at him. He took his time filling his pipe. I saw just his fingers moving, carefully lighting it, his head leaning to one side, one finger on the pipe to make it draw. He looked at me out of the corner of his little blue eyes. I knew he was going to come out with something shitty, but I wasn't afraid. I was boiling inside, and was sure I could give him an answer for everything. Raymond and I always talked to each other "man to man."

He took a puff on his pipe without saying anything, then he began.

"Momone . . ."

So I knew this was going to be serious. He never called me that —I was always just Simone. I had a hollow feeling inside, like when the elevator goes down too fast. He was nervous, and cracking his knuckles. He had dry, rather beautiful hands, an artist's hands.

"Little Momone . . . you've always thought I didn't like you. You're wrong. I'm quite fond of you."

"You can keep your fine words and your pity! Get to the point."

"O.K., it'll be easier that way. You know I'm doing everything for Edith. I've bet on her. I believe in her. And . . . you're not good enough for her."

"The evil genius! You've already said that. There may be something to it, but you'll have to prove it."

"The example you set isn't good for her. You run around, you get drunk, you lead her on. I've gotten her two contracts, one at the Sirocco, and the other in a club on the Champs Élysées, on the rue Arsène Houssaye. She's going to appear at the A.B.C. too. She's got to change her life, and her friends. She mustn't forget what she's learned. You're her past. With you around it's there all the time, right under her nose. She's got to forget it. If you stay, she won't be able to. It's not a question of your not seeing her any more, but . . ."

"Why . . . you've got a hell of a nerve!"

"You mustn't live with her any more. The two of us are going to the avenue Junot, to another hotel, alone. I didn't get a room for you."

"Is that all right with her?"

"Yes."

"Is that why she went out? She knew you were going to give out with all this crap?"

"Yes."

"Well, then, I have nothing more to say."

I packed up my few rags and cleared out. I didn't want him to see me crying.

I was too young to understand he was playing his own game, that he was lying to me. He was counting on my pride. He wasn't wrong there. Much later, talking with Edith, I found out she'd asked where I was when she came home and he'd told her:

"She's gone. She found a guy."

"Without saying anything to me? The bitch!"

This was the sort of thing Edith couldn't stand—being abandoned. She was willing to drop other people, but wouldn't have it done to her.

I left and didn't come back. I went up the rue Pigalle, our street, by myself. My footsteps, my loneliness and my heartbreak had taken me from Pigalle to Ménilmontant—it's straight down the boulevard. I went to my mother's without even knowing why. I found two almost loving arms there to hug me close. For the first and only time in my life, I hadn't come back to "my mother's" but to "mama's."

In those few moments I forgot everything: her hardheartedness, her toughness, her greed, her indifference; everything. She hugged me to her. I was finally the child I'd always dreamed of being. But I had no illusions. I knew her tenderness wouldn't last long.

I took up the sort of life I'd had before meeting Edith. During the week I worked at one of the stores at the Félix Potin chain, putting chocolates in boxes. On Saturdays I went to the swimming pool, and on Sundays to the movies.

I was lost, at loose ends. I'd lived with Edith for years, lived her life, her loves . . . and now! It was all over between Edith and me, I was sure of it, and I needed to be loved. She'd loved me. She'd been the only one, in fact.

I needed love so badly that I found it with a boy I'd met one Saturday at the pool, in the water that smelled of chlorine. After all, it disinfected me from Pigalle, the pimps, the whores and the soldiers. . . . I felt cleaner and I was cleaner, because he believed in me right away, believed in my innocence. It was so nice to see him respect me. He didn't dare touch me. He'd called me "mademoiselle." I wasn't used to that.

If I became his wife before being his fiancée, it was because I couldn't bear being alone any more. I needed to talk, to hear an echo of my thirst for love, to feel something human near me. So I got married, just like that! Without saying a word, without any wedding announcements or wedding banquet, without the fancy wedding cake. Just like that, one Saturday, along with twenty or so other couples waiting their turn.

I was out of my mind; I hadn't realized it wasn't possible to forsake Edith. A nice quiet life, the factory, weren't for me. One day I got up my nerve and phoned her.

"It can't be! Is that really you, Momone? Come on over. I've got a nice setup here—you'll see. I've got a bathroom!"

"No, I'd rather see you somewhere else."

She didn't make a fuss. She must really have wanted to see me! We agreed to meet in a café, the Wepler, up by Clichy. It'd be more elegant!

When she came in, I could see by her smile, her eyes, her

clothes, that things weren't going badly. She was in a good mood, as radiant as when she was cheating on one of her men. She was cheating on Raymond by seeing me.

She wanted me to tell her everything. But the story of my marriage belonged to me. It was such a nice clean thing, I was keeping it for myself alone.

I stopped talking. Edith didn't even notice. She had too many things to tell me about her new songs, her plans, Raymond's advice. It's funny—I didn't hold anything against him. I knew he was a useful transition for Edith—her chance. We saw each other like that several times. One day when she met me, her face was drawn and pinched with anger.

"Momone, I have to tell you. He can't get away with it! Do you remember the legionnaire?"

I had only a vague recollection.

"Explain."

"You know! The story of Riri the legionnaire? From the Porte des Lilas?"

Suddenly it all came back. It had been four or five years ago. It was at the very beginning, when we were singing in the streets and working the army barracks. You had to really be on the lookout because the guys would try to sneak out without paying. Edith stationed me at the entrance to the canteen with an empty tin can in my hand.

"Look stern, Momone! You have to assert yourself." It wasn't exactly an easy job when I was only fourteen and four feet ten inches tall!

This time all the soldiers were already sitting down when a legionnaire came by, with his white kepi, his red sash, the whole outfit. He looked down at me and said, "I'm not giving anything."

Then he said to Edith, "I'll see you afterward."

He wasn't all that handsome, but he had blue eyes. The three of us left together. It's not far from the Porte des Lilas to the rue Orfila. We went straight back to the Hôtel de l'Avenir. Riri went back to the barracks at seven the next morning, and got locked up for four days.

We didn't know anything about it. Edith had a date with him at six o'clock that same night. Since she liked him, we arrived on time at the Porte des Lilas. We asked for him at the sentry's.

"What do you want with him?"

"I'm his sister," Edith said. "I've come to see him."

"And is she his sister too?" the sentry asked, looking at me.

"Sure, since she's my sis."

"He's being punished. Come back some other time."

"I can't; I have to talk to him about my mother. She's sick."

She handed the guys at the sentry box such a line that the corporal called the sergeant.

"You'll have to see the adjutant," he said. The adjutant said it wasn't according to regulations. "But since it's in a good cause, I'll send for him," he added.

They brought us Riri, the legionnaire, flanked by marines with all their paraphernalia: rifles, chin straps, gaiters, everything. The bastard didn't even look at us, as if he'd never seen us before.

But Edith threw herself into his arms and whispered, "You're my brother!"

"You've got a nerve!" he answered.

All the sentries laughed. They weren't taken in. Riri made a date with her, while the sergeant was bawling out an order:

"Kiss your sisters, you poor fool! Better than that!"

That was the story of Edith's legionnaire. I had no idea why she seemed so damn furious.

"Listen, Momone. While we were having fun with Riri at the Porte des Lilas, Raymond, whose name I didn't even know, was writing a song that was *my* story. He called it *'Mon Légionnaire.'* Isn't that something? How's that for a coincidence?"

> *J'sais pas son nom, je n'sais rien d'lui,*
> *Il m'a aimée toute la nuit,*
> *Mon légionnaire!*
> *Et me laissant à mon destin,*
> *Il est parti dans le matin*
> *Plein de lumière . . .*
> *Mon légionnaire!*

I don't know his name, I don't know anything about him,
He made love to me all night long,
My legionnaire!
Leaving me to my fate,
He left in the
Bright morning light . . .
My legionnaire!

"That's the song, Momone; And do you know who sang it first? Marie Dubas. Raymond gave it to her! Isn't that a puky trick?"

I tried to explain to Edith that Raymond wasn't guilty, that before he knew her he was free to do what he wanted with his songs. She wouldn't listen to a word.

"The '*Légionnaire*' is mine, nobody else's. He should have kept it for me. It was *my* song, *my* story!"

When she got excited, she was always unfair. I knew Edith too well not to know that Raymond had had to listen to that business about the legionnaire song given to Marie Dubas day after day . . . and, above all, night after night. She pounded the table with her little fist.

"I don't give a damn. I'm going to sing it, you hear? I'll make people forget Marie Dubas!"

Nobody remembers now that Marie used to sing that song. . . .

What kept Raymond and Edith together wasn't a gold wedding band, but singing. Edith soon gave Raymond back everything he'd given her. It was thanks to her that he became famous. But, like the others, Asso didn't last more than eighteen months with Edith. The only difference was that long after they'd stopped living together, people still kept saying, "Piaf and Asso."

In Paris the A.B.C., on the Grands Boulevards, was *the* vaudeville theater, the most famous stage of all. There was none better. It was run by Mitty Goldin, a guy who was tops in his profession. He'd come from Central Europe to Paris, with nothing in his bags but his Hungarian genius. He could boast of having launched all the big singing stars. They all appeared there, but there weren't many who'd begun at his place. They wouldn't have dared offer their services to A.B.C. Even the performer in the curtain raiser had already been on another stage. There were plenty of them: the Concert Pacra, Bobino, the Gaîté-Montparnasse, Wagram, the Alhambra, the Moulin Rouge and so on, not to mention the little neighborhood vaudeville theaters, the ones in the suburbs, and the big movie theaters: the Rex, the Baumont-Palace, the Paramount. And Mitty didn't pay much either. But you knew you'd really made it when you appeared at the A.B.C.

In those days, you made your name on the stage. Records came later, and were just something extra. It was exactly the opposite of the way it is now. Singers didn't use a microphone either, and had to have a completely different technique. It took a voice and a good gut. Just try murmuring "I love you" with feeling for an audience of two thousand people. Edith carried it off every time.

I got quite a shock when Edith hit me with:

"Momone, it's happened—I've got the A.B.C.! And guess what spot I've got on the bill."

"The beginning of the second part?"

"*Costar!*"

Costarring straight off—I couldn't believe it!

"It wasn't easy. Raymond really is somebody. Didn't you know that? The first time he talked to Mitty Goldin about it, Goldin laughed.

"But you know Raymond; when he gets an idea in his head . . . He kept going back. I can just see him, smoking his pipe and sitting in the old broken-down bench in front of Mitty's door.

"Mitty comes out and asks him:

" 'What are you waiting for, Raymond? Do you want to talk to me about a song?'

" 'No, I've come about a contract for la môme Piaf.'

" 'You might as well leave.'

" 'I'll be back tomorrow.'

" 'Tomorrow and the day after tomorrow it'll still be no.'

"Mitty Goldin didn't change his tune for weeks. Raymond paid him a visit every day. The old bastard made him wait for hours, on purpose. I don't know how long it went on, but it was a long time. . . .

"Mitty was getting fed up with the whole thing.

" 'O.K., Raymond, just for you, she can be in the curtain raiser on the early show.'

" 'No—you're going to make her a costar.'

"Tough old Mitty finally gave in. Let's drink to it, Momone. Come on! Drinks for everybody!"

Luckily we were in a little bar and there weren't many customers. We had a lot to drink. Then Edith said:

"The party's over. We're going up to the Sacré-Coeur to light a candle to the little sister from Lisieux."

So off we went, a little tight, lurching along gaily. It was a good thing we were on the rue Lepic, right near the Butte and uphill all the way, so there was less danger of flopping on the ground than if we'd been going downhill.

While Edith was at it, she also lit a candle to the Sacred Heart, to the Holy Virgin, to more or less everyone. She simply had to share her happiness. She thanked all of Paradise!

When we came out, we stopped. Edith was holding me by the arm, very tightly. How little the two of us seemed, with the whole huge city of Paris at our feet, and its lights! You'd think the sky and all its stars had turned upside down. . . . Edith had sobered up. She spoke in her strong, low voice.

"The A.B.C. is the first step, Momone. I'll climb so high we'll be dizzy."

I looked at her and was afraid she'd get too big for me.

"Don't leave me at the bottom. . . ."

"Are you crazy? Listen! My life's something serious now."

What a thing appearing at the A.B.C. was! We were far from the days when we knitted Edith a dress. Another time was coming: a time of success, of millions, of traveling, of glory.

Edith would phone me at my concierge's any hour of the day or night. The old biddy complained, but I didn't give a damn. Edith would say:

"Come over right away, Momone, I've got news for you. I have to tell you."

And I'd dash over.

"I've done it, Momone—I've met the 'Marquise' and the 'Marquis.' They invited me into their office, like a buddy."

We'd been waiting for that a long time! M. and Mme Breton of the Raoul Breton music publishing house were kings in the profession. Nobody could succeed in the field without their help. They were the ones who discovered Charles Trenet, who'd pushed him. Their music catalogue was the "Who's Who" of singing.

Edith and I had often struck poses in their lobby, telling ourselves that maybe they'd notice us. But we were too shabby, too tiny. . . . I hadn't forgotten Mme Breton though: a thin, lively little brunette, with intelligent eyes and the elegance of a marquise. She was always loaded with jewelry, with bracelets that jangled.

"When Raymond and I went into their office—it's more like a living room—I said to myself, 'There's something different this time!'

" 'So you're going to appear at the A.B.C. Are you happy?' asked the 'Marquise.'

" 'It's wonderful!' was all I could answer.

" 'There's only one slight difficulty. You're just under Charles Trenet, but your name, "La Môme Piaf," doesn't look right next to his. Not at all.'

"That's what she said—polite but curt. I couldn't get over it. It was like with Leplée. I was about to change my name again.

" 'I have something to suggest. "La Môme" is a cabaret name, and it's already passé. What about "Edith Piaf"?'

" 'Fine,' Raymond answered.

"We drank champagne; she even poured some on my head.

" 'I baptize you "Edith Piaf" in the name of Song.'

"Here, Momone, touch my hair; it'll bring you luck. And I brought you the cork—keep it!" (That cork traveled everywhere with me until one day I lost it.) " 'Edith Piaf'—what do you think of it?"

It was all right with me because she was happy, but I really minded dropping "La Môme." It was like giving up a bit of the past, and it made me feel sad.

When it came to dresses, hairdos and makeup, Raymond had nothing to say any more. The "Marquise," who always liked Edith a lot, had taken over. Before the premiere at the A.B.C., she took her to a great couturier, Jacques Heim. Edith couldn't get over it.

"If only you could have seen, Momone. The salons, and the salesladies, and the dresses! It's so beautiful! When I have dough, you'll get your clothes there too. Remember how we drooled when we looked in the windows of the cheap dress shops on the Champs Élysées coming home from Gerny's? Their nineteen-franc dresses really knocked our eyes out. We weren't hard to please in those days—we didn't know anything.

"The 'Marquise' said I couldn't go all over town in my stage dress. She said I had to dress like the other dames for cocktails and receptions—all that elegant jazz they go in for. What do you think?"

I wasn't thinking any more. I was stunned, completely out of it, and, breathless from keeping up with Edith, I didn't have any more air in my lungs. I had to breathe twice as fast.

The "Marquise" had chosen a purple dress with a cape lined in Parma violet for Edith. She looked pretty in it. No question about it: Mme Breton had taste. She had also taken Edith to a beauty parlor: Anna Pegova's. But there they had trouble. Edith complained:

"I don't say their creams and stuff aren't good: they're soft and they smell good. But I can't get used to the way they make you up. When you leave you're even uglier than when you came in. Anyway, I know my face. It's an old chum. When I see this unknown clown's face smiling back at me from a mirror, it gets on my nerves."

Three weeks before the dress rehearsal, Edith couldn't sleep, couldn't eat, couldn't drink.

"I can't stand Raymond any more, Momone. The guy drives me nuts, he's so know-it-all. He wants me to take singing lessons—*solfège*. Never. I told him no! It'd make me lose everything I've got going for me."

She stood firm. She was ready to learn anything connected with her profession, but she never changed her mind about this.

"He bugs me with his advice. He gives me headaches. 'Do this, don't do that, say it like this, sing, don't holler! . . .' He pounds away at me so hard I can't hear a word of what he's saying.

"I've decided to take lessons, but in my own way, all by myself. Marie Dubas is on at the A.B.C., just before me. I'll go hear her and you'll come with me."

I was working in a factory. I had a husband. It was no easy job being Edith's sister! When she made up her mind about something, she never paid any attention to other people. I was too proud to bother her with my little life. She would never have understood; it was too far removed from her. She'd have made fun of me.

So I managed to arrange things, and for two weeks, every day, and twice a day when there was a matinee, we went to hear Marie Dubas.

"What a lesson, Momone! Just look at her! Listen to her!"

At the last show Edith was still discovering tricks of the trade she'd never seen before. It was Marie who made Edith realize that gestures, the way you came onstage, the way you walked around, the pauses, the silences were the punctuation of a song.

"Look, Momone. When she comes on, she hasn't even opened her mouth yet, but she's already *there*. Raymond can explain it to me, but it's not the same. I *see* her. I understand why she does this or that. It all makes sense."

It wasn't a question of imitating her. Edith never copied anyone. She just wanted to check on what she herself was doing. To Edith, Marie was like the touchstone you check your gold jewelry against at a pawnshop.

Edith was an admirer of Marie's till the very end. She often used to go to Marie's dressing room and sit in a corner listening to her criticize herself. That was a lesson too. Marie Dubas would have barely left the stage, right after she'd made a big hit, and she'd say:

"No, in the last verse of 'Pedro,' when I repeat 'Pedro, Pedro . . .' it's flames, sun, castanets and at the same time an attack. I didn't put it across strongly enough. And don't you think I use too much emphasis in '*La Prière de la Charlotte*'? It should stay very simple. Charlotte isn't doing that for a man. She's doing it for something up in heaven, so it doesn't need to be jazzed up."

"That woman's a lady," Edith used to say. "When I listen to

her, I see everything I don't have." It was Marie Dubas's example that gave Edith an artist's awareness.

The dress rehearsal was only a few days away. Edith's and Raymond's nerves were on edge. He'd finally written her a song about her pals the legionnaires.

"Momone, this one really belongs to me. I'm finished with begging. I'm not singing other people's songs any more, I'm singing my own!" What triumph there was in her voice!

> *Ah! la la, la la, belle histoire,*
> *Là-haut sur les murs du bastion,*
> *Et dans le soleil plein de gloire,*
> *Et dans le vent, claque un fanion:*
> *C'est le fanion de la Légion!*

> Ah, what a great story,
> Up there on the walls of the fort,
> And in the glorious sunshine,
> In the wind, a pennant is waving:
> The pennant of the Legion!

How lucky I was to be part of the A.B.C. adventure! I really saw Edith change before my very eyes. Looking at her was like being at the movies, when they show you an ugly caterpillar turning into a butterfly. At first you see the little tips of their wings, all stuck together, moving just a bit. You're not sure what it is. And then they get bigger, they stretch out, they unwrinkle, and presto! they're ready to fly, they're silky, they're velvety, they're full of glory.

Every day something changed in Edith. I'm not talking about Edith the woman—*she* never changed. The proof of that was she had long since cheated on Raymond with guys who didn't matter. No, it was Edith the performer who was growing wings and was about to try them out in the spotlights of the A.B.C.

Three days before the premiere, Edith said to me, "We're rehearsing all night tonight. I'm going to run through my whole act, with the dress, the lighting, everything. You've got to come."

"But what about Raymond?"

"You can sit in the back of the theater. He won't see you."

I was pleased. But how cruel those words seemed to me!

"It's important, Momone. Tomorrow you'll have to tell me everything you've seen. Since there are lots of things Raymond's taught me that you can't understand, I'll explain them to you.

"First of all, there's an order to the whole performance. You can't follow one song with another just like that and trust to chance. It's like a pearl necklace—it's the position of the pearl that shows off its beauty.

"Then there are the lights. You'll see—they change with every song, depending on the style. Papa Leplée's simple little spotlight shining straight at you was just child's play, it seems. I've got blue lights, red lights and mixtures—and they don't turn them on full. Really bright lights overpower me.

"There's one funny thing—fake curtain calls. At the end of the fifth song you close the curtain as if your act was over. The audience is supposed to clap and yell for you to come back. If the clapping is only lukewarm, it doesn't matter; you raise it again right away. And then after that you have more fake curtain calls at the end, the bows, the encores. . . .

"I'll have stage makeup on because of the lights. Take a good look at me. I don't trust Raymond for that. I've got my own ideas on the subject. He'd turn me into a Marlene Dietrich if he could. Not that he's blind or stupid, but he's a man, and they can't ever look objectively at the woman they sleep with. It's either too much or not enough!

"I'm sure I have to look the way I did on the streets: pale, big eyes, a mouth and that's all. And there've been squabbles about the dress too. He wanted a touch of red, like a scarf. I said to him, 'Are you nuts? I suppose I ought to do an apache dance like Mistinguett!' "

She talked to me that way for over an hour. The next night, in the theater, hunched down in a corner, I savored my happiness all by myself: Edith on a real stage.

The curtain was all lit up. The velvet looked like it was alive.

Something was moving behind it. You could hear the stagehands talking.

Raymond came on, in front of the curtain. It gave me a funny feeling to see him there after nine months—the time it takes to make a kid. He had his pipe in his mouth. His face was usually dry, but now it was shiny with sweat. He was wearing a turtleneck sweater. He looked like a kind of worker, like a prole who's had an education. That night I thought he was good looking. He put his hand in front of his eyes. "Lower the three and the five in the balcony, and strike number one of the two downstage. You mustn't overpower her, you guys, you've got to set her off." By God, the bastard really knew his business!

From his seat in the third row, Mitty asked, "O.K.? Ready?" Raymond jumped down off the stage and yelled, "Go ahead!"

And the orchestra began to play. That really impressed me—eighteen musicians for Edith! They were there for her, they were playing for her. It was as beautiful as church to me, and I had tears in my eyes.

This dark, empty theater, smelling of dust and stale tobacco, was like a magic cave! The curtain opened and Edith came on. The light picked her out and went where she went like the wing of a guardian angel. The orchestra leader's eyes never left her. She began to sing. She'd told me to watch closely, and I couldn't. I collapsed on the back of the seat in front of me, my head in my arms, and sobbed all during the first song. It was too much. But later I opened my eyes and ears wide and took note of everything. I felt like a recording machine going clack, clack, clack. It was all taking place in my head. It seems to me today that that's the way a computer's memory must work.

What a night! When she'd finished her act, my hands were itching to clap. But that's never done at a rehearsal—it brings bad luck.

When the curtain came down, there was silence. Then Mitty yelled, "It's good, Edith. It's very good!"

Raymond started acting like a big shot. He got out his notebook. Edith was standing there in front of him, so little and looking so much like a well-behaved child, her big eyes raised to him as if she were in front of the "master." He was really playing the boss!

"On song three you don't pause long enough. You don't come across; you pick it up too fast. I went up to the peanut gallery. You don't look at them enough up there, Edith. They're the ones you're singing for. It's the proles who're going to make you a success. When you bow, give them the feeling you're looking them straight in the eye.

"On six, '*Les Fanions*,' the full spots aren't on her fast enough, you guys! There's a gap. She's finished singing before the light hits her. It's all got to get off together: that's the moment of victory."

I realized that night how much work Raymond had done. My leaving had paid off.

Mitty shouted:

"O.K., kids, that's all for tonight. See you tomorrow."

And the theater grew cold and dreary again.

The next day I was there ahead of time for our meeting. I hadn't slept all night. For quite a while we'd been meeting in a bar in Montmartre—Chez Jean Cyrano. Jean was a crooner who'd had a little success, really no more than that. He went in for sugary stuff. But that wasn't why we met at his place. It was because he had blue eyes! Edith would say, "Jean's eyes are like a little patch of sky, they're full of blue, it brims over!" And she'd add, "They're not like Raymond's eyes. If he didn't have black lashes to set off the blue of his eyes, they'd be sort of gray. . . ."

It was plain to see Edith had made it with Cyrano. And for the few weeks it lasted, "Blue Eyes" stood us all our drinks.

The minute she arrived and sat down, Edith said, "Well, how was it last night, Momone?"

"It was terrific!"

And we kissed each other.

"Is that all you have to say?"

That's the way Edith was. Compliments rubbed her the right way, they made her feel good, but she needed criticism, she had to have it, she asked for it. That's how you can tell a real star.

"As far as the songs go, you can trust Raymond. He knows

what he's doing." It went a little against the grain to say it, but it was true.

"Your hairdo's all right. As for the makeup, be careful about your mouth. You just slap on the lipstick any way at all; you don't outline your lips, you just smear it on."

Edith had always put her makeup on without looking in a mirror.

"My style is not to put anything on my face, Momone. I offer my face bare to the audience the way I would to a lover. What about the dress?"

They'd had a black dress made up for her in a kind of puckered material that was all the rage. It was a very simple skirt and top, with long sleeves and a little white collar.

"I don't like the collar."

"But I wore one at Leplée's."

"It wasn't the same. When you wore a little collar of imitation lace with a sweater, it looked sort of dressy. But onstage, with the careful lighting you have, I'd rather see just your bare face, like you say. See what I mean: the only thing white, the only bright thing, would be your face and your hands."

"I like that. I think you're right. I'll have to make Raymond swallow that. Right now, you know, he thinks he's God the Father. . . ."

(The night of the dress rehearsal, she wore her dress without the collar. I had my victory too!)

As she left, she gave me a box. "This is for you, for tomorrow night. It's a coat. Don't take it off."

I don't know how I could have! I had nothing decent to wear underneath.

The next night, wrapped in my dark garnet-colored coat with a fox collar, I felt sure of myself. But when I saw the packed house, the mixture of workers and Paris society, I was scared stiff! What if they didn't take to my Edith?

Her career hung in the balance. She had about thirty minutes to make it. If it didn't work at the A.B.C., she'd have to start all over again. My eyes were burning as I stared at the curtain, about to go up. Then she walked onstage looking as sure of herself as she'd been in the street! But I knew all about her stage fright.

I felt a tremor pass through the audience. That little dame standing there, a bit forlorn, almost poor, in a short dress (those days women sang in long dresses), with her beautiful, pinched face, white as bright light, and a voice that had everything in it—their troubles, their joys, their loves—she went straight to their hearts. To the working people she seemed one of them. And to the others she was something they didn't know, something they might come across on a street corner without wanting to see it.

They clapped from the very first song. I could hear them holding their breath, around me, above me, inside me. Edith's voice was like a strong wind sweeping over them, filling their lungs with intoxicating air, with air they'd never breathed before. At the end people were screaming and shouting, "One more! One more! . . ."

I could see Edith trembling as she bowed to them, way up there on the stage. She looked so fragile you'd have thought she was going to collapse. After that she had other successes, great successes, but this one wasn't like the others. It was the one that swept her to glory, like a storm.

Sitting there in the audience with a lump in my throat, I said to myself, "She won't be like she was before, I'm sure of it. Something'll change. There's going to be a barrier between us. This success is like a Maginot line separating us."

I felt like shouting to all the people applauding her:

"I'm right there with her!"

I was drunk with a crazy pride. I sat there in my seat like everybody else. This was now where I belonged. Up there on the stage, in the light, was where she belonged. All that space separating us scared me. And at the same time all that madness, that delirium around me, made me tremble with happiness.

That night at the A.B.C. a page of poverty and filth had been turned over. But we'd lived this misery together, and I clung to it. We were bound by almost eight years of living together. And that night I knew she'd laugh and drink with others. . . . I was too young, too sensitive to realize that it didn't matter, especially as far as Edith was concerned. And if I didn't go to her dressing room afterward, it was because I'd decided not to. She had said:

"Come give me a kiss when it's over, Momone."

But I couldn't. I knew what would have happened. Raymond would have taken me by the collar of my fine new coat and lifted me up in front of everybody to show he was stronger than I was, and he'd have made some beautifully shitty remark.

But that wasn't all. The A.B.C. was his triumph; he was happy. He was in his element, being the "boss," the creator of a "star." I wasn't going to spoil his pleasure.

Poor Raymond; he was in his glory as he hovered around Edith. But he had no reason to be: she was done with him.

Edith wasn't ungrateful. She was fond of him, but he'd more than served his time. She kept her friends for life, but not her lovers. She never forgot what she owed him, however, and she was always thankful to him, but that's not a feeling that keeps you in love. Whenever he needed her, she was there. Later, when he became a sick old man, she didn't let him down.

As far as love was concerned, though, it was over and done with, and Edith never went back to a man. She didn't believe in patching things up; she needed someone new. "The only time you really love somebody is the first time, Momone. . . ."

The next day the newspapers carried stories about her. I'd bought them all. It broke me! One of the critics wrote: "Last night, on the stage of the A.B.C., a great singer was born."

That was the night Edith's destiny began. In her professional life, no more gaps, no more tumbles, no more going backward.

Chapter 7

᭡
᭡ ᭡
᭡

Paul Meurisse: Le Bel Indifférent

Edith's life, her nonprofessional one, was hardly what one would call orderly. Everything was all mixed up together: friendships, passions, one-night stands and, above all, love affairs. She no sooner finished one when she began another. But she had principles in love, especially when it came to breaking up.

"A woman who gets herself dropped is a poor sap, Momone. There's no lack of men—the streets are full of them. But you have to find a replacement first, not after. If you wait till after, you're the one who's been cheated on; but before, it's him. And that makes one hell of a difference!"

Edith always applied this principle with a clear conscience. No man was ever able to make her change. She'd cheat first, and then see what happened. Sometimes she'd tell them; other times she'd just laugh watching them. And if any man thought he'd cheated on her first—boy, was he wrong! She'd already beaten him to the punch. As long as the new guy wasn't ready to shack up with her she didn't say anything; she kept the old one. She had to have a man around the house.

"Can't have a house without a man, Momone. It's worse than a day without sunshine. You can get along without the sun—there's electricity. But a house without some guy's shirt lying around, where you don't run across a pair of socks, or a tie, where there's

not a nice warm jacket thrown on a chair, it's like a widow's house
—it gets you down!"

Raymond didn't know it, but he was living his last days at the
Hotel Alsina. After his success at the A.B.C., he was sure of his
future with Edith. He thought she couldn't get along without him.

Edith was happy. She had reason to be: she was in demand
everywhere. Her profession was like a house of stone. Or better
still, a sort of solidly built arch of triumph.

For her to be perfectly happy, she needed a new man. And
she'd just found one.

"I've got to tell you, Momone. I've taken up with a weird sort
of guy. Not like the others."

I thought, "Oh, great, here we go again!"

"What does he do?" I asked.

"He sings in a club."

"What's his name?"

"Paul Meurisse."

The name didn't mean a thing to me.

"Don't you recognize the name? That doesn't surprise me—
you don't know anything that's going on any more!"

It was on the tip of my tongue to say, "Whose fault is that?"
But I decided to keep my mouth shut. I wanted to hear her story.

"You know I'm appearing at the Night-Club, on the rue Arsène
Houssaye. Every night, before I go in, I stop by for a drink at the
Caravelle. It's nearby, and I meet my pals there.

"Well, you know me. I was sitting there, not thinking of anything special, when I saw a nice-looking guy at the bar, got up like
an English fashion plate. Handsome, really handsome. Dark, shiny
hair plastered down like a crow's wing. Black eyes. Yes, dark eyes
—you've got to change once in while! And refined as hell. A little
too much like a fashion model, but that can probably be fixed. I
gave him one of those long looks. You know, my wide-eyed look,
all innocence, the one that makes me look like a kid you can have
for two cents, but who's got a big heart. It didn't work. He never
batted an eye; he didn't even smile.

"He may have been worth it, but I dropped the whole thing.

Anyway, he was there the next day at the same time. I asked a few questions.

"The barman told me he sings every night at L'Amiral. 'He comes here for a drink before he goes on like you do. It's M. Paul Meurisse,' as much as to say, 'He's a prince in disguise.' "

She started laughing.

"You can't imagine. You've never seen a man like him. Listen, Momone, I don't want to look like I'm making advances, but couldn't you drop by and ask about him? I'd like to know where the guy's from."

The next day I had all the details. He was twenty-six, born in Dunkerque, and his father was a bank manager. He'd studied law in Aix-en-Provence and had clerked in a notary's office. After starting out singing popular songs in the Marseilles vaudeville theaters, Paul came up to Paris and became an insurance investigator—and he sure looked the type to investigate disasters! He was dying to sing in a vaudeville theater, so he turned up for an amateur contest at the Alhambra and won. Mitty Goldin took him on as a chorus boy, and in addition he sang in various cabarets every night.

I told Edith what I'd found out, and she said:

"Not exactly what you'd call a 'flaming' past. And he doesn't make you dream of adventures either. But I don't give a damn; what I like about him is how really earnest he looks. Anyway, you can't imagine how well he talks!"

"Have you gotten that far already? Aren't you afraid you're rushing things?"

"Don't make fun of me. He spoke to me yesterday. You know, I've got intuition. So I went to the Caravelle all by myself to encourage him. Talking to a woman who's horsing around with her pals isn't easy for some guys. Maybe Paul's shy.

"I no sooner sat down, playing the role of a tearful babe waiting for somebody to console her, when he gave out with one of those cold, distinguished smiles that'd make a polar bear shiver. But it made *me* feel good! 'He's taking the first step,' I said to myself. And I was right. He walked over quietly and said, 'May I offer you a glass of champagne?' That's all I was waiting for. He sat down next to me, and I think we were both equally embarrassed. See, I didn't want to throw myself at him—he's not the type. We were so 'refined' we didn't say more than ten words to each other. Finally, to thaw him out, I said, 'You've got nice eyes.' What I'd been thinking about those eyes from the very beginning I kept to myself: 'I'd like to see them when they go wild!'

"He seemed to be touched. He took his time and answered, 'I noticed yours right away, and your smile. When you smile, you look as if you're letting yourself go. It's very moving.'

"He said it so well that I thought, 'Wow! He's learned all those words by heart!'

"The ice was broken. He was nice enough to spend half an hour talking to me. At the end, he said:

" 'You must come and hear me. I'd be pleased to have your criticism.'

"I pay attention when he talks to me so I can repeat what he's said, because if I didn't tell it to you word for word, it'd lose all its charm."

I followed their story like a movie serial—*The Three Musketeers* type. You know how it ends, but that doesn't keep you from watching anyway. And I really got a kick out of it. Seeing Edith mixed up with a fellow like that was kind of a riot.

The next day there was the climax. It began with a fiasco, but what an ending it had!

"I went to hear Paul. I didn't like it. The guy's not going to make it singing. He's too deadpan, with a stony face and a neat jacket buttoned all the way to the top. He sang:

> *Ah! viens, viens, ma Nénette,*
> *Faire un tour sur les chevaux . . . de bois.*
> *Ça fait tourner la tête,*
> *Et ça vous donne la gueule . . . de bois.*

> Ah! come, come my Nénette,
> Take a ride on the wooden horses.
> It'll make your head swim,
> And give you a hangover.

"There's not much of a public for a style like that. He won't make the twenty-cent seats laugh with that! But I thought he was handsome, the beast! So I went to his dressing room. As he was tying his tie, he asked if I'd liked it.

"I gave it to him straight: 'No, not much.'

" 'Well, you can't please everybody.'

" 'How about pleasing me?' I asked.

" 'That's different,' he said. 'But I don't intend to charm you with my verses. . . .'

"And then—hang onto your chair!—he bent over and kissed my hand. . . . It was like acting in a play! But I was annoyed. I couldn't help asking:

" 'Listen, Paul, are you angry?'

" 'Not at all. Why?'

" 'You didn't really kiss my hand. I didn't feel a thing.'

"He burst out laughing. 'But it's only pretending. Only a boor *really* kisses a woman's hand. You brush it with your lips, but that's all.'

"Did I look like a fool! But I quickly managed to get out of it. I looked him straight in the eye and said:

" 'It's not the same with you. *You* could have . . .'

"Momone, we've still got things to learn. I never would have thought that kissing someone's hand was that complicated!

"And then Paul really knocked me out. He asked me, just like that, to go to bed with him.

" 'Edith, the sooner the better, it seems to me,' he said. 'I don't see why one has to beat around the bush, or why women have to say no before they say yes. Do you want to come have a drink at my place some night?'

"I felt like answering, 'Two drinks'd be better than one.' But I couldn't be personal with him right away like that. So I went into my princess routine:

" 'Do you have any doubts?'

"He laughed like a kid. I could have hugged him.

" 'I'll pick you up at the end of your act, Edith,' he said. 'You're adorable. I kiss your hands.'

"And he kissed them both—really kissed them this time. But that's the story."

"What now?" I asked.

"There's no 'what now' about it. It's happened. He's my lover. He's a change from the others. You don't have any idea what nice manners he has. He holds my coat for me. He's always behind me. He lets me go in front of him. I'm not used to that. It seems almost as if I've got a flunky."

I knew what she meant. With those pimps we hung around with, we were the ones that stepped aside to let them go first. We respected men. With Raymond, it depended on the mood he was in. . . .

"How about Raymond? What have you done about him?"

"I'm waiting. I have no way of knowing if it's going to last with Paul."

I was sure it was going to last. I saw from the start that Paul impressed Edith. There'd never been a man before who'd surprised her. She'd admired them; she had to, in order to love them. But she always knew ahead of time what a man's gestures and reactions would be. With Paul, she had no idea what he was going to do or say. He was an exotic beast. If he'd eaten orchids for breakfast, she'd have thought it was natural.

I was really anxious to meet him. But when?

I've never forgotten the date: September 1939.

Edith and I had never been very interested in world events. Politics was way over our heads. In 1938, at the time of the Munich agreement, I'd tried to tell Edith there were newspapers on the stands that were talking about war. She'd answered:

"Don't worry about it, Momone. It's not your business to make history. It's small fry like you who get screwed and have to pay for the damages if they don't watch out. Anyway, it's no use getting upset about things you can't change!"

Her opinion on that score was always the same. It was true that in our position we didn't have a goddamn thing to do with the way the world was run. Our subjects of conversation weren't compli-cated, and didn't cover much territory. We had to scare up cash every day for a five-pound loaf of bread and a bottle of cheap red wine, and once we had it, to hell with wars and the end of the world. We weren't interested in strikes. We weren't workers. Our class didn't even have a name. When we were kids, the only one who'd ever mentioned politics or stuff like that was our old man. And that didn't go very far!

But it wasn't the same in September 1939. I have reasons not to forget the date. My husband had been called up. I'd gone with him to the Fort of Vincennes the night before. It was wide open: people kept going in and coming out. There were noncoms and officers in uniform, and infantrymen with all their gear. And then there were the others, looking like real freaks: military jackets and fatigue caps mixed in with civvies; uniform pants with civilian jackets; dressy brown shoes; clocked socks with hobnailed boots, with or without puttees.

Also, those odd-looking soldiers were standing there talking or sitting on the ground and leaning against the walls. Some of them were eating; others were going hungry. I didn't have the least idea what it was all about, but I tried to make it jibe with the memories of my father, who'd been in the infantry in 1914. And I couldn't really see any connection. They sure didn't look as if they were going off to victory!

That was the way I left my husband in the courtyard of the Fort of Vincennes—in the middle of those men shuffling their feet, coughing, spitting, swearing and not paying a goddamn bit of attention to the adjutants' yelling. We kissed each other. We were young; we didn't understand. I had his picture in my purse, and he had mine in his wallet. I never saw him again. He was one of the first to be killed. So I never talk about it. He just wasn't lucky. Maybe I wasn't either. . . .

So, obviously, the morning after he left I wasn't in any mood to have fun. The concierge hollered in the courtyard, "Mme Simone, your sister's on the phone."

I rushed downstairs. Edith—what a blessing! And there she was on the other end of the line, a real chunk of ice. No hello, nothing.

"Simone, how come you stood me up?"

I'm not usually short of breath, but I was speechless.

"Come back right away."

Those four words took me back several years, when I'd run away and Edith ordered me to come back like a little kid.

"Come where?"

"To the Hotel Alsina, you dope, where I live."

That suited me just fine! When you're singing "*Les Mômes de la cloche*," you couldn't care less about the war, but when you're a worker in a factory, it's not the same thing. Before they get organized, they bounce you, and you don't know where your next meal's coming from. Anyway, instead of moping around all by myself, I was going to be with Edith. That was an idea I'd given up. I had my life and she had hers; we were at opposite ends of the earth.

"But what about Raymond?"

"Never mind. He's been called up. Are you coming or aren't you? Bring your stuff, take a taxi and leave the key with your concierge."

As usual, she'd thought of everything, except asking me if I was free. She didn't give a damn about my private life; I belonged to her. Raymond had left and she was alone; I wasn't with her and I was wrong not to be!

A sort of joy came over me in the taxi with each turn of the wheels; my heart was bursting. I was going to see Edith and take up my life with her again. I realized that the life we'd led together was as strong as a drug: it wasn't easy to get along without it.

Before I'd had time to get everything straight in my mind, I found myself in Edith's bathroom at the Hotel Alsina, sitting on the bidet, watching and listening to her. It was a staggering change. I'd never seen a private bathroom that close up before, and this one was Edith's, now ours. I suddenly realized that "sessions in the bathroom" were going to play a big part of our lives.

"Are you happy, Momone?"

"Am I ever!"

"Good. Now hand me the bobby pins."

We'd started all over again. . . .

Edith made all the important decisions about her life in her bathroom. We were alone there; no man would have dared come in and bother us. We chattered like real magpies for hours at a time, and about everything—her profession, her plans, her shifting from man to man, her great resolutions, her solemn promises. Edith told me her ideas about everything. As she saw different people and different things, her horizon broadened and her subjects of conversation increased.

Her men never got to know her. The only line she took with them was love; that was all she talked to them about. It was all they had the right to hear from her. Their business was loving.

Edith always gave the impression that she wasn't a flirt, that she couldn't care less. She perfectly well realized that it was part of her image, of her publicity.

"I'm the simple sort of girl. A child of the people . . . natural . . . a sidewalk flower . . . and not even very pretty!"

And she'd modestly add:

"I'm ugly. I know I'm not beautiful. I'm not Greta Garbo!"

But she didn't believe a word of it. It was part of her legend, and she knew how to keep it going! People kept writing that she was an insignificant little dame (they practically said she was a hunchback!), that her beauty lay in her talent, that that was what made her the greatest of all. So Edith went along with them. But she didn't really like it. When we were together, she'd set things straight and draw up her own list.

"Look at me. My eyes are an unusual color; they're violet. And my mouth, it's alive, it's beautiful. Maybe my forehead's a little too big, but I like it better than a little low narrow one. At least it's broad. It doesn't make me look like an ass or a half-wit. Anyway, it's no big drawback; look, a few curls over it makes it smaller!"

She used to get terrific laughing fits that cracked the beauty masks she put on her face.

"Hey, Momone," she'd scream, "get a load of my plaster façade! It's shot to hell. Never mind, I'll try another one. That one wasn't worth much anyway."

Edith was the ideal customer for beauty products. Nobody was taken in the way she was.

"Momone, look at this ad in the paper: 'Charm every man with Doctor X's strawberry cream . . .' 'eternally young with So-and-So's cellular cream . . .' 'removes all your wrinkles like an eraser,' " and so on. "Do *you* believe all that?"

I didn't tell her what I really thought. "Well, you know, you don't really need them," I'd say.

And she didn't. She had marvelous soft, white, dewy skin. It was a gift of nature, and it could take a lot of beating. The rare times she washed, she used bars of cheap toilet soap that stank and were so strong you could have scoured an oven with them.

I also admired her ears—tiny as a baby's, nicely curled and sort of transparent, like porcelain. But what were really extraordinary were her hands—small, delicate, soft and marvelously warm. When she took your hand, that warmth went straight to your heart and filled you completely.

I'd sit there happily, passing Edith bobby pins, rollers, jars of cream. I listened to her chatter away with a feeling of happiness and complete security. And the world under our feet was about as solid as Vesuvius erupting.

When I came out of the bathroom that first day, I saw a Chinese sitting in a chair, and a guy in a silk dressing gown lying on the bed reading the newspaper. I said to myself, "It can't be—she's got two of 'em, a white one and a yellow one. There'll be four of us in bed!"

Before I could think any more about it, Edith said:

"Momone, this is Paul Meurisse. He lives with us. And this is Chang, my cook."

Paul got up, not looking very pleased.

"If you'd told me beforehand, Edith, I would have put a jacket on."

It couldn't be! A jacket! The guy sure wasn't normal!

As for the cook, I didn't understand. I hadn't seen a kitchen anywhere. Chang rose, picked up the bag at his feet and went into the bathroom. I hadn't thought of that. It was very simple. He put a board over the tub and did the cooking on alcohol stoves. His specialty was steak and french fries.

"What do you think of that?" Edith asked me. "Having a Chinese cook is pretty classy, huh? Besides, you save money."

I had no illusions about that. Edith's "good housewife" routines had always cost a lot.

The more I looked at her Paul, the more I thought that the three of us really couldn't share the same bed, and I wondered where I was going to end up.

"I got you a room next door, Momone. Come on; we'll go unpack your suitcase."

Paul stooped down and picked up the suitcase.

"I'll carry it for you. May I call you Simone? Edith has told me so much about you."

Out of the corner of my eye I could see Edith grinning like a fool. No, I'd never seen a man like that! Could he be real?

"What do you think of Paul?" she asked me later.

"Amazing. He was really polite about the business of the suitcase. But the silk dressing gown to lounge around in in his room—I thought that was only in the movies! He seems to do it so naturally."

That night we went out to "dine," as he put it. He held our chairs for us and waited till we were seated. He put his napkin on his lap. We were chilled with admiration. Edith didn't seem to be very used to it yet. And I said to myself, "The guy's going too far? He's piling it on!"

I had been sure we couldn't learn anything more than Asso had stuffed our brains with, but now I saw there was still more. . . . I was uncomfortable. I was afraid of doing something wrong when I ate. For Paul it was all so natural. He must have had centuries of good breeding behind him. He was elegant, but I didn't find him much fun. I often envied Edith her men, I thought she had taste, but I didn't understand this one. I was wrong though, and Edith was right. Paul gave her something she had been missing: class.

When the headwaiter asked us what we wanted, Edith started to say, "I think I'd like . . ." But Paul glared at her and took over.

"Madame will have . . ." and he reeled off our whole menu, ending with the words: "Send the wine steward over." Then he said to Edith in a scolding voice, "You know very well that a woman chooses but lets the man give the order. Just as I mustn't order the wine without asking you about it."

We'd never heard that. Life with this man was going to be fun!

Raymond didn't know he'd been replaced. For Edith a soldier off fighting was far away! But men who'd been called up did get leaves, and I couldn't rid myself of the thought that Raymond was bound to show up sooner or later.

"Listen, Edith. What are you going to do about Asso?"

"I'm keeping him for the songs and dropping him for the rest."

"And what if he doesn't agree?"

"Don't ask foolish questions. A man's never stayed with me when I didn't want him any more."

Saying that was one thing. It was true, but the kiss-off didn't always go smoothly. I'd seen some real scenes!

Just as I'd foreseen, Raymond turned up on his first leave. He didn't knock—this was home. The first unpleasant shock for him was opening the door and seeing me, looking like I belonged there.

"Are you back?" he asked.

"You can see I am."

"She took you back?"

"It looks like it."

"Where is she?"

"I don't know."

But I did know. Edith was with Paul in the room next door.

"Listen, Raymond, how about a bath? It's restful when you've been fighting a war."

"What are you giving me? Do you know where she is?"

"No. I'll see if she isn't around the neighborhood somewhere."

"I see she quickly went back to her good old habits. It's time I came home."

"So you're coming home, are you? Well, I've got some advice for you: don't be in any hurry."

I wanted him to get mad so Edith would hear him yelling. I

managed to. He hollered so loud Edith came running. She greeted him with:

"Do you think you live here, shouting like that? If you've come to get your things, go ahead and take 'em—there aren't all that many!"

"What do you mean, Didou?"

"Don't call me Didou, or Didi, or even Edith. Don't call me anything. I've had it. And what the hell are you doing standing there listening to me, Simone? Is this any of your business? It's not, so go next door."

Raymond didn't miss that one.

"What's next door?"

"A room—Simone's room. Does that interest you?"

"Yes, a lot. She's got a room now? You don't bed down together any more?"

"Listen, I don't ask you who you sleep with. You fled the coop. It's none of your business any more."

"I was called up."

"Well, stay called up. And clear out. You've got no business being here any more."

I left them screaming at the top of their lungs, and I found Paul in the room next door, sitting on the unmade bed in his dressing gown, filing his nails. He'd picked a good time!

"Is it Raymond Asso?" he asked.

"You can hear."

"Only too well."

There was a real battle going on in the next room, and I was wondering if it was time to call the cops when I saw Paul put on his jacket, grab his hat and umbrella, and leave. That made one less!

The scene lasted at least an hour. The two of them eventually calmed down. I heard Edith crying; she must have got slapped. That was the only way to handle her, and Raymond had never minded doing it.

I heard her say in her little-girl voice:

"You know, Raymond, you had the best part of me. Deep in my heart you'll always be the one I'll never forget."

"Even so, my little girl, you shouldn't have done that to me while I was in the army."

I was sorry for Raymond. I put myself in his place. It couldn't have been any fun to come home on leave and discover your woman in your bed with another man.

I couldn't hear much any more. They must have been talking about singing. Raymond was probably giving her advice, for the last time.

Edith saw him again later. They became good pals again. But even though she was without regrets, Raymond was never the same again. He knew he was only a songwriter whose songs Edith might or might not take.

It wrung my heart that day when he left, because there was no way of knowing how it would all turn out, since after all we were at war, and he might get killed tomorrow! And seeing him leave, looking a little bit round-shouldered in his uniform . . .

He died twenty-nine years later, in 1968, five years after Edith almost to the day, in a hospital bed. He was sixty-nine years old. The last thing he did for Edith was to write program notes for her last 45 rpm record "*L'Homme de Berlin.*" He was still taking care of things for "his little girl." A few hours before he passed away, my old Raymond was still talking about her to anyone who would listen.

"Edith always used to tell me, 'Don't ever leave me by myself!' "

Poor Raymond, he clung to those words, which Edith said to every man she loved. He believed them. He added, "She was right. I should have held out against everything and everybody. If I'd been there to take care of her, I wouldn't have let her die at an age when she should have been having her greatest triumphs. . . . She was made for recitals, with a concert piano, not for big deals with a large orchestra and choruses. . . ."

It's heartbreaking and depressing to think that even as he lay dying Raymond still wanted to have a part in Edith's life, giving her advice, telling her what she ought to do.

Raymond hadn't always been nice to me, but I respected him. And I felt for him, maybe because we were of the same breed. Whereas with Paul I always had the feeling I was living with Louis XIV.... It was a real show!

Edith went off to sing that night, just like any other night. When we came home, Paul wasn't there. He probably hadn't swallowed Raymond's visit! Edith began to complain.

"If Paul tries to play games with me, he's gonna have some real trouble. If he gets jealous just when I'm getting rid of Raymond, I'm gonna let him have it, the conceited darling!"

She'd barely got the words out of her mouth when Paul opened the door as if he were entering Maxim's, with exactly the proper polite and distant smile.

"My dear Edith, I hope you'll pardon my being a little late, but I needed some solitude, some time to think. And this is what I've decided: You shouldn't live in Montmartre. It lacks elegance. You expose yourself to unfortunate encounters which are not to my liking. When one has a name like yours, one lives at L'Etoile."

Making an entrance like that after the scene there'd been . . . well, I took my hat off to him! The guy had real class. He'd gotten around her by taking her by surprise.

"It's charming and very picturesque to have a Chinese cook in a hotel, but an apartment would be more suitable for him, and for you too."

An apartment of her own! The idea pleased Edith immediately. She'd not only never had one, but the thought had never even crossed her mind.

"What do you say to that, Momone?"

"I think Paul's right. It'd give you class."

Our dream had been to have two rooms and a kitchen someday. Living at L'Etoile would be putting us right up there with all the moneybags. That's why we moved to a furnished apartment at 14 rue Anatole de la Forge, on the ground floor. A fine neighborhood near the Etoile, and a nice location, next to a bar, the Bidou-Bar, which soon became our headquarters.

Paul knew how to do the right thing, I must say. When we got there with Chang and all the stuff, Paul held the keys out to Edith. He'd seen to everything.

"Open the door yourself. This is your home."

Edith melted and threw her arms around his neck.

"Oh, Paul, you're a darling!"

The only trouble was that Paul did it all looking, as usual, like an English clergyman, and Edith's spirits drooped like a bad soufflé. She began to find it tiring being refined all the time. . . .

The way Paul moved in wasn't at all what we were used to. He arrived with leather suitcases and put everything away himself! When there was a man around the house, we were used to taking loving care of him. We unpacked his things and put them away. It was the only time, in fact, that Edith ever tidied up. Mostly she liked filling out their wardrobes the way she wanted. She adored dressing her guys. Even when she didn't have much money, she gladly paid for what they bought. Edith's pimps had encouraged this trait of hers and had no trouble exploiting it. She gave for her own pleasure.

With Paul it was out of the question. He had everything custom made: suits, shirts, shoes. He chose his own socks, his own underwear. And his handkerchiefs, his pajamas, his scarves and his ties were silk. He was the only one who had good taste. That annoyed her.

"I would have liked to buy him a suit, shirts, ties. . . . We don't have the same taste, but I've got as much as he has! Maybe he's got good manners, but he's not tactful. He could wear one of my ties just once!"

Edith's choices were rather startling. They looked like Picassos. Which is fine for paintings, but ties are something else! You had to have nerve to wear them, and it was just too much for Paul.

We'd look at all his nice things, not daring to touch them; they were laid out the way they'd be in an elegant shop.

"Did you know there were men who dressed like that, with everything custom made? Maybe you've met some, O.K., but you've never lived with them. What a change! It's the first time I've ever had one that didn't smell like a man. Paul smells of toilet water, and lavender, and fine leather. He shaves twice a day—our old man only shaved when he was downright filthy. And then Paul uses an English lotion. It feels cool when you kiss him. You think all that's normal?" She laughed. "After all, he's not a broad!"

Paul fascinated us with his elegant manners. But it wasn't always fun. After Raymond's lessons, we had to cram ourselves full of Paul's.

"Where are you going, Edith? Are you going out looking like that? Aren't you ashamed of yourself?"

"What's wrong?"

"Spots. You're covered with spots. A woman called Edith Piaf doesn't go around in dirty clothes. Being well groomed gives you class, even if you're wearing a cheap little dress."

He was so clean it worried Edith and me. We didn't understand. He forced us to do what he did, to wash our hands before sitting down at the table. We hardly knew that such a thing as a toothbrush existed, but Paul made each of us get one and use it twice a day. Edith especially, since he kissed her, and she used to eat pickled herring full of onions all night long!

"Come on, darling, let's go to bed," Paul would say, looking impeccable in his silk pajamas and dressing gown and smelling of toilet water. Edith would come in in a nightgown that was always too big for her. You could have put three women her size in one of them. (This wasn't surprising since she bought them any old place, any old way.) She dragged around in slippers and usually wore an old wool coat, because she always felt cold. In a nice way Paul would look behind Edith's ears to see if they were clean. As if they'd had time to get dirty! He used to ask, "Have you washed?" As if you had to wash up to sleep!

I wouldn't have liked that. She went along with him; she loved him. When Edith loved a man, he could ask anything of her and make her do anything.

But all this cleanliness worried Edith.

"Don't you think there's something sick about washing yourself like that all the time?"

You may smile, but it was rather pathetic. When we were kids, people around us thought dirt and lice were protection, like a vaccine against illness. Later on, when she'd got rid of her vermin, Edith would take a cat, the dirtier the better, put it on her lap and dreamily look for fleas. . . .

We were sure Raymond had taught us everything there was to know about table manners. So the day Paul said to Edith, "Darling, I want you to behave differently at table and eat English style," we looked at each other dumfounded.

"Look how I hold my knife." He held it like a pen. "I use it to push my food onto my fork."

"So what. I'm not left-handed and I'm not an acrobat. I eat with my right hand."

He laughed, something he didn't do very often.

Edith couldn't stand it. She answered straight out:

"Paul, you give me a swift pain. All this crap about eating; you can keep it!"

It wouldn't have mattered if Edith and Paul hadn't basically been strangers to each other. When I was a little kid and saw a guy who wasn't from our neighborhood, from our world, I'd take a good look at him, and just from the way he dressed and behaved and talked, I'd say to myself, "There's a guy with a diploma; you can tell."

It was a border I had no passport for. Edith thought the same thing. When she'd ask me, "What do you think of him?" and I'd answer, "He's got a diploma," she'd say, "He's not for us. You've got to be careful; when you haven't been to school, you really seem simpleminded. It's dangerous, Momone; I might lose him!"

Only later did Edith realize that talent compensated for a lot of things, that it was at home anywhere, that you could be intelligent even if you weren't educated. But in Paul's day we didn't know that yet. He awed us. Anyway, he knew how to talk, and Edith was very aware of it.

"Just listen to him, Momone. How well he talks! He talks like people write. It's beautiful! And never one word louder than the next, no temper tantrums, no vulgar words. A well-bred, refined man like him is restful. It was a good idea to come and live at

L'Etoile. I guess what he calls class comes from having the right address, the right telephone number, a servant—and other little things we'd never have thought of without him. See, there aren't any surprises with Paul: he comes home, puts on his dressing gown and listens to the radio in his slippers. He belongs to his little woman body and soul. The guy's not a skirt-chaser. Boy, is he restful!"

But Edith wasn't going to stand that sort of restfulness very long.

I slept in the back of the apartment. Edith was in the bedroom with him, in a lovely bed covered in blue satin. It was the way it should be, but I wasn't used to being alone. I'd waked up too many mornings with her next to me.

But that's all that had changed. In the morning, man around or not, I was the one who woke her up—and it was a whole ritual. I liked to watch her sleep; she looked like a baby. I'd slip one finger in her hand—she always had her fists clenched—and she'd squeeze my finger and murmur:

"Is that you, Momone?"

She'd open one eye, then the other. She'd hold out her hand and I'd give her her coffee, black and very strong. Then she'd sit up, settle down against the pillows and begin to take a cautious look at life.

"Is it nice out? Open the curtains. Not too fast."

She paid no attention to the man lying next to her. He could either go on sleeping or wake up; she didn't give a damn. I'd sit on the bed and we'd start yakking. She'd vaguely look at the mail and at the articles about her, raging or laughing—living, I called it. Then she'd toss off the covers, uncovering the guy, who was grumbling, and then traipse into the bathroom in her oversize nightgown, me along with her.

Edith would look at me and laugh and turn on the faucets. The noise was cheery—it sounded like a waterfall. Like a kid who's afraid of getting scolded, she'd wet the washcloth and the soap, and throw the towels on the floor in a heap as if they'd been used; that way, Paul would let her alone. Then we'd get down to serious things—the jars of cream and bla-bla-bla. It was Edith who made that one up. With us it wasn't "arsenic and old lace," but "jars of cream and bla-bla-bla."

When she felt like spoiling the boss because he'd been good in bed that night, and when she hadn't been so tight she forgot it, she'd say, "Go fix Paul's breakfast," but usually he managed to get it himself.

You have to admit this isn't exactly the sort of awakening a lover dreams about.

Paul dreamed of little tête-à-têtes, of scenes like Manon's "little table," with candles. If they'd had one, it would probably have looked like Zola's Gervaise having dinner with the Chevalier des Grieux.

When he got too fed up with having three of us at the table, he'd look at me and say:

"I don't want her here; let her eat in the kitchen."

If Edith was in a good mood, she'd shrug her shoulders or tap her forehead with her finger, meaning, "He's batty; don't pay any attention, Momone."

But if she was cross, she'd grab her plate and follow me.

"I'll eat in the kitchen too."

Paul would sit there stubbornly on his tailbone, finish his meal, smoke and read as he had his coffee. That didn't make the atmosphere any warmer, especially since by that time we'd come back from the kitchen horsing around and going on with our conversation. As if by chance, the subject always happened to be an old boyfriend.

"Say, Momone, remember Riri the legionnaire [or Jeannot the gob, or my fiancé on the Paris-Mediterranean train—he sure was a a good kisser, the bastard!]."

And there were plenty like that, plenty—a real fourteenth of July parade of them.

Edith would light into Paul:

"Why aren't you laughing? Doesn't it amuse you?"

"Not exactly."

"I wonder what it'd take to get you to laugh."

"Certainly something besides your stories about sleeping around."

"You don't like my love stories? But I've got some beautiful ones, really beautiful. Right, Momone? Well, aren't you jealous?"

"Your past doesn't interest me—it's got too many people in it."

"Why don't you call me a whore while you're at it?"

No matter what she did—and no one could be more unfair than she could—Paul kept his cool. Edith would begin to get worked up.

"He's an iceberg, Paul is. I must be absolutely nuts to have fallen head over heels for a guy that's a handbook on etiquette. Do *you* feel like kidding around with some undertaker? I don't. I'm going to make him forget his good breeding. He's going to smack me yet, do you hear? I'll get my smack out of him."

Once she'd made up her mind to get slapped, I was sure she would be someday. But how? As far as I was concerned, when they made Paul they'd forgotten to put the nerves in. Only the guy's head really worked, and the only thing in it was good manners.

Edith adored fights and scenes and screaming. Things had to be hopping around her, inside her—it was her way of living. She sang about fun, love, jealousy, separation, not cozy firesides. And what she sang was always something of her life, and lots of herself.

We'd sneak out to the Bidou-Bar next door, creeping past our windows on all fours so Paul wouldn't see. When we came in at ungodly hours, either tight or pretending to be, Paul would grit his teeth and not say a word. It would have been a blow to his honor to come get us, but it was just what we deserved; what's more, he should have dragged us home by the skin of our asses!

Paul's way of not saying anything got Edith so mad she'd throw anything handy at him. And Paul would say to me, cold as an icebox:

"Simone, there are still some plates in the kitchen—go get them." Then, with an air of great dignity, he'd stretch out on the bed with a book and turn his radio up full blast. The neighbors really went for that! The radio was his bosom buddy—he adored it. He'd listen for hours to classical music, music we didn't understand a note of, and the news, naturally. This bugged Edith no end!

The "phony war" was in full swing. Except for the air-raid wardens and the little smarties who went around with their chests puffed out in their preposterous uniforms and all those who were supposed to be "somewhere in France" but really were always close to Paris, nothing much was changed. And since it was absolutely necessary to see that the troops got a rest and had their morale kept up, all the nightclubs, vaudeville shows, movie houses and theaters were full of people.

Spring that year had been very beautiful, promising a good summer. Edith, who never paid any attention to the weather, kept saying to me, "It's lucky I have Paul. This spring weather knocks me out and the days are too long."

I always thought Paul had lots of talent in bed. But that didn't stop Edith from wanting to horse around. It didn't take much to put her in a black mood. There was no doubt about it—something was happening around us that we could feel but couldn't see.

One day I had a brilliant idea for getting her mind off things.

"Let's go to all the bistros on the rue de Belleville—up one side and down the other."

And we were off. We went into every joint going up the street —and there were plenty of them—but coming back down was out of the question. By the time we got to the place des Fêtes, we were crawling on all fours. All the concierges in the neighborhood still remember it.

When we got back, Paul looked very disapproving. Edith insisted he had to get tight too. Drunks always made her gay.

"That's enough of that, Edith. Go sleep it off somewhere else. I don't want a drunken woman in my bed."

"You're a pain in the ass, a damn party pooper. You're as fucking dull as an All Saints' day; you smell like chrysanthemums."

Paul left without answering and, his radio under his arm, closed himself in his room.

"So that's the way it is, is it? You shit, you bastard," Edith

Edith (on the right) age 4. Taken at Bernays. *(Séruzier)*

Edith and Simone in the "work clothes" they wore to sing in the streets of Pigalle.

Papa Gassion, contortionist. (Séruzier)

GASSION

CONTORSIONISTE-ANTIPODISTE

L'HOMME QUI MARCHE LA TÊTE A L'ENVERS

Simone Berteaut,
age 14.

With Papa Leplée who named Edith "La Môme Piaf." *(Séruzier)*

1938 in Montmartre with Raymond Asso (to Edith's left). *(Séruzier*

Edith and Paul Meurisse as they appeared in *l'Etoile sans lumière* in 1941.

Jean Cocteau and Edith. *(Serge Lido)*

Edith with Yves Montand after a performance at l'Etoile. *(AGIP)*

Jean-Louis Jaubert of Les Compagnons de Chanson, Edith and Simone in Holland, 1946.

In New York with Marcel Cerdan and Simone the night of the Middleweight Championship bout (1948).

At the Versailles in New York a flock of celebrities came to see Piaf perform.

From left: Faye Emerson, Sonja Henie, Judy Garland and Ginger Rogers.

With Lena Horne.

Gary Merrill
and Bette Davis.

Danny Kaye and Helen Hayes.

Edith and Dean Martin.

Winner of the Grand Prix du Disque in 1952, Edith is greeted by Edouard Herriot, President of the National Assembly, and Colette.

Charles Aznavour after his show at the Alhambra in 1958. *(Photoworld-FPG)*

Marlene Dietrich, matron of honor, escorts Edith into St. Vincent de Paul's in New York for her wedding to Jacques Pils in 1952. *(Photoworld-FPG)*

Félix Marten and Marguerite Monnot. *(Globe Photos)*

Rehearsing with Francis Lai. *(Photoreporters, Inc.)*

Piaf performs. *(Globe Photos)*

Théo Sarapo and Edith were married October 9, 1962.
(*Photoreporters, Inc.*)

"The last smile." (*Agence France Presse*)

screamed, white with rage and booze. It was one of those alcoholic furies when you feel up to attacking the Eiffel Tower.

She opened the door, rushed in, grabbed the radio, threw it on the floor and stamped on it, so mad and so soused she was hiccuping.

Paul got up—she was finally going to get clobbered—picked up the pieces of his radio, looked at Edith standing there swaying, and grabbed her by the shoulders.

"I'm disappointed in you; what you've done is very wrong." And he left.

We hadn't sobered up enough to be ashamed. The next day Edith gave Paul another radio. It was lucky she bought it then, because a few months later radios were very hard to come by.

She wasn't happy though. Maybe it was a little childish but she missed that walloping she'd so much deserved. It wasn't long before she got it.

Edith would have left Paul for sure if she hadn't met Jean Cocteau.

We were having dinner at the "Marquise"'s one night and next to Edith was Jean Cocteau. Mme Breton had naturally told Jean the same thing she'd told Edith: "Darling, I want you to meet someone really unique." She hadn't misled either of them. Each in his own way was truly extraordinary. Jean Cocteau was a marvelous man.

When we turned up for dinner at the "Marquise"'s, Edith wasn't completely at ease.

"What will I look like compared to a man like Jean Cocteau?"

It didn't take long. Jean took her hand.

"Edith, I'm so happy to meet you. You're the poet of the streets. We're made to get along."

With a beginning like that, Edith melted. Mme Breton was beaming. The streets were starting to be a memory of the past. Edith was feeling very much at ease now, laughing and talking with Jean.

He was a poet, a dramatist, a writer and an artist. He understood music, singing and the dance. He juggled with words; he made all sorts of things come out of them the way a magician pulls things out of a hat. She didn't know much; he knew everything. I couldn't take my eyes off their hands. Like Edith, Cocteau had very beautiful hands, and both of them made gestures that became words, that took flight like birds. It was a pretty sight to see them talking with their hands!

When he said good night, Jean added:

"I live on the rue de Beaujolais, at the Palais-Royal. You must come and see me. We'll talk together; little Piaf, you're very great. . . ."

Edith couldn't get over it. She said:

"You saw how Jean Cocteau spoke to me. I'm going to see him again. He's not like the other men I know. With him you learn without his giving you lessons!"

Gilbert Bécaud wrote a song recently, with Louis Amade. called *"Quand il est mort le poète."* Every time I hear it I see Jean again, with his mania for drawing stars everywhere, on paper table-cloths, on programs, on books. He marked everything with them. They bloomed like flowers wherever he went.

"See, Momone, what I've been missing was a poet in my life, a real one. Well, now I've got one."

We liked the way he sort of looked like a Pierrot, with the wild thatch of hair above his forehead. Some critics called it his "clown's toupee." That made us mad because we thought it was more like a halo.

"People don't realize it, Momone, but that man's a saint," Edith said to me very seriously. "He's so good! Never nasty, never a mean word about anybody. He's always ready to forgive, to under-stand."

She said to Paul:

"I want to read Jean Cocteau's books. Paul, buy me some."

I don't know if he did it on purpose, but he came back with a book called *Le Potomak* that we didn't understand a word of.

"It's crazy! When the man talks you understand everything, but when he writes, you can't understand a thing. I'm going to ask him why."

"Don't do that," said Paul. "You'll make a fool of yourself."

She did though. And Jean, kind as he was, explained that it was natural she didn't understand. He gave her *Les Enfants terribles*. We liked it a lot, and didn't think the part about the stone in the snowball unusual. Kids in our neighborhood used to do things like that.

It was surely Jean Cocteau who, in an article, wrote the most beautiful things about Edith:

> Look at this little creature, her hands like a lizard among the ruins. Look at that Napoleonic forehead, those eyes full of wonder like a blind man who can suddenly see. How will she sing? How will she express herself? How will she squeeze those great wails of the night out of that narrow breast? But then she sings; or, like an April nightingale, she tries out the first notes of her love song. Have you ever heard a nightingale? She labors, hesitates, rasps, chokes. The notes rise and fall back. And then, suddenly, she sings. You are entranced.

Edith thought this passage so beautiful, she cut it out and read it to everybody. To her, when a man like Jean Cocteau wrote that about you, you'd climbed another rung.

We'd got into the habit of meeting Jean at the Palais-Royal. In the basement of Cocteau's house on the rue de Beaujolais there was a *cave*, a kind of private club, where performers, writers and painters got together. We felt at home there. It was the very first *cave*, years before the ones in Saint-Germain-des-Prés. There was one other advantage—you could stay where you were during air-raid alarms. They were long, the blacked-out nights in our disfigured Paris, wearing the blue glasses of a blind man. How sad those little blue lamps were! How far back in the past was the City of Light!

But we could forget down there in the *cave;* we were really among friends. Jean would come down from his apartment, like a neighbor, in a warm bathrobe, along with his friend Jean Marais, whom we called Jeannot. What a handsome beast he was! He adored Cocteau. Christian Bérard, the set designer, whom we called Bébé, would come with them, with his round, pink doll face and a beautiful beard flowing down his velvet jacket. He drew bits and pieces of stage sets all the time and all over. And there was Yvonne de Bray, with her dark, sparkling, intelligent eyes, perhaps the greatest actress of the day. They were the headliners of Jean's group. Edith was very proud to be part of it, because Jean, in spite of his kindness, always was the grand bourgeois, brother of a stockbroker, and an expert at getting rid of you if he didn't like you.

Edith and Jean clicked immediately. She didn't hide anything from him—she told him everything that went through her head. The great concern of the moment for her was Paul. She still loved him. So she told her troubles to Jean.

"Paul's driving me nuts. I feel lost with him. Why is that?"

"My darling," Jean answered, "you never understand the people you love when you're with them. You don't accept them for what they are; you expect them to measure up to your dreams, your desires. . . . And these are rarely the same ones they have."

Edith didn't philosophize about love; she wanted a man who loved her. It was so simple!

In the taxi on the way home Edith said to me:

"Jean's a great guy. He's not only intelligent; he's kind. When he talks to me, when he explains Paul to me, I tell myself he's right —that I've got to try harder."

When she got home she asked Paul if he loved her.

"Of course," Paul answered with the air of a gentleman who's been asked an indecent question.

"Is that your only answer? You say 'I love you' the same way you'd say 'The veal roast is served.' If you don't give a damn for me, say so! A guy like you's impossible. I've had a bellyful of that pasty white smile of yours." And on it went, all night long.

The next night she'd meet Jean again and make more good resolutions. Then she'd go home, plow into the iceberg and it'd start all over again.

Sitting between Yvonne de Bray and Jean one night, Edith began to weep on their shoulders. Edith was more emotional when Yvonne was there, because together the two of them used to finish off the whole supply of red wine in the rack.

"You don't know what it's like. I tell him I love him, and he reads the papers on the bed in his dressing gown. I tell him I don't ever want to see him again, that I adore him, that he has to get the hell out. He reads the papers. It's unbearable. I smash everything, I throw things at him—words and anything I can get my hands on. He reads the papers! He's driving me crazy. . . ."

"Darling, calm down. I'll fix all that. Just be a little patient."

"I don't dare ask Jean what he's up to, Momone."

A few days later Jean phoned.

"Come on over, Edith; I have something to read you."

We made it fast to the rue de Beaujolais. Jeannot, Yvonne de Bray and Bébé Bérard were there. Jean Cocteau read us *Le Bel Indifférent,* a one-act play he'd just written. The play was based on Edith's troubles with Paul.

"A shabby hotel room, lighted by the neon signs on the street. A studio couch. A phonograph. A telephone. A small lavatory. Posters. As the curtain rises, the actress is alone in a simple black dress. She is watching out the window and running to the door to keep an eye on the elevator. Then she sits down next to the phone. Then she puts one of her own records on the phonograph, '*Je t'ai dans la peau,*' and stops it. She goes back to the phone and dials a number. . . ."

The character was Edith, a successful singer, jealous of everything about her lover. . . . It was so true to life I could almost hear her voice.

"Once, in the beginning, I was jealous of your sleep. I'd wonder: 'Where does he go when he sleeps? What does he see?' And you smiled, you relaxed, and I began to hate the people in your dreams. I'd often wake you up so you'd chuck them. And you liked to dream and were furious because I'd waked you up. But I couldn't stand your blissful face."

"Do you like it?" Cocteau asked her.

"It's terrific, Jean."

"It's for you, Edith. I'm giving it to you and you're going to act in it with Paul."

"I can't. I don't know how. I'm a singer, nothing else. And acting with Paul! Oh, no! Jean, I couldn't."

That's the way Edith was. She never had any doubts and yet

she was always afraid she wouldn't know how: she had no confidence outside her profession.

Jeannot laughed. He had magnificent teeth and a warm smile. He said to Edith:

"It's easy. Paul doesn't say anything, and you play the scene you have with him every day."

It seemed simple enough. She was the only one who spoke. But a monologue lasting a whole act tends to drag. It wasn't as easy as all that, we realized at the first rehearsal.

Paul naturally agreed to play the part. A play by Jean Cocteau, directed by Jean and Raymond Rouleau, wasn't something to sneer at; it was important. Giving a silent role presence was a tour de force that pleased him.

One character talked too much, the other not at all. The trouble was that the one who knew how to talk onstage had nothing to say, and the one who knew how to sing talked. At the first rehearsal Edith went to pieces. Luckily Paul wasn't there, Jeannot was standing in for him.

Her diction wasn't right. And though she knew how to express everything in a gesture or a word sung on the stage, she couldn't walk any more, and her hands were useless. It was a disaster! She was completely lost.

"The theater isn't for me, Jean. I'm sorry. I would have liked to do it, but it's no good. I'll never be able to."

It was no use that Jean told her, "It's only the first reading; you'll manage eventually. It's your play, your role; I wrote it for you." Edith was stubborn; she still said no. I saw she was close to tears.

"Boy, is Paul going to make fun of me!"

Jean looked at Yvonne de Bray, sitting hunched over in a corner, not saying a word. Those two understood each other. . . . She said:

"Edith, you're going to act. I'm going to teach you how."

And what a beautiful job Yvonne did! I think that in her hands even I could have managed to act! It was fantastic to see Yvonne take Edith's role apart, sentence by sentence, piece by piece, like the little wheels of a watch. Once all the pieces were put back in place, the watch ticked like a heart.

At the end of the play, the handsome indifferent man gets up, puts on his overcoat and picks up his hat. Edith clings to him, begs him:

"No, Emile, no, don't leave me. . . ." He disentangles himself, pushes her away and slaps her. He leaves, and Edith stays onstage with her hand on her cheek, saying:

"Emile . . . Oh, Emile . . ."

At rehearsals Jean would complain in his own way—kindly, politely.

"No, Paul, that is no good. She irritates you. Her love exasperates you, it's unbearable to you, so you give her a slap, a really good one, as hard as you can make it. . . . A slap from a man, not from an aristocrat slapping a marquis in the face with a glove before a duel. . . . Come on, go to it!"

Paul gave Edith a polite, elegant slap. Edith started giggling.

"It's not his fault. He doesn't know how. I'm going to show him."

And she gave him a superb double whack on both cheeks. If he could have squashed Edith, I think he would have! Very calmly, very much the actress, she explained to him:

"The first whack just works up momentum. Then on the return trip, hit with the back of your hand. That's the slap that hurts. . . . See what I mean?"

"I see," Paul replied, continuing to look dignified but gnashing his teeth all the while.

"Perfect," Jean chimed in. "Once more."

Paul was afraid his anger would get the better of him. He again gave Edith his usual nice little love tap.

Edith laughed. I did too.

And she needled Paul so much that on the night of the dress rehearsal at the Bouffes-Parisiens, he laid on a really good one, and it wasn't acting.

In the dressing room, he said offhandedly to Edith:

"That's what you wanted. Are you pleased?"

She shrugged. "It was only acting. . . ."

I think if I'd been Paul I'd have sliced off her head! But he got his revenge another way.

She'd gone to lots of trouble to get her slap. Now she got one every night, and I've always thought that Paul was getting rid of his repressions!

The play was the hit of the 1940 season. There was another Cocteau play on the bill, *Les Monstres sacrés*, starring Yvonne de Bray, with sets by Christian Bérard.

Edith was very proud of being an actress; it had given her even more confidence onstage. For Paul it was more than an interesting experience. *Le Bel Indifférent* got him other plays and even films. The critics said: "Paul Meurisse, in a thankless role, proves to have exceptional gifts as an actor. He is not satisfied just to be the foil for Mme Edith Piaf; he gives the character he plays a very definite personality."

Edith ended the period of the "phony war" with a "victory." She had been asked to take part in a gala benefit performance for the Red Cross and its work for soldiers at the front. The names of the greatest singing stars were on the bill at Bobino. The gala performance began at midnight and ended around five in the morning. That was the only time Edith was ever on the same program as Marie Dubas, who sang *"La Madelon,"* and Maurice Chevalier, who sang his hit of the moment:

> *Et tout ça, ça fait*
> *D'excellents Français,*
> *D'excellents soldats . . .*

As usual, Edith had worked hard on her number, and it hit everybody right in the gut. She sang *"Où sont-ils tous mes copains?"*

> *Où sont-ils mes p'tits copains*
> *Qui sont partis un matin*
> *Faire la guerre?*
> *Où sont-ils ces petits gars*
> *Qui disaient: On en r'viendra,*

Faut pas s'en faire.
Tous les gars d' Ménilmontant,
Ils ont répondu: Présents.
Ils sont partis en chantant
Faire la guerre.
Où sont-ils?
Où sont-ils?

Where are all my little pals
Who left one morning
To go to war?
Where are those little guys
Who said: "We'll be back,
Don't worry"?
All the guys from Ménilmontant
Answered: "Here."
They left singing
To fight in the war.
Where are they?
Where are they?

At the last "Where are they?" the back of the stage lit up red, white and blue. It started out no bigger than a rosette, then filled the whole stage, and at the end Edith seemed to be wrapped in the French flag. It was Edith's idea. The people got to their feet, yelling for an encore and joining in on the chorus; there were even some who saluted. In the wings Paul and I had such lumps in our throats we didn't dare look at each other.

After Edith had been on, we stayed in the audience and listened to the others. Everyone felt like staying together. That night at Bobino we believed in victory; it was ours. It wouldn't have taken much to get us to sing the "Marseillaise." When we left, even though we hadn't had anything to drink we were intoxicated with hope. As we came home down the rue Anatole de la Forge, day was just beginning to break, all rosy on the horizon.

"This is the first time in my whole life I've ever felt like laughing when I saw the sun rise," Edith said.

Paul opened a bottle of champagne. We drank to ourselves and all our hopes. Paul was relaxed and smiling. All three of us were happy; we felt fine.

Mechanically he turned on his beautiful brand-new radio, raised his glass and said, "To today, the tenth of May."

Just then we heard the announcer's ominous voice saying:

"At six o'clock this morning, German troops crossed the Belgian border. Panzer divisions are advancing into Belgium. . . ."

The fun was over, all over.

The following weeks were very short. Paul kept his ear glued to his radio. Edith and I didn't understand much of what was going on. A few names stood out: Paul Reynaud, Daladier, Weygand and then Pétain.

Paris was a sorry sight. We discovered what air-raid alarms were like and were petrified. Edith didn't want to go down in the basement. She was scared of being buried alive. So we went to the Bidou-Bar. It was forbidden, but they took us in anyway. They turned out all the lights because of civilian defense, and we waited. Paul used to go with us—he never left us now.

We saw weird-looking cars go by—first, refugees from Belgium, with two or three mattresses on their roofs. Edith and I thought at first it was because they wanted their beds with them, but it actually was on account of airplane bullets. Then came people from the North and East. All those poor people were just passing through; they didn't stay. They were sweating with fear; they had terrible stories to tell about the Krauts. Above all, they told us Paris wasn't safe. It was hard to believe. People were leaving Paris. They poured out of all the neighborhoods, the elegant ones first of all—ours became deserted—and then the working-class districts. The ministers and the government had withdrawn to Bordeaux.

On the walls of the capital we saw posters proclaiming the defense of Paris, stone by stone, so panic drove out those who were still there. Later on, there were other posters declaring Paris an open city.

There were announcements on the radio asking people to stay home, but they couldn't; they'd lost confidence. Paris was behaving like a belly in a state of panic.

We didn't have any idea what was going on. We'd snuggle up next to Paul and cling to him. We didn't leave. The days seemed to collapse one upon the other.

My God, how sad Paris was on the morning of June 13, 1940! From behind our closed blinds we watched people piling their most precious possessions into their cars. The old concierge across the street set out on foot with her suitcase in one hand and her cage and canary in the other. I don't know where she was going with no car. And there was no métro any more either.

We listened to Paul's radio in a room at the back of the apartment. We left it on day and night. It talked of bombardments of strongholds: "Our heroic force . . ." The poor buggers—what were they fighting for? We couldn't have told them.

"Leave?" Edith had said. "Where would we go? We don't even have a car. Walk? Our feet would be worn to the bone before we got very far. Anyway, it'll be the same all over."

How right she was! It was true Edith had no thought for anything but her profession and her love affairs, but when she was interested in something, she always had good judgment.

Besides, what did we have to defend? Our skins? They didn't seem important to us.

Ever since we'd heard about those Germans and their slogan "Guns, not butter," we'd told ourselves they were sure to be hungry. I could see them descending on us like those battalions of red ants that eat an ox clean in no time. And then Edith, always the practical one, had said:

"We have to buy things to get by on: bread, canned goods, cigarettes, alcohol, because those guys percolate on schnapps."

Paul had protested:

"I hope you're not going to offer them something to eat!"

"No, but I'd rather have them rape the larder than me. And we're bound to need stuff like that for ourselves. This way we'll be all set."

Paul clenched his fists so hard you could see his bones. He wasn't thinking about washing his hands or filing his nails any more. He hadn't even shaved. All that was unimportant now.

Edith and I no longer looked at him in the same way. He wasn't a mannequin any more. I watched him, sitting there hunched over his radio. He was listening to the last sobs of our dying country with a bitter taste in his mouth. I can't remember why Paul hadn't been called up; I think he was 4-F because of his heart. One thing's sure; he was delicate.

The Germans were about to enter the city; it was only a matter of hours. We didn't know what they'd do with apparently healthy men. Concentration camps? Prison camps? Make them hostages? . . . And Paul was staying there with us. I felt sorry for him. He couldn't fight, but, like the others, he smelled of fear, the war, sweat —he finally smelled like a man.

He was doing his duty; he'd stayed to protect us. He wasn't a coward, and we were sure he'd have got himself killed defending our virtue—though just between us, our virtue didn't amount to much.

Edith hadn't lost her cheek. Paul, in his usual simple way, said: "We are living days that will go down in history."

To which she answered, "Shit! If this is history, I'd rather read about it than make it."

The streets were empty; not a soul around. There were thick black and pink clouds in the sky. Reserves of gasoline were burning in Rouen and almost everywhere else, to delay the German advance. That sticky fog falling all over Paris made the deserted city an even sorrier sight.

Night fell. There was a deadly silence, with an occasional slow step in the night like a cemetery guard's. It was reassuring; we told each other we weren't all alone.

Suddenly, in the morning, *they* entered Paris singing, like a circus parade—guys bursting with health, blond and suntanned, in black uniforms. Behind this first contingent were trucks filled with green uniforms and more happy guys laughing and playing the accordion. They didn't look hungry. How could it be? They'd lied to us!

Edith and I cautiously made our way to the Champs Élysées, watching from a distance. All the cafés and shops were closed, with their iron shutters drawn. Seeing the Germans in the sunshine like that, we wondered why we'd been scared. Edith said to me, clutching my arm:

"See, it's over. There won't be any more fighting!"

It's true it was a circus. If only it had been just the parade! We were about to live with fear that empties your gut. It was to be a horrible spectacle. Willingly or unwillingly, we were to watch it without a word, without a gesture, for four long years.

We saw the people on our street coming back day by day. The Bidou-Bar reopened. We never saw the old concierge across the street again. A month later, at Fouquet's on the Champs Elysées, guys had started cooking up deals with the occupation troops. "Collaboration" had begun.

Like all performers, Edith had to report to the *Propagandastaffel* that had been set up in the Champs Élysées. She met lots of other performers there. You had to go, otherwise you couldn't work.

Life began again, but it was no longer the same.

Maurice Chevalier was among the first to come back to Paris. He refused to use a car; when he got in at the Gare de Lyon, he took the métro like everybody else.

Edith had never had as many contracts and proposals for benefits of all sorts: galas for prisoners, the Red Cross, the vaudeville theaters. . . . People stood in line for everything—for bread as well as for movies, plays and vaudeville shows.

I don't know whether it was the shock of the occupation or what, but Edith was very nervous. She found that Paul was no longer the same as he'd been at the time of the defeat. He'd become quite the gentleman again, looking as if he'd just stepped out of a bandbox. He was more withdrawn than ever, clutching his radio tighter, listening to the BBC. To make him mad, Edith would say:

"There's no point in it any more; everything's shot to hell. I don't know why you listen; they don't play music."

Or she'd plant herself in front of him with me as a witness.

"You think this guy knows how to talk? Maybe the gentleman unbuttons outside, but not here. We're not good enough for him!"

Paul loved Edith though. It was just that their ways of loving didn't jibe.

It was unbelievable, the things Edith could invent to rile him.

She turned him over and over on the grill. She made dates with guys in cafés and fixed it so Paul would know. He'd secretly follow her and stand outside, freezing, waiting for her for hours at a time.

Edith even went to a fancy place where people go to make love. When she came out, she found Paul on the sidewalk, waiting with a cab. He took her by the arm.

"You're coming home right now."

"No," screamed Edith.

"Get in this cab this minute."

"No," yelled Edith even louder.

I don't know how he forced her to get in, but the next day she was full of bruises, a real field of periwinkles!

To get even, Paul took up with a girl, a little singer who was doing pretty well. She'd been chasing after Paul ever since he'd been living with Edith, and was rather pretty. When Edith talked to Paul about her, she'd call her his "old lady." Anybody over twenty-five was ancient to us.

Paul went to see her, and Edith found out. She waited till he'd left and, talking in an affected, simpering way, all politeness, she called up his babe.

"Can we see each other?"

"Oh, no, I'm sick in bed," the girl replied suspiciously.

Then Edith said to me:

"Come on, Momone, we're going over there right now. A chance like this comes only once in a lifetime."

Since Marguerite Monnot was visiting us, we took her along. And though she followed us trustingly enough, she did ask where we were going.

"We're going to give Paul's doll a little party."

"I didn't know you liked her enough to celebrate her birthday."

Not realizing that by "a little party" Edith meant a sound thrashing, Marguerite, still completely in the clouds, and as sweet as ever, had misunderstood.

The girl was in bed; she hadn't been lying. And we gave her a hiding that we hoped would make her fed up with Paul for the rest of her life. We turned the poor girl over, and while I held her down, Edith gave her a good spanking.

Marguerite looked at us flabbergasted. She'd never seen anybody wish anybody a happy birthday that way! She was simply not with it, and kept saying:

"Not so hard, dears; you're going to hurt yourselves."

It was the only time we ever found Paul out. If he cheated on Edith, he did so quietly, without making a big thing of it. Personally, I could see why he needed a change once in a while, especially since he got sister Simone along with Edith. From the very beginning, she'd warn her guys:

"You'll have to take both of us; we're not splitting up. Momone's the bonus. Anyway, if I leave her by herself, she'll do some damnfool thing."

"Aunt Zizi" (that's what I used to call her when she gave me too hard a time) wasn't always pleasant to me or easy to get along with. After Cécelle died, I'd sort of become her kid. She kept tabs on me, in her own way, and it wasn't much fun. And then I'd clear out. I needed to be alone, to live my own life.

This time I left to let Edith and Paul be by themselves. Even before the occupation, the "Marquise" and even Marguerite had said things like: "It's easier for just two people to get along," or "From time to time a couple needs a little honeymoon."

I said to myself, "I really owe Edith that. Maybe if I'm not around they'll patch things up."

If I'd said anything to Edith, she'd have screamed, "I forbid you to leave. Stay out of it." So I flew the coop.

Walking around in a Paris that wasn't like it had been before, I thought of home, other times I'd run away; I often ended up at a carnival. A carnival's fun. But I couldn't count on that any more. The only music there was came from the Jerries. Every day on the stroke of noon they marched up and down the Champs Élysées. I didn't feel like seeing them. As I walked along, depressed as hell, I was thinking, "This time I won't find any merry-go-rounds to make me dizzy."

Usually I felt better once I'd got past the first corner. I was myself at last, not somebody's sister. A guy would look at me, and I wouldn't lower my eyes—I knew I had nice eyes. And he might take me to a carnival.

It was great to go riding on a merry-go-round till you were breathless, eat a bag of french fries in the hellish racket and end up with a turn on the dance floor. I'd let myself go and waltz with love itself in my arms. What happened next isn't hard to guess. You go around full circle faster with a man than you do on a merry-go-round . . . only, rather than living Edith's love affairs, I was living my own for once! It was *me* that was getting told "You're beautiful" and "I love you."

Then suddenly I'd look at my old shoes, my crumpled dress, and want only one thing: to go home. How scared I was at the idea. But that was part of the game. I knew I'd hurt Edith, that she couldn't understand how I needed something else besides her.

So I'd go back. It was always the same. Edith would rant and rave. I didn't hear a word; I didn't give a damn. She could yell, pace around the room, throw herself around, and I'd count inside my head—one, two, three, four—waiting for her eyes to meet mine, for her to stop looking at me sideways. The moment always came when she'd look me in the face. It was over. She'd hug me and we'd cry for joy. . . . The worst was over. She'd take me by the hand and say, "Come on, you ass. . . ."

What a loving word!

But this time there was no rejoicing in my heart. How sad my Paree was! I didn't give a damn for men. I didn't feel like horsing around. So I went and looked up my father.

He lived in a hotel on the rue Rébeval. Edith paid for his room and bought his clothes for him, so he was clean at least. He'd begun to look worn out, the poor old man. He was awfully glad to see me.

"What have you done with your sis? Edith doesn't come very often. She's got her work, of course."

He was more than a little proud of his Edith, and he made no bones about making a little money thanks to her. He'd say, "I'm Edith Piaf's father." People would buy him a drink and slip him a few coins. He'd show off the gold watch Edith had given him.

"My daughter sure spoils me! Isn't that some ticker?"

The people would laugh and get him to tell stories about when Edith was little. Our old man had no scruples about embroidering a little—he gave them their money's worth.

He was happy to see me again. We'd eat at a restaurant, and he'd tell me stories, especially about Edith. She'd become important to him. Sometimes he'd ramble a bit. He couldn't even do acrobatics any more. He was very tired—hardship and booze had taken their toll. I liked being with him.

I'd given myself two weeks; I managed one. When I was back, I got my scene.

"This time I've had enough! You can leave again for all I care; I'm fed up. You're a little bitch. Where have you been?"

"I stayed with the old man for a week."

"Why didn't you say so? You did right to come home. It's time you showed up."

"What about Paul?"

"He gives me a swift pain."

I realized I'd failed. My clearing out hadn't fixed anything.

After playing in Paris, they went on tour with *Le Bel Indifférent*. It was no fun. Nothing was heated, neither the trains nor the hotels. People who have never been on tour during the occupation can't have any idea how miserable and grim it all was. . . . The stations in the night with the loudspeakers bawling in German: *"Achtung! Achtung! Verboten!"* Everything was *verboten*— laughter, light, wine. . . .

We didn't always have a seat when we traveled. Often we sat on the baggage in the corridors or vestibules of the train. Hunched over on her suitcase under Paul's coat, Edith looked so little, so miserable, it wrung my heart. If he hadn't been there, we'd have easily found a way to huddle up next to some guy and be nice and warm. But there was no use even thinking of it. Paul kept a close watch on us. What exasperated us was that Paul got off the train looking like he'd traveled in a bandbox, while we looked more like we'd been following the band, and been boxing into the bargain!

What we liked was passing the line between the occupied and

the unoccupied zones. After the checkpoints, we could at last breathe in free France again.

Le Bel Indifférent had kept Paul in Edith's life a little longer, but the whole thing was over as far as she was concerned.

"Mustn't be ungrateful, Momone. Paul brought me something. He hasn't been useless in my life. Without him, I'd still be living in a hotel, and I wouldn't have a secretary." She'd had a secretary for several months. Paul had explained to Edith that she couldn't get along without one, that it was useful, that it gave her class. That's how Mme Andrée Bigeard came into our lives. She was a brunette with short hair. Apparently she tended to business. It was hard to say though, since she had nothing to do but answer the phone.

It would go something like this:

"Who's calling?"

"Mr. So-and-So."

"I don't know him," Edith would say. "Let me talk to him."

When she did know him, she'd yell, "What are you waiting for? Let me talk to him!" The third solution was: "Momone, you take it." One can hardly say that we *had* to have a secretary. . . . Answering the telephone wasn't much of a job. There was no endless stream of calls; we hadn't yet reached real glory. The secretary was one more pal for Edith, that's all. We didn't have any precise idea of what there was for her to do.

When she got there in the morning, it was practical; it allowed us to snooze more peacefully. Edith also sent her out on errands like buying the newspapers so she could cut out the articles about her. That was one of Paul's ideas. As for the bills (and did they pour in!), the first thing old Bigeard asked Edith was: "What should I do with them?" And Edith answered, "File them!"

Poor Paul! That was the only mark he left on our lives—a secretary.

Edith wasn't happy; she didn't have anybody around any more to write her "custom-made" songs. She couldn't live without having a song manufacturer handy. She needed one around to be able to work. She needed someone to give shape to her ideas and her desires, understand them, and create for her. Raymond, who was in the service, didn't have the time to do very much.

There was the Michel Emer episode, of course, at the beginning of 1940. He came into Edith's life through the window. One morning she was in a bad mood and feeling very edgy. She was getting ready to appear at Bobino; the dress rehearsal was to take place the next day. There was a ring at the door. Edith shouted to me:

"Don't open it. I don't want to see anybody."

I let the bell ring once, twice. But whoever it was didn't keep on ringing; it was somebody shy. I was lounging around in the front room, a sort of combination living room and dining room, when somebody rapped at the window. I looked out. On the sidewalk was a soldier who looked like a puppet in his uniform, gesturing at me. It was Michel Emer. He was wearing big thick glasses, the Marcel Achard kind, and behind the huge lenses his eyes were shining like two little fish at the bottom of an aquarium. I liked his face, like that of a kid who's grown up without noticing it. He was touching.

Edith had met him in 1939 in the halls at Radio-Cité. She'd thought he was nice. He seemed intelligent, but what he wrote wasn't for her; it was full of blue skies, little flowers and birds. It was pretty, but it didn't have punch to it.

I opened the window.

"I'd like to see Edith."

"No dice. She can't. She's getting ready for Bobino."

"Tell her it's me, Michel Emer, and that I've got a song for her."

I went and told Edith.

"Get rid of him, Momone. His songs aren't my style. I don't want them."

I went back to him, standing there quietly on the sidewalk, all clumsy in his uniform. There are men who look glamorous in a uniform, but he wasn't one of them. He had no presence at all— just another lost sheep.

"She's got too much work, Michel. Come back tonight or tomorrow."

"I can't. I'm a patient at the military hospital at Val-de-Grâce; I have to be in before six. Please. I've got a very good song; I'm sure. Tell her the title: '*L'Accordéoniste.*'"

I felt too sorry for him.

"O.K. Come on in and play your song," I said.

I opened the window for him and he leaped into the room. He sat down at the piano and sang *"L'Accordéoniste"*—badly. The minute he played the first few bars, Edith appeared.

> *La fill' de joie est belle,*
> *Au coin d' la rue, là-bas.*
> *Elle a un' clientèle*
> *Qui lui remplit son bas....*

> The whore is pretty,
> On the corner, down there.
> She has a clientele
> That fills her stocking with money....

Michel had finished. He peered out at us from behind his portholes with a worried look. He was dripping with sweat.

"Did you write that, little corporal?"

"Yes, Mme Edith."

"Why didn't you tell me you had talent? Take off your coat and tie and get comfortable. We're going to work. Start over and give me the words. I'll sing it tomorrow at Bobino."

He had come at noon. It was five in the morning when she let him go. She kept up his morale with salami, Camembert and red wine. He was in good shape for a sick man. Feeling a bit high, he kept repeating:

"Edith, I'm going to get court-martialed . . . desertion in wartime. I'm in for it, but I don't give a damn. I've never been this happy!"

"Don't worry about it," Edith replied nobly. "I know some generals."

She didn't know a one. But it was a sure bet that if Michel had been in danger, she'd have gone to see the Minister of War. Edith had colossal nerve.

We didn't know how he managed it, but the next night he was at Bobino and Edith sang his song. It wasn't the immediate success we'd thought it would be. The end disconcerted people—they thought the song wasn't over. But *"L'Accordéoniste"* went on, and did it make up for its slow start! Some 850,000 records of it were sold, an extraordinary figure for the time. She sang it for twenty years, from 1940 to 1960.

Edith had said to Michel, "Swear you'll bring me more." He swore he would. But when we met him again, much later on, Michel was no longer the same boy. I saw right away things were going badly for him. He had the face of a hunted man and was sweating with fear.

"Edith, I'm done for. You won't even have the right to sing my songs. I'm Jewish; I have to wear a yellow star. That's the way it's going to start, and then later . . ."

There wasn't any later. Edith fixed things: she paid to get Michel into the free zone. We didn't see him again till the liberation. He wrote some very beautiful songs for her: *"Monsieur Lenoble," "Qu'as-tu fait de John?" "La Fête continue," "Télégramme," "Le Disque usé," "D' l'autr' côté d' la rue."* Edith admired Michel's talent, and she continued to call him "the little corporal."

"What I like about Michel is that he writes and composes at the same time. When he brings you a song, it's all done, and that's rare. Anyway, he's got a real gift. You remember the melody right away —as though you'd already heard it sung in all the streets." They worked a great deal together.

But to go back to 1941, Edith was looking for a songwriter. She kept pestering Marguerite Monnot on the phone.

"It's your profession, Guite. Find me somebody."

"What for?" Marguerite would ask.

"To write songs. Not to make love—I've got what I need in that department."

"I'm looking, Edith, I'm looking."

Edith would hang up. "I'm crazy to ask her to do that; she's already forgotten what I wanted."

Ten minutes or an hour later, Guite would call back.

"Did you find somebody?" Edith would shout.

"That's just why I called, dear. I wanted to ask you to remind me what I was supposed to be looking for."

Edith had met Jacques Larue though, a charming boy who was

later to write her some very pretty songs: *"Le Bal de la chance,"* *"Marie la Française."* But a date she'd missed when she sent me in her place had delayed their getting to know each other.

It was a movie that brought her what she was looking for: a new songwriter—and a lover. Piaf-Meurisse, the couple starring in *Le Bel Indifférent*, had attracted the attention of a director, Georges Lacombe. The play had had a three-month run in Paris, and had gone well all over France. The public knew Paul and Edith—why not capitalize on the fact? Lacombe brought Edith a film scenario called *Montmartre-sur-Seine*. Edith had already been in a movie in 1937. She sang in *La Garçonne*, with Marie Bell. Nobody had been terribly impressed. It was different in *Montmartre-sur-Seine*. She didn't just rush through a song. She had a role to play, a real one, her first.

Paul had seemed happy to be making a film. I don't know if Edith's presence as his partner made him enjoy it more, but in any case, since they were working together, Paul had stayed at the apartment, where he continued to lead a quiet life—no more scenes. This period of calm before he took off for good wasn't unpleasant. Paul had now become indifferent to the two of us.

Being in a movie amused Edith. The only bad part about it was that we had to pry ourselves out of bed very early in the morning. The studio car came to pick the two of them up, and me too. Edith couldn't have stood being alone in her dressing room.

The very first day in the studio canteen, Georges Lacombe had introduced Edith to a handsome, tall, well-dressed fellow with a touch of silver in his hair, and a bit of the hoodlum in his eye and in the way he lit his cigarettes: Henri Contet, the public relations man on the film.

Georges said to Contet, "You're in charge of her." No sooner said than done. If Paul didn't pack his suitcase right away, it was only because Henri couldn't move into the apartment. I could see at a glance that this one was more like we were, that he was a guy for us. It didn't take long. That very night in our bathroom talk session, Edith asked me if I liked Henri.

"He's just fine. I think he'll fill the bill."

"O.K., agreed. He's a newspaperman with *Paris-Soir* and a film review, *Cinémondiale*. We've never had a newspaperman; it'll be a change for us. Anyway, he'll be useful."

On August 8, 1941, Henri Contet wrote:

No doubt about it. The motionless, serious little woman over there under the gray stone arch is Edith Piaf. I surprise her in spite of myself, because I'm very early for the appointment she gave me. Piaf isn't alone. A man is there, facing her, and I'm immediately struck by his cruel, hard expression, an expression that sweeps away any notion of pity, of forgiveness, of indulgence. It seems to me I recognize Paul Meurisse.

. . . Still, she's not weeping. She looks more like an unhappy child waiting, yearning for something—the happiness of fairy tales or a simple and innocent love as in street ballads. I feel like making up a song for this Piaf:

> *Celui que j'aimerai*
> *Aura les tempes grises.*
> *De l'or à son poignet*
> *Et de belles chemises.*

> [The man I'll love
> Will have gray temples.
> Gold on his wrist
> And fine shirts.]

She hasn't spoken yet, but I already know what she's going to say. I can see it. For suddenly in her eyes, on her forehead and in her outstretched hands is a prayer that I recognize, an age-old prayer, as old as the world, a heartbreaking, useless plea.

"Keep me . . . I still love you. . . . You're all I've got . . . stay."

What is Piaf's heart made of? It's certain that anyone else's, in its place, would already be dead.

Edith leans her head, her head that's too heavy, a little more to one side. I see her cheeks, grown hollow, her eyes that no longer want to look at anything.

. . . What should I do? Console her? How? I think of all the songs that this star has given her tears to, her immense heart, and all the admirable strength she's able to find within herself, in her lungs and in her life.

Will she manage to be strong? Her shoulders seem so sorrowful to me. In spite of myself, the first words of another song pop into my head:

> *Elle veut savoir si la Seine*
> *Peut endormir toute sa peine;*
> *Et lorsqu'elle a sauté,*
> *N'a plus rien regretté.*

> [She wants to know if the Seine
> Can lull all her grief;
> And when she jumped,
> She regretted nothing any more.]

But I hear the sound of a stream, the liquid laughter of a river. Edith Piaf is crying, with little choking sobs.

I never saw a man who could resist Edith. There was no reason for this one not to take her in his arms. And he lost no time doing it. Several times a day I'd say to her, "Oh, Edith, how fine he is!" That made her happy, and I didn't have to force myself; that's what I really thought. It was continual fair weather, it was happiness; you'd have thought she was a little seamstress who'd just gotten engaged to the Prince of Wales.

She had a pure and very sentimental side that came from when she sang in the streets. She'd look at the flower vendors near the subway entrances. "Do you think a man will ever bring me a little bouquet he just went and bought as he passed by?" She received flowers later on—more than enough. She was satisfied; it was proof of her success, but . . .

"You can't make me believe that centerpieces like this come from the heart; you just need dough to buy them," she'd say. "You have to think about a bouquet of violets, you have to put your hand in your pocket, and then carry it without being afraid of looking silly. That's what I call a gesture. . . ." And Henri made that gesture, quite naturally. Edith burst with joy. She'd found the man of her dreams.

The official separation from Paul came off without any fuss. Edith and he had finally worn each other out; being weary is good for breaking things off. It really helps.

They both waited till the movie was finished. They weren't sorry to leave each other. Paul packed his bags very carefully. He kissed Edith and wished her lots of happiness with Henri. You have to give him credit—he wasn't blind. When he left I felt like bowing to him as if he were a marquis, he behaved so much like one.

Chapter 8

The Bidou-Bar

With Paul gone, we changed apartments. We didn't go far—we took one across the hall, directly next to the Bidou-Bar, so close we could have had a door cut through the wall we shared; and there were nights when we could have used it to get home: we wouldn't have had all that trouble finding the keyhole!

When she switched men, Edith liked to change her surroundings too. She said to me, "The morning after always leaves you with a sort of hangover. It's only later, when you've had time to clean up some, that you forget everything that wasn't very nice."

She and Henri clicked right off the bat; they were of the same breed. Besides, he wrote a bunch of articles about her. She liked that. She'd realized immediately that publicity was part of her profession and was very useful.

"Momone, a name's like a lover. If it's not seen, if it's away for too long, it's forgotten."

To Edith, Henri was most of all a handsome guy she was fond of. She had no idea he was going to be the songwriter she needed so badly.

Henri was just the opposite of Paul. He didn't flee from the Bidou-Bar—he made it his headquarters. And I didn't bother him either; he wasn't afraid of the three of us being together. He liked me; we were pals from the start.

One evening when we were sitting in the Bidou-Bar, he said to Edith:

"I don't know whether this'll amuse you, but I've written songs. I was twenty years old. There was one that was set to music by Jacques Simonot: '*Traversée.*' Lucienne Boyer sang it, but it didn't go over—it wasn't her style."

"Thank heavens. That means you don't go in for charm and sweetness and light. Have you got any others?"

"Well, I got disgusted, so I stopped. But since I've known you, I've felt like writing them again."

Naturally Edith threw her arms around him. Along with Raymond Asso, Henri Contet wrote the most songs for her, and the best ones. His songs stayed in Edith's repertoire. Among them was "*Y'a pas d' printemps,*" which he wrote on the corner of a table in twenty-five minutes, because Edith had bet him he couldn't. He also wrote "*Coup de grisou,*" "*Monsieur Saint-Pierre,*" "*Histoire de coeur,*" "*Mariage,*" "*Le Brun et le blond,*" "*Padam . . . Padam*" and "*Bravo pour le clown*":

> *Je suis roi et je règne,*
> *Bravo! Bravo!*
> *J'ai des rires qui saignent,*
> *Bravo! Bravo!*

> I'm king and I reign,
> Bravo! Bravo!
> I've got laughs that bleed,
> Bravo! Bravo!

This did the trick for Henri, although there was going to be trouble—serious trouble—between them. Edith wanted him all to herself, and he was living with another singer.

Edith wasn't in the habit of sharing *her* man very long. But she forgave Henri everything; he knew how to make her laugh. Though he was Edith's lover, he was never *really* one of her men because of this woman. It was too bad; if he had been, it surely would have prevented us from the period of madness we went through from 1941 to 1944.

We were right in the middle of the occupation. The restrictions, the raids, the black market, the hostages, the posters and the *Ausweis*—identification cards—stamped with "the crow on pedals," the name the street people gave Hitler's eagle and swastika, got to us and made us unbalanced. We had such an overpowering feeling of uncertainty that we lived any old way. We horsed around when we could. We drank more than ever. You had to get warm and forget. The occupation stuck in our throats. Laughter seemed temporary, and left you with a fuzzy taste in your mouth.

Edith's name was beginning to be worth money. She didn't lack for contracts; she was in great demand. Her price was three thousand francs. It wasn't bad, but it should have been better. The thing was, there was nobody to look out for her interests at the time. Sometimes she appeared in two places at once. Days like that she made six thousand francs, which was great. But money slipped through her fingers like sand. There were many ways for it to dribble away. The Bidou-Bar ate up a lot. And the black market, too, siphoned off quite an amount of dough. A kilo of butter was worth four to five hundred francs, and in 1944 it went up to twelve and fifteen hundred francs. Chang, the Chinese cook, filled the icebox at night, and in the morning it was empty. He'd worked out a clever routine: "Mamamiselle no likes butter; Mamamiselle no likes leftover beef or lamb, so I take away." He'd take it home so as not to throw it out. Good old Chang; he had a wife and five kids to feed.

Then there were all Edith's pals: those she took up with for an evening or for several nights, each with his song and dance for getting dough out of her.

One, for instance, was sitting there looking like death.

"What's wrong with you?" Edith asked. "Cheer up, have a drink."

"I can't, I don't feel like laughing, I've got problems."

"Your love life?"

"No, money."

"Well, if that's all, it can be fixed"—just what the guy'd been counting on.

Others would whisper, "My old father is Jewish. We have to get him to the free zone; I'm afraid for him. I don't have a cent." "How much?" Edith would inquire. The going price was from ten to fifty thousand francs, and sometimes fifty or a hundred thousand, to get to Spain. Edith couldn't always scrape up the whole amount, but she'd give part of it. There were also dames whose sons didn't want to be caught by the STO, the forced labor service in Germany. If the amount of dough Edith donated for all these good causes is any indication, smuggling people across the border was a great way to make a living! A month or two later the same people would show up with another story.

A great many stalags or *oflags* in Germany asked her to be their "godmother." Edith sent packages. When it came to the camps, Edith's heart was red, white and blue, and her purse was always open. "I've loved soldiers too much, they've given me too much pleasure for me to let them down."

Then there were those who didn't hand her a line, but fobbed off all kinds of stuff on her, useful or not. Edith wasn't vain, but she was proud of her name, so they took advantage of it. It was "Mme Piaf" here, "Mme Piaf" there. You have to know what it was like to be called "La Môme" ("Hey, La Môme, come here, you've got nice orbs," or "O.K., La Môme, get the hell out, we've had enough of you") to know how impressed she was when somebody called her "Mme Piaf."

"When one is Mme Piaf, one has to wear white fox," they'd say.

"You think so, Momone?" When you see a kid's eyes gleam in front of a Christmas tree, how do you tell her: "That's not for you"?

If only that was all! The second apartment on the rue Anatole de la Forge was worse than a railroad station. People went in and out and sacked out all over the place, in our beds, on the floor, in the armchairs. It was easy. Since there was a curfew and no more métros running when we left the Bidou-Bar in a group, already half plastered, Edith would say, "Sleep here. We'll have one last drink and a little snack."

We were defenseless; we needed a man. It was too bad we didn't have Henri for a boss. He was a fine guy and good looking. The wrinkles on his face were intelligent and as well structured as a map of Paris. They gave him class and helped counteract his street-urchin manner that pleased Edith so much.

"You see, Momone, that's the type who gooses you so politely you can't get mad at him. It's even nice!" She wasn't lying. Edith and I could never go up a stairway in front of Henri without—wow!—nice and quick, getting a pat on the ass. When it was he who did it, it seemed rather a polite gesture.

With Henri it was the hesitation waltz; he wanted to come live with us but his woman kept him from it. There were scenes because of it. Every once in a while he'd announce, "Listen, dears, this time I've made up my mind. Get everything ready; I'm coming. I'll move in next month." So we'd buy him underpants, socks, handkerchiefs, shirts, pajamas, everything he needed, at the top price, without ration coupons. We'd put it all away in the dresser drawers, feeling very happy.

But Henri didn't come. So Edith would get mad and toss everything out of the dresser. She kicked the underwear so high it flew in the air like her hopes, and she'd scream, "Throw all that crap out!"

Next month it started all over again. On the crucial day, back came Henri. I looked at his hands—no suitcase. He'd blown it again. What a good actor! A distressed look came over his face, and his eyes filled with tears. "My Edith, forgive me. She wept, she clung to me and I gave in. Let's let her have a few more days."

For months he dragged out the business of "I'm coming to live with you next month." Edith was so anxious to believe it, she'd get her hopes up all over again after every disappointment. Finally we realized it wasn't going to happen any time soon, that in fact it would never happen.

Henri liked singers, but he also liked his comfort, and the other woman was a singer-housewife. She kept her guy cleaner than clean—shirts nicely ironed, impeccable creases in his pants and gleaming shoes. Henri, who was as well groomed as Paul, had nothing to complain about. . . .

All this was hard for Edith to swallow—all the more so since she had girl friends who had strange ways of cheering her up. Léo Marjane, for instance. Léo was a good singer. She was really popular, with hits like "*J'ai donné mon âme au diable*," "*Mon ange*," "*Seule ce soir*," "*Mon amant de la Saint-Jean*." To lord it over us she'd drive by in her horse-drawn carriage—the last word in elegance those days. She often wore breeches and boots, which she'd tap with her whip.

"Hello, Edith. I was in the neighborhood, so I stopped by to see if you were finally living with your hairdresser." (She meant Henri Contet.) After Léo left, Edith would say, "My hairdresser! She'd sleep with him in a flash!"

During the day everything was more or less O.K. Henri would pass on all sorts of stories and gossip—he was in a good position to—about his pals, all the stars of the day: Jean Tranchant, Johnny Hess, Georges Ulmer, Léo Marjane, Roberta, Andrex, André Claveau, Maurice Chevalier, Georgius, Lucienne Dellile, Line Clevers, Marie Bizet, Lucienne Boyer and many others. . . . Edith adored it; she was a real gossip with a wicked tongue and a cutting wit.

But there was more to it than that. Edith worked hard with Henri and Guite, who was always somewhere around the place. There was nobody more demanding than Edith when it came to her work. Her accompanists at the time were Daniel White, a young man about twenty-seven, and Walberg, who was older. Edith made them slave like convicts. But nobody complained. In her work that little wisp of a woman had the authority of a dictator. In the middle of the uproar around the house and her crazy escapades, she kept a clear head. She'd throw herself into her work the way an Olympic swimmer dives into a pool. She always had a record to beat and she had an iron constitution. I kept wondering what she was made of, where she got all her strength. . . .

Work sessions began around five or six in the afternoon and ended early the next morning. Raymond may have taught her the technique of her profession, the grammar, but it was Henri who helped her to use it, to go beyond her professional knowledge and become "the Great Piaf."

Asso had been dictatorial, a teacher with no flexibility. Contet didn't give orders and wasn't pigheaded; he did his best to understand. He knew how to listen to her and talk things over with her. That was a great help to Edith in finding what she was looking for. It was with him that she began to acquire, without knowing it, the claws and the fangs of a boss, of one who, in turn, would train others. Edith read hundreds of songs. By this time she had a very clear idea of what a text should give her. "A song's a story, but the audience has to believe in it. For them, I'm love. It has to rip people up, it has to break their eardrums—that's my image. I'm allowed to be happy, but not for long; my physique won't permit it. I've got to have simple words. My public doesn't think; what I scream goes straight to their guts. I have to have poetry, the kind that gets them dreaming."

When Edith had chosen *her* song, she had someone play it for her. She learned the words and the music at the same time, never separately. "Both have to work their way inside me together. A song isn't words off on one side and a melody on the other." When people tried to give her advice she didn't "feel," she'd answer, "My conservatory is the streets. My intelligence is instinct."

When she finally knew her song, things got dramatic for the lyricist and the composer. Their martyrdom began. In the middle of rehearsals Edith would stop short, so abruptly the pianist would go on playing. She'd shout, "Stop!" or "Shut up! It's not right, Henri; change this word. It doesn't sound right coming from me, and anyway, I can't say it; it's too complicated." And at the same time she'd attack Guite, who'd be sitting there dreaming, waiting for her turn to come.

"Guite, wake up! Listen. You know the part that goes 'tralalala, tralalalaire'; it isn't right. It's too long, it's too wishy-washy, it stretches out like a marshmallow. I don't sound like I'm crying; I sound like I'm melting away like an old candle. I need a cry there. Something like 'Tralalala lala!' More abrupt at the end, shorter. It has to stop short because the girl can't take it any more. If she went on, she'd start bawling, so she cuts it off. See?" They could all see, but they had to do something about it, find the right thing. It'd last for hours.

One day we had one of the very best sessions of this sort. They were rehearsing "*C'est merveilleux*," I think. The words were by Henri Contet and the music by Marguerite Monnot.

> *C'est merveilleux*
> *Quand on est tous les deux*
> *Le bonheur nous surveille.*
>
> *C'est merveilleux*
> *Quand on est amoureux*
> *Les beaux jours se réveillent.*
>
> *C'est merveilleux*
> *La vie est peinte en bleu*
> *A grands coups de soleil*
> *Puisque je t'aime*
> *Et que tu m'aimes.*
> *C'est merveilleux!*

> When we're together
> Happiness watches over us.
> It's marvelous . . .
>
> When you're in love
> Beautiful days dawn.
> It's marvelous . . .
>
> Life is painted blue
> With lots of sunshine
> Because I love you
> And you love me.
> It's marvelous!

Henri hadn't made it enough of a street song to suit Edith, and Marguerite's music was too celestial. Guite adored violins; whenever a song was about happiness, she immediately scored it for a symphony orchestra and was back being a child prodigy. They battled for ten days!

Once this period of feverish activity was over, Edith practiced her song all the time: in the bathroom, in bed. She'd wake up Henri or somebody else and sing them her latest song over the phone. While she was learning it, the gestures would come to her. She didn't chase after them; she waited for them to come to her from the words, quite naturally. She used them very sparingly—the very opposite of the way she lived. "See, gestures distract your eye and your ear. When you watch too closely, you don't hear as well. I don't want to be seen; I want to be heard."

Once a reporter asked, "Do you practice your gestures in front of a mirror?" She never laughed so hard. "Can you see me in front of a mirror working on my gestures? I'm not a comedian; I don't practice effects to get laughs."

As for the staging of her songs, Edith would only work that out onstage. Then she'd improve the song itself face to face with the audience. And if she noticed she was thinking about something else as she sang it, she'd take it out of her repertoire. "I'm doing it all by heart; it's not worth anything any more, it's mechanical."

It was during this unusual period that Edith discovered and perfected her own best way of working. She later gave it a few finishing touches, but she never again varied her method. That and her fierce will were what made her the great lady of song. Papa Leplée, Raymond, Jean Cocteau and Yvonne de Bray had all opened her mind and taught her something; now she was coming out with it. It was that strenuous work, the locust working like an ant, that made Jean Cocteau write: "Mme Piaf has genius. She is matchless. There never was an Edith Piaf and there never will be one again. Like Yvette Guilbert or Yvonne George, like Rachel or Réjane, she is a star burning up in the lonely night sky of France."

When she'd worked hard, Edith was happy, she was comfortable; she'd coo when she was with Henri. But just when she felt like keeping her guy with her, snuggling up next to him all nice and cozy and spending the night with him, he'd say, "Edith, I have to go home." "Stay a little longer," Edith would beg, "just this once. . . ." But Henri knew how to get out of it with style. "My Edith, my baby . . . the curfew . . . it's not safe at night." And she'd give in. "Go quickly, love. I'm too fond of you; don't let anything happen to you."

And Henri would disappear into the grim night of occupied Paris. He wasn't taking much of a risk though: as a reporter, he had a night *Ausweis*. I'd seen it, but Edith never knew about it. It was better that way; she'd have been hurt too much or she'd have screamed bloody murder.

Edith and Henri had cooked up a whole system of telephone signals so she wouldn't worry. When he got home, he'd call us, let the phone ring twice and hang up, then call us back, let it ring three times and hang up again. We knew then he'd arrived safely. We also knew he wouldn't be back till the next day.

The whole business was to reassure Edith. I'd look at her and see the nasty pout on her face. She was imagining Henri with the other woman. It's not the sort of thing anybody likes very much.

But you have to give Edith credit: she never let up on her rival. She called Henri at home at any hour of the night. If the woman answered, she'd say, "Let me talk to Henri; it's about work." Then she'd talk to him about songs or love, depending on the mood she was in. When she hung up, she'd say to me, "Do you think she listened in?"

That's how one of Henri's and Edith's best songs came about: "*C'est un monsieur très distingué.*" "Henri, I've got an idea. I'd like us to do a song about Paul Meurisse. Come on over."

"I can't, Edith. It's after curfew. Tell me about it; I'm listening."

"Well, a sentence came to me: 'He's a very distinguished gentleman.' I don't know what's next. But in the song she—that is, me—might be a poor kid who's not very smart and he might awe her by his good manners and make a damn fool of her. See what I mean?"

"Yes, we'll talk about it tomorrow."

"No, we mustn't let it get cold. I know I've got some ideas. I can go out at night—I've got an *Ausweis*. I'll take a cab and come pick you up. They don't stop cabs."

That's what she did. She was beside herself with joy. "I've got the better of him, Momone! Boy, must his dame be furious!" Naturally the two of them didn't get very far on the song that night.

"I want a whole night with you," she said. "I've certainly got a right to one."

Two days later, Henri came with a book. "I've brought you

Back Street to help you write our song. It's a story you'll understand."

They came close to a nasty breakup over this book. Edith had read it at night without having anything to drink—she couldn't read when she'd been drinking. Ever since childhood her vision hadn't been too good, and when she drank, everything got blurry.

The next day in the bathroom, she unloaded everything that was bothering her—and it was a lot. Sitting on the edge of the tub, she told me the story of *Back Street* and the poor girl who spends her whole life on the fringe of the life of the man she loves.

"What does he take me for, giving me that book? That poor sap in the book is me; I'm 'Mme Back Street.' And as if that wasn't enough, he's added insult to injury with that song. '*C'est un monsieur très distingué*'—the same story indeed! He's laughing his head off at me. I'll sing the song because it's too good to drop, but is he gonna get it! He's made me pay through the nose for my night of love. When I think that I gave him breakfast in bed! You watch; I'm not going to let him get away with this!"

When Henri came, he had a bunch of violets in his hand; he often used to bring Edith one. "Put it over there," said Edith. "You look like a guy who's been stood up." He leaned over to kiss her and she pushed him away.

"It's no time for smooching. Sit down. Why did you give me that book to read? Am I the poor idiot wasting her life waiting for you? So your majesty wants me to stay here, crying and knitting, and cooking up little dishes he won't come and eat. Well, you're one hundred percent wrong. I'll show you how I play *Back Street*, how I play the poor inconsolable sap who's let herself be ruined by bastards like you. Can you picture me with the hangdog expression of a woman whose life's been sacrificed? And who to? To someone in curtain-raisers! Me, Edith Piaf! You sure as hell haven't ever looked at me. I didn't wait till you came along to have men. And the list's gonna get longer; it'll have as many as the telephone book. . . . I swear I'm going to give you such a pair of horns they'll reach to the neighbors' upstairs!" With a text like that, Cocteau could have written a new play if he'd been there.

I knew, unfortunately, that she'd keep her word. Edith had a neat way to get even just staring her in the face. His name was Yvon Jean-Claude. Actually, he'd already filled in a few times. Unless she was dead drunk, Edith couldn't go to sleep without feeling a man's leg next to hers. When it came to getting herself a guy to sleep with, she thought more or less the way a man does.

This Yvon Jean-Claude was a nice guy, a young singer. He was tall, and dark, and looked a little like a mannequin from a fancy department store.

For "*C'était une histoire d'amour*," Edith had had an idea for staging the song that called for a man's voice. She'd heard Yvon and liked him. Every night he'd stand behind the backdrop, and when Edith would sing:

> *C'etait une histoire d'amour . . .*

Yvon would sing:

> *C'était une histoire d'amour*
> *C'était par un beau jour de fête . . .*

It hardly took much out of him, and afterward he'd come home with us. Edith didn't pay him, but he slept at the apartment. He was entitled to meals, to the Bidou-Bar and sometimes to share Edith's bed.

On the night of the *Back Street* scene, Edith said, "You'll see, Momone. Henri's going to suffer as much as I have. He'll get to know the hell of jealousy. It's gonna hurt, believe you me."

Unless Henri was blind and deaf, he couldn't have helped but know that Yvon was sleeping with Edith too.

One afternoon Henri opened Edith's bedroom door, said, "Oh! Sorry," and shut it again. I felt myself turn green. I thought, "This is it, disaster, it has to be."

But no. Henri went into the living room to wait. When Edith joined him, he looked as if nothing at all was wrong. He laughed and kidded around, and then left as usual.

The next day he didn't come by and he didn't phone. Edith didn't want it to show, but she was eating her heart out; she kept glowering at the phone. Every time it rang, she'd shout to Andrée Bigeard, "Who is it?" She was really worried; I was too.

"What do you suppose he's going to do? Is he going to chuck his babe?" It seemed to me that in Henri's place, it was Edith I'd have chucked.

The next day Henri came back with a song, "*Le Blond et le brun*":

> *Dans ma p'tite vie y'a deux garçons,*
> *Y'en a un brun, y'en a un blond—*
> *Qui m'aiment tous deux à leur manière.*
> *Le brun a l'air triste et sérieux,*
> *Et le blond rit de tous ses yeux.*
> *Je crois bien qu'c'est l'brun que j'préfère;*
> *Oui, mais le blond n'a qu'à s' ram'ner,*
> *Avec son air de rigoler,*
> *C'est pour lui qu'j'ai envie d'êtr' belle.*
> *J'crois bien qu'c'est l'blond que j'préfère.*

> In my little life there are two boys,
> One's blond and the other's dark—
> They both love me in their own way.
> The dark one looks so sad and earnest,
> And the blond's eyes laugh.
> I really think I like the dark one best;
> Yes, but the blond only has to turn up again,
> With his cheerful air,
> I want to look beautiful for him.
> I really think I like him best.

The song, however, ended with the death of the blond, the one who laughed all the time. He killed himself. You didn't have to be a college graduate to understand: the blond was Henri. Actually he had light brown hair with a few gray strands mixed in. Edith liked it. She'd say, "Look at him in the light. Henri, turn your head. Gee, it's pretty . . . he's a silver blond." Well, if she said so . . .

Henri left his song, said, "Good-bye, dears!" and went off. Naturally Edith never missed a chance. She read "*Le Blond et le brun*" to Yvon. I saw Yvon's eyes fill with tears and he ran out the door. "What's the matter with that idiot?" Edith asked. "One more guy off his nut. Go see what's the matter, Momone."

Poor little fashion plate for a department store catalogue—he was crying like a kid, repeating one of the lines from the song: "I like the blond best."

"It's Henri, he's the one she loves. I don't mean anything to her!"

It wasn't easy to contradict him. I'd have liked to console him, but he really wasn't my type.

Henri never blew up a storm when he was mad; he waited till he'd calmed down. The next day he lit a cigarette, the match in the hollow of his hands like when there's wind; it made him look like a man in the streets lighting his cigarette before making his move. The gesture suited him, and he knew it. He looked around the room as if he were panning the place with his eyes and threw away his match.

"So you'd like me to come here? Really, just look around! What a housekeeper! You're not keeping house, you're keeping a brothel! You're an assistant madam who's made a comeback and keeps on screwing customers for pleasure." That was nasty, and the two of them screamed at each other for quite a while. Then Henri burst out laughing.

"It can't be! *You're* going to make *me* jealous—of *you!*" He *was* jealous, but it couldn't change anything any more. Edith became her old impossible self again. And there were times when it wasn't much fun. The two of us would go out for a walk, see some guy with his pal and have a drink with them (Edith always took the best one and left me the dog); then we'd go to the lavatory and she'd say, "Listen, Momone, if you don't sleep with the pal, he's going to tag along with my guy and me; we won't be able to ditch him." It got to be a bore; I wasn't always in the mood. But she'd say, "Be a good kid, Momone. What difference can it make to you? It's not important. Doing that or gulping down a glass of wine—it's all the same!" *I* thought there was a difference. But when she said, "Do it for me, Momone," I couldn't say no.

Edith was still mad at Henri. She'd decided to give it to him good. She played every card she had.

Once Edith made a date with a guy who lived at Pantin and whose name was Hémond. Henri was at our place relaxing, spreading his toes, drinking a liqueur and warming it in his hands: perfect bliss. Edith had told me what she was up to. "Not a word to Henri, Momone. We're sneaking out. I'm going to meet Hémond."

Edith was in good spirits. It excited her to be plotting something against Henri. To get herself in the mood, she'd drunk a lot at lunch. On the stroke of three she broke the news:

"I'm going to the theater."

"In your condition, you won't understand a word," replied Henri.

I was pretty soused myself. Henri was annoyed but nice about it and took us to the door of the theater. "I can't leave you alone. I'm going in with you," he said.

Naturally we were late; the play had already begun. "Too bad," whispered Edith, "I won't see my Hémond."

The first line we heard was: "Let us love one another." Edith began to laugh uncontrollably and to shout, "Hémond's the one I want. Hey, Henri, do you hear?" Henri walked out on us in a rage. I was tight, but not so far gone I couldn't hear people saying, "Shhh," "Quiet," "Sit down," all around us. The usher was trying to seat us. It was dark and we were about to break our necks. The actors went on, and Edith shouted, "They really could stop until I sat down. We're not gonna understand a word of this play. . . ."

Finally the guard on duty and the usher managed to get us seated, but they couldn't get Edith to shut up—she just wouldn't. I've never seen anything like it. As we sat there in our seats, we played with the actors. Edith answered them back and gave them advice, shouting:

"Don't let him get away with it! Tell him you don't want him, that he's too ugly. . . . Good for you, Joe, that's really telling 'em. Right, Momone? Boy, is this a scream! What a play! They're good actors, but what they're saying couldn't be assier! Look, Momone: I'm him and you're her. You say to me, 'Go away.' What do I answer?"

" 'Shit!' "

And we doubled up with laughter. We'd never seen a funnier play. I don't remember the theater or the name of the play or the actors, much less how it all ended. They must have kicked us out.

Edith had decided she was in love with Hémond. It was even true for twenty-four hours. She wasn't a cheater (in anything— and she paid for it with her life). To her, every guy had something interesting: a nice tie, beautiful eyes, a special mouth or hands or laugh. Each had something attractive about him.

Hémond lasted barely two weeks. But Edith believed in her passion and that's what drove Henri crazy. How pleasant it is to hear your mistress tell you: "I love him, he's not like the others. Henri, you've got to understand."

This time he really got angry. He called her a madwoman, a lush, a whore, a psychopath, a hysteric, a nymphomaniac. . . . He had quite a vocabulary. I didn't understand it all, but I was full of admiration.

An hour after he left, Edith was in despair; she'd completely forgotten about her passion for Hémond. "Listen, Momone, I was wrong. But Henri just can't do that to me. He'll call. He knows I'm afraid for him. I can't lose him for this Hémond guy; I don't give a damn about him, he doesn't count, but Henri . . ."

It went on and on. I began to be as nervous as she was. She wept, buried her head in the pillow and tore the sheet with her teeth. It was a real crisis.

"Call him up, Momone. Tell him I've got a song we've got to work on right away."

I phoned. Edith listened in.

"Hang up, Momone, it's his babe."

She cried so hard that the next day she had eyes as big as hard-boiled eggs. "Go see him, Momone. I can't live without him." I'd heard that before about others.

I phoned Henri. He told me to meet him in his office at *Paris-Soir*. There, I must admit, he was really somebody. And did he make his job look like serious business! The phone rang all the time. He gave orders. Not a bit of his big-screen production was lost on me.

"If you had me come here to watch you, just say so," I told him. "I've got all the time in the world."

He laughed, and that was the end of it.

"You're real dolls, you two, a couple of jokers. Come on, let's have a drink."

"No, come to our place. Edith's waiting for you."

Coming home with him that day, I understood Henri. I was as aware of what he was thinking as if I'd been him. I saw the apartment with his eyes—a real shithouse. It was one-thirty or two o'clock. There were people lying all over the place: poor Yvon Jean-Claude, as usual; his sister Annie Jean-Claude, who married the filmmaker Dorffmann; old lady Bigeard, who was doing something or other in the midst of all the chaos; Chang, who was cooking (he'd learned to cook beans and chicken); an unknown guy strumming on the piano; another drinking. . . .

It was sad enough to make you vomit. You had to be Edith Piaf to keep a *decent* man in the middle of such a pitiful mess. You also had to be Piaf to dare ask him just to come over in the middle of all that.

Edith was still in bed when Henri came in. She shouted, "Henri, it's you! I love you!" When a man heard that in the voice of la môme Piaf, he felt weak in the guts.

She made up with Henri, but nothing was right between them. Edith made one last effort though. She wanted to have something of him she could keep: a child. "You see, Momone, it'll be good looking and intelligent. You should always choose the father—you shouldn't leave a thing like that to chance."

Edith never talked about Cécelle. Just once, on the thirty-first of January, Saint Marcelle's day, she said to me, "My little girl would be ten years old today. If your mother'd taken her when we brought her over to her, maybe the kid'd be alive today." She was fooling herself. I knew what my mother was worth as a nursemaid.

Edith was very calm, very serious that morning as she said to Henri, "Dear love, I know you'll never come live here; it's hopeless. So I want to have something from you that'll always be with me. I want a child."

Henri was terribly touched. He kept saying, "You want a child, a child by me?" over and over again like a big idiot.

It wasn't all that easy, otherwise she would have had one a long time before that. When she had her little Cécelle, they'd told her, "It's a miracle. You'll have a lot of trouble having any more." We went to see a big doctor, the very best, now that she had the means. He told her there wasn't very much wrong, that all she needed was a little gynecological operation, that she'd only be hospitalized forty-eight hours. "O.K.," said Edith, "I'll go to your clinic, but I'm taking Momone."

The evening before she was to go, Edith said to me, "Come on, we're going to do something we'll enjoy." We bought shirts and diapers and pants and bonnets and little shoes, even a christening dress. We bought two of everything, one in pink and one in blue. We didn't know if it was going to be a boy or a girl. Only Edith would have dared do that.

Acting very much like the "prospective father," Henri went with us to the Belvedere Hospital in Boulogne. As he was leaving, Edith clung to his arm and said, "After my operation, you'll make me my child." We were all deeply moved, so we drank a bottle of champagne.

When the nurse saw us unpacking the whole layette, she thought we were two nuts.

"But, madame, you're not expecting a baby."

"Not today," answered Edith, "but this is to help me believe I will. And this way, when it comes, I'll be sure my kid won't need anything." She wasn't joking any more.

"I had a little girl, mademoiselle, Cécelle. I didn't have a cent to my name. I couldn't buy her a thing; the only clothes she had were given to her. Now that I have the means, I want the nicest things there are. But you can't understand; you have to have gone through it. This time my kid's going to have everything."

The nurse didn't know what to think. But she was closer to tears than to laughter.

I put the whole layette away in the closet. It was pretty, with all the piles arranged by color. I said, "Maybe it'll be twins, a boy and a girl."

"Leave the closet door open, Momone. I'll be able to see all the little things from my bed and it'll give me courage for tomorrow."

We'd also brought our ammunition. The only drinks hospitals ever have are water and tea. You can't celebrate with that.

"You know, Momone, this is serious business. I've got to get ready for the shock of the operation." Edith's technique was surely unfamiliar around there; it wasn't the way *they* went about things. To get ourselves in shape, we drank toasts to each other, to the future kid, to Henri—we certainly owed him that!

To create some atmosphere, we'd brought our phonograph and records. They didn't much appreciate that at the hospital. They came and told us to shut up and gave us some sedatives. But it was sad without music, so we got up and wandered down the corridors in our nightgowns, bottle in hand. We made a racket, we horsed around, we offered the nurses a drink—a real scandal! Finally they put us to bed by brute force, and the nurse on the morning shift found us snoring like angels who'd really hung one on. . . .

When the doctor saw Edith in that state, he kicked us the hell out. Apparently alcoholic cures weren't his specialty. We had to leave, bag and baggage, just when we were sleeping the soundest.

And that's how Edith did not have a child with Henri. But she'd got the idea in her head, and with every new man she'd say, "He'd be a good one to have a baby with . . ." or "This one's worth nothing . . ." meaning that, in Edith's mind, he was going to be deprived of a child. This got to be a way for her to size up a guy. She kept the ones who passed muster longer, and they never knew why!

The Contet period lasted a little over a year. In order to keep things straight and not forget dates, the various guys ought to have got certificates! The love between Edith and Henri was over and done with, but she kept him as a friend and songwriter. What's more, she had a good time with him. That former engineer was far from being a bourgeois and wasn't a conformist. He was at ease with everybody, in every sort of situation, and had contacts everywhere, which were later to be very useful to us.

On the rue Anatole de la Forge we'd never have won a popularity contest. The neighborhood was too stuffy to put up with Edith's way of life. And she didn't pay her rent either—it was too much bother. When the concierge came by at the end of the month, all mealy-mouthed and full of sweetness and light, Edith would say, "Put the bill over there. Simone, pour madame a drink." And then she'd add, royally, "I'll have a drink with her," and slip her a generous tip. Several months later, the bills would still be "over there." All her life she was ridden with debts. If she didn't pay immediately, it just waited. Poor Andrée with her pile of bills— what a lot of trouble she had! She's the one who got it from all sides. You couldn't talk about money with Edith. She earned it, and that was enough. She didn't want to know if her expenses were more than her income.

Everything was falling apart. The Contet business hadn't worked. We were cold; the heat in the building had been cut off, our coal stoves smoked and we let them go out, and we forgot to lay in stocks of coal from the black market. Edith couldn't bear the cold; she'd bundle up from head to foot in woolens and it put her in a bad mood. So when the owner of the building kicked us the hell out, we were rather pleased.

The vulture didn't weep too much over his accounts. The fact that Edith hadn't paid her rent made it easier for him to get rid of us. The list of our misdeeds was apparently long: disturbance of the peace at night; drunk and disorderly; and so on. In spite of the drinks and the tips we'd given her, the concierge had said we behaved like whores, that men came and went at all hours of the day and night, and, in short, that this was no way to act in a bourgeois building.

When Edith said to Henri, "We're leaving because, according to the owner, we've been acting like whores," he replied, "This is exactly the time for it, dears, because I'm moving you to a brothel."

"A real one?"

"Not exactly. A place where prostitutes take their customers. In an elegant neighborhood, in the rue de Villejust [today the rue Paul Valéry]. You'll be on the top floor, and it'll be nice and quiet. You'll have all the services of the house at your disposal. Only the best people go there. You'll be as cozy as tarts in an oven."

"Tarts! Always one for a laugh, eh?" Edith answered.

"My dears, you're going to like it there. You'll make a hit with the management, I'm sure. It'll be swell! You'll be nice and warm; in houses like that the customers are afraid of drafts. Besides, you'll get rid of your whole gang. You'll be able to straighten out your finances."

When the two of us moved in, along with Mme Bigeard, the manager and his wife threw their arms around us. We hugged each other like buddies from the same regiment. They were called Fredi; they surely had another name, but I never knew what it was. He was an Italian who looked like a taller and not as cute Tino Rossi. She was a fat bleached blonde, who traipsed around all the time in a nightgown falling off one shoulder and one tit hanging out. Her flesh was a little flabby. She called her girls "dearie" and "darling," but that didn't keep her from having eyes like a hawk. She didn't let a thing get by her. "Listen, dearie, you weren't in good shape today; M. Robert wasn't satisfied"; or "Darling, be more careful about your underwear. You wear the same things too many times in a row, and the customers don't like it. M. Emile told me so. You mustn't disappoint the customers; the reputation of the house is at stake." It was a discreet house; the girls knew their customers only by their first names.

We clicked with the Fredis, male and female, right from the start. "I don't have any money," Edith said to them as soon as we moved in. "Well, it doesn't matter; we'll wait," they said.

They gave us credit, but when we had dough, they caught up, and with interest! They practically conked us over the head. But we were warm and had all the food we wanted, right in the middle of the occupation. And we weren't alone; we felt that we had a family.

We had a bedroom and a bath. Mme Bigeard also had her own room and bath. We were in a brothel, but we had our secretary. "That's real class, Momone!" There was wall-to-wall carpeting and nice furniture—and what you call all the modern conveniences. Edith was delighted.

We met a whole bunch of new pals that very night. The young ladies' "workrooms" were on the floors below ours, and the drawing room was on the ground floor, above street level.

The house did two sorts of business; the Fredis were no fools. During the day they used the call-girl system: the girls weren't there; they were requested by telephone. In the evening it was more "classical"—something like the deluxe prewar brothels, the "One-Two-Two," "Sphinx" or "Chabanais" type. The customers had dinner or supper in the drawing room. There was a pianist there all the time. It was pleasant; everyone felt comfortable. The first time, Edith closed her eyes.

"Be quiet, Momone, let me listen to my memories. The pianist, the smell of perfumed women . . . It's not the same songs, or the same perfumes, but it feels like a brothel, the way it did when I was blind. It's been more than seventeen years now, but it seems to me I'm about to hear Grandma's voice saying, 'Edith, you've listened to the music long enough. Come to bed.' "

There was an unusual atmosphere about this house. It was quite lively. We were good pals with the girls. They weren't at all like the whores on the sidewalk or in cheap brothels. They knew how to talk about lots of things: books, music, the theater. They had to. The men who came there were big wheels in the occupation government and in the black market, or they were collaborators. The Jerries who patronized the place weren't underlings, but generals and colonels, discreet and "correct," as we used to say, never in uniform. And big-time gangsters (French and German) high up in the Gestapo. The rue Lauriston, where those shits worked, was very close by. Between interrogations or torture sessions, they'd come there to relax their overtaxed nerves. Nobody liked them, but the Fredis were too afraid of them not to let them in. I've kept the best till last: guys in the resistance—incognito, naturally. We didn't know this till much later. M. Fredi quietly had his foot in both camps. And he milked them both, let me tell you.

Henri Contet was happy as anything there. He liked this carnival and didn't miss any part of it. He even had the nerve to go listen to BBC broadcasts in Edith's room while General Von "Zo-and-Zo" was cuddling downstairs with "Mamoizelle Franzaise."

We didn't have a man living with us; not a one came with his suitcase. Men passed through Edith's life the way they passed through her bedroom: like gusts of wind. "I'm fed up with loving; it hurts too much. I've put my heart on vacation; I'm giving it a holiday," Edith would say. She put a good face on it, but deep down she was a little depressed.

Between work and visits, we didn't have time to think. We had every sort of visitor. Even one of our old pimps, Riri, the most faithful of them and our favorite, brought Edith a superb bouquet of flowers.

"It's for you. You gotta keep 'volving in life."

Did we laugh! Our pimp had made it; he'd "evolved"! He had a big hunk of ice on his finger; not fake—real! And here he was with flowers!

"Business is good, eh?" Edith said to him. "What are you in now?"

"I've still got my good earners, nice girls who work hard. But that isn't what brings in the most. I've gone into business." We didn't ask him what sort of business. In that world, keeping your mouth shut keeps your feet dry. We never forgot it.

He bought us a bottle of champagne and we talked about the good old days. He gave us news of old pals. "You know some of 'em went wrong. They're with the Gestapo. And others who were unlucky are in the camps or were hauled in for dealing on the black market. Fat old Fréhel has had troubles too. She was singing in Hamburg when it was bombed. The phosphorus ran in the streets; the pavement melted. People were burned up in it, standing there like torches. Houses collapsed. The flames lit up everything— you could have read a newspaper if you had one. It seemed like the whole town was screaming. There were fires all over the place, and Hamburg stank like roast pig. Fréhel had all her hair, her eyebrows, her eyelashes burned, and her legs. When she talks about it, you tremble, you're scared shitless. You know how sensitive I am; I was sick to my stomach. I don't think the Nazis can win the war after blows like that. We've got to be sharp and make a lot of dough off 'em."

He left, saying, "Kids, I'm happy to leave you here in a nice, warm, decent place."

Guite came all the time. She'd arrive on a motorbike (we were all riding two-wheelers) with a scarf on her head so as not to muss her hair (it was a big fashion; we even made turbans out of them). But Guite's hair was always flying about anyway. "I don't understand," she'd say. "My head's always a mess." We laughed, and Guite got mad. "I don't see why you're laughing. I'm not absentminded; I'm just thinking about something else, that's all."

She may not have been absent-minded, but one day she came by on somebody else's motorbike.

"Dears, I'm all upset. I just noticed I've got the wrong motorbike. I've taken one that doesn't belong to me."

"All you have to do is give it back."

"But to whom?"

"Take it back where you got it."

"I don't remember where it was."

Edith and I always thought Guite didn't realize we were living in a brothel. One day she said, "There's a lot going on in your hotel, but it's good and warm. They're very nice here; they let you in very politely." She thought the Fredis were the concierge and his wife! Charming, adorable Guite, so in the clouds you felt like taking her by the hand and leading her around.

Edith had a lot of visitors. She didn't see singers very much. She preferred actors, and they came by in an endless stream.

Her great friend was Michel Simon. What an extraordinary man! He was ugly, but nobody gave a damn. I spent hours listening to him, and forgetting what he looked like. . . . I'd have fallen in love with him, just because he was so intelligent, but I wasn't his type. He was very keen on the little whores on the rue Saint-Denis. Those he liked. But he came to our place to chat with Edith. To me, they were two monsters together; they fascinated me.

Michel didn't talk a lot about his profession, but he told us about lots of things that had happened in his life. There were so many! He also talked about animals, especially his pet monkey, which he loved like a woman. He was a great storyteller, and his unusual, very special voice added something true, something painful, to what he said. He couldn't stand his face; his ugliness haunted him.

"With a mug like mine, only whores will have anything to do with me (they're good girls), and only animals love me. My monkey thinks I'm good looking. She's right, because she'd have a hard time finding a male monkey as handsome as I am! Anyway, it's better to have an ugly mug than none at all. . . ." That made Edith laugh. But it made my heart ache a little.

Michel Simon thought Edith had a face like his and looked as dreadful as he did. It reassured him; he wasn't the only one any more. "You see, Edith, we don't have to be beautiful to be a success."

What was astonishing is that after a while I ended up seeing Edith through Michel's eyes. I'd always thought she was pretty, but now I told myself there really was something abnormal about her —her narrow shoulders, her big forehead, her little face. Yet she was better-looking offstage than on. She no longer looked half starved; you noticed she had round hips and good thighs.

She and Michel used to tell each other their life stories. They also liked to say a lot of damn foolish things and tell each other silly jokes. They didn't mind at all if their jokes were corny, and they were good drinking partners. As I'd be swallowing my first Cinzano, they'd already be on their tenth drink. They held their own, each of them. As Michel said, "We're ugly, we're not beautiful, but we're not weaklings!"

Boy, did we have a lot of visitors!

Jean Chevrier would come with Marie Bell, from the Comédie Française. She looked quite the socialite, but that didn't keep her from coming to our brothel. We'd receive them in the drawing room, then she'd go discreetly upstairs with her Jean. They weren't married at the time.

Marie Marquet would come too. When she and Marie Bell would meet, they'd be a little catty. They didn't like each other much. Edith admired Marie Marquet; she thought she had great style. She was in fact quite a dame, from every point of view—her size (when she stretched out her arms, both of us could pass underneath them) and her talent. No one recited poetry the way she did; it was a dream! Edith listened to her respectfully. "Marie, when I hear you I take lessons, because a poem is a song without music; the problems are the same."

It was pretty funny to see that very elegant woman wander about our brothel, not shocked at all. She'd tell us extraordinary stories. She was the one who introduced us to Edmond Rostand's plays: *Cyrano de Bergerac, L'Aiglon, Chantecler.* . . . She used to tell us about the house at Arnaga, near Cambo, in the Basque country, where Edmond Rostand had lived. She and the poet had been very much in love. It was a very beautiful love story, which enchanted Edith.

We also had our regular visitors, like Madeleine Robinson and Mona Goya. Madeleine Robinson was Edith's best pal. They had two tastes in common: men and drinking. The binges they went on together are still famous. But they were most extraordinary and instructive when they talked about men. Listening to them, I learned lessons that came in very handy.

As for Mona Goya, she was a riot. She laughed all the time. She was chic; she was pretty; people liked her; and she was a real man-eater. She and Edith worked out a pretty funny routine. On the nights when they were short of men, they'd leave the curtains open and the light on. The cop on the beat would blow his whistle, and they'd just sit there. The guy would finally come upstairs and, if he was good looking, they'd offer him a drink for his trouble and keep him awhile. . . .

It wasn't funny all the time though. We had a little of everything.

One day in 1943, Edith was called to the police station because of her mother. It wasn't the first time, but it was to be the last. Ever since Edith had become famous, her mother had caused one scandal after another. More than once we'd found her in Fresnes prison; she'd been picked up on the streets, dead drunk or doped up, a real bum. We'd go and get her and reoutfit her from head to foot—and it'd begin all over again.

Once when Edith was appearing at the A.B.C. in 1938, a woman dressed like a tramp came and clung to the door of Edith's taxi. Her hair was hanging in her face, she'd been drinking, and she kept screaming in a terrible, drunken, hoarse voice, a voice of destitution: "She's my daughter . . . she's my daughter." Raymond Asso had got mad and had Edith get rid of her for a time. But then she began whining all over town that Edith was her daughter, that Edith had left her without a cent even though she was rolling in money.

She threatened to go to the newspapers. And in fact she did go, in 1941, to ask for help from the charity services of *Paris-Soir*. She put on a good act, but it didn't work every time because she never sobered up and they didn't take her seriously. By 1943 we were so used to it that this time Edith said to me, "You take care of it." At the police station, the cops told me she'd died a terrible death—in the gutter.

She'd been living in Pigalle with a young man—a poor little drug addict, a derelict. It was drugs that kept them together; the two of them used to sniff dope together. One night the boy got up out of their lice-ridden cot to go get a fix. As he left, he glanced at Edith's mother, who was snoring away. When he came back up to their room, she was still lying there in the same position. He touched her and she was cold. Scared and high on drugs, he took her body and dumped it in the street. She'd died just as our old man had predicted—in the gutter.

Henri and I took care of everything. Edith had her mother buried at Thiais. She wouldn't come to the funeral or visit her grave. "My mother's been dead a long time as far as I'm concerned —ever since she abandoned me, a month after I was born. She was never anything but the mother on my birth certificate."

It was true. There was really no love lost between Edith and her mother. They both tried, but their hearts weren't in it. Edith's mother only saw her when she wanted something.

Edith worked hard. In her profession her contacts with the occupying forces sometimes came close to turning out rather badly. In spite of her first name, there was nothing about her that resembled the heroine Edith Cavell. But she was too much of a cheeky Parisian urchin, a kid off the streets, to stand for anyone interfering with her freedom and to not be irreverent.

The night of the dress rehearsal at the A.B.C. in 1942, there naturally was a whole mess of German officers there in uniforms of every color—green for the Wehrmacht, black for the SS, gray for the Luftwaffe, blue for the Kriegsmarine. But all those officers with their decorations weren't the only ones there; the A.B.C. was crammed with all kinds of Parisians. At the end of her act, Edith threw *"Où sont-ils tous mes copains?"* right in their kissers, with the French flag projected on the backdrop. The whole house went mad.

The next day there was an instant reaction from the Germans. Edith was sent for, and those Jerries really raked her over the coals.

"Take that song out of your repertoire."

Edith was scared silly, but she answered, "No."

"Well, then, I'm going to forbid it."

"Go ahead. But all of Paris is going to make fun of you."

They finally compromised. The French flag was removed.

The Germans liked what she did. They invited her time and time again to come sing in the big German cities; she always said no. But she was always ready to sing in the stalags, and she never kept the fees she earned: she turned them over to the prisoners. She'd come back heartbroken from these trips. All those soldiers, those men, belonged to her, they were the ones she'd always loved. They welcomed her like a princess.

Andrée Bigeard had asked to take my place during all this traveling.

"Are you that fond of the Jerries?"

"I like to travel," Andrée replied.

"She's lying," Edith said to me. We weren't such dimwits we hadn't noticed that Andrée Bigeard invited lots of men up to her room. In the beginning Edith had laughed. "This house has made Andrée lose her mind. Boy, the number of men she invites up! I'd never have believed it of her!"

Later we realized she made use of being in the heart of enemy territory to help the resistance, and that the men who came to see her were "terrorists," as the Jerries called them. So those trips across the Rhine were very useful to Andrée, but they weren't exactly safe for her.

One day when Edith was singing in a stalag, a high-ranking German officer said to her, "I hope you're pleased, madame, and appreciate the hospitality of the Reich. What do you think of Germany?"

"I'm glad you asked," Edith replied. "Our room is ice cold, the windowpanes are broken, the food stinks and we can't even get any wine. Germany's crappy!"

The guy turned beet red. He grabbed the telephone and started yelling into it in German. Edith said to herself, "This time I've gone too far." But no. An hour later, she was moved to the best hotel and served a decent meal with a bottle of very French Bordeaux.

Another time, in another stalag, Edith had learned that the French prisoners had set the following words to a Hitler anthem:

> *Dans le cul, dans le cul,*
> *Ils auront la victoire.*
> *Ils ont perdu*
> *Toute espérance de gloire.*
> *Ils sont foutus,*
> *Et le monde en allégresse*
> *Répète avec joie, sans cesse:*
> *Ils l'ont dans le cul,*
> *Dans le cul!*

> Up the ass, up the ass,
> They'll get their victory.
> They've lost
> All hopes of glory.
> They're damn well done for,
> And the world, happily,
> Joyfully, keeps saying:
> They're getting it up the ass,
> Up the ass!

At the end of her act Edith announced, "To thank the officers, I'm going to sing you a German song. But since I don't know the words, I'll just hum it." And she started off in the loudest voice she could. With an impressive scraping of boots, all the Germans got to their feet and stood at attention listening to Edith, who was actually singing them *"Dans le cul."*

As the atmosphere was friendly, Andrée Bigeard said to Edith, "Ask permission to be photographed with the whole group of prisoners." After clinking glasses with the commandant of the camp—"To Stalingrad," "To victory," to whatever they wanted —Edith said:

"Colonel, I'd like to ask you a favor."

"Granted in advance," he answered, clicking his heels.

"I'd like to have a souvenir of this fine day—a photo with all of you and with *my* prisoners."

The German agreed. Back in Paris, Edith gave the photo to Andrée. It was enlarged, and each French soldier's head was removed separately and pasted onto false identity cards and papers of volunteer workers in Germany. Edith asked to go back to the stalag and was given permission. And Andrée, using Edith's double-bottomed makeup box, smuggled all the false papers in and saw to it that they got to the prisoners. Those who managed to escape were helped greatly by these documents. Some were saved by them. Edith and Mme Bigeard carried out this operation whenever they could. Edith used to say, "No, I wasn't in the resistance, but I helped my soldiers."

We would have been happy to stay in our deluxe brothel till the end of the war. But unfortunately Papa and Mama Fredi went a bit too far—too much black market. Toward the end, the occupying forces became virtuous and were getting rid of black market guys to serve as examples. There were also girls who had conned some of the customers, among them a German officer. The bastards from the Gestapo came to see them for ugly reasons now—not just to have a ball. Things were going rotten and decaying, and one morning in the spring of 1944 Henri came to bring us up to date.

"Listen, girls, I smell trouble; you've got to get out."

Edith, who was always quick to make up her mind, said; "We'll retreat to the Hotel Alsina."

We left owing the Fredis two million francs, in spite of all the dough we'd already given them. When I said they cost us a lot, I wasn't fooling. They'd got dough out of us so regularly, even though they'd extended us credit, that we practically had none left.

The day after we left, the house on the rue de Villejust was surrounded and the owners thrown in jail. Our days of living it up were over!

Chapter 9

First Discovery: Yves Montand

At the Alsina we went back to our old habits. But at first it wasn't a very good time for us.

The war was not going so well for the Germans. They'd put up posters with a black border and the names of hostages who might have been our neighbors. This put quite a damper on our spirits. To the Germans we were all terrorists, even the old granny who sold newspapers on the corner. There wasn't a free zone any more. The Jews were rounded up and shipped off like cursed cattle. It was the end of the "proper" occupying forces whose job it was to charm the population. You could feel fear in the streets.

Our morale had fallen to pieces. We didn't have any money. And no more Chang. And we'd said a tearful good-bye to Mme Bigeard. Keeping careful accounts and cutting down made Edith cross. On the rue de Villejust she'd lived like a madwoman: every penny had gone for food and drink. Since we'd been in constant debt to the Fredis, we hadn't even bought clothes. We were wearing whatever we had left, which wasn't all that great.

No more dough; and no more pals: Edith wasn't treating them to drinks any more. It was no fun. It might have been a lesson for her, but no. When she had dough again, she didn't change; she let everybody take advantage of her once more.

One night Edith went off to sing in a stalag. I remember how the Gare de l'Est stank of the soldiers' leather boots, with all the sweat and rancid grease. The smell of boots was the smell of the German army. The train had left long since, but I just stood there, brooding about the misery of that flock going off to the slaughter-house on the Russian front. For them leaves and girls and their country were *fertig*. They were the occupying forces, but they were also human beings, and it wrung my heart.

When I got back to the Alsina, the porter said, "Mme Piaf's father's valet telephoned and asked you to call him back right away."

The business about that valet was a funny story. Edith hadn't dropped her father. One day he'd said to her, "Now that you've made the big time, I'd like a valet. It'll impress my buddies." Boy, did we laugh! But since it fit in with Edith's way of thinking, she put an ad in the paper right away. "The poor old guy, he's prob-ably not long for this world. So let's give him his valet. But we'll have to pay him a lot to hole up on the rue Rébeval!" she said. It was true. Our old man had never been willing to leave his filthy, seedy, rundown hotel, with none of the modern conveniences. A valet in a place like that was unthinkable—but he got one.

I don't know why, but I was worried. Our old man used to go down to the corner café to telephone. Since it was usually to ask for money, he'd make the call himself. I phoned the valet, who was probably waiting for my call, and got him right away.

"I just wanted to tell you, madame, that your father is dead." I didn't realize it, but big tears were rolling down my face. I had really liked the old guy. Anyway, a whole part of my life was about to be buried in the grave alongside Papa. I immediately called Henri Contet, and we went to the rue Rébeval together. There was no way to get word to Edith. She did get back in time for the funeral though. It all made her pretty miserable.

There was a whole bunch of relatives waiting for us at our old man's hotel—cousins and second cousins we'd never seen. They all wanted souvenirs. When our old man was alive, they wouldn't have given him a glass of water! Edith gave Papa Gassion's fine gold watch to the valet. She told me to give the others his pipes, so I handed out the smelly, caked pipes he loved so much.

They put him in a grave at the Père Lachaise cemetery. The girls from the brothel in Normandy were there. They bawled heartily and didn't dare give Edith a hug. Henri was with us. The guys from the funeral parlor had put him among "the gentlemen of the family." Seeing the dirt fall on the casket made me feel awful. Edith gave my hand a hard squeeze. We each knew what the other was thinking. It was our whole childhood, our youth, being buried.

Nothing was going right. When Henri came to see us, he was all gray and dull. He didn't feel like writing songs. Everybody was burrowing in. Even Guite, who never came any more. She'd lost her last motorbike and there was no piano at the hotel. The only way Guite could talk was with a piano under her fingers.

It wasn't the right moment, maybe, but Henri suggested to Edith that she join SACEM—the Association of Lyricists, Composers and Music Publishers.

"It'll keep you busy. You've already written songs. Since you can't sign them, you don't get anything from them. Join SACEM, and when you've been accepted as a member you'll get royalties."

"Are you nuts, Henri? I couldn't possibly pass an exam!"

I kept after Edith to do it. She didn't want to, but she went.

"I applied, Momone. Boy, is it serious business! Those guys don't kid around. You have to have your birth certificate, your police record and a photograph, and you have to pass a weird test: just like that, right away, you have to write a three-verse song on a subject they give you. I've got the jitters."

Early in 1944, Edith Gassion, better known as Edith Piaf, was summoned to take the exam.

"I can't do it, Momone. I've never taken an exam in my life. I'm going to flunk for sure. And in front of all those bearded guys who're going to judge me." (To Edith a judge or a professor was somebody with a beard, and she hated beards.)

An hour before the exam she was numb with fear. To screw up her courage, she had a few drinks. Then she went down to rue Ballu to SACEM. They shut her up in a little office with some paper and her subject: "The Street by the Railroad Station." She panicked. "Momone, that piece of paper kept swimming in front of my eyes. The words 'Street by the Railroad Station' kept making zigzags on the paper. They didn't mean a thing to me any more. Boy, did that goddamn street bug me! All I could think of was stuff like:

> On the street by the railroad station
> A girl wanders by,
> She's lost her heart
> And with it her happiness . . .

Dumb, assy things. I couldn't write words any more. And I hadn't thought about spelling mistakes! My mind was all confused. I left without the slightest idea of what I'd written, all upset and with a godawful headache! I flunked. I shouldn't have had those drinks. But you know, Momone, I have no ideas when I'm cold sober." She'd blown it!

If ever there was a man who came into Edith's life at the right time, it was Lou Barrier. And he stuck with her right to the end. He was a great guy. Even the way he showed up was sensational. The concierge at the hotel phoned Edith: "There's a M. Louis Barrier to see you."

"All right. I'll be down." She hung up. "Do you know a Louis Barrier, Momone?"

"Never heard of him."

We didn't have many visitors. So we rushed down and found a tall, pleasant-looking blond with a bicycle, and bicycle clips on his pants, standing quite calmly in the lobby.

"Hello, Mme Piaf. I've come to see you because I'm an impresario."

We looked at each other and burst out laughing. The impresario we'd been waiting ten years to see come along in a Rolls with a big cigar stuck in his face had arrived on a bicycle, with little clips on his pants. . . . It was so funny he couldn't have helped but make a hit with us. He had nothing at all in the way of references —just an honest, sincere look on his face. Edith immediately got one of her well-known "shocks": she took to Louis.

"I'd like to manage you. I know you don't have anybody; no

one to protect you or your interests. You've never had an impresario. Now you need somebody. You really do. You're on your way straight to the top, and this is the right moment. So here I am!"

Imagine having enough savvy to say that to us, just when we thought we were about to become bums again!

"O.K.," said Edith, "I like you." They didn't sign any sort of contract, not the tiniest scrap of paper. They didn't need to. Edith always trusted Loulou completely, and he was as devoted to her as a Saint Bernard. He was one of the few people who never said *tu* to her, only *vous*. He was always the one who got her back on her feet, and Edith wasn't easy to deal with.

That very night she decided to sleep with him. "You never know a man, Momone, till you've tried him in bed. You know more about a guy in one night in bed than you do in months of conversation. When they talk, they can pull the wool over your eyes as much as they please. Just try and see! But in the sack they can't cheat—it's the real test. It's when they think they've mastered us that we really control. Sometimes I've had a real ball in bed, let me tell you! Men have given me some good times, but not always the way they think!"

Since she'd made up her mind to, she tried Louis out (and from then on called him Loulou). It was easy; he was more than willing. But it was all over before it began; the little love scene came to nothing, and in a way, that was really too funny.

Edith agreed when he asked her to come visit his bachelor apartment. I wouldn't have remembered their leaving for their little tryst if Edith hadn't come back so soon. I've never laughed so hard! She was hopping mad.

"Momone, pour me a drink. I'm choking with rage."

"Didn't he give you anything to drink?"

"Be quiet. Never mention that idiot's name again! He may be a good impresario, but he's out of luck as far as anything else is concerned! What an ass! We went up to his little two-room apartment. It wasn't bad, and I said to myself, 'He's got taste.' He'd planned it all nicely—champagne, a snack, flowers—and things got off to a good start. We had one drink, then another. He's

the affectionate type. He took me in his arms and whispered sentimental things. I could feel myself melting—you know, just the
right moment! And then he got up.

" 'I'm going to give you a little atmosphere.'

"He put a record on. Guess what he had the nerve to play,
Momone. A song by Henri's old girl friend! For me—after all I'd
put up with with Henri because of her! It was worse than a slap
in the kisser! But I held my temper and said sweetly, 'That's
pretty. Who's singing it?'

"And he mentioned the name of that drip of a girl.

" 'One of your chums? Is she your babe?' I asked.

"And then he got a self-satisfied look on his face—he thought
I'd be impressed! I leaped to my feet and told him off:

" 'If you've got her, you don't need me. For all the contracts
you could get *her* in a year, you won't even make enough dough to
buy yourself bicycle clips!'

"As I took off, I yelled at him:

" 'Keep your atmosphere for her. And don't be afraid of wearing out the record; there'll always be plenty of 'em in the stores!
You should've found out what the score was before pulling that on
me!' "

By next morning our Loulou had got all the dope, and arrived
on our doorstep feeling miserable.

"Edith, please forgive me. I didn't know."

She laughed in his face.

"Don't look like that. I'd forgotten all about it an hour later"—
which wasn't quite true. "Never mind; I'm keeping you. Take
good care of me."

Barrier took wonderful care of her. He was very important in
Edith's career. His time as a lover may not have lasted any longer
than a falling star, but he was very efficient as an impresario. We
could see that right away from the results. These were hard times,
but he got her a two-week contract at the Moulin Rouge, one of
the great music halls of the day. We were working feverishly again,
though we still had some time to talk. I'd sit on the bidet in the
bathroom and listen to Edith. She liked that.

"No one else listens to me the way you do, Momone. You've really got terrific talent when it comes to that." She was sentimental that day. We were floating around in memories of old love affairs, avoiding the rocks. She adored talking about her men.

"Remember José, the little Spaniard? He only lasted one night, but I haven't forgotten him. He was between Jeannot the gob and Riri the legionnaire. . . ."

"No he wasn't. It was long before."

"You think so? That's funny. I'm mixing them up a little."

You'd have had to give Edith's guys numbers to keep them straight. Even she got them all confused. She forgot what order they came in, but she didn't give a damn. What counted was what she was about to tell me. It would begin with:

"He wasn't all that bad. I've had better, but . . ."

The silly thing was that she could never decide which had been the best. Whenever she'd start analyzing one, she'd say, "He wasn't all that good!" But she always ended up with:

"He loved me . . . oh, how he loved me! Right, Momone?" She hardly ever said, "Boy, did I love that one!" After they were gone, she couldn't tell one from the other, except for the stars. All the beads in her rosary of love were the same size.

She decided once to file them by period: "the streets," "the sailors and the colonial troops," "the pimps," "the flings." "Asso and Meurisse'll be the 'professor' period. Contet's the 'brothel' period. And then, after that . . ."

But even with the filing system, we couldn't keep track of them all. The next period was to last a long time. Edith called it her "factory" period, because she began to manufacture singers on an assembly line. She began it with Yves Montand.

Loulou had said to Edith, "They won't assign you a costar any more. It's you who'll choose one now. They've suggested Yves Montand for the Moulin Rouge."

"No, I don't know him. I want Roger Dann; he's a pal of mine."

Roger wasn't in Paris. It was out of the question to bring somebody in from the provinces; everything had become too difficult. It was July, a little more than a month before the liberation.

"All right," said Edith. "Bring your Yves Montand in for an audition. I'll come and hear him."

Edith sat waiting at the back of the Moulin Rouge Theater. We saw a tall guy with dark hair, an Italian type, come onstage, good looking but badly dressed in a loud checked sports jacket and a little hat like Trenet wore. What's worse, he sang old American stuff, fake Texas songs. He was copying Georges Ulmer and Charles Trenet. Boy, was it awful! I looked at Edith and was sure she'd cut out before the end.

After three songs, he came downstage and said peevishly:

"Should I go on or is that enough?"

"That's enough," Edith shouted. "Wait for me!"

That one was sure going to get it. Edith knew he was wild to have an audition with her, but also that he went around calling her a "blues peddler," a "realistic singer off the streets," a "first-class pain in the ass."

Seeing them from a distance was funny—him standing there at the edge of the stage with her down below, so short that her nose came up to his ankles. He probably thought it beneath him to lean down to her. What Edith had to say didn't take very long.

"If you want to sing, come see me in an hour at the Hotel Alsina."

Yves was out of breath, and so furious he was deathly pale. But an hour later in the room in the Alsina, he had all the wind taken out of his sails. Edith didn't handle him with kid gloves.

"We'll begin with your good points—it won't take long. You're damn good looking, you've got presence, your hands are expressive and you've got a good, low, warm voice that'll make women melt. You seem like a go-getter and you seem intelligent. The rest is a total loss. Your clothes are fit for the circus—you look ridiculous. Your Marseilles accent is horrible, you drawl your *o*'s and you wave your arms around like a puppet. Your repertoire's worthless! Your songs are vulgar. All the American stuff makes me laugh."

"It's popular. It's been a hit."

"In Marseilles: they haven't seen anything down there for four years. And in Paris the public's pleased when you make damn fools of the occupation forces. It's not you they're applauding—it's the Americans! You'll look like a sap next to them once they get here. You're already old hat."

Yves choked back his rage. You could hear him grit his teeth. Edith was having a ball.

"Thanks, Mme Piaf. I get the message. You don't want me. I'm not your type."

"You're all wrong there. You are my type, and I don't want to keep you from making a living. Two weeks with you will be over pretty fast."

He was so mad he was choking but he didn't say a word. As he was on his way out, Edith caught him.

"Wait a minute, I'm not finished. I'm sure you're a singer, a real one. I'm ready to make you work. If you'll listen to me, and obey me, and trust me, you'll be the greatest of them all."

"Thanks a lot!" he answered, and left, slamming the door behind him.

I was bowled over. It hadn't lasted more than fifteen minutes. And in that quarter of an hour I'd discovered a woman I'd never known. I'd never even thought this Edith existed. The way she'd just pulled the guy apart made him seem like a pea pod she'd opened and picked the best peas out of. She'd seen through everything ridiculous and fake and bad about him. It knocked me out. Edith had always astonished me, but never to that degree. She sat on the bed looking at the door. And I could see she was thinking fast about a lot of things.

"Not my type! Boy, can men be stupid. . . . The fathead's so good looking he's a dream. That guy's going to revolutionize singing, Momone. He's the one the public's been waiting for. He's what's new; he's the guy for after the war."

"Do you think he'll put up with your lessons?"

"Yes."

I wasn't so sure. Yves had pride. What's more, he was an Italian. They don't like taking orders from a woman; they're not used to it.

The next morning at the rehearsals he'd taken off his jacket and was singing in his shirtsleeves. Then came Edith's turn. She went right for him when he left the stage, and asked:

"Have you heard me sing before?"

"No, Mme Piaf."

"Well, then, how do you know I'm a 'blues peddler'? Call me Edith, and listen to me. That way you can judge for yourself."

He stayed right to the end, then disappeared without a word. Still, Edith waited for him. She was right. He came to the Alsina.

"Listen, Edith, if you're still willing, I'm for it."

"It bothers the hell out of you, doesn't it, to take orders from a woman?"

"No. I heard you sing. Now I see what you mean. You know all the things I don't know."

We poured a drink, toasted each of us and began to work.

"Have you thought about what you're going to wear?"

"Yes, but . . ."

"You don't have the dough? So what? You're not going to sing in a tuxedo! It's wartime, so you're going to dress very simply—a shirt and a pair of pants. Not a white shirt; you'd look like you never did a lick of work. Anyway, it'd cut you in two. And don't look a mess; you've got to respect the public. A shirt the same color as your pants. You're tall and slim, you've got haunches like an alley cat's, so use 'em."

I couldn't get over Edith's air of authority. She seemed to know the lesson she was giving him by heart.

"Your Marseilles accent busts people up. Leave that for those who haven't got anything else on the ball. Here's an old actors' trick: put a pencil between your teeth, then talk and speak your songs with it. And I've made you a list of words full of *o*'s. You're going to recite it to me several times a day."

"With the pencil? I'll look like a fool."

"No one's ridiculous when he's working hard. Come on."

It isn't easy to talk with a pencil between your teeth. Yves drooled and swore, and Edith just laughed. It was really a riot seeing his handsome mug plugged up with the damn pencil.

When Yves was there, there was no more room in the place.

He took up every inch of space with his six feet one and his 180 pounds. Seeing him standing there, docile and willing, with his forehead wrinkled like a puppy with problems, touched me. He was afraid of looking like an ass, but he did it anyway. That pleased me.

The two of us became pals right away. He was a change for me from the other guys we'd had. He made me yearn for fresh air. He faced life like a strong young wolf, with his flat belly and his long, hard muscles. He had an honest, direct, sincere smile, and laughed all the time, as if the weather were always sunny.

After the lesson we'd go out together. We'd walk along side by side, down the avenue Junot. With a kick of his old shoes—he wore at least a size twelve—he sent a pebble flying one day, then stopped, both hands in his pockets, and said, very seriously:

"I think I can trust her. I'm going to work hard."

And he started in right away. In two weeks, even with the rotten songs in his repertoire, Yves made unusual progress. True, he was now taking his lessons in what had become his home. He was the new "boss," and Edith was very much in love with him. Once again I told myself she really had good taste and knew how to pick her men. Yves is still a handsome guy today, but at twenty-two, when he came into a room the sun came in with him.

Being in love with him didn't keep Edith from making him work. He slaved twice as hard, and she didn't let him get away with a thing. She'd decided he'd get to the top very quickly, and she couldn't be wrong! Since she never got tired when she was working, their sessions lasted for hours. Sometimes she was really a pain in the ass. Yves and I would look at each other and feel like getting out. But we couldn't; she held the two of us tightly in the palm of her tiny hand.

"Either stop distracting him, Momone, or get out. When he's finished, I'll give you both an hour to take a walk."

We needed it. The room was too small. Edith loathed having the windows open, and after half an hour Yves, with his athlete's lungs, had breathed up all the air. It got unbearable.

He had no right to go out by himself; she wouldn't let him. I'd

go with him. Edith didn't distrust him, but she was taking precautions. She wanted me to stick right with him every minute.

"The guy's got too much life in him, Momone, too much good
health. We can't let him loose to wander around." I was beginning
to think that tagging after him wasn't going to be much fun.
Though he was all smiles, he wasn't the sort of guy who lets you
put a collar and a leash on him.

They went about their work like two friends. When one of
them wasn't attacking, the other was. Yves kept asking for more!
He had a good solid jaw and nice long teeth, and patience was
hardly his strong point. Even though he didn't know anything yet,
he was already asking:

"O.K., Edith. I need a new repertoire. Where are you going to
find songs for me? How will you do it? Who are you going to
ask?"

"Don't worry, love! Things are moving. It's working."

"What do you mean? Who's it working with? I've got a right
to know."

Yves wasn't an easy person to get on with. He and Edith both
had strong personalities; each was as pigheaded as the other. There
were some great wrestling matches in store. When she got fed up,
Edith would cut things short.

"Do you trust me or don't you?"

How many times I was to hear those words! The two of them
were always ready to question everything. Edith liked things to
hop; that was what pleased her. She was going to get what she
wanted. Yves was a real battler.

I knew she was lying to him; she still hadn't tried to find a
single song for him.

"See, Momone, I don't know anything about his life. The only
things you sing well are what you've got in your gut: all that's hurt
you or made you dream. He thought he was a cowboy, just like a
kid who goes to the movies. He's got his head stuffed full of old
prewar Westerns. I'm sure he thinks he's Zorro! He's got to talk to
me. He's got to tell me about when he worked with his hands or
just lolled around. What he thought about—a little girl friend,
Sundays, going on the stage. Everybody else has to see himself in

him. For that to happen, he has to want the same things they do. And there aren't many people past the age of twelve who dream of riding some nag over the western plains! I have a pretty good idea of his style, but I've got to be sure."

As I listened to Edith, it seemed to me I was listening to Raymond Asso making her work in the little room in Pigalle.

"Come with me and listen to him talk, Momone," Edith said. So several evenings I went to the theater to listen to Yves. I liked it. He knew how to tell a story. Onstage his gestures weren't right at all, he made too many of them; but offstage he was faultless, perfection itself. I knew Edith thought the same way I did. "Boy, how great his gestures are, the beast!"

"You know, I'm Italian, a spaghetti eater," Yves told us. "I was born in a little place thirty miles from Florence on October 13, 1921. Mama baptized me Yvo, and my father's name was Livi. When I came on the scene, I already had a brother and a sister. My parents said life was very hard for them. Life meant poverty and unemployment. I didn't realize it though; I was two years old in 1923 when my father took off for France with all of us. He didn't like fascism. He was afraid his sons would be forced to join the fascist youth group that took in kids starting at the age of six. 'My boys aren't going to wear those Italian mourning shirts.' He was right. Italy in black shirts was really mourning its sons and its women in advance.

"We got as far as Marseilles. We didn't have any more money, so we couldn't go any farther. But it was supposed to be only temporary. My old man wanted to go to America; for us Italians, you know, it's the promised land, where you make a fortune. All of us in Italy have a relative in America who's written how he's really made it there. We don't know how, and we don't know if it's true, but we believe it. It helps us go on living.

"You kid me because I copy the Americans, but I've always heard talk about their country being a paradise. When things were going very badly, my father would say, 'Wait till we get to America!' and the whole family would start dreaming.

"*La mamma* saved money penny by penny for the trip. But again and again, when hard times would hit the Livi family, it'd all disappear. So that was that. But we're tough people and stubborn, and we'd begin saving pennies again. For a long time I put in my share. Then one day I realized it wasn't going to happen; we'd never go; we were paying for our dreams with our poverty. So I took off."

"Did you play around in the streets when you were a kid?"

"I wasn't allowed to. I went to school and *la mamma* watched to see what time I came home. She was strict about the time; she didn't like to see me dawdling around. People here think that in Italy, because of the sun, you're little jokers and lazy bums who don't give a damn. But that isn't true. Life is very hard there, especially in the North. There are a whole bunch of things an Italian family doesn't joke about—work, the virtue of women and young girls. . . . A boy who's lucky enough to go to school has got to walk the strait and narrow. People always think that if he gets an education he'll be able to eat his fill, and his family will too, because Italians have a strong tribal sense."

"So you went to school?"

"Yes, I learned quite a lot. There were some things I liked, others not so much. I remember one of my teachers wrote on my report card: 'An intelligent student but undisciplined. Clowns around and imitates American animated cartoons.' What a bawling out Papa gave me that night!"

Neither Edith nor I could understand Yves's life. He'd been a little boy, but a type we hadn't come across before. It irritated Edith, who kept saying:

"You had no idea what the streets were like! I don't know, but in Marseilles the streets must be like being in the middle of a festival. Full of noises, colors, smells . . . It must lead you on and go to your head. I couldn't have stayed inside."

"I caught up later, when I left school. My father was having a hard time of it. Three kids and a wife to feed isn't easy. So I went to work when I was fifteen. I had all sorts of jobs—waiter, bartender, worker in a pasta factory (paradise for an Italian!), and since my sister had a beauty parlor, I was even a ladies' hairdresser. Can't you just see me?"

He laughed and you could almost see him with a curling iron in his hand. He waved it in the air and curled a lock of hair with it. His smile had changed; it was full of pomade. I laughed, but Edith never took her eyes off him. I knew she was working.

"Wait, Yves, do that again; that's good."

"If that's why you're making me tell the story of my life, it's no fun any more."

Edith wasn't a fool; she dropped the subject.

"Darling, you're so silly! I love you. Give me a kiss. . . ."

Once the intermission was over, she came back to the subject and wouldn't drop it.

"You didn't sing very much in all that!"

"Of course I did! I wasn't slaving away just to have something to eat, but to be free, to be able to do what I wanted. I spent all my dough buying records of Maurice Chevalier and Charles Trenet. I was dying to be like them. To me they were the greatest! I knew all their songs by heart. I went to see them when they came to Marseilles, and I'd practice all their gestures in front of my bedroom mirror. I worked at it for hours, and I was happy. Then one day I got to sing on some seedy stage in the suburbs; but to me it was already the Alcazar.

"It was on account of that place that I changed my name. The manager told me 'Yvo Livi' was no good. It was funny the way I found my new name. Like I told you, when I was a kid, *la mamma* didn't like to see me hanging around outside the apartment house. She didn't speak French very well, and would yell, 'Yvo, *monta* . . . Yvo, *monta*' when she wanted me to come up. I remembered it. So I translated my first name into French, Yves, and *monta* became Montand.

"I worked in lots of tenth-rate little theaters and finally I made the Alcazar. M. Emile Audiffred was the manager and the one who got me started on a career. He was really great to me. He'd say, 'You'll see, my boy, you're going to be a world sensation in Marseilles,' and we'd both laugh. But did I suffer from stage fright on the first night!

"When people go to the theater in Marseilles, they bring along car horns, tomatoes and rotten eggs, expecting to use them if they don't like the show. I got along all right; I was a success at the box office. But I didn't earn much of a living. They know my name though. I could go back tomorrow and you'd see.

"The war didn't help matters at all. I took a job as a metal-worker. My specialty was sanding. It's very bad for your lungs. I was entitled to three quarts of milk a day. Then after that I was a longshoreman down at the port."

"Why? Didn't you like milk?"

"Yes, but in a factory you have regular hours. You've got to punch a time clock. Longshoremen's hours aren't that regular, so I could sing without getting fired.

"I knew I couldn't make a career for myself in Marseilles. So I dropped everything and came to Paris. I got my chance last February and appeared at the A.B.C."

"That's funny. We might have met there. Did it work?"

"Not very well. I got called a zoot-suiter by the peanut gallery because of my jacket."

"And what did you do from February to August?"

"I worked in movie theaters and whatever else I could find. I had a pretty tough time of it." Yves opened his big hands in a typical Piaf gesture. "See, I haven't had an easy life; I've had a hard life."

Edith and I looked at each other. It was like being flooded with memories. *We* knew what a hard life was. The thought of going to school till you were fifteen; what a dream! We'd never had a mama who wouldn't let you hang around the streets, a papa who worked, a *real* family. This guy we thought was so close to us suddenly seemed miles away because of his memories. His childhood set him apart from us.

But what happened later on we could understand. Edith had had the same dreams he'd had—her name on a poster, the stage, the curtain opening, the lights, *success!* They were of the same breed after all, with a rage to live, to conquer, to be better than the others, which ate at their guts.

When they were face to face like that, I used to wonder which of them would devour the other. For the moment Yves was on his best behavior. He loved Edith and expected everything from her. But it couldn't last long. Yves thought she'd ask him questions about women, about his conquests. Edith didn't give a damn, and that annoyed Yves. He wanted her to realize that he was a lady-killer, that girls would just look at his handsome mug and get weak in the knees. It didn't interest her. She was sure the men in her life had only slept with whores before they knew her. Love began with her.

To Edith, Yves was a new experience. She discovered a power she'd never known—making a star. It was stronger than booze, and got her more tipsy. After a few days she decided she knew enough about him. "You've got to sing about all the things you've told me. Show me your hands."

He opened them, as though he were about to have his fortune told.

"They're the hands of a guy who's punched a time clock going in and out of a factory; a longshoreman's hands. You've had blisters on them and you mustn't forget it. Your hands come from the workers, and they've got to know it. Now we're going to have to find guys to write for you, and it's not going to be easy. You need songs that tell a story, that'll allow you to create an image and bring it to life. But to really get inside its skin, you've got to feel comfortable in it. I want you to sing about love; you're made for that."

"No, I can't!" shouted Yves. "I'm a man. Bleating about love is all right for a woman. I'm not a Piaf!"

I thought Edith was going to jump on him. She began yelling so loud it echoed all through the hotel. This was the first time Yves had ever seen her angry, and he just stood there looking at her like a big dope. Finally, he began to laugh.

"Wow, the lung power you've got!"

"Don't you see, one's just got to sing about love. That's what the public wants. There's a place waiting for you right next to all those Pierrots crying for the moon. People are just waiting for a man, a real man, shouting out his love—they're begging for him! I'm fed up; do you trust me or don't you?"

When he got a notion in his head, it was hard to get it out again.

Besides, he was as jealous as a guy in the days of the Crusades and would have liked to buckle a chastity belt on Edith. He immediately detested the first rival he could find, Henri Contet.

"Don't you ever ask that guy for a song for me. I'd never forgive you."

Of course, that made things easier. . . . It was the beginning of August 1944, and we still had Henri. The day had started off rather badly. The phone rang. I saw Edith cup her hand around the receiver and whisper. I was standing right next to her and heard her say, "Yes, five-thirty. O.K., here. Come right up." Yves was looking out the window and didn't seem to have heard.

"Who was it?" he asked.

"Is that any of your business?"

"Yes."

"Loulou Barrier."

I was sure Edith was lying. Around five Yves said, "I'm going out for a little walk, Edith."

"Come back soon, love."

"Don't worry."

"Aren't you taking Momone with you?"

"I've got a right to be alone, don't I?"

Edith was indeed expecting Henri. He hadn't been there one minute when Edith looked at me. We'd heard a slight noise in the next room, my room. She began to smile, and I saw a gleam in her eye that I knew well, the one that meant she was about to play a nasty trick on somebody and take swift revenge. She raised her voice a bit and said:

"I had you come over, Henri dear, because I want you to write me some songs."

"Well, with everything that's going on now, I don't feel very inspired."

"It just happens that I need some powerful songs, songs for a guy who's got lots of talent—Yves Montand."

Henri broke up.

"God, you make me laugh! So what people are saying is true then? You're looking out for that fake cowboy?"

"That's what I mean. He's dropping that style."

"Listen, Edith, I'll be frank with you. Your guy's worthless, he's a sap. He has no presence. He's vulgar, and his accent is frightful. He gestures like a singer from 1900. He's impossible. . . ."

Instead of scratching his eyes out, Edith answered sweetly:

"Do you think so?"

"I'm sure of it. Go ahead and sleep with him if it amuses you, but he's no good professionally."

"You're right, Henri; I think I've made a mistake. He's a dud."

At the door, as Henri was leaving, they were still on the subject:

"I was right to see you, Henri; you've opened my eyes."

"Your Yves will never fill a theater. . . ."

He'd no sooner gone than Edith opened the door to the next room. Yves was behind it, white with rage.

"That'll teach you to eavesdrop behind doors!" said Edith. "Oh, you've hurt yourself!"

Yves had pieces of a broken glass in his hand. He must have squeezed it so hard it broke. He was bleeding like a bull in the ring, and so mad his voice was strained, all flat and toneless.

"Don't you ever do that again, do you hear me? Never. I felt like killing you."

During the next few days we had to deal with other things besides songs. August 20, 1944: the Allies had made rapid advances along the roads since the landing in Normandy in June, and Paris had a 104-degree fever as it waited for General Leclerc and his Second Armored Division to enter the city.

The German army was clearing out. What chaos! The Parisians called it "green diarrhea." Tricolor armbands of the French Forces of the Interior suddenly bloomed on the arms of all the men—old ones, young ones, kids. The smell of gunpowder went to your head. It was the smell, at last, of victory. Flags were out all over Paris.

And Edith was waiting for General Leclerc to arrive, like a kid waited for a fourteenth of July parade. To her he was the real liberator. De Gaulle didn't interest her. "He's a politician, not a real general. He doesn't march at the head of his troops!"

The day de Gaulle marched from the Arc de Triomphe to Notre Dame to hear the *Te Deum*, Edith couldn't sit still. Yves wasn't with us. I think he was with the FFI. In those days the men left home when there was news. It was only to be expected, and the women weren't jealous; they just took up where they'd left off when the men got back. We took advantage of our freedom and walked down from Montmartre to the Etoile, like in the good old days when we sang in the streets.

"Come on, Momone. I want to see Leclerc with his cane. I want to kiss that man."

What a great day! Everybody was our pal. We didn't see a thing at the Arc de Triomphe, and barely caught a glimpse of General de Gaulle's reddish-blond hair. There wasn't a sign of Leclerc. But what a crowd! People were climbing up on the tanks with names of French places: "Lorraine," "Alsace," "Belfort." Like all the girls, we kissed soldiers and sailors, the red berets, the black berets—everybody. They didn't know they were kissing Edith Piaf, but she made a hit with them. We would have liked to stay with them.

Like all the performers who'd sung during the occupation, Edith had to appear before the Purge Committee. They didn't give her any trouble. Life went on as before, but we could breathe easier now.

Yves and Edith were more and more jealous of each other. And "Aunt Zizi" had given me my orders:

"I'm counting on you, Momone. Don't let him out of your sight. I know the type—he's a skirt-chaser. He could pick a girl up right under your nose without your even noticing. Don't go into bistros; you'll be in bad company. Make him walk—it'll do him good."

It was easy! I took three steps to his one. Yves laughed. "Listen, this is all I need to do to shake you," and he'd lope off, turn the first corner and I'd lost him.

Sometimes he sat me down in a bar. "Wait for me—I'll be back in five minutes." It was almost the truth; I never had to wait too long. I had a way of blackmailing him. "If you're gone too long,

I'll drink. And if I'm tight, I won't answer for anything. I'll babble when I get home. . . ."

I didn't ask him what he'd been doing. I didn't want to know. When he came back, with a twinkle in his eye, we'd drink the last one together, because of Edith. She was suspicious, and smelled our breaths when we got back. "You've been out drinking again. . . ." It didn't matter that we'd been drinking, but if I'd been the only one with alcohol on my breath, it would have been fun and games!

They'd begun work again. Edith would meet Henri out somewhere. The episode of the broken glass had been almost enough for her, but she hadn't given in altogether. Nothing could keep her from doing what she'd made up her mind to do.

"I'm having real trouble with Henri. He doesn't want to work for Yves. It's too funny! Now that we've been split up a long time he's jealous! That's all I needed!"

Henri gave in. She made him do what she wanted.

"I've done it, Momone—I've got some songs! Henri wrote them with Jean Guigo. 'Battling Joe' is the story of a boxer who's unlucky and goes blind. '*Gilet rayé*' is about the life of a hotel valet who ends up in prison. I've also got '*Ce monsieur-là*,' a petit bourgeois whose only way to get over his troubles is to commit suicide. And 'Luna Park,' the story of a worker from Puteaux who finds happiness in an amusement park. We've got to get going now. We won't be working in a vacuum any more. Yves! Come quick!"

He was having a quiet snooze in the next room, but he came. What a good-looking animal he was, standing there in the doorway, as if in a frame that was too small—barechested, with his wide shoulders, his narrow hips, his flat belly. . . . I understood Edith.

"Listen to me, Yves." And she hummed him the songs one after the other.

"They're great! Singing those'll be terrific! Who wrote them?"

"Jean Guigo and Henri Contet."

Yves took a deep breath that sucked in his belly. Then he came out with an enraged "You've won" that said a lot.

"So now we've going to get to work, love." And they did.

Onstage his accent was gone, but offstage it came back when

he wasn't paying attention. "Careful, Yves," Edith would say. "Your dash of garlic's coming back!"

He knew how to sing. That part of it was going fine. His voice was well pitched and very beautiful. But he still had to work on staging the songs. His gestures were the biggest problem. He'd picked up some bad habits. Edith would work him over for hours. The sweat would pour down Yves's face, but he'd go on. He was the only one who could work as long and as hard as Edith. They often put in fifteen hours at a clip. At that point, no one else could see straight any more. The guy at the piano would be playing like a machine. And the two of them went on. . . .

"No, Yves. The beginning's not right. Punching around in the air doesn't make you a boxer. One blow is enough; the audience'll see the whole fight. If you put up your fists, they'll know perfectly well you're not a fisherman! You don't have to move around all the time. Come on. Start over again with '*C'est un nom . . .*' "

> *C'est un nom maintenant oublié,*
> *Une pauvre silhouette qui penche,*
> *Appuyée sur un' canne blanche . . .*

> It's a name that's forgotten now,
> A pitiful stooped silhouette
> Leaning on a white cane . . .

"Bad! You look like a doddering old man. That's not what a blind man is. Battling Joe's still a man. He's had it, because he can't see any more. That's what you've got to show us. Work on the gestures. Your characters are caricatures."

"You give me a swift pain," Yves would answer.

But the next day he'd work on his gestures in front of the mirror. Edith loathed that method; it was against her principles. But Yves couldn't work any other way: it was how he'd learned. What was funny was that he couldn't see all of himself in the wardrobe mirror; the room was too small. He had to stand in profile in the bathroom door. Since he never could see himself full face, when we went out walking in the streets I'd see old Yves stealthily trying out a gesture in shop windows as we passed by.

To fill out Yves's act, Edith had written two songs for him.

"You see, I've written my first love songs for you. There's '*Elle a des yeux . . .*'

> *Elle a des yeux,*
> *C'est merveilleux,*
> *Et puis des mains*
> *Pour mes matins.*
> *Elle a des rires*
> *Pour me séduire*
> *Et des chansons*
> *La la la la . . .*

> She has eyes,
> How marvelous,
> And hands
> For my mornings.
> She has laughter
> To charm me
> And songs
> La la la la . . .

"And '*Mais qu'est-ce que j'ai? . . .*' "

> *Mais qu'est-ce que j'ai?*
> *A tant l'aimer*
> *Que ça me donne envie d'crier*
> *Sur tous les toits:*
> *"Elle est à moi!"*

> What's the matter with me?
> Loving her so much
> I feel like shouting
> From the rooftops:
> "She's mine!"

He'd hung onto a few American songs though, like "*Dans les plaines du Far West.*" "They wouldn't recognize me without them, Edith." So Yves finally had his repertoire. The most important part was over, but not the hardest.

"Yves, now you're going to have to polish it all up in public. But don't make a big thing of it. You're ready! And don't forget that there are both men and women in the audience. The guys have to think you're handsome, that you're everything they'd like to be. Of course, with a mug like yours, the women'll be easy; they'll be making love to you during your act. Be careful though; don't let them do it till the very end. Save some feeling for the last song. Then the guy sitting next to the lady will take her hand and they'll be happy. He's the one going home with her, not you. And it'll be just one heart applauding you. You'll see how pleasant it is on days when the audience's got talent."

It was only September 1944. In two months Edith had created a new Montand. Now, when I listened to Yves, it wasn't the same. He got me in the gut, just like Piaf. His gestures shattered me. In his chestnut-colored shirt and pants, he was all the men in his songs. You believed in him. It came straight at you; you took it and yelled, "More!" The little guy from the Moulin Rouge was left far behind. You'd have to be a professional to realize how much work they'd done. I think I admired them both equally.

Edith had got Loulou Barrier to make a place for Yves in the tour she was to go on all over France.

"Make him my costar."

"Be reasonable, Edith. He's not up to that yet."

"That's where Yves belongs. I won't have him anywhere else. If they want me, they'll take Yves."

"Don't you think it'd be better for him to first have a go at it all alone? I'll get him to tour the south of France. They know his name there."

"Are you nuts? If you suggest that to him, it's all over between us, Loulou. Me separated from Yves for over a month! On a tour where there'll be girls running after him before he's even thought about it! Now listen to me: that guy's mine. I'm the one who made him. He's staying with me, and that, in this profession, is what you call a start!"

"Do you think it's easy to appear just before you?"

"Don't be a pain; it's all decided."

Loulou shut up; the boss had spoken. Barrier wasn't wrong though. Going on just before Edith, with a repertoire very much like hers, would be more than a challenge.

The first city on the tour was Orléans. Edith had ordered me to sit in the audience while Yves was on and report everything to her. Some job!

When the curtain went up and Yves came on stage, people liked the way he looked. He stood there so tall and straight, he looked so strong, that you'd have thought he'd reach the sky, the world of the stars, and hang there! People like strength. They liked him, but he didn't come across. Some little thing was missing, but what? He was only a middling success.

When you saw them onstage on the same program, you knew right off the bat that Yves was Edith's pupil. He had a tendency to roll his *r*'s and he stood in the spotlight the same way she did. They had more or less the same lighting. And most of all, he had gestures that were "Piafesque." I'd had a feeling this was so at rehearsals, but in front of an audience it struck you right away. That night he was at his wits' end. So was Edith.

"I could tell it wasn't working, Edith. Why? You think we were just damn wrong?" Yves asked.

"No. One city isn't all of France. This was the first of them. You're just starting out. Still, they've never seen anything like it."

"Just starting out—don't make me laugh! I've appeared all over the south of France, on the Riviera and even up as far as Lyons. I was a terrific hit everywhere!"

"And in Paris you fell flat on your face. If you don't like it, just forget the whole thing."

Montand's act had its ups and downs. I was scared stiff every night, and it wore me out. During the day Yves went around with an almost nasty look on his face. He was chewing over a lot of things he just couldn't digest.

"Never mind," Edith said. "He's going through a crisis."

We came close to catastrophe in Lyons. Before going on, Yves had got his smile back. "This has always been a good town for me —this is my audience. You'll see, I'm going to get my revenge."

Poor Yves; he was so close to being razzed I couldn't swallow. Edith was white with fear. During Yves's performance she was the one who took over in the wings. She took complete charge of the lights and the curtains. If she'd given him a "false curtain" that night after the fifth song, it wouldn't have worked. The curtain wouldn't have opened again. He'd never have got any further.

When he came offstage, he was woozy, like a boxer after a bad blow. For the first time, I didn't watch Edith sing. She'd shouted, "Go with him, Momone; don't leave him."

The minute I entered his dressing room, Yves got aggressive. He had his wits about him again. "I'm an ass to have thought they'd believe in me or understand me. I don't give a damn. It's *me* that'll get *them*—not the other way around." He'd yanked his shirt off, and his naked chest was gleaming with sweat.

"Hand me my other shirt. I'm going to change and go hear Edith. She has to see me standing there by her and realize they don't scare me."

I'd been so petrified, I felt like laughing now. Yves realized it. He put his big hand on my shoulder and gave me the smile he wore on good days—the ones when we were in cahoots.

"People shouldn't get me angry, Simone. They got me fucking mad tonight. You heard them asking me to sing my old songs. They want crap, and they're not going to get it! That's all over with. I'll never sing songs like that again. What I'm doing is good, I know it, and they're going to have to like it!"

The fight was on. Yves wasn't going to give up.

We were appearing in the Variétés in Marseilles, but I had the jitters anyway. At rehearsal Edith made Yves work with a sort of frenzy. They were equally tough. If it wasn't Edith saying, "Do it over," it was Yves who wanted to.

That night she sat at the back of the theater with me, squeezing my hand. Our stage fright was worse than his. When he came on, the audience applauded. It didn't mean anything; they were clapping because one of their own had come back. That's why they were going to be all the tougher. From the very first song, Edith's fingers tightened on my hand. We'd realized he wasn't going over. They'd known him and his American songs, and had loved him.

They didn't understand this new Montand. They practically booed. Or what was almost worse, they sat on their hands—and they were from Marseilles!

Yves was waiting for us in his dressing room, sitting on a wobbly chair.

"You saw them, Edith! And when I think that I was a real hit here!" Seeing our downcast faces, he gave one of his healthy laughs, the hearty laughter of a giant.

"I don't give a damn, my darling, my love. I'll get them yet. The next time I come back, they'll give me an ovation and beg for more. Meanwhile, I've got a surprise for you—we're having dinner at my parents'!"

Boy, did I like the Livis' little kitchen, filled with all the sounds of Marseilles! And his family—they were so nice! When Yves introduced Edith to them, he said, "This is my fiancée." She had tears in her eyes. What luck to have a family like that!

The next day Edith stunned me. "Last night watching Yves, Momone, I wished I were a virgin."

It was true; you wanted to be brand-new for him. No man had ever made her feel like that before.

Yves was obsessed with marriage. He kept saying, "Edith, let's get married. I'd like you to be my wife." The way I see it, they didn't get married because Yves didn't go about it the right way. He didn't ask her at the right time—only when there were people around, or when they were eating, or when Edith was drinking and felt like having a ball. This made him sentimental, and Edith loathed that. To Edith fifteen minutes of sentimentality or just a little bouquet was enough romance. To her a man with tears in his eyes wasn't virile.

What she liked about Yves was his strength, his liking for a good fight, his youth. There wasn't any great difference in age between them. But she'd already lived so much, and he'd lived so little!

When we came home early in the morning, she'd put up her hair in the bathroom, try out different hairdos, look at herself, and once satisfied with what she saw in the mirror, she'd say:

"Really, I'm not worse looking than any other woman. . . ."

She wasn't indulgent or complacent about her body at all. She looked at herself critically, and sighed philosophically. "I'm not Venus. . . . But what the hell, I can't get mad at my body. It's been used a lot. . . ."

There was only one thing that really annoyed her, and she often harped on it. "I've got sagging breasts, a low-slung ass and little drooping buttocks. I've had 'em for a long time. But I can still get men." And she'd go to bed happy. She'd laugh. Edith's laugh was really something. She laughed the way she did everything else— louder than anybody.

"How Yves adores me! And I'm mad for him, Momone." It must have been true. He was the only man she never cheated on. . . .

When she came back from the tour, Edith appeared at the Alhambra, with Yves as her costar. Paris wasn't the provinces. It might be better and it might be worse.

Loulou Barrier, Edith and I were none of us in very good spirits. We might be the day after the opening night, but meanwhile we needed a real pick-me-up. Edith sat at the back of the theater, the way she had in Marseilles. When Yves came onstage and smiled, his teeth were so while I said to Edith, "Look, his smile is blue!"

We realized right away he had it made. The tour had been very hard on him; he'd suffered so much he was ready for anything, and it had given him a masterful presence. Onstage he really came across.

"It's not the same, Momone. Remember how he was at the beginning? Look at him. I'm not going to be able to hold on to him. . . ."

As Yves was the big surprise of the evening, he got top mention in the papers the next day. He moved around the room at the Alsina like a hurricane. We felt like twitching our ears, like dogs, he was buzzing about so.

"Read this, Edith: 'A name not to be forgotten: Yves Montand.' Look at this, Momone: 'A star is born.' Edith, I've done it: 'A revolution in singing.' You were right, Edith, I'm 'At last, the singer everyone's been waiting for!' You're pleased, aren't you?"

"Sure," Edith answered, irritated by this mad dog. "I know what it's like."

"I know—you made it before I did."

That was the little knock that cracks the china. . . .

"They're really not such damn fools as they are in the provinces."

"Watch it, Yves. You get your start in Paris, but it's the provinces that make you!"

"You can't spoil my mood—I'm too happy!"

That evening, outside the Alhambra, he looked at the poster.

"You should have insisted that my name be bigger."

"After your 'triumph' in Marseilles that would have been easy! They just couldn't wait!" she answered dryly.

Montand had that pitiless, savage hunger of young people. In life, as at the table, he had a hearty appetite. But Edith wasn't the type to let herself be eaten alive.

She had to put up with Yves's jealousy. I told myself, "His success will calm him down; he'll think about other things." How wrong can you be! Edith was his property, his private preserve. . . . He was like a gamekeeper guarding his doe, rifle in hand. He wasn't going to let any poacher get her.

He'd wake her up at night. "Who were you dreaming of? One of your old lovers?"

She'd tell him to go to hell, but the next day she'd say to me, "See how he loves me?"

That was O.K. once or twice, but not all the time. If she looked at a guy or let him prowl around her, strutting about, Yves went into a cold rage:

"Don't you see what a creep he is, a poor sap who doesn't give a damn about you?"

She'd tell him off, and they'd battle for hours. Then for twenty-four hours they'd adore each other. I loved them, but they were beginning to really get on my nerves.

They were in even more of a fever because after the Alhambra they were to appear at the Etoile (after the liberation, the most elegant music hall, the one that was really "in"). A few days before the premiere, they were so happy they were floating. I was trying to get my strength back—I needed to, between the morning sessions in the bathroom and the walks with Yves, I'd had a bellyful of their confidences and their spying on each other. Each of them would take me aside and say, "Stick with him every minute," or "Watch her when I'm not around and tell me everything."

Their work together, though, went along as smooth as silk. Yves's name was in letters almost as big as Edith's, in spite of Loulou Barrier. "Watch out, Edith," he'd say. "He's dangerous on the same program. Don't give him too much leeway."

"Don't worry. The 'M. Piaf' of song who can gobble me up hasn't been born yet. The Etoile is going to be the crowning piece in my fireworks. I want him to succeed. Afterward . . ."

She put everything into it. She made more than a hundred phone calls in a few days—to all her friends, to reporters, to the most important people in the profession. Edith always did things big!

Yves had money very soon. And no wonder, since he knew the value of it and didn't just throw it around. He never sponged on Edith; he was too proud for that. She did buy him some suits and alligator shoes though, and accessories to make him "Piaf's man"—the lighter, the watch and chain, the cufflinks.

As usual, Edith didn't keep track of what she spent, so that on the night before the dress rehearsal at the Etoile she had only three thousand francs left. The two weeks at the Alhambra hadn't done much for our budget.

We hadn't been able to buy ourselves anything to wear since we'd been at the Alsina. And as we'd come there with practically nothing, we were hardly much to look at.

"I want to be beautiful for Yves tomorrow night, Momone. Come on; I'm going to buy myself some clothes." We hadn't got as far as the door when Yves asked:

"Where are you going?"

"I'm going to buy myself a dress, gloves and a hat." She'd never worn a hat, but that night she had to have one. She thought it would be more chic.

"That's ridiculous. You don't need anything. I forbid you to spend money. You won't have a cent left." Which was true.

"Shit!" answered Edith.

We left to go shopping without paying any more attention to him. He was furious. When we got back, we didn't have a franc left. Edith jubilantly laid one pair of gloves on the bed. We'd been in fifteen bars on our way to the store! Because she was feeling happy, she'd not only had lots to drink herself, but had bought rounds for the others. She didn't give a tinker's damn about Yves's "I forbid you's." But she was wrong. He flew into a terrible rage, like a husband whose wife has filched all his dough. That wasn't the case, but Yves had principles; a woman should obey her man.

"You're up to your neck in debts. You throw dough out the window. You'll end up a bum. . . ."

"Seeing as how you won't be around, what's it to you?"

"I'd forbidden you to; that should have been enough."

"Nobody's ever forbidden me anything."

They were yelling so loud they weren't even listening to each other any more. Finally Yves gave her two gorgeous slaps across the face, hard enough to unscrew her head. He was no weakling. She cried and he went out, slamming the door. When he came back they kissed each other. A circus! Then both of them said, "It's good relaxation before a premiere!" Still, they'd screamed so hard they were hoarse, and an hour before the performance they were both gargling in front of their sinks.

That night Edith stepped in front of the footlights and introduced Yves Montand to the audience. It was the first time she'd done that. When Yves came on, the house—packed with a mixture of Paris society and workers—was electrified.

Edith again took charge of everything for him in the wings, even if she did have to go on right after him. Every time Yves made an exit, Edith sponged him off and handed him a glass of water. After the final curtain, we figured he'd been called back thirteen times. "That's a good sign," murmured Edith. "It'll be a lucky number for him." She could breathe easy. Her troubles were over—her champ had won.

Too bad there always has to be a next day! We were treated to a repetition of the Alhambra morning, but this one topped it. . . . Yves crowed like a rooster after his victory. The press was raving, and so was he. He was the center of attention.

The same thing twice was once too often for Edith. I could see it in her face. But she'd asked for it. She snuggled down in her pillows and her eyes followed him. I could tell by her smile that she was about to come out with something filthy mean.

"It's good to see you happy. You needed it, love. You still have a few little things to learn though. . . . One doesn't perspire onstage —it makes you look like a longshoreman. One—"

Yves cut her off, raging mad:

"You're the one that makes me sweat. Last night *I* pulled it off, nobody else!"

In spite of the squabble, Yves beamed with joy that night in his brand-new dinner jacket at the dinner Edith gave. Again he was the center of attention; you couldn't get a word in edgewise. He was so proud of himself, like a kid who's won a race, it made me laugh. Not Edith.

"Wow, did I have curtain calls! Thirteen! Simone counted them. Didn't you, Simone?"

Edith cut in. "You're beginning to bore the hell out of us with your curtain calls!"

An icy chill went through the room, freezing Yves's enthusiasm. It was a painful lesson for a twenty-two-year-old boy. Yves swallowed it, but it was some time before he could digest it.

At home, nothing had apparently changed. But I didn't like the way Edith eyed him. She seemed to be watching his every move. I'd never seen her like that, and I was sure she was up to something. Yves was worried too.

"What's happening, Simone? It's not the same with Edith and me any more. Why?"

I knew why, but how could I tell him? He'd become a big star too fast. He was slipping out of the fragile hands that had created him. It was singing that was cracking that love I'd thought was so strong. And he just couldn't resist the bravos. I felt like shouting at him, "It's your profession that's making you destroy your happiness." But it was too late. Yves had already become a kind of monster too. There was nothing to do but let it go.

One morning Edith blew up.

"I can't stand it any more, Momone. I can't bear Yves's "Ris-Organis" * bit any longer. He acts like an old ham telling about the good old days. 'Did you see me at the Alhambra? . . . at the Etoile?' In a year all I'll be good for is shining M. Montand's shoes!"

"It won't last, Edith. He'll catch on. Give him time. It's natural, his head's reeling—he's intoxicated."

"Maybe. But I don't like men who can't hold their liquor. He'd better watch it! I'm going to fix his wagon, and fast! I'm going to take a lover who'll talk to me about love, not about my profession! *That* I can do all my myself."

That same day she told Loulou Barrier, "I don't want any more contracts with Yves on my program."

"High time," replied Loulou. "It's become impossible for theater managers to have you on the same bill."

When Edith was in love, it was always for the first time, and for life. There'd never been anything like it before. It seemed to me the only thing that changed was the guys. Love with Edith was like a temperature chart. At the start it shot up to 105 degrees, high enough to break the thermometer. Then the fever would start to go down, zigzagging all the way; I called it the "roller coaster" period. Then it would drop straight down to below normal. Below 85 degrees she was cold, her heart was chilly, and she'd look for somebody else to warm it up. To live with Edith you had to be in good health! The last high fever she had with Montand was during the Etoile engagement.

There was a naïve side to Yves. He had thought Edith would be bowled over by his success. He was wrong. For her to accept it, she'd have had to go on being the boss, and he'd have had to be constantly attentive. It didn't work out that way. He'd say, "I love you," true. But he slept around all over the place, and Edith knew it. I saw her cry too many times. She'd say, "That guy hurts me

---

* A rest home for variety performers.

too much, Momone; I can't take it any more." That's what she'd say, but it wasn't true. Yves was going to be around a good while longer.

Actually Yves didn't try very hard. There were scenes he could have prevented. One evening he came home as if nothing had happened, looking quite pleased with himself. Edith didn't let it pass.

"You might have told your babe to clean you up when she sends you home. You're goddamn filthy. Look at your shoulder." Yves's jacket was full of powder and makeup. "I don't like rejects. When I think stuff's fresh, I'll swallow it, but not when I know it's leftovers!

"I'm fed up to here with your acting like a Marseilles gangster! Fake tough guys make me laugh. I know what a real man's made of. You're not laying down the law in my house. So if you've had it, go pack your bags; I'm not stopping you. Go back to your babes—they'll take care of you!"

This time it looked serious. Yves backed down, and in a hurry. He laughed too loud; it didn't sound natural. He took her in his arms and cooed tender things in her ear. He had a way with him, the rat! He held her tight and pressed her against him, and gave her the "I love you" routine. She didn't weigh much in his arms. She was so delicate I said to myself, "She's just got to give in to him!"

"Dear Edith, you know you're the only one I love. The bastards who've told you I've been cheating on you are just jealous. Our happiness keeps them awake nights. You're my whole life. You believe me, don't you?"

She smiled blissfully. "Yes," she said, as if sighing with pleasure. Too bad he continued laying it on so thick. He was off in some dream world, not paying any attention.

"When we're married and they see our names on the posters, both the same size, they'll realize that with us it's for life. . . ."

Edith wrenched herself out of his arms. He'd made a direct hit. With her little sad smile of the street urchin who's had it, she said:

"Oh, you know, eternal love, it doesn't always last with me."
Then she drew away, keeping her distance. "As for both our names
on the same poster, forget it. That's over! I've given Loulou my
orders."

Even when you're six feet one and built like a leader of men,
an answer like that shrinks you down to the ground. . . .

But it wasn't the end of their two names on the same poster,
and because of her. During the occupation, Marcel Blistène had
had an idea for a film for Edith. He'd talked to her about it and
she'd said, "It's a swell idea. I'll make your film; I promise." It
never got made though, because Blistène was in hiding. But in
December 1944, Marcel turned up again with his scenario. It was
a simple one, and custom made for Edith: a great singer takes a
guy into her life, loves him, trains him and then goes off by herself. When she read it, Edith laughed!

"Marcel, you didn't kill yourself writing it, but you guessed.
You predicted the future. O.K., I'll do your film. But Yves Montand
has to be in it."

Marcel Blistène agreed, but the producer didn't. A cast like that
didn't appeal to him. He was the one who had to put the dough
up, after all, and a movie poster with Edith Piaf and Yves Montand
wasn't going to make people jump for joy.

When Edith wanted something, she knew how to get it. On the
fifteenth of January, 1945, she gave a cocktail party for the producer at the Mayfair, on the boulevard Saint-Michel, where Yves
was appearing every night. Yves sang. Blistène asked Edith to
please sing one of her songs. They'd arranged it in advance. She
pretended to be reluctant. "Only one, and just for you. . . ." She
sang, and the backer was astonished.

"She's a genius, and the boy has a very good build," he said to
Marcel. "It's O.K. with me."

That was how *Etoile sans lumière* came to be made. Marcel
Herrand, Jules Berry and two beginners—Serge Reggiani and
Yves Montand—were in the cast with Edith. A few years later,
when Yves said, "I owe Edith everything," he wasn't kidding.

Yves may have had the appetite of an ogre and a desire to

devour everything, but in everyday life he wasn't sure of himself. On the day of the screen tests he was sort of pale.

"Don't worry. You're a natural for films; you're a born actor. It'll really work," Edith assured him.

She was right again. The shooting of the film went smoothly, except at the end. *Etoile sans lumière* ends with a shot straight out of Chaplin. You see the great star leave the studio, all alone, and her little silhouette, seen from the back, gets smaller and smaller on the horizon. . . . For just this one time, I was the big star. Edith was a little tight that day. She started off all right, but after walking three yards she began swaying. "Walk straight," shouted Marcel.

Edith laughed. "I can't. I'm too miserable!"

"You look more like you're plastered."

"Stop bugging me, and use Momone!"

Marcel looked at me and said:

"Put her clothes on. We'll do your hair like hers and from the back nobody'll know the difference." It was no use telling myself that people would only see my back; it still really upset me walking in front of a camera. Edith thought it was a riot.

"I've found you a profession. You'll be my stand-in. Marcel, you'll have to give her a fee."

Yves talked a lot about the film. It preyed on his mind. He was right: it was more important for him than for her.

We were still at the Alsina. Things seemed to be going all right between them, but I knew it wasn't going to last long. Edith was living *alongside* him, not *with* him. They were living together, but you could tell it was more or less out of habit.

After the liberation, Marguerite Monnot—Guite—had come back into our lives. And she loved Yves. "He's as good looking as he is talented," she'd say. That pleased Edith. When she told Guite about her love affairs, Guite always thought they were wonderful. You wouldn't have had to push her very hard to set them to music.

Edith had a plan, but it wasn't easy to talk about it to Guite. She came out with it anyway.

"Listen, I don't dare tell you this, but when words to a song come to my mind, I hear music with them. What I mean is, the whole thing comes to me at once. Do you think I could try to write a simple little song?"

You had to be Guite not to tease Edith. She didn't even know her scales! Saying a thing like that to a composer like Marguerite Monnot was going too far, and took a lot of nerve.

"Try, Edith! I'll help you."

"You won't make an ass of me? I have a little melody that keeps running through my head. Should I play it?"

"Go ahead."

And just like that, Edith played us the melodic line of what was going to become "*La Vie en rose.*"

"I don't feel it," said Guite.

"So you don't like it?"

"What about the words?"

"I don't know what they are. It's just a little tune I can't get out of my head."

"Well, in any case, it's not a melody for you. You'll never sing it yourself. But keep on. Why don't you take the SACEM exam as a melody writer?"

"I've already flunked the words test. With the music I'll go down for the count."

Guite laughed.

"That doesn't matter. They failed *me* the first time . . . and there have been others!"

We couldn't get over it: Marguerite Monnot had failed! That gave Edith new courage.

"I'm going to take the exam again."

"*La Vie en rose*" was apparently anxious to be born. It was ready to come out in the world. Edith had a pal, a singer, Marianne Michel, who'd come up to Paris from Marseilles. Her "protector" was the owner of a cabaret on the Champs Élysées, and things were beginning to go well for her. But like all beginners, she had no repertoire. Edith used to have a drink with her here and there. And Marianne kept pestering her.

"I can't find any good songs," she'd complain. "I need a hit to get me started. Couldn't you write me one, Edith?"

"I've got a melody that keeps running after me. It's your type. Listen." And Edith hummed her the melody she'd played for Guite.

"It's great. What about the words?"

"Wait, I think I've got 'em. . . ."

And right then and there, just like that, Edith wrote:

> *Quand il me prend dans ses bras,*
> *Qu'il me parle tout bas,*
> *Je vois les choses en rose . . .*

> When he takes me in his arms,
> And whispers low to me,
> Everything looks rosy . . .

Marianne didn't care for it much.

"Do you like where it says '*choses*'? How about putting '*vie*'?"

"Good idea! And the title will be '*La Vie en rose.*' "

The song was finished the next day. But since Edith wasn't a member of SACEM yet, she couldn't sign her name to it.

We rushed over to Guite's.

"Here. I've got words for that little melody I played the other day. Listen."

Guite exploded.

"You're not going to sing a silly thing like that, are you?"

That was the end. But since Guite was against it, she had to make a go of it. Edith couldn't bear people saying no to her. We had a little pal with lots of talent, a nice boy and a good composer who was broke at the moment: Louiguy. Edith had him come over. Out of her little refrain he made "*La Vie en rose*," and he was never sorry he had.

Marianne Michel introduced "*La Vie en rose.*" The song was a hit the world over, one of the biggest ever. It was translated into a dozen languages. The Japanese version made us laugh the most. "Are you sure he's not singing 'Life looks like rosy fish'?" Edith asked.

American stars like Bing Crosby and Louis Armstrong put it in their repertoires—and they didn't have a soft spot in their hearts for French songs. It was used in the sound track of the film *Sabrina* with Audrey Hepburn, Humphrey Bogart and William Holden. Over three million records of it were sold in one year at the time, and it's still selling. A Broadway nightclub took the name "La Vie en Rose." It was the most popular song in New York; Edith and I often heard it being hummed and whistled in the streets. Her song was such a success that Edith complained, "What an ass I was not to have sung it myself!" She did sing it finally, but two years later.

At the house (the place we lived was always "the house" to us, even hotels and furnished apartments—we didn't make any distinction—and that way of talking astonished Yves; *he* knew the difference), things were falling apart in the love-life department, although they were booming professionally.

"You're daydreaming too much about your films," Edith told Yves. "You say they'll get you to America. Maybe. But you can get there by singing too. Anyway, you're made to succeed in both. A recital at the Etoile will make you 'the one and only Montand,' 'the greatest.' "

Edith wanted to go all the way and make him a really solid success. Yves was her creation. She didn't mix sentiment with work, even if things were going badly with him.

Yves had lost his domineering ways before his recital at the Etoile. He didn't show off any more. He rehearsed enough to make his legs cave in and his voice hoarse. Every time he thought he'd hit a snag, he'd shout:

"Edith, that's not good, is it?"

"Sure it is. Don't stop. Run through the whole thing for me."

Yves finally collapsed. "I can't see straight. I don't know where I am any more. I'm scared stiff. . . ."

She looked at him. You should have seen the expression on her face. It had everything in it—satisfaction, revenge. . . . She turned to me and said, "You see, Momone, he's getting there."

What she loved about him was the way he could dig in and work. "He's really tough when it comes to singing. He'll soon be making the rules." And at night she'd cuddle up close to him. It gave their love a sort of fresh start—the kind that comes from working feverishly together.

You had to have real nerve to give a recital at the Etoile in 1945 —a show lasting two full hours with just one guy onstage from beginning to end, when the audience was used to variety acts. Even Edith Piaf hadn't done that yet. I think the only one before Yves to have appeared alone on a bill was Maurice Chevalier. Yes, it took some nerve!

So even though we were confident, we were in a funk. And did Edith look after her Yves! How she hovered over him! His stock with her had gone way up, and he was all she was interested in.

Henri Contet had given him two new songs: *"La Grande Ville"* and *"Il fait des . . ."*

The morning of the premiere, Yves said, "Listen, Edith, I'd like to ask you something. Would you light a candle for me?"

"I already have, you idiot! And I'm going back again with Momone."

So back we went to the Sacré-Coeur and lit a candle to little Saint Theresa of Lisieux. It was getting to be a habit. . . .

That night she said to him outside the Etoile:

"Are you pleased? Your name's the only one on the poster."

Yves answered, somewhat bitterly:

"And if I fall flat on my face, I'll be all alone."

Edith didn't abandon him: she stayed in the wings the whole time. I was sitting with the Livi family, who'd come up from Marseilles. I looked at them sitting there in their plush seats, bursting with happiness. It must have been great for them to see that big guy, their kid, onstage. They'd forgotten America. You can strike gold in France too.

I dashed to Yves's dressing room at intermission. Everyone else was being kept away, but not me. If I live to be a hundred, I'll never forget the way his eyes questioned me: "Well?"

"It's working!"

"Didn't anybody leave? They're not fed up?"

"You've got 'em hooked solid. Keep it up."

I stayed in the wings. He did keep it up right to the end. The second part was the hardest. The audience might suddenly get tired of watching the same guy all the time. We were so nervous we were shaking all over. When Yves sang:

> *Mais q'est-ce que j'ai?*
> *A tant l'aimer*
> *Que ça me donne envie d'crier . . .*

he turned his head toward Edith for a second. That cry of love was for her—a gift from him to her. I saw big tears streaming from Edith's eyes.

At the end the whole theater, stuffed with snobs, with people in the profession who'd come to see the lion tamer get eaten alive— why not?—rose to their feet, applauding and shouting, "Encore, encore!"

When he came offstage after the last curtain, Yves took Edith in his arms and said, "Thanks, thanks. I owe it all to you."

All the Parisians who usually attend opening nights filed through his dressing room. "It's all over now," Edith told me. "He doesn't need me any more." Those words were like a great wail of solitude. They sent a chill through us.

He didn't need Edith any more, but once again she started looking after his future. Marcel Carné often used to come to the Alsina bar. He liked to chat with Edith. He'd been at the Etoile and they talked about Yves together.

"Montand's got a great physique, and tremendous presence," Carné said.

"Don't forget his name. He's not just a singer; he's a good actor too. He's made for films."

A year later, Yves was playing the lead in *Les Portes de la nuit*, with Nathalie Nattier, directed by Marcel Carné. Neither Nathalie nor Yves was supposed to be in it; the roles had originally been intended for Jean Gabin and Marlene Dietrich.

Edith was working hard; Loulou made sure she had engagements. Yves was still jealous and didn't like the idea of leaving her. But he couldn't stay; he had engagements too. Singing, which had brought them together, was driving them farther and farther apart.

Edith was singing on Christmas Eve. Yves and I waited for her. For some reason, we weren't in a very festive mood. We stood there waiting. But for what? Edith, of course, but there was something else in the air and we could feel it. What's more, Edith and I had never liked this kind of holiday very much. You had to have celebrated it when you were a kid, and we hadn't. We hadn't been allowed to. We'd watched other people's happiness behind the windows of toy stores and pastry shops and restaurants. . . .

The three of us spent the rest of the night together and had a nice time. Edith still seemed to be very much in love. Things were going all right, but Yves said to Edith rather clumsily:

"We'll have to make our Christmas Eve celebration count double, because on New Year's Eve I'll be at my parents' in Marseilles."

She seemed to take it all right at the time, but the next day she was furious.

"Can you imagine, Momone! He bores me to death with declarations of love, but I come after his family! In spite of all his fine words, I'll always come after something."

We found ourselves all alone New Year's Eve, like two damn fools. After Edith's performance, we went to the Club des Cinq, in Montmartre.

The "Cinq" were five guys who'd met in General Leclerc's Second Armored Division and had started a sort of elegant private club. They invited a different star to appear every night. They'd asked Edith several times, but she'd never been able to.

That night she said, "I don't want to stay at the hotel. Come on, let's go there."

We were completely out of it. There wasn't much of a crowd, and, worse luck, we didn't know a soul. So we just sat there, feeling lost without a man. And to make it even grimmer, everyone kept throwing confetti and paper balls at each other.

Paper hats had been stuck on our heads. Edith had a sailor's beret on, and I had a kind of Directoire thing. We felt so out of it all, we didn't even get tight. You've got to be in the right mood for that; you have to feel like horsing around or be really depressed. We didn't feel anything—just empty. At midnight we kissed each other. The party was over and we'd begun a new year.

"You know, Momone, some people say the way you begin the year is a sign of what's going to happen for the next 365 days. Some time we're going to have in 1946!" I don't know if that's true or not, but the year was certainly getting off to a pretty bad start.

Yves hadn't been back even three days when they had a serious battle—their last.

Edith was rehearsing before leaving on tour. As usual, she was all wrapped up in her work. She didn't have any makeup on, her hairdo was falling down, and she was got up in an old sweater and skirt, with her mind entirely on her singing. Suddenly we heard Yves's voice, as cutting as the guillotine, cry out:

"Stop! It's all wrong!"

Edith stopped like an obedient machine.

"What's wrong?"

"What you're doing is worthless. It sounds fake; too tricky. It doesn't come from here or here"—and Yves tapped his belly and his head.

"Just say that again." She had her hands on her hips and her neck thrust out. Drawing herself up to her full four feet eleven, she looked at him. She couldn't believe her ears.

"It's no good. If it were me, I'd—"

"*You're* not going to do anything at all. You know where you can shove your 'if it were me's. They make me sick. The day I decide to take lessons from anybody at all, I'll let you know. Right now, I'm going to waste one minute more and give you one last polite tip. What you sneeringly call 'fake' and 'too tricky' . . . well, I just hope you have enough of that sort of thing on tap, because you're going to need it someday—like all the rest of us—to hedge your bet the night you don't have anything left in your gut. And clear out. I've had enough of you."

Edith was able to take Yves's advice five years later. But not that day. She left for Alsace on tour before they could *really* make up.

I knew there were nine boys called the Compagnons de la Chanson with her on the first part of the program. She'd met them, that's about all. We'd heard them sing during the occupation at a benefit at the Comédie Française, organized by Marie Bell.

Edith immediately baptized them "the Boy Scouts of Song." People liked their act because it's always pleasant to see nine fairly good-looking, well-built boys cheerfully singing songs that don't strain the audience's mind; some people actually find Sunday school stuff refreshing!

So when I found out she was going to join them there, I didn't think anything about it, though I always had her and her men on my mind. Still, nine of them were a hell of a lot to take on! "What's she going to bring home to me this time?" I wondered.

I hadn't gone on tour with her. She'd told me she wanted to leave the Alsina, and that I was to stay behind to take care of the new place Loulou was supposed to be looking for. I was surprised, though, when he told me:

"Edith phoned me from Alsace to ask me to find her an apartment right away. She wants lots of rooms for some reason. Do you have any idea why?" I didn't have a clue. "So I've found her something at 26 rue de Berri. Come have a look at it."

The building was very plain. I never suspected so many things were going to happen there, thanks to Edith. There was a courtyard, and at the back a sort of town house with a little garden and trees that seemed to weep with boredom and dream of the countryside. To amuse them, after we moved in, we gave them a dwarf rooster, Pupuce, and his mate, Nénette. But the trees didn't look any more cheerful for all that! They continued to look lost, as if they didn't know why they'd been born there. I was fond of them; they were very like me. I didn't know what the hell I was doing there either.

To enter, you climbed three steps. It was all on the ground floor. I don't remember how many rooms there were, but it was big and not badly furnished and cost quite a bit.

"Do you like it?"

For some reason I wasn't excited about it. "It's not bad, but it's big."

"That's what she wants."

"I hope she's not going to move the boy scouts in!"

We laughed, but I don't think either of us was convinced she wouldn't.

Knowing Edith, you couldn't be sure whether she'd move in or not when she got back. So the night before she was to arrive, I took a few precautions. The only thing she'd said to me on the phone was: "Come and meet me at the station." So I put some flowers around anyway, and moved in some of our things. I waited for her to get back, feeling a little confused. I could smell something I didn't like in the air.

I went to meet her at the station. As she usually did when we'd been apart, she said to me with a suspicious look in her eye, like a mother who thinks her daughter's taken advantage of her absence to lose what she's got to offer, "You don't look well. I hope you haven't done some damnfool thing!" Then she took me in her arms and kissed me. Right away, I was *her* Momone again.

Once we'd got in a taxi, she said to the driver:

"Twenty-six rue de Berri."

I was flabbergasted. We weren't going to the Alsina. It was lucky I'd thought of the flowers.

"Aren't we going to go meet Yves?" I asked shyly.

"It's over. I've made some resolutions. He doesn't need me any more. He knows how to play his cards all by himself. You'll see I'm right, Momone. And I've got lots of ideas. I'm going to look after the Compagnons. I'm going to work up a terrific act for them, something nobody's ever seen before. We're going to give people something new."

"Is that O.K. with them?"

"They don't know it yet. I figured it all out on the train. But they'll go along with it."

"Listen, Edith, nine of them at once is a lot. You'll be lost in the middle of them. Nine boys that age can be voracious."

"Don't worry. You have to change—it's the secret of staying young."

We arrived at the rue de Berri. Edith was really surprised. She seemed to like it. But what was uppermost in her mind was telling me about her chorale. The "boss lady" had ambitions. It wasn't just one man she needed now, but nine.

"They're not ready yet. I'm going to have my troubles, but their whole act's going to change."

I was waiting for her to mention one of them by name. But she didn't. I wondered whether she was going to try them all out, one at a time, before making up her mind. With Edith, it was more than possible!

"Listen, we've got to look up Chang and hire him back. And I want a secretary too."

There was no doubt about it: we were moving in. I kept thinking about Yves. He knew she was coming back that day. He didn't know it was the rue de Berri, but Loulou would give him the address. What was he going to do?

I saw him. And their break-up was one of the most painful of any I'd witnessed.

When Edith didn't come back to the Alsina that night, he came to the rue de Berri and timidly rang the doorbell. "If that's Yves, don't open up," said Edith.

I was sick about it. I watched him through the closed blinds. He rang the bell like a madman, and then began pounding with his fists. The wood resounded; it was dismal. Then he stopped making a racket, put his mouth up to the door and said in a loud voice, "Open up, Edith, I know you're there. Open up," and then just stood there without moving. I felt really sorry for him.

I kept walking back and forth from the window to Edith's room. She'd stuffed cotton in her ears and put her head under the pillow.

"I don't want to have to listen to him," she shouted. "I don't want to start all over again with him. Make him go away, Momone, otherwise I'll never get over him!"

She still loved him, but she didn't want him any more. I suffered as much as they did. We'd had so many good times together. I'd have been quite willing to open the door and see them fall into each other's arms, happy yet in despair, and to begin their fights all over again.

I liked Yves. He was straight with you; you knew what he was thinking. When he looked you in the eye, with that nice healthy mug, you didn't feel like lying to him. He was a man, a real one. So it made me sick to see him suffer like that.

I don't know how long it lasted. I finally saw Yves leave, looking very dignified, all straight and stiff. I felt he was having a hard time not breaking down. He crossed the courtyard with the tired look of a tomcat that's lost a battle.

I stayed up watching the dawn break. Edith was sleeping like a child. But when she woke up and I straightened her pillow, it was wet with tears.

Chapter 10

Conquering America

The Compagnons came next in the "factory" period, and promised to last a good long time. We were about to have some new experiences, both good and bad!

Nine guys take up quite a bit of breathing space. One guy is absorbing enough, but when you multiply by nine, it gets a little tiring—especially when pleasure isn't multiplied by nine: that you only get from one at a time.

I wasn't overjoyed when I saw the whole troop march in with their suitcases. Boy, were there going to be complications! They lived there in one sense, and didn't in another. They'd rented a place together on the rue de l'Université, so they came and they went, and, as always with Edith, anybody who wanted to slept there.

The new secretary was called Yvonne (I think), a nice little thing. She was so astonished by it all, her eyes rolled in her head. She'd never been any place like it.

Chang, though, came up with a bit of very Chinese wisdom: "All this please Mamamiselle? All this please Chang!"

As for me—well, to tell the truth, I felt lost for the first time. There were just too many for me. I can't love people in bunches; I have to take them one at a time. I said to myself, "Wait and see. One of them is bound to come out on top." Edith was perfectly happy. Her skin glowed the way it always did when she was in love.

In the evening you'd have thought we were huddling around a campfire, with all of them sitting in a circle around Edith. And there was no doubt about it—she was the flame. She'd told me, "Listen to them carefully. You'll see, each of them has his own story to tell. I don't know what I'm going to do with them yet. I have to get to know them first." This was a tried-and-true technique with her.

"But what are you going to do with your troop? Are you going to play scout leader?"

"I'm going to make them over. They're still singing in short pants. I'm going to teach them to wear long ones."

"And will they go along with that?"

"To a man."

That was what bothered me. Who was going to be the boss? There couldn't be nine fairly handsome, normal guys holed up in the house without one of them coming up from the ranks and slipping between Edith's sheets. I was soon to find out which one it was. But before that happened, Edith's first attempt to change them was something of a flop.

The little campfire-style talk sessions, the kind of wolf-cub horsing around, the great glee of kids being allowed to run loose in the woods—all that wasn't unpleasant; it was like a "rejuvenation" treatment. And it amazed us, because when you're brought up in the streets, you're soon playing house, not loving nature; and our songs were about pavements rather than about "poppies in the field."

Then Edith started talking shop to them. That's what they were there for, after all.

"Listen, your repertoire's not worth much. With the songs you sing, you'll never get beyond appearing in the provinces, where people still have a taste for Sunday school. That's as far as you'll get. I don't have anything against your old French songs—'*Perrine était servante*' is sweet. But you won't hear any delivery boys whistling it in the streets. And unless they do, you're not a success."

Jean-Louis Jaubert, the manager, interrupted her.

"Listen, Edith, street songs aren't for us. We're not soloists, we're a chorale. We need pieces for a vocal orchestra. Just what we *don't* need are people singing our stuff in the street. They come to hear us the way they go to a concert."

"You're dead wrong. And how about records—have you thought about them? If in all of France you find a thousand retired idiots who'll buy your records, you'll be lucky. Either you sing for a specialized audience, or you sing for the general public. You've got to choose."

"We've already chosen. We've filled theaters with people who want to hear us. We're not out for fame."

"Well, then, you're a bunch of jerks."

It seemed to me there was a certain coolness in the air that night. . . .

Edith had decided she'd make them over and she simply had to succeed. If she was being stubborn like that, it was because she found one of them to her taste. Meanwhile she did some serious complaining. Professionally they were out of favor.

"You've no idea how narrow-minded they are, Momone. Nobody's going to be ringing any bells when they come to town. Hey, that's it—I've got it! *'Les Trois Cloches.'*" At one time Edith had asked the songwriter Gilles to save "The Three Bells" for her, and she hadn't sung it yet. She liked it, but she didn't "feel" it. In ten minutes she'd rounded up all her guys.

"I've found a song for you. Listen.

> *Une cloche sonne, sonne,*
> *Sa voix, d'écho en écho,*
> *Dit au monde qui s'étonne:*
> *'C'est pour Jean François Nicot!*
> *C'est pour accueillir une âme,*
> *Une fleur qui s'ouvre au jour,*
> *À peine, à peine une flamme,*
> *Encore faible qui réclame*
> *Protection, tendresse, amour!'*

> A bell is ringing and ringing,
> Its echoing voice

Says to an astonished world:
'It's for Jean-François Nicot!
It's welcoming a soul,
A flower opening to the light of day,
Barely, just barely a flame,
Still so weak it calls for
Protection, tenderness, love.'

"Well?"

They stood there not saying a word and looking at Jean-Louis, who was so bossy he'd begun to get on my nerves.

"No, Edith, absolutely not, it's silly," he said.

"What if we worked on it together and I sang it with you?"

"That's different."

I could see very well what was different: there'd be Edith's name, and I knew how much weight that pulled. I could also see that Jean-Louis was going to be the new boss. She talked about him too much and he had too many good points! The leader was the guy she'd picked for herself. I should have realized it right away, from the moment she'd decided to make them over.

Every time we were alone, she really went at it.

"What do you think of him, Momone? He isn't like the others. He's pure. . . . You know what I mean? He hasn't got a past, he hasn't been around. . . . It's idealism that makes him want to sing. . . . I was glad he refused to change his repertoire and wanted to be just another musician. . . . He doesn't give a damn about fame. What counts with him is singing. . . . Anyway, he's good looking. . . . And you can tell he's a banker's son. . . ."

When you think what luck she'd had with another banker's son, Paul Meurisse! She raved on and on till my ears were ringing.

The work Edith put in to stage "*Les Trois Cloches*" was something quite out of the ordinary. Since it was scored for orchestra and grand organs, the background music was astonishing—it kind of knocked you out. And then there was the presence of that simple little dame standing in front of those tall guys, all dressed alike in white shirts, midnight blue pants and cummerbunds, mingling the voice of a woman who'd really lived with their young voices. It was a hit.

But in spite of that, her dear Compagnons didn't go along with everything Edith suggested. They didn't trust her. They sang well, but somehow they just weren't with it. They lacked warmth.

It was the help of Jean Cocteau that once again changed Edith's life. First of all, he told the guys they sounded very fine. And they were dumfounded. Then he did even more. He wrote in an article: "It is a pleasure to hear them and to hear her voice mingling with theirs, running through their bronze and gold bell like a vein of agate. . . ."

The next day everything was changed. The guys had finally decided to listen to Edith and follow her advice. They weren't wrong. "*Les Trois Cloches*" was a success in every country in the world. Over a million records of it were sold in France. In America, where Jean-François Nicot was called Jimmy Brown and the record was known as "Jimmy Brown's Song," the first pressing of sixty thousand was sold out in three weeks. As far as the Compagnons were concerned, Edith could now do no wrong. They realized she knew the right recipes. They began to trust her, and their repertoire changed.

When "*Les Trois Cloches*" began to ring out wildly to announce their joyful success, they tolled my death knell.

Having been the winner and having found a place in Edith's heart, Jean-Louis Jaubert got the royal treatment—the watch, the chain and all the rest of it. In the midst of all those guys who walked around as if they owned the place, I looked more or less like the poor cousin you let stay there out of pity. And I'd never liked pity or charity.

In my part of town, when I was a kid, benevolent ladies used to come by. They didn't do us any good—in fact, they did us harm. When they were there, you couldn't forget you were poor. They gave us ugly, shabby things that had already been worn, disgusting rags that only we would wear. To them we weren't of the same breed. We didn't have the same color skin as their kids.

I would have done anything for Edith—except crawl in front of her men. That, never! If I'd been willing to be a sort of crummy general maid, I might have been able to stay. But when Jean-Louis said coldly, "I don't want her around," I didn't make a fuss. The guy could live with nine people; a triangle was too much for him. I didn't hold it against him. From his point of view, he was surely right—I was in the way and he didn't like me. So I cleared out.

When I came back to Edith, just a little over a year later, she told me what had happened with Jaubert and her trip to America. Edith knew how to tell a story, with all the details. It really seemed as if you'd been there with her. She was funny. She could bear being separated from me (always because of her men), but I simply had to know about her life, as though I'd been right there with her.

"I've got to tell you the whole story right away, Momone. I'll never remember as clearly later. You're my memory. So pay attention. Don't forget a thing." And I didn't forget a thing, as she realized when she casually checked up on me a few months later.

"Momone, having those nine guys with me was like having my own orchestra. Not an orchestra accompanying me, but one I conducted. All those voices that sounded like musical instruments were terrific! At the beginning, I horsed around with them at the house. We got along fine. It was as if I had a whole bunch of brothers to take care of me. I'd never lived with guys that way. We'd kid around, and I'd laugh so much my belly ached.

"That's how we came to make the film, just for fun—*Neuf Garçons . . . un coeur*. Lucien Nat, Marcel Vallée and Lucien Baroux were in it. It wasn't a work of genius, just a simple little thing we did together—you know the kind I mean. It was shown in neighborhood theaters, with no particular fuss. The boys were a bit disappointed. And I'd done it to please them, so . . ."

As had happened with Yves, Edith had asked Loulou to manage the Compagnons, to get them on the same bill with her. They'd appear first on the program, and she'd sing *"Les Trois Cloches"* with them. Then she'd come on as the star.

"Loulou complains every time I don't appear alone. We had a kind of fight and he partly got his own way. So I opened in Paris in October 1946, without the Compagnons. That was the way it should have been—Loulou was right."

Edith had never had such delirious press notices. "The great Piaf years" were beginning.

Pierre Loiselet, who was very popular on the French radio, said: "A large, rather pale face, and a voice that seems to be washed in all the water flowing down the gutter. . . ." ("The guy's an ass," Edith said. "I don't have a large face!") Then he went on: "She's come back . . . in a very simple little dress . . . with her strikingly high doll's forehead and a wig that doesn't quite fit . . . her apostle's fingers . . . her humble eyes—her poor girl's eyes—wild eyes that protect themselves from the bravos raining down on her. . . . A little girl lost in the woods . . . a sweet, distraught face . . ."

Léon-Paul Fargue wrote: "She sings because there's a song inside her, because there's drama inside her, because her throat is fraught with tragedy. . . . When she evokes the triumph of love, the harshness of fate, the panting anguish of trains, the joy of light or the heart's mortality, she rises to ultimate, vibrant tones, pure, clear touches that escape her like those divine brush strokes in the dark narratives of Goya, Delacroix or Forain. . . ." And Charles Trenet called her "the white dove of the working-class districts."

"They said unusual things about me, didn't they, Momone?

"After that I sometimes worked with the Compagnons and sometimes by myself. You know Loulou! I'm the one who gives the orders, but that doesn't keep him from doing what he wants. He's such a pain in the ass, with all his talk, that I finally end up saying yes. That's how he got me to sing by myself in Greece, and I wasn't sorry. I even felt like changing my life and never coming back. . . . You've got to get to know that country someday, Momone. It's not like the others. It's hard to explain, but when you're there, you don't think the same way you do here—you can't any more.

"When I saw all those old stones piled one on top of the other in Athens, on the Acropolis, that thing full of columns in the sky, I realized there was something else in the world besides the Sacré-Coeur. It was impressive, believe me. And even more, because I was with a guy as handsome as a god!

"It was the sort of thing I like. I'd been singing for three days, and every night I found a bunch of flowers in my dressing room. No name, not a word, nothing. I said to myself, 'It's some guy who's loaded and too old and ugly to show his face. . . .' But he was handsome as a god, and hardly had a cent to his name! On the fourth night there he was—with curly hair, deep dark eyes, a build like one of their statues, and proud as a feudal lord. His name was Takis Menelas, and he was an actor.

" 'I'm the one who dared send you flowers,' he said. 'I wanted them to talk to you before I did. I would like to show you my country.' Nothing could have pleased me more than seeing anything at all with him! That same night he took me to the foot of the Acropolis in the moonlight. We climbed up to it on a little path that smelled of all sorts of warm things. The sounds of the city were like an orchestra, a kind of music rising from below. He explained that wandering among all those huge columns were guys in peplums who were his ancestors. I could see them after a while. And he kissed me. . . . Ah, Greece is beautiful!

"You can't have any idea how I loved that boy! For two weeks . . . What could I do? That's how long I was there. A few days before I left, he really upset me. He kept begging:

" 'Stay. Don't leave. I won't ever see you again. You're my whole life. Stay! We'll get married. My country's made for goddesses, and you're one of them. You're Love. . . .'

"I was so taken with him I wondered if this wasn't *real life* after all—forgetting everything for one man! . . .

"The next day I got a cable from Loulou that really jolted me. 'Tour in the U.S. Have accepted Boston, Philadelphia, New York. With Compagnons. November 1947.'

"I phoned him.

" 'Are you nuts?' I asked. 'I don't have what it takes for America.'

"And then—you know me—I said right after that, 'O.K., I'll do it, but it'll be something they've never seen the likes of.' With a thing like that, a tour in America and all the work I was going to have to do, it was the end of Takis. I really cried when I left. I'd never had a handsomer guy or a better one in every sense. I was sure I was leaving him forever. But I wasn't. I saw him again in New York. He'd just turned down a very good contract and was going back to Greece. And he was just as handsome as ever."

Several years later, when Edith was so sick and the papers said she didn't have any more money. Takis sent her back the gold good-luck charm she'd given him with these words: "For you. You need it more than I do." That impressed Edith. "You see," she said, "I have a feeling I missed true love, the great love of my life. . . ."

When she came back from Greece, she began to get ready for her trip to the U.S.

"Ah, Momone! Was I sorry you weren't there! It would have been something if you'd gone through it with me." That I didn't doubt. "I had the jitters, you know. America isn't France!

"Loulou had got us staterooms on a ship. I was at the captain's table. You had to behave yourself and just nibble at your food as if everything they served disgusted you. And that went for the conversation too. It wasn't very relaxed. Luckily the purser soon got to be a pal of mine; he was a little guy with dark hair and not badly built at all. But I didn't make the most of it! A ship's not that big, and you don't have very much freedom. Anyway, I began to realize that Jean-Louis was keeping tabs on me and wasn't in any mood to kid around. . . . He kept talking about what was going to happen in New York, and boring me with all his questions: 'Do you think it's going to work? Do you think they'll like us? . . .'

"My first contact with America was a big disappointment. I thought I'd get a big bang out of the Statue of Liberty. Well, let me tell you, it isn't any more impressive in New York Harbor than it is back in Paris on the Pont Mirabeau. Everything around it's so tall, it looks tiny.

"What overwhelms you are the buildings. It's like what Jean Cocteau wrote: 'New York is a city standing upright.' Next to theirs, our houses would look like bungalows. We think we rush around like mad things in Paris, but it isn't true! We just stroll. In New York everybody's out to break the world record.

"Loulou had booked a suite for me at the Ambassador Hotel.

When I got there—let me think, it was in November 1947—and found myself all alone, standing there in the middle of my suitcases, I could have bawled. I decided it was time I boned up on my English. I'd bought me a book, *English Without Tears*. What a laugh!

"There's the *th* sound, first of all. It's impossible to say. It's no use putting the tip of your tongue between your teeth—it doesn't work. Since I'd begun studying in France, I was already up to: 'A woman is waiting for a sailor who promised to return to her when he became a captain. . . .' Boy, that was going to do me a helluva lot of good! I laughed so hard my sides ached.

"Clifford Fischer, my American agent, a very nice guy, sort of like Loulou, had organized a press conference with a big crowd of men and women, all writing down what I said. The first question they asked me was:

" 'Miss Idiss'—they couldn't pronounce Edith the French way —'you've just arrived in the United States. Who's the first person you'd like to meet?'

" 'Einstein. And I'm counting on you to get me his phone number.'

"You can't imagine how happy Clifford was—like a dog who'd been tossed a bone. He stood there chewing on his cigar and laughing. When they left, he said:

" 'The Einstein bit was terrific! You really came up with a good one!'

"It was my turn to laugh. I really *did* want to see Einstein."

The guy behind the Einstein business was Jacques Bourgeat— our Jacquot. We'd kept on seeing him since the Leplée days. He came and went in Edith's life. When she needed advice, really good advice, she'd call on either Jean Cocteau or Jacques Bourgeat. He was an old man now, but he was the only one who could get complicated things across to Edith. Thanks to him, there was a Bible, a copy of Plato and a book on relativity alongside a framed picture of Saint Theresa of Lisieux on Edith's night table. She mixed them all up a little in her head at first, but she gradually got it straight. Edith had a very open mind and adored learning things.

"This relativity business is awfully complicated, Momone, but it opens your mind. Boy, am I amazed when I understand something. And Plato's simple. You shouldn't read it all at once like a novel, but you get along fine if you read it bit by bit. That M. Einstein is a genius. If I go to the U.S., I'll phone him. . . ."

"The press conference was a good start," Edith went on. "But believe me, that evening at the Playhouse, on Broadway, was no fun at all. The Compagnons went on and didn't do badly. But the audience whistled when we sang '*Les Trois Cloches*.' I turned white with despair. Nobody had thought to tell me that whistling was better than applause in the U.S.!

"When I came on, I was wearing my usual little black dress. That was the first disappointment for the Yanks. They thought I'd worn it as a sort of disguise—you know, to look as plain as my boy scouts. To them, a star, especially one from Paris, home of the cancan, the Tabarin and the Lido, ought to have the means to pay for feathers, sequins and furs. I don't look anything like a glamour girl! I must admit, compared to Rita Hayworth or Marlene Dietrich, I didn't look so hot!

"I realized later that they think a woman from 'Gay Paree' has her hair done by Antonio, her face done by Jean d'Estrées, and wears a twenty-five-thousand-franc dress. I'm telling you this so you'll get the picture and have some idea of the atmosphere. The Compagnons were voices. It didn't matter whether they were understood or not. They were good-looking guys. Even if they weren't built like Hercules, they had what it takes—good stage presence. The audience didn't have to beat their brains out to understand. They just listened, it sounded nice, and that was enough.

"Then I came on in my short little black dress, with my mousy hair done up any old way, and my pale face. From a distance I guess I looked black and white. It was such a huge theater! If you'd circled the stage four times, you'd have easily had your daily quarter-mile walk!

"It was so quiet you could have heard a fly sneeze. I'd thought of a way to give them a jolt. I'd had two songs translated into

English and learned them by heart to please them and so that they'd understand a little. Was it a success! That evening some guy said to me, 'I really liked those two songs you sang in Italian. . . .'

"To top it all off, while I was singing, the MC would talk into a microphone and explain the songs. He'd come up with things like: 'She's unhappy because she's killed him and been put in jail.' I can't say it was exactly a disaster, but it came close. It was a miserable disappointment, to say the least!

"I was in such a state I couldn't get back on my feet again. I didn't hold it against the audience though. We just weren't the same breed, we couldn't understand each other. When an American goes out at night, he wants to be entertained. He's been fighting all day. He doesn't come to a show to hear someone sing about having the blues or being poor. He wants to leave his worries in the checkroom.

"He's sentimental on principle and also to keep healthy. So this little French girl, forcing him to remember that there are people who suffer and have reasons for being unhappy, didn't go over at all! That's the way it was for the ones who partly understood the words, and the others could feel it in my voice.

"What's more, my music was nothing like theirs. I didn't have any gooey melodies, easy on the ears. And my songs weren't jazz either. So what was I? That's what the few reporters who were kind enough to write little articles about me wondered. They wrote things like this: 'This plump little woman wears a lot of mascara and has a mouth made for swallowing a cup of tomato juice in one gulp. . . .' Not the sort of thing to advertise your talent and make people come running!

"I'd never been in such despair. Jaubert, though, was in his glory. I could have used some of his good reviews. The 'French boys' went over well. *They* represented a wholesome France—the buddies of the GIs who'd liberated us. You can just picture it: The 'Marseillaise' and 'The Star-Spangled Banner!' I went on like that for several evenings, feeling depressed. Then I said to the Compagnons:

" 'Listen, guys, I'm getting out. It's silly to be stubborn in our profession. They don't like me. So long, pals. Finish the tour without me. Keep on, and good luck! I'm taking the boat home.'

"You know me, Momone—I'd already reserved a stateroom. Besides, they didn't try to hold me. But believe me, I had a heavy heart. The damned thing really ached! I've suffered when I've been in love, but no man ever hurt me like that.

"And then suddenly everything changed, and I got my chance. Virgil Thomson, a music critic, who never wrote about popular performers, wrote a two-column review about me on the front page of one of the biggest papers in New York. He 'explained' me to the Americans. Everything they needed to understand me was in it. To him everything about me was song—my voice, my gestures, my build. He ended the article with the words: 'If we allow her to leave on the heels of this undeserved failure, the American public will have given proof of its ignorance and its stupidity.' The guy really rolled up his sleeves when he wrote that!

"I hadn't even had time to get all of it translated when Clifford Fischer came into my room with his hat on his head and the newspaper under his arm. What a great guy! You'll see what I mean when you meet him—you'll like him right away. He's got all the good qualities of the nicest Americans—direct, frank, quick-witted, and a good poker player.

"He tapped his paper and stood there chewing on that stinking cigar—which before breakfast turned my stomach—and bellowed:

" 'Idiss, it's great! This article's worth thousands of dollars. Don't leave. People here appreciate courage; it always pays off. I'm going to go to the most elegant, the most snobbish nightclub in Manhattan—the Versailles, on East Fiftieth Street. And they'll sign a contract with you. Order us up two bourbons to celebrate, and I'll tell you what I'm going to do to get you a high price.'

"Clifford and Thomson had suddenly bolstered me up. I could have drunk twelve bourbons—except that I didn't like that stuff of theirs much—and climbed to the top of the Empire State Building.

" 'The way I see it, Edith, you have to appear alone. Several reporters have said you're only a voice in the Compagnons' chorus! When a woman appears onstage with chorus boys in this country, she dances and sings and is more important than they are. They're just there to set her off. But with you and these guys it's just the opposite, and that's not good. And when they've left the stage, you're a sorry sight out there all by yourself. Americans have a horror of anything that looks cheap. Let the Compagnons go on with the tour. And I'll tell the guy at the Versailles, "When people have got used to her little black dress and realized that a Parisienne onstage isn't necessarily a chorus girl with feathers on her head and a dress with a train, they'll be fighting to get in to hear her." I'll even tell him, "If she costs you money by the end of the contract, I'll pay the difference!" '

"Fischer gambled on what he thought was a winner. When he finally got me a contract, he made me work every day for two weeks. I took English lessons. I worked on my two translated songs with a teacher, and believe me, it was no fun.

"The first time I went to the Versailles to rehearse, I was really bowled over and thought Clifford had gone nuts. Me in that setting—it couldn't work. Imagine the palace of Versailles as seen by a Hollywood set designer for a Technicolor musical comedy. Filled with statues and clipped trees, with mirrors and thousands of doors and windows! And the whole thing in pink and white plaster! I'd already had a tough time of it on a stage with simple backdrops, so I was sure nobody'd notice me in the midst of that whole mess of stuff.

"Fischer told me I didn't know what I was talking about, that it was a very French setting (the only one Americans had ever heard of, except for the Moulin Rouge and the Eiffel Tower) and that it suited me perfectly.

"It was O.K. with me; I shut up. No point annoying the only man trying to save me. Anyway, what would one more fiasco matter?

"Fischer and I decided not to have an MC. That way there'd be one less problem to deal with. But it wasn't enough to save me from stage fright. It was no use for Fischer to say, with that American cordiality that tosses you in the drink with a hearty slap on the back, 'Don't worry. It'll work. It's in the bag. Your audience knows

who you are now. You mustn't surprise Americans without warning. They have to know what they're supposed to think and then
they go along with you. They're conditioned to swallow anything!'
I was in a cold sweat. I had an attack of stage fright as spectacular
as their nutty interior decorating.

"Fischer and the guys from the Versailles had softened the
public up, I must say. The ads in the papers described me as the
singer that GIs had discovered in Paris (I don't think there were
many who ever heard me) and—don't laugh—as 'the Sarah Bernhardt of Song.' The guys had shot the whole wad.

"Marlene Dietrich, Charles Boyer and all of New York society
were there. And among the French, the Craddocks, and Jean
Sablon, who'd come to lend me moral support. I sure needed it!

"But I really made a hit. People shouted, 'Bravo!' and 'Vive la
France!' and 'Paris!'—any old thing—even though lots of them
hadn't even been able to see me. I was so tiny in that enormous
place, all they could see was the top of my hair—and that's not my
best feature, is it, Momone? So the next day they raised the platform for me.

"Marlene came to my dressing room to give me a kiss. That's
how we became pals. Did she get me publicity! She was wonderful
to me.

"After the flop at the Playhouse, I *had* to be a success at the
Versailles. I'd been hired for a week, and I stayed twenty-one.
Imagine that!

"Four months in New York is quite a hunk of time. I couldn't
stay in a hotel. They watch your room there like you're a nun
who's taken a vow of chastity. Irène de Trébert, my pal from Paris,
had a little two-room apartment on Park Avenue and turned it
over to me. I had plenty of friends who'd come and horse around
with me there. Still, I felt lonely. I spent nights that seemed endless,
that just dragged on and on.

"Jean-Louis had finished the tour we were supposed to be on
together, and went back to Paris with the boy scouts. That's how I
divorced the Compagnons, with no fuss at all. Luckily all my pals
passing through the city came to see me. The one I was happiest to
see was Michel Emer.

"When he turned up at the Versailles with that frightened owl face of his, was I pleased! I was so happy I teased him. He rushed over to kiss me, and I pushed him away, saying sternly, 'Have you brought me a song, little corporal?' And he answered, 'No,' with his guilty kid's look. 'I'll say hello to you when you've written me a song.' I left him standing there and went off to sing.

"He was kind of mad at the time. Sitting in my dressing room, he could hear me singing from a distance. That got him all wound up again and he began to write '*Bal dans ma rue*' on my dressing table. When I came back, he handed it to me. 'Kiss me. I've written you your song.' "

> *Ce soir il y a bal dans ma rue*
> *Et dans le p'tit bistrot*
> *Où la joie coule à flot*
> *Des musiciens sur un tréteau*
> *Jouent pour les amoureux*
> *Qui tournent deux par deux,*
> *Le rire aux lèvres et les yeux dans les yeux.*
>
> Tonight there's a dance on my street
> And in the little bistro
> Overflowing with joy
> Musicians on the stage
> Play for lovers
> Dancing two by two,
> A smile on their lips, gazing into each others' eyes.

"All he'd had to do was listen to me!"

That was true. "If I don't see you, if you're far away, I can't write for you," Michel used to say. So he'd come to the house. "Edith, talk to me. Sing me anything you want." And the next day he'd bring her a new song. He wrote over thirty of them like that for her over the years.

"The next day we had lunch together at my place and got to work," Edith went on. " '*Bal dans ma rue*' was good, but I wanted another one. I wanted something sad, the story of a guy who dies at the end. I explained what I had in mind to Michel, and he sat down and wrote me '*Monsieur Lenoble.*' "

Monsieur Lenoble se mouche,
Met sa chemise de nuit,
Ouvre le gaz et se couche;
Demain tout sera fini.

Monsieur Lenoble blows his nose,
Puts on his nightshirt,
Turns on the gas and goes to bed;
Tomorrow it will be all over.

"He'd been in New York twelve hours and he'd come up with two songs for me!"

That didn't amaze me. Edith, with her extraordinary power over people, made them give her the best they had in them. They couldn't get over it themselves. She kept asking you for more—and you gave it to her!

I was no different than the others. You wanted to please her; there was only one recipe for that—bringing her something. Not money—she didn't gave a damn about it (she gave it away to others). What was important to her, what she needed, was to be admired. I liked to shock Edith, both in big things and in little ones.

In 1950 I had a very serious operation. The doctor told Edith I had a month to live. Thirteen days later I was on my feet again. She was happy to see me, but even happier that I wasn't like other people. "You're a little soldier, you are!" she said to me. That was the biggest possible compliment.

And she was proud of me. "Wow, what Momone can put away!" she kept saying to everybody, and kept feeding me crazy things like toast with marrow. It was so rich I loathed it, and it made me horribly sick.

She used those concoctions with marrow to test her men. She'd order some for them, and if their mugs turned pale, she'd say, "Ask Momone; she'll tell you how good it is." There were guys who'd have killed me if they could have. That made Edith laugh. And what a laugh! It could shatter windowpanes.

And I did everything she did. I didn't put sugar in my coffee for thirty years. I hated it that way, but Edith didn't take sugar, so I didn't either.

That's how our friendship was: it showed in everything, big and small. Affection like ours, so long and so perfect, can't be explained. It's not even friendship: it's a rare feeling. When you've experienced it, everything else seems washed out and colorless. I took anything from Edith and still had the feeling I owed her something.

The Americans couldn't understand Edith. Her personality was too new to them. They didn't know people like that existed. And they didn't catch on to how talented she was till after Fischer's Barnum and Bailey–style poker game, when he'd said to them, "Step right up, ladies and gents!"

But when she came home at night, no one was there. Edith, the woman, was alone. When she gave a party it was Edith the star they came to see. Her little apartment would be packed. And when the last guy staggered out, it was all over. There was nothing for her to do but hit the sack and sleep.

Marlene became a great pal of hers. "I've never met a more intelligent woman than Marlene Dietrich—maybe some as intelligent, but none *more*. And beautiful!—like the ones you only see in the movies. Every time I was with her I thought of *The Blue Angel*, the part where she sings in her black stockings and her top hat. Marlene was a real movie star, so perfect you couldn't believe she ate. So when she told me she liked to cook and that her favorite dish was French boiled beef, I thought she was pulling my leg!

"The two of us often had dinner together. At first I was damn careful, because I was afraid of sounding like an ass, but she gave me confidence the day she said, 'Let yourself go, Edith; for me you're Paris—in fact, you're Paree. And besides, you remind me of Jean Gabin. You talk like him, eat like him and, as delicate as you look, you give me the same feeling of strength that he does.'

"That impressed me, because as an actor and as a man, there's no one better than Gabin. I must have reminded Marlene of her big, strong Gabin the night she took off the gold cross with emeralds she was wearing and hung it around my neck.

" 'Here, Edith, I want it to bring you luck, as it's done for me. And this way it'll get around Paris, just as it did with me.' Her gesture brought tears to my eyes."

Edith wore the cross for a long time, but after Marcel Cerdan's death she took it off. She'd decided that the little green stones had brought her bad luck.

Her friendship with Marlene helped fill her life, but it didn't absorb her. Edith's heart was empty and it couldn't be filled by a hasty, casual love affair.

"You can't imagine how hygienic love is with those guys. They go into maneuvers—one, two! one, two!—lousy lovemaking, over before you know it, and then they're asleep. You also run into some perverts who, because you're French and from Paris, want you to do all kinds of things you don't feel like doing and who can't believe it when you refuse. Or else they're so sentimental they bleat. They think you're 'mother,' and pretend they're little boys, snuggling in your arms and bawling, because they're so plastered. But that doesn't make it any better in bed!

"The funniest thing that ever happened to me was with John Glendale, the movie actor. The guy was handsome, the way only Americans are—tall, with the trained muscles of an amateur athlete, elegant, well dressed, relaxed and uncomplicated. He was a little conceited, but I thought, 'He'll get over that in bed. He'll have something else to do and to think about!'

"I invited him over, with a few pals. We laughed and drank; no more than that. I wasn't tight at all. I wanted to keep my wits about me for him. I liked him too much to ruin it. Everybody finally left and I stood at the door politely saying good night. There was no sign of John. This guy's got tact, I thought. He's discreet about it. I came back inside, sure I'd find him waiting for me. I could already see his smile, and feel his arms around me. I was very excited: the thought of sleeping with a guy like that always turns me on a little. No one in the living room. I went into the bedroom. What did I see? John Glendale, stretched out naked between my sheets, smoking cigarettes. I can't tell you how I felt.

" 'Come on, I'm waiting,' he said.

"I grabbed the whole pile of clothes he'd dropped and damn well threw 'em in his face. He was stuttering, 'But . . . isn't this what you wanted?' And I yelled at him, 'Get the hell out, and fast!

I'm no whore . . . I'm no whore. . . .' He didn't stay for more but I cried all night alone in my empty bed."

That was the last time Edith was insulted like that. A young boxer—Marcel Cerdan—has just shown up in New York.

Chapter 11

"La Vie en rose" with Marcel Cerdan

I was in Casablanca, invited there by my fiancé. I was happy. It's always nice to have a husband in view! I was still lonely, though, because my fiancé, his family and the rest of it didn't seem all that important. I didn't really give a damn. You only love once in your life, and I already had! The man I loved was killed in the war when I was twenty. You don't ever forget things like that.

I'd been in Casablanca almost six months, and I'd had a bellyful of the sun. I'd never seen it so close. When I was in Paris, I hadn't really believed the legionnaires and their stories, but here I could understand them. Now I knew why they were so depressed, why they went nuts and why so many drank themselves to death later.

Forgetting Paris isn't easy when it's in your blood. To stay sane, I had to blot out the memory of Edith, her laughter and her songs. I didn't have anything to hold on to. I'd given up on the future husband; he was already past history!

If only I could have forgotten I was so far away. But I was the one who'd asked for it. I could have gone to live in the suburbs of Paris: Fontenay-aux-Roses or Bobigny. But from there I'd have phoned her and we'd have met in secret, like lovers. We'd done that when Asso was around, but I couldn't do it any more. I'd either be with her right out in the open, or not at all. And it was not at all.

I knew from the newspapers what she was doing, more or less, and I could fill in the details myself.

I was fed up with thinking about it. You can't even wander around in a city on the sea because you always end up at the seaside: that's what attracts you. I really felt like throwing myself into that water beating against the rocks so noisily. That awfully loud music became Edith to me—Edith onstage at the A.B.C., or somewhere else, accompanied by a big orchestra. I could hear her voice singing: "This sun that pierces the skin, this sun . . ." The drone of it was tapping on my skull, tapping on my heart. I began to drift helplessly. . . .

One night, stretched out on the sand, I looked up in the sky to find the Big Dipper. The legionnaires had told me you couldn't see it in this part of the world; you saw the Southern Cross instead. But there were too many stars in the sky, all shining so brightly I got confused and couldn't find anything at all. My head was swimming. Then a cool breeze touched my forehead and refreshed my heart. I began to feel better. I was alone, but my mind became one with the stars!

Suddenly I heard the sand crunch. Someone was passing by. No, someone was coming toward me—to ask the time, maybe? I saw him. He was no Apollo; he was better. His face looked pale in the moonlight, like in a spotlight. His eyes sparkled. The Southern Cross I'd been looking for was right there, gleaming in his eyes. I was sensitive and had a fertile imagination.

He stretched out next to me without a word. It was funny—he felt like telling me his life story, and I felt like telling him mine. It began so simply.

"What are you doing here?" he said.

"I'm on vacation."

He said *tu* to me from the very first sentence. So what? We felt like we knew each other.

"Are you from around here?" I asked him.

"Yes."

"What do you do?"

"I'm a boxer."

He said it with a strange accent. No doubt about it. He was from around there. He propped himself up on his elbows in the sand and leaned his head on a hand so white it was hard to believe it belonged in a boxing ring. Then he triumphantly announced:

"My name is Marcel Cerdan."

He seemed like a kid. He was so proud of his name, of what he did, or what he hoped to become, that I swear he seemed like a male Edith. To him boxing was his life, it meant a lot, even though the articles about him at the time were only fillers.

Boxing, to me, was unknown territory. I didn't care a hang about it. Vaudeville and singing were my world, but sports! Maybe the Tour de France . . . but beyond that I knew absolutely nothing.

My silence impressed him. He was sure he'd left me speechless. But not at all! I was just thinking, "If he sang, his name would look good on a poster. Even if the names were listed alphabetically, his would be among the first."

Just like that, because of a night spent together on the sand, we became pals. We didn't say a word about it to anybody, and nobody ever knew. We often met each other in little bars for mint tea or coffee. The first time I had a Cinzano, but after that I drank nonalcoholic stuff, like him; Marcel didn't drink.

Boy, was he serious! He never took his mind off training. He was a homebody, with his wife, Marinette, and his kids, Marcel and René and Paul. I think I was his only sin. I brought him a whiff of Paris. He'd already breathed that sort of air and wanted more. . . .

I talked to him, and told him everything about myself. He'd listen to me for hours. I've never met a gentler, a more patient man. He sat there facing me, calm, a bit awkward in the small chair. He always tried to make himself look small. When he wasn't in the ring he always seemed amazed at how strong he was. He was never bad-tempered or impatient or angry. If you'd stepped on his toe, he'd have said, "Excuse me." One day I said to him:

"Seeing you like that, and knowing you, it's hard to understand how you can earn your living knocking guys around."

He laughed. "But I don't hit to hurt them; I just fight. And I fight clean." I felt like apologizing.

Marcel wasn't the least bit lazy. He put everything he had into his work. When I saw him in training, he looked like a big bruiser, with muscles so solid that if you stabbed them with a needle, you'd have broken it. He moved so fast on his feet, he was like a dancer. And he smacked his sparring partners so hard I felt sorry for them.

Marcel's job was to punch hard, but he was always afraid of going too far.

"Are you O.K., buddy?" he'd ask his sparring partner, who couldn't catch his breath.

"Sure, Marcel. Go ahead, hit me."

The funny thing was that Marcel couldn't bear to be hurt himself. It drove him wild. He always thought the other guy had done it on purpose.

I never had with any other man what I had with Marcel—understanding. We didn't need to talk. He knew all about me, except for one thing—Edith. It never occurred to me that this boxer from Casablanca would finally bring me back to Edith. . . .

While I was eating my heart out in that lousy place, thinking she was still with Jaubert, Edith met Marcel. While I was thinking I'd been forsaken, Edith was yakking to Marcel about her sis. Later on, each of them separately told me how they'd met.

Edith was very proud of her man, her Marcel. She was dying to show him to me. I wouldn't find a single fault in this one. After all, I was pretty much a pain in the ass, and when I didn't like her guys, I sure didn't hide it. I could always figure them out the minute I laid eyes on them. I had experience and didn't get seriously involved very often. When it came to men, especially Edith's, I had a cold eye. I didn't make it any easier for them. But Marcel wasn't like the others; I was going to be impressed. Edith was very anxious to introduce him to me.

She'd pulled out all the stops when she told him how lonely her life had been.

"I don't have any family, you see. All my mother ever wanted was my dough. You'd never understand what it was like. Ah, here's an example. One day when I was with Momone, I said to her, 'After all, I do have a mother!' We went and got her address from my father. I was fifteen, just a kid, singing in the streets with Momone.

"We went to the address he'd given us. My mother looked at us; not a move, not a kiss.

" 'Oh, it's you. Who's that with you?'

" 'It's Momone.'

" 'I see. Come over here! Are you filthy!' And she touched our hair with her fingertips. 'You've got lice!' They didn't bother us; we were used to them.

"She sent us to the drugstore to buy some Marie-Rose, a lotion that sends lice to a sweet-smelling death. She poured a whole mess of it over our heads and locked us in for two days. When we'd washed our hair, she said:

" 'You can go now. Here, buy something to eat.' And she slipped us a few pennies. Not a single kind word. Nothing. Not even a kiss. Don't think it got any better later, Marcel. In about 1932 or '33, she was singing at the Boule Noire. Since I wanted to see her, I went there. Nothing had changed.

" 'So it's you again, and with her?'

"This time my mother wasn't alone. She had a young girl friend called Jeannette living with her. A really nice kid who tried to clean us up and to help us. It was a little like having two fathers —Gassion and Jeannette. She was devoted to my mother. She'd work the streets sometimes when they were broke, and with my mother they were more often than not. The poor kid died of tuberculosis. So you see, I didn't really have a mother. My only family is Momone."

What could Marcel do after all that? "You'll have to bring your sister back here," he said.

Edith would have loved to, but she didn't know where I was. By then I'd returned from Casablanca and was working the gas pump at a suburban garage. One night the boss sent me out to get the paper. On the front page was a picture of Cerdan, Edith Piaf and "Miss Cotton," an American, getting off a plane.

I didn't put two and two together at the time. I probably thought Marcel was with Miss Cotton, but I really didn't think about it at all. I noticed one thing—that Edith was back, and there wasn't a sign of Jaubert in the photo.

I phoned all over town and discovered she was staying at the Claridge, where I'd gone when I was just a kid. I phoned her.

"Come right over!" she said. I wept for joy. I couldn't live without Edith.

The concierge announced me as "madame's sister," like in comedies, but I didn't feel like laughing. Standing there in front of her door in that fancy corridor, I put my hand over my heart to keep it from jumping out. Also, I was scared. Our reunions weren't always pleasant, and it was a long time since I'd seen Edith.

I knocked and heard her voice saying, "Come in."

She was standing at the window with her back toward me, looking out through the curtain, which she clutched with one hand. It was like a scene in a movie. She turned to me and said, "You see, Momone, I'm still waiting." It was true—she spent her whole life waiting.

I stood there like a fool. I looked at her and felt uncomfortable; it had all happened too fast. An hour earlier I'd been at my gas pump, my hands covered with grease. And now I was face to face with her. Edith looked at me . . . I'd changed; I was sadder now, and with good reason! How beautiful she looked, how pleased she was in the midst of her new-found happiness!

She stood at the window and I stood at the door, just a few yards of carpet separating us, though to me it seemed like thousands of miles. But in a few seconds I was in her arms. She wept for joy, kissing me.

"You'll never know how happy I am, Momone. You can't know. I'm in love with the most marvelous man on earth, and he loves me, and now you're here. . . . It's awful, Momone; I think I'm going to die of happiness. . . ."

But happiness isn't like unhappiness. You recover from it!

She inspected me from head to foot. I wasn't exactly a gorgeous sight! She opened her closet. Something was wrong. There were dresses in it, and that was unusual. It meant nobody was sponging off her. In a detached tone she said, "Take your pick. You can have any one you like." Then she ordered up two high teas. What with the dresses and the hot tea, I was lost. I didn't recognize her.

She wasted no time. "Look, Momone, this one I really love." I knew what that meant: I wasn't to raise an eyebrow at him or criticize him; this was serious. I couldn't wait to see the guy, and after two endless hours he finally arrived. He knocked, and Edith called, "Come in!" When I heard her say, "Marcel Cerdan, this is Momone," I felt the earth open up under my feet.

He walked over to me with his angelic smile and held out his hand. Edith watched us anxiously to see whether we'd like each other. What courage it took for me to look her in the eye and say, "You're right; he's wonderful."

Neither Marcel nor I brought up the past. It was all we could do, since she was standing there like a kid. Telling her the truth would have been like telling her Santa Claus didn't exist. No one budged—it was like Madame Tussaud's. Edith was bursting to talk to me about her new love. She had to serve it up, nice and hot, right then and there. Luckily Marcel had the bright idea of leaving, and we were alone. She asked me only one question:

"What have you been doing all this time?"

"I'll tell you later."

That's all she was waiting for. She was off:

"First I have to tell you how I broke up with Jaubert. It's too funny. Marcel was in my apartment in New York. Jaubert often phoned, because he thought it was taking me a long time to get home. I wasn't there that night, and when Jaubert heard a man's voice answering, he asked curtly:

" 'Who are you?'

" 'Marcel Cerdan,' replied Marcel with his slight accent.

" 'What are you doing there?'

" 'I can't tell you what I'm doing, but it'd be better if you don't come back.' Then he hung up and went to bed.

"When I got home I found a note on my pillow: 'Jaubert phoned and . . . never mind, it takes too long to explain. Wake me up.' Don't you think he's terrific?"

I did. Without knowing it, Marcel had helped me get revenge on Jaubert. And I felt good about it for a long time.

Several months later Jean-Louis Jaubert still hadn't come around to see Edith, even though his contracts with her hadn't run out. Edith continued to sing with the Compagnons de la Chanson in a cabaret, so she also continued to see Jaubert. But I felt I'd got even with him, and every night, when we left the cabaret, I couldn't resist saying, "Good night, Jean-Louis. We're going home early because I have to take care of Marcel tomorrow morning." He was furious.

For once we weren't in the bathroom for a talk session. Edith was sitting on a kind of couch in the far corner of the room with her legs tucked under her. Wearing just a sweater and a skirt, she looked the way she had at the beginning—the way she always looked, our way. Except that this skirt and sweater had cost dough. Her hair was shorter. She'd cut it herself one evening in New York, when she'd been very hot and had no hairdresser handy; since she never liked to wait, she'd cut her hair all the way around her head with a pair of scissors. It left her rather short neck bare, but she'd kept the hair long on top and now it fell over her forehead. She never changed that hairdo, which had been the result of chance and a fit of impatience.

What, I wondered, was different about her? She was calm. A contented woman. That's important! She was such a tiny thing she didn't take up much room there in her corner. Her hands were motionless, but her eyes were like shining lights. They were beautiful.

"When I met Marcel . . ."

"She's finally going to tell me the story," I thought to myself.

". . . it was one evening at the Club des Cinq, around the end of 1946, when I was introduced to 'the Moroccan Bomber.' There's fate for you—a handshake right in front of everybody!"

Their first meeting was touching. Marcel was shy. They were introducing him to "the great Edith Piaf." That was the way he saw her, the way he was always to see her. He didn't at all realize that he was "the great Marcel Cerdan," as great in his own field as she was in hers.

"And Momone, I said to myself, 'This guy has really unusual eyes.' Then—you know I wouldn't lie to you—I didn't think any more about him. There wasn't much chance we'd meet again; our jobs were so unrelated. It was America that did it!

"I was at the Versailles, and Marcel's manager, Lucien Roupp, had arranged some fights for him in Madison Square Garden. I was feeling pretty lost in my New York apartment. Then one day the phone rang. It was Marcel.

" 'Marcel *who?*' I asked him.

" 'Cerdan. The boxer. Don't you remember? We met at the Club des Cinq in Paris. I'm here in town.'

"It was funny! There were pauses in the conversation, and he must have been really sweating.

" 'Of course I remember,' I said. 'I haven't forgotten you.'

" 'And I haven't forgotten you either,' he said. He was so relieved, he began to laugh. 'How about dinner tonight? I'll come get you.'

"You can bet I didn't say no. I piled on the makeup and got into my most elegant dress—you know, the very simple kind that costs a fortune. I was barely ready when he arrived. 'Let's go,' he said. 'I'm famished!'

"He didn't have a car and there weren't any taxis. 'It's only a little way,' said Marcel. So we started off on foot. I couldn't keep up with him—he should have been a long distance runner. And he didn't even notice; the guy was really dense.

"We went into some seedy drugstore, and I hoisted myself up on a stool. First long distance running, then mountain climbing! I found myself face to face with a plateful of what they call 'pastrami'—a kind of dried and boiled beef you wouldn't dare give a bum in Paris. The mustard began to make my nose itch. Then they served me a peppermint sundae, and some beer to wash it all down. It was enough to make even jailbirds puke. Then Marcel plunked down forty cents.

"No manners, and stingy to boot!

"Marcel looked at me with a good-natured smile. He hadn't noticed a thing.

" 'Shall we go?'

" 'Oh, this was just the first course!' I said. 'Well, it didn't cost you much. Is that what you call taking a lady out to dinner?'

"He turned beet red and took me by the arm, not squeezing it but keeping a good grip on it so I couldn't get away. . . . 'I'm sorry . . . I didn't realize,' he said. 'That's what I usually do for dinner. But you're right; it's probably not the same for you.' We got into a taxi. Not a word during the whole ride. He even tried not to look at me. And suddenly we were at the most elegant restaurant in New York, the Pavillon. That's how I ate two meals on my first date with Marcel! After that, we never left each other. Boy, was he shy with me! *I* had to make the advances. Yet he's a man, a real one."

For Edith it was too good to be true. She had a man who adored her, who did everything she wanted, not because he needed her, or because he was afraid of her screams and her scenes, but because he loved her.

He was as famous as she was. He had his public and she had hers. When they were together and people applauded them, they shared it equally. They were lucky not to be in the same profession. Their names would never appear on the same bill.

"Nothing else mattered when he began to love me," said Edith. "Marcel's faithful. Marinette—his wife, the woman who gave him his sons—is sacred. But I'm the one he loves. She must loathe me. If I were her, I'd have kicked up a fuss long ago. But she knows she'd lose Marcel if she did. He doesn't talk about her, but he thinks about her. You know what I mean?"

Edith couldn't know how well I did. I knew Marcel was a decent guy who played it straight and couldn't possibly tell a lie. I knew he must be unhappy in his own simple, uncomplicated way. And I knew my Edith. It wasn't hard for me to imagine what she was going through. When she loved a man, she had to show it. "You know me, Momone. I can't hide my feelings."

"One night we had a marvelous time," Edith went on. "Marcel suddenly had a great idea. 'Come on, we're going to go to a carnival.'

"It was past midnight. 'You're nuts! There's no carnival in this hole.'

" 'Sure there is—Coney Island.'

"Nobody'd ever told me about it. Coney Island's a huge amusement park, covering acres and acres. And in America they don't go for tame little merry-go-rounds. After you've ridden in circles on one of their contraptions, your legs keep on waltzing for hours. Your head goes one way and your stomach the other! It takes a while to get them back together again! We ate hot dogs and some sort of waffles and ice cream. I didn't want the night to ever stop singing, whirling around me, laughing. . . .

"Marcel took me on the scenic railway—an American-style roller coaster as high as a skyscraper. Marcel shouted for joy, and just for fun I cuddled up next to him. Nothing could happen to me in his arms; I was safe. Screaming was part of the fun!

"When we got off, hundreds of people began shouting, 'It's Cerdan! Wow!' Then they recognized me and began to stamp their feet and yell, '*La Vie en rose!* . . . *La Vie en rose!* . . .' And I sang, Momone, just like that. The way I used to sing in the streets. It smelled like a carnival, of fried food and sugar and sweat. We heard all sorts of music mixed up together. You can't imagine how great it was!

"Another night, I went to see Marcel fight. He'd wanted me to.

" 'No, Marcel, I'm scared.'

" 'So am I when you sing, but I come to hear you. Maybe it's because you're the best. Boxing's my business. You have to see a man when he's working, otherwise you don't know what he's really like.'

"His reasons are always so simple, you just can't resist. At first I closed my eyes. I could hear blows landing on skin. It hurt me. I was afraid Marcel was getting them all. The audience screamed and whistled. The place was full of smoke. Everybody was gobbling popcorn and spitting out peanut shells. It was awful. I finally opened my eyes. Curled up there in a seat that would have held two people my size, I yelled, 'Go get him, Marcel!'

"It was Marcel and then again it wasn't. He was squinting, with a hard, intense look in his eyes, and they never left his opponent. He'd never looked at me that way. He won, but there was a cut on his cheekbone and he had a pretty banged-up eye. I could have cried. I rushed over to console him, like a mother when her kid comes home bloody. He gently pushed me away. 'No, Edith, it's nothing. This is part of my job too.'

"Wasn't that beautiful? He's great—if only you knew how great he is!'"

I knew.

"The reporters pestered us and ran after us so much that one day Marcel agreed to hold a press conference. 'The romance of two French celebrities in New York.' They could write the story blindfolded.

"Every reporter in town was there, chewing gum and smoking, with or without a pencil in hand. Marcel didn't beat around the bush. He always went straight to the point. If you could have heard how he gave it to them! He didn't want me to be there. But I wasn't going to be left out; I wanted to hear. I stationed myself behind the door. Marcel was in front of it, so there was no way of any curious onlooker getting by him and opening it.

" 'Well, here we are. You're interested in just one thing, so let's not waste each other's time. You want to know if I'm in love with Edith Piaf. Yes, I am! As for her being my mistress, if she's only that it's because I'm married. If I weren't married and didn't have children, I'd make her my wife. Anyone here who's never cheated on his wife raise his hand.'

"The reporters were dumfounded.

" 'Now you can ask me all the questions you want, but I've said everything I have to say on that subject. I'll see tomorrow if you're gentlemen.' The next day there wasn't a single word about us in the papers, and I got a basket of flowers as tall as a skyscraper with a card on it saying: 'To the lady who's loved best, from the gentlemen.' They wouldn't have done that in France!

"You won't recognize me, Momone. Marcel's changed me. He's so pure, when he looks at me I feel as if I've been washed clean of everything. You get clean again with him. I always wanted to start all over again with the others, but with him I've done it."

There was also another change, an important one. She never paid for anything when she was with Marcel. He was the one who opened his wallet. "You know, it's not easy to get him to accept a present, but I've found a gimmick. When he gives me a present I give him one. Look here, Momone, he bought me my first mink coat. Isn't it beautiful?"

It was great. No, better than that: it touched my heart, seeing those little hands fondling the fur, burying themselves in it, grabbing it by the handful. It wasn't the coat's quality or the price; she didn't give a damn about that, she didn't need anybody to buy her a mink coat. No, it was Marcel's love she was fondling and losing herself in. . . .

"A mink coat . . . It would never have occurred to me. But it did to him.

"I didn't waste a second. I went straight to Cartier's and bought him a pair of cufflinks. The finest ones they had, with diamonds, and also a watch, a chain, everything I saw! Nothing was too good for him. When I gave them to him, he laughed like a kid. He grabbed me, lifted me up in the air and whirled me around like a madman.

"I'm nuts about him, Momone; he's made me lose my mind. What's hard on me is our not being together very much. We've got our jobs, and then there's Marinette. There's no use telling myself he's right not to leave her; it's just killing me.

"Tomorrow we'll get up early and go to a tailor. Marcel doesn't know anything about clothes. He doesn't have any taste. He's a real Arab. I have to teach him. We're going to outfit him."

It was as simple as ever; everything was beginning all over again. I could tell. "We're going to outfit him"—I'd heard those words so many times. Edith always adored dressing her men, and they all went through it.

Poor Marcel turned up at the Palais des Sports one day wearing a gray suit with stripes as wide as your little finger. Edith had one just like it made for me. I still have it, though I never wore it. It was so hideous. Even worse, Marcel had a purple shirt and a kind of horrible tie with orange in it. . . . Marcel, the nicest man I ever knew, gentleness itself, said, "Darling, do you think I can wear this?" And she replied, "Listen, Marcel, you don't have any taste; you don't know the first thing about clothes." Then she turned to me. "How does he look, Momone?"

I couldn't possibly say he looked awful. Edith wouldn't have understood; she'd have thought I wanted to hurt him, to make a scene. So I chickened out and answered, "Marvelous! Do you look handsome!"

"O.K., then," said Marcel with his slight Algerian accent, looking all confused, doubting his own eyes. "If you say it's all right, I'll wear it."

But he was unhappy. He really suffered. A lot of others suffered too, but not as much as he did. He was convinced that Edith was very superior to him intellectually. He counted on her to give him an education, to instruct him, to teach him how to behave. He expected everything from her.

In the wings that huge lummox made himself very small, and looked and listened. He fascinated me. What amazed Marcel the most was Edith's voice. Every night he'd say to me, "Just look at that. She weighs a third what I do. If I just breathed on her, I'd hurt her. Such a tiny woman with such a strong voice—it knocks me out!"

Every time Edith sang, we had to bring along a bunch of stuff: her glass, her nose drops, her handkerchief, towels to take her makeup off, a bottle of aspirin, her pencil, her notebook, her English books and so on. She left almost nothing in her dressing room. We'd take everything home with us and then bring it all back the next day. So when Marcel was around, he checked up on everything. "Have you got all her stuff, Momone? You've at least got her dress?" Long after he died, I could still hear Marcel's voice in Edith's dressing room: "Where's her dress?" I never knew why Edith had only one dress to wear onstage. She had it with her wherever she went, and I was the one who was supposed to take care of it. She couldn't stand having it hanging in a theater dressing room. I'd iron it and clean it every day at the house and take it to her every night.

Once in New York I panicked. Edith was in her dressing room in her panties, all made up, her hair all fixed. As she bent down to put on her pumps, she shouted in her booming voice, "My dress!" I turned around to get it off the hook, and felt an icy chill come over me. Her dress wasn't there! I'd left it on Park Avenue. Just to help matters, the stage manager announced, "Five minutes, Miss Piaf!"

I dashed out without a word, grabbed a taxi, got the dress and came back. Traffic's no better in New York than in Paris, but Americans are sticklers about beginning on time, and the cops don't fool around when you speed. What a mad race! I thought Edith would raise hell when I got back with the dress. But seeing how upset I was, she kissed me, squeezed my hand and went on to sing. Jeez, what a relief!

Edith couldn't love someone without looking out for him, so she decided to make Marcel read. When they first met, she'd caught him reading Mickey Mouse comic books. It really did look silly seeing Marcel with his huge boxer's paws reading kid's stuff.

Edith forced good old Marcel to read books, real ones—*Via Mala, Sarn, La Grande Meute, La Recherche de la vérité*—not necessarily amusing.

"Why do you force me to read that, when it's so beautiful out and I feel like taking a walk?"

"That's the way I learned, Marcel."

And he'd plow ahead courageously because he was sure she was right, sure she couldn't be wrong. The only things he had doubts about were the suits—and how right he was!

We weren't living at the Claridge any more. Edith had rented a small town house on the rue Leconte de Lisle. It was the first time she'd had her own furniture. For us this was a real step up!

"Don't you see? A hotel, even the Ritz, is all wrong when you've got a man like him in your life!" Edith exclaimed.

She wanted to be the best, the most beautiful, the most everything for Marcel. And one evening she was. She was appearing at the A.B.C. when Princess Elizabeth and the Duke of Edinburgh came to Paris. Princess Elizabeth had never heard her sing. She asked Edith to sing at Carrère's, where a private but unofficial performance was to be given. To be singled out by the future Queen of England was really something! One morning a guy phoned and said, "I'm Monsieur de So-and-So, from the Quai d'Orsay." We didn't know what the Quai d'Orsay was; we'd never heard of it!

Edith shook her head no to old lady Bigeard, who was back with us. She put her hand over the phone and quickly explained to us that it was the French Foreign Office.

When Edith hung up she was bursting with joy.

"Princess Elizabeth wants to see me."

It was a Sunday. Edith did her act as usual, appearing at two matinees and in the evening. But as we drove down the boulevards to the rue Pierre Charron in the ambassador's car, Edith was impressed. And it took a lot to impress her! The streets are a strange school; you learn not to be shy. But you don't meet queens there! The chauffeur was an Englishman, so we couldn't get a word about his boss out of him.

Before she went on at Carrère's, Edith crossed herself, touched wood and went through the whole usual rigmarole. "I have to be the best," she said. "I represent France, and the Queen of England's gone out of her way to see me." To Parisians like us, Elizabeth was already the Queen.

Edith sang with all her red-white-and-blue heart. When she got back to her dressing room, the chief of protocol was there waiting for her—a pretty attractive guy. In phrases we didn't hear every day, he informed her of "Princess Elizabeth's wish to have her at her table." He sounded like it was Edith giving Elizabeth pleasure. That's what's meant by the courtesy of kings.

Edith said yes, but I could tell it was time to slip her that final drink you give a condemned man. Suddenly she got panicky. She looked at me.

"No, I can't do it, not all alone, not without my sister." As I was a member of the family, no one objected, and the chief of protocol left us alone a few minutes to fix our hair and things. Edith fell completely apart. She tried to glue herself together again, but there wasn't much chance to; and I was as limp as a rag.

"How do you make a curtsy, Momone? How do you talk to a queen? Oh, hell, let's go; she's no different from any other woman!" She said it, but she didn't believe a word.

Elizabeth held out her hand with a lovely smile. Edith made a quick little bob, a kind of genuflection. The chief of protocol had probably never seen anything like it before. The Princess had Edith sit next to her, and I was seated opposite Elizabeth and Philip. I didn't dare drink and neither did Edith. The conversation was really weird. I listened in a fog.

"You see," said Edith, "it wasn't as perfect as I wanted it to be for you, because I had two matinees today and then the evening performance. Forty-two songs between three P.M. and midnight isn't beans! Your voice gets tired. . . ."

The Princess smiled, and went to great trouble to reassure Edith, in better French than we'd ever managed to speak. She kept saying things like: "It was perfect," "You mustn't worry," "You're very talented. . . ." And through my panic I could hear Edith saying over and over, "Yes, but if you could only hear me when I haven't had two matinees . . . you'd know what I mean."

She went on and on. It was all she could find to say. Here we were, two girls who used to work at Lulu's, sitting at a queen's table; we were paralyzed.

Elizabeth had a radiant smile, very English, but charming. She kept saying to Edith, "I understand." She said it, but it couldn't have been true. What did we have in common with a woman who was fed court manners in her baby bottle?

Finally the Princess informed Edith that her father, George VI, wished to have Edith's records in his collection. She wasn't trying to get Edith to make her a present of them; it was simply a nice way of letting her know that the King liked her, Edith Piaf. I heard Edith answer, in all innocence:

"O.K., I'll have them sent to you in the morning. Where are you staying? . . ."

Then the party was over, and we left. It had been like in a dream. We never knew how long it had lasted. Sitting at that table was like being suspended in space.

When we'd both recovered, Edith said, "Her guy's terrific looking! Just think—I had a drink with the Princess and her Duke. Too bad Marcel couldn't have seen me; boy, would he have been proud! I was a little soppy, though, wasn't I, Momone? But from a distance I must have looked pretty fine sitting there next to her. . . ."

Cerdan's famous fight with Tony Zale was coming up. Marcel was training very conscientiously, and so were we. Edith took the training seriously, and when she took something seriously, you did absolutely nothing but that.

Marcel's manager, Lucien Roupp, was being a pain in the ass. "You love your champion, so don't sleep with him too often. Making love slows a guy down, and Zale's fast on his feet." Lucien was nice, but he wouldn't let up on his Marcel. His advice rained down on us like a thundershower:

"Watch his diet when he eats at your place. Above all, don't keep him up at night; he's got to sleep ten hours, like a baby."

When Marcel was in Paris, we had an odd sort of life. He went to bed with the chickens. Edith, who was working, went to bed at four in the morning. I did too, but I got up before Marcel, around eight, to fix his fruit juice for him. Then bang! In two seconds he'd be on his feet in great shape. Still half asleep, out I'd go in a blue "French team" sweatshirt just like his, following behind him as he did his jogging. It must have been quite a sight to see me galloping after the champ.

At home the fever was rising. Edith, who didn't know anything about sports and cared less, asked everybody what they knew about boxing. If they answered, "Nothing," she'd complain, "I don't understand why some people aren't interested in boxing. You must really have no curiosity at all to be like that. People should know everything in life. Really, that's true! Some people don't give a damn about anything."

Of someone else she'd ask, "Tell me, what are Marcel's chances?" As long as he told her lots of stuff in Marcel's favor, she was pleased. Any fan of Cerdan's could ask Edith for anything and get it. Some of them did. I won't mention any names—there were too many. But Edith was radiant and bubbled with laughter.

Very patiently, Edith spent a lot of time on the rue Leconte de Lisle waiting for Marcel, who divided his time between Casablanca, Paris and his training camp. This probably was the time in her life when she knitted the most. She made sweaters for her boxer that were so ghastly you wouldn't believe it. She knitted well, but she chose colors she liked—gay ones, so loud they made you feel like howling with laughter. So Marcel wore them as sweatshirts while he was training. And with his extraordinary kindness, he'd say to her:

"Edith dear, if I fight well, it'll be because of your sweaters. I've never had such warm ones or such big ones." I could see a twinkle in Marcel's eye, but Edith was so happy! She'd beam, grab her needles and her yarn, and knit for all she was worth!

No one can possibly know how thoughtful the man was. He didn't have an education and nobody had ever taught him anything, but he always knew what to do so as not to hurt anyone. He was unfailingly tactful. I never heard him boast. Everything he did he did simply, and he never told you what he was up to, either before or after, so as not to put himself in a good light.

Marcel's world was no more saintly than ours. It was just as rotten—just as full of shady deals, cruddy knifings in the back and sordid foul schemes whose only aim was to pass dough from hand to hand. Yet Marcel had made his way through this world without dirtying himself. Not because he didn't know what was going on— he saw everything. He'd say to Edith when she got irritated, "Don't pay any attention to those guys, they're so petty. You mustn't waste your strength crushing weaklings."

"I didn't discover the real Marcel in bed," Edith told me, "but in the street one day when I met an Arab childhood friend whom Marcel was holding by the arm because he was three-quarters blind. He took him to an oculist every morning and saw to it that he got proper care. He was a boxer from Casa, down on his luck. Marcel sent for him and paid for everything—his hotel, his trip, his medical expenses, everything.

"You know how jealous I am. I'd noticed that Marcel often left me by myself. He'd look at his watch and say, 'I'll be back in an hour. I have to meet someone.' Finally I got fed up; I wanted to know where he went. When I said I met him, I lied. I'd shad-owed him. Marcel saw me in the street (by chance, he thought—I wouldn't have dared admit I was following him), and told me the whole story. He'd hidden it even from me, but he hadn't lied—he really did meet someone. In addition to seeing that his pal got cared for, he'd go over to see him so he didn't feel lonely. I know how long days in the dark are! I was so happy I cried. I didn't think a man like that existed. And when I think there are damn fools who say, 'Boxers are all brutes,' I'd like to have Marcel's fists so I could smack them in the kisser."

I loved Marcel too, in a different way perhaps, but just as much. He was my friend. I didn't have any pocket money. Edith didn't want me to. She was quite willing to pay for everything for me, but she didn't give me a cent. I never had twenty cents of my own, and was treated like a little kid. "You do some pretty damn foolish things when you have dough," Edith would say. "You don't need anything as long as I'm around. Money just slips through your fingers." She was one to talk—she who never had any idea what she did with her own. But although she couldn't save any money for herself, she made deposits in a savings account for me.

I didn't even have enough to buy myself a newspaper or a pack of cigarettes or a drink. So Marcel took pity on me and slipped me a little cash. Not a lot, but often. He'd found a way to do it. "Don't you have any cigarettes, Momone?" he'd ask. If I said I didn't, he'd give me what I needed.

As luck would have it, Edith had a contract for seven thousand dollars a week at the Versailles in New York at the same time Cerdan was fighting there. Marcel had to leave before she did to go into training. Edith would have gladly tagged along after him, but Lucien Roupp didn't want her to. "Don't be silly. You can't arrive together. There'd be stories in all the newspapers," he said.

Loulou Barrier agreed. "It's not good for you. As far as the Americans are concerned, Marcel is married—and not to you. You two can have such a romantic love life that all the secretaries in the skyscrapers weep, but you can't get off the plane together like a married couple."

"O.K.," said Edith. And that very night she asked me to go with Marcel to keep an eye on him.

"I'm turning him over to you, Momone. Take good care of him. He can't do anything by himself. This terrifying boxer's just a kid."

"I've traveled by myself before, Edith, I assure you," Marcel objected.

"Leave it to me. Who's going to put away your shirts and socks and suits? I don't want any woman, even a hotel maid, touching your things." So I went with Marcel, got him settled in his hotel room and went back to Paris to get Edith.

Naturally, when we arrived in New York three days later, Lucien Roupp jumped on us. "I'm counting on you, Edith. This is the fight of Marcel's life. He can't flub it."

"Nobody knows I'm here. My contract doesn't start for ten days yet. I came to see Marcel and I'm going to see him."

"Don't start getting irritated. It's all arranged," Roupp told her. "Marcel's about a hundred miles from New York, near the training camp at Loch Sheldrake. He's stopped off at the Hotel Evans before going there, and I've found you a little boardinghouse close by."

"Why not the same hotel?"

"Come on, Edith, you know what America's like. A man and a woman can't sleep in the same room if they're not married. You'd ruin Marcel's career doing stuff like that. You'll stay in the boardinghouse for two days, and while Marcel's in the training camp you'll come back to New York and wait for him quietly."

"Well, if you've arranged things that way, it's O.K. with me," Edith said with a false ring to her voice. We took off as if we were in the race at Le Mans—we didn't want anybody to recognize Edith. This time we had an adventure that was almost too much to be believed.

When Lucien said, "I've arranged this" or "I've organized that," there wasn't a word of truth in it. It was Marcel who wanted things that way, and the first thing he did was to find us a boardinghouse close to where he was staying. Lucien was to serve as a messenger, shuttling back and forth between us.

He got us settled in the boardinghouse, where everybody thought we were two sisters traveling together. While we were unpacking our bags the dinner gong rang, and we rushed downstairs. It was the first time in her life Edith had ever been on time for dinner. It amused her; she'd never been in a place like that before, and neither had I. Fleabag hotels or luxury hotels, yes, but

never a boardinghouse. When we got to the table we were introduced to the others; nobody knew anybody else, so there was no
sociability. Edith didn't touch a thing all during dinner, but quietly
slipped everything onto my plate, forcing me to eat her food and
mine as well, apparently so as not to hurt the landlady's feelings.

"Be polite, Momone. We're in a foreign country." This was
rich, coming from Edith, who never gave a damn about anything.

Finally dinner was over. Finished. But no, it wasn't! Horrors!
It was the birthday of one of the landlady's little boys, and since
we were all one big family, they brought out a monstrous, hundred
percent American birthday cake. It was made of whipped cream,
coconut, chocolate, currants, almonds, peanut butter, maple syrup
and sponge cake; I'd never dreamed you could put all that in one
cake. It was huge, so big I looked around and counted the other
boarders. I was so busy counting I didn't see a serving plop onto
my plate and run all down the sides. It was ghastly! I looked at
Edith's plate and discovered she'd been served just as much. I said
to myself, "She can't possibly expect me to eat both of them!" But
by God, she did.

"Momone, take it away. It makes me nauseous. And eat it; it's
a birthday cake and we can't be rude."

Rude or not, that night I thought I'd croak. Every time I closed
my eyes I could see the monster cake and was sick to my stomach!

Edith horsed around as much as she could, and sang "Happy
Birthday" to me. . . .

With some difficulty, Lucien and Marcel had shaken the reporters and found a place to meet Edith. As soon as Marcel saw the
expression on her face, he realized she wouldn't stay around. Happy
as she was to see him, she couldn't help making a scene.

When Edith, too sweet to be true, asked, "Where is our room?"
Lucien answered, "It wouldn't do, you know that. Training,
discipline . . ."

Edith cut in. "Listen, you! I'm getting sick to death of you.
When we ring for you, you can start acting like a big shot, but not
before. You're not my husband or my lover; you're not even my
impresario. So shut up, and fast! I'm not going to hurt your cham-

pion; but a bed—our bed—is our own damn business. Now get out! We've had enough of you."

And old Lucien, not at all pleased, kept his mouth shut.

In a very gentle voice Marcel explained to Edith how important training was and how one had to respect the rules of another country when it came to sports. Since she adored him, she quieted down.

"All right, if you think we have to, Marcel, if it's for your own good. But I couldn't bear to stay without seeing you."

"Just trust me, Edith. I'll fix the whole thing by tonight."

That shy boy, so respectful of rules and regulations, suddenly got carried away and engineered an outrageous and dangerous scheme. He decided to sneak us into his training camp, in spite of the fact that it broke every rule in the book. He was not supposed to see anyone but his trainer and his sparring partner. If anybody had found out that Marcel Cerdan had hidden two women in the camp, he'd have been disqualified immediately. The scandal would have ruined his career.

The next morning we said good-bye to the birthday-cake baker and left in a taxi. It was just like in the movies. The driver was rather amazed when we asked him to leave us along the edge of the road near an intersection. Being curious, he asked, "You walking back to the city or hitchhiking?"

We answered him in our halting English. "Yes, Buffalo Bill comes back with his horse." He got a good laugh out of it. A few minutes later, Marcel arrived alone, without Lucien. It couldn't have been easy to shake him. Marcel drove down a little road, put us both in the trunk of the car and locked it. "If anybody asks me to open the trunk, I'll say I've lost the key and am going to go look for it." Luckily, American cars have trunks as big as ship holds.

At the Loch Sheldrake camp each boxer had his own bungalow. Marcel had spotted an empty one, quite a distance from the others, and that's where he let us out. Still, if you think about it, it took real nerve to pull off a stunt like that. We were at the mercy of any guy who might decide to do some cleaning or fix the plumbing. We were all crazy.

"You understand, Edith, it seems that making love is very bad for boxers in training," Marcel explained with a laugh. "It weakens their legs and ruins their wind and everything else they've got." He proved exactly the opposite! He spent all his nights with Edith, and he'd never been in such good shape for a fight.

So there we were, Edith and I, settled down in the bungalow. Since no one knew it was going to be occupied, there wasn't anything to eat and no hot water. We waited till evening to eat: Marcel would bring us sandwiches he'd hidden in his jacket. And since lovemaking works up an appetite, he'd gobble down some of them during the night, and the next day we'd starve. All we had to drink was tap water. Luckily they hadn't shut it off. Every time she took a drink of it, Edith was moved. "See how much I love Marcel? I couldn't possibly drink this stuff otherwise. I'm sure it's going to be the end of me."

Then she'd get dramatic.

"There are millions of microbes and crap in it. Did you ever see a drop of water under a microscope?"

"No, have you?"

"No, but I know it's true. The guy who told me that was an army medic on his way home from the colonies. So you see."

"But this isn't the colonies. It's America!"

"That makes it even worse. They dump so much disinfectant in it, it eats out the lining of your stomach. See where love leads you—to suicide!" And we laughed, but not too loudly. Someone might have heard us.

This water cure was hard on Edith, who had always been a drinker. Some days she drank more than others, but she drank every day. She didn't get drunk enough to pass out on the floor, because she could hold her liquor. But still, she'd always get a little high. Drinking water may indeed have been the greatest proof of her love that Edith ever gave a man.

We lived in the dark most of the time. During the day the blinds had to be closed; at night we couldn't turn on the lights. We went to bed at sundown, and we couldn't talk loudly. It was an impossible way to live.

In the evening Marcel would arrive, beaming and in a good

mood. Once or twice he managed to get some beer. The other times he brought us milk. That made Edith laugh. "You think we're calves!" He'd take her in his arms and waltz with her—he loved that—her feet dangling in the air, while she hummed, "Happy with everything, happy with nothing, as long as you're here. . . ."

She may have had good reason for singing, but I didn't have Marcel in my bed and I was fed up with our "vacation" at the camp. Two days of living like cloistered nuns was quite enough for me. I couldn't stand it any more.

Edith was happy at night, but how she complained in the day-time! We all got our reward at the end of two weeks though. For Marcel, the world championship; and for us, freedom!

Marcel sneaked us out of the camp the way he'd got us in—in the trunk of the car. This was Edith's "official" arrival in the city. The Americans never understood how she got to New York with-out coming through La Guardia Airport.

When we got to the city we found two furnished apartments, one above the other. It was practical and kept up appearances. Marcel was watched very closely by the Boxing Commission, which didn't kid around. They called it "protecting" him. The hotel swarmed with cops looking like Al Capone–style gangsters in movies made during Prohibition.

We finally got frightened though. Marcel had received threaten-ing letters and phone calls, like: "No use training; you'll never even get in the ring," or "We'll get you before you can touch Tony." Marcel just laughed. Lucien was nervous, Edith even more so. "They're all gangsters here. You're not in Paris. Be careful, Marcel."

Edith readily imagined someone poisoning Marcel. She solved the problem by making me the guinea pig. She'd order a steak and say to me, "Eat half of it, Momone." The other half was for Marcel. She did the same with fruits and vegetables. "Here, cut this pear in two and eat half," she'd say, and Marcel would eat the other half. This went on till the day of the fight. I wouldn't have done it for any of the other guys she'd had. Not for a single one of them, I swear. But Marcel was different.

A world championship in New York is something that has to be seen to be believed. It draws millions of people of all kinds—big shots, small fry—and oceans of dollars.

It wasn't long before the sportswriters began attacking Edith. "Marcel isn't leading the ascetic life of a champion. He'll pay for it." "The title's not in his pocket yet." "His love affair is interfering with his training." Edith was worried. She was afraid it would be her fault if he lost. She prayed to Saint Theresa of the Infant Jesus and made vows. She didn't tell me what they were; that way she could change them later. She was in a terrible state. She was starting to panic, and so was I. Edith had unearthed a church with a statue of Saint Theresa, and we lit more candles to her in one day than she usually got in a year.

We didn't see much of Marcel the night before the fight or on the big day itself. We couldn't—he was being watched too closely. Lucien stuck with his boxer every minute of the day and night. The tension had mounted so high, no one could have stood it for very long. These Americans weren't so kindhearted or easy to deal with.

On September 21, 1948, without any fanfare, Marcel drove us to Madison Square Garden, where the fight was being held, while Tony Zale made a spectacular entrance with flashbulbs, cheers and the shouts of the crowd. The Yanks were in high spirits! The guy in the parking lot said, "It's not worth parking your car. The fight with that Frenchman won't last long. It'll be over in a couple of minutes." He hadn't recognized Marcel, who calmly turned to Edith and said, "See, I'll be home early." Then he kissed her and walked away from us with his usual unhurried stride, his broad back filling the door of the locker room. Lucien showed us to our seats.

It was stifling in the Garden. Boxing arenas are pretty cruddy places. Even though the fight takes place up above you in the ring, like a stage in a theater, they don't care much about the spectators' comfort. Sports fans are tough; they're thick-skinned. But I'm not.

The two champions entered the ring, and the crowd shouted and whistled; in fact, they yelled and stamped their feet so hard the seats trembled. Edith's little round face was pale white and puffy with anxiety. She took hold of my hand, the way she did when things got serious. I tried to put a good face on, but I didn't look any better than she did.

I can still hear the bell clanging in my head, in my whole body, the way it did that night. And then there were the things people around us were saying. They were all boxing experts, of course. Luckily we didn't understand much of what was going on or we wouldn't have been able to stand it. There were dames in fur coats with their men in tuxedos. And hordes of guys with hats rammed on their heads, smoking cigars that stank, sucking on butts, chewing gum and spitting all over the place. There sure was plenty of atmosphere. All this suddenly disappeared in the smoke and the darkness as the big white spotlights lit up the ring like an operating table.

"I'm going to close my eyes, Momone. Tell me when it's over." But she didn't close them for a second. Every time Tony landed a punch on Marcel, her fingernails dug into my skin. I couldn't feel a thing! It was as hard on me as it was on her. At the end of the first round we could see Marcel suck in his belly, making his chest swell. It was impressive.

"You think he's winded?"

"No, of course not. He's getting his strength back."

"He's saving his energy," said a guy who understood French.

The second and third rounds were over, and in the fourth Tony Zale turned nasty. At that point Edith went out of her mind. Tony practically sent Marcel sailing, and the Americans were delirious. Edith called on Saint Theresa for help, yelled insults at Tony, stamped her feet on the floor, and pounded her fists on the hat of the guy sitting in front of her. Apparently nobody sitting around a boxing ring is normal. The guy didn't even feel it; he didn't say a word.

The bell rang. Zale was on the ropes, and Marcel started to his corner. In the middle of the ring he turned around and stood there tall and straight. Zale was slowly collapsing, like a melting candle. Then Marcel went over to his trainers, looking green. The referee came over and led him to the middle of the ring. He raised Marcel's arm and shouted, "Ladies and gentlemen, Marcel Cerdan, the new world champion!"

A thing like that hits you right in the gut! French flags were raised on the flagpoles and the band struck up the "Marseillaise." Everybody was standing. Edith was deathly pale and didn't say a word. She was holding my hand, and hers felt soft as wax in mine. I looked at her. We were alone among all those Americans standing there around us, laughing and shouting. Many of them had recognized her, and besides, we were French. They turned out to be good sports with a sense of fair play. They lifted us up in their arms, bellowing, "French girls! French girls!" We couldn't understand the rest—it was too noisy. We were so drunk with emotion and so exhausted we didn't know where we were any more. In fact, Edith was so worn out she felt like she'd won the world championship herself! A tiny part of Marcel's victory *was* hers. Once in a while I thought to myself, "Poor Marinette. She's the one who ought to be here, not Edith." But as one of Edith's songs went, "*C'est la vie!*" This was no time to think about that.

The guy whose hat Edith had squashed made her laugh when he gave it to her. "Here," he said. "It's no use to me any more, but what a souvenir for you!" We couldn't get to the locker room to find Marcel. It was worse than the subway at rush hour, and Edith had to go on at the Versailles. When she came onstage, the audience gave her a standing ovation. She wiped away the big tears in her eyes and said, "Forgive me, I'm just too happy!"

During her act a burst of bravos suddenly broke out. It was Marcel coming in. He was very embarrassed, and sat down quietly at one of the tables. When we joined him, he had a drink with us. Everybody in the audience at the Versailles would have liked to be in our shoes. We were very proud. He was *our* champion. That was all Marcel did the night of his championship. Hundreds of people would have given anything that night to have had him at their table. People everywhere went mad just at the sound of his name.

And after saying no to everybody's invitations, he went peacefully home through the streets of New York, holding Edith's little hand in his—the hand that had just knocked out a champion. It was like another honeymoon for them. They had never loved each other so much.

Marcel had to return to France, where they were clamoring for him to fight. Edith finished her contract and they went back to living the way they had before. They often had to go their separate ways. When Marcel was in Casablanca, Edith had worked out a scheme for keeping in touch that was effective, but expensive and tiring. She'd write a letter to Marcel and I'd take a plane and deliver it to him. He'd answer it and I'd take his letter back to Edith. I did it a good three times a week and was the best-known passenger on the airline.

"I don't want any strangers touching our letters," said Edith. "Anyway, I don't trust the mail. Post office employees are no different from anybody else—they might steal my letters."

Life with Edith was pretty tiring. She wore out everybody who lived with her. She not only dreamed up schemes like the one that kept me traveling, but she also had no set hours for anything, not even sleeping. When she decided she was sleepy, I had to put her to bed, tuck her in and give her her ear plugs and a black mask for her eyes. She couldn't stand the least little ray of light. Only then would she finally say to me, "Go to bed, Momone." And when she woke up, I had to be awake before she was, before I even knew she'd opened her eyes.

If she decided she didn't want to sleep, I had to stay up with her. Once when she was exhausted and her nerves were shot, a doctor pal of hers gave her some sleeping pills, a dose strong enough to knock a horse out for forty-eight hours. But she kept dashing around having a good time and making damn fools of us. So he gave her an injection. She shut her eyes and we put her to bed, stealing out of the room on tiptoe. Ten minutes later we were all sleeping like babies, when suddenly a terrifying voice woke us up.

"What the hell are you all doing, sleeping like that? Poor saps. Come on, Momone, let's make coffee for this pack of idiots." It was six in the morning!

While Marcel had been training for his championship bout, Edith got all excited about the fight. She wanted him to be better than the other guy. Out of love for him, she agreed not to stay up all night and to lead a more regular life. But it was against her nature—she'd always done her living at night. When Marcel wasn't there she returned to her old habits, and when he came back she dragged him out with her. "Marcel, you're not going to bed! You're not going to leave me. How can I have a good time without you? I see you so seldom. Take advantage of it while you're here. You owe me all your time—it's all mine. You're in great shape— you've proved it. Do your training when you're not with me."

Once she even said, "You make me unhappy. This is no life, the one we're leading. I never see you, and when I do you desert me."

Marcel was mad for her, so he gave in. Some people began to say that Marcel was turning into a playboy boxer, and that La Motta, who was going to fight him for the title, might well give our champion a lesson. Lucien kept falling into terrible rages. But what the hell! Marcel and Edith were living their love and couldn't care less about anything else.

One night Edith flirted with destiny. Marcel was in Paris, where he'd finally begun training in earnest for his fight with La Motta, which was to take place soon in New York. Edith had become almost reasonable again. The barometer read "fair" around the house. The date for his leaving had been set, and Marcel had said good-bye to all his friends, also our friends— M. and Mme Lévitan, Mme Breton and her husband, and the others we ran around with.

We were still living on the rue Leconte de Lisle. The back of the dining room was lit up by a huge, luminous aquarium that took up most of the wall. Edith's decorator had told her it was the chic thing to have. On the other side of the aquarium was a hall. The night Marcel was leaving, Edith invited to dinner everybody he'd said good-bye to the night before. She was in a very good mood and had thought of a trick to amuse her guests—a thing she adored doing.

The dinner was very gay. Mme Breton spoke of Marcel and of seeing in the evening papers pictures of him leaving for New York. "Marcel must just be arriving at La Guardia. He'd be having a better time with us."

"Well, I'm going to knock three times and produce Marcel for you," said Edith. "Look behind the aquarium." The smartest guests thought, "We're going to see a photograph of Cerdan." Edith ceremoniously knocked three times and Marcel himself appeared behind the aquarium. It was very effective. I started to shiver. In the pale green light, with the soft seaweed and the fish swimming in front of Marcel's face, he looked like a drowned man.

Two months later he was dead.

He left the morning after Edith's party. La Motta beat him and Marcel lost his title. When he came back, he wasn't quite himself. He was obviously asking himself questions. He was a conscientious boxer and knew that champagne and sleepless nights weren't the right recipe for winning in the ring.

The next morning didn't help things any. There was a big headline in one of the papers, reading: EDITH PIAF HAS BROUGHT BAD LUCK TO CERDAN. That wasn't the only article; there were also others openly accusing Edith. Marcel, always sweet, consoled her.

"Don't listen to them. It's true I wasn't in good condition, but that can happen to anyone. I'm going to get my revenge and we'll do everything necessary to beat La Motta, won't we, Edith?" It was just like Marcel to reassure her instead of bawling her out, as anybody else would have done.

"It's not Edith's fault, you see," he explained to me. "It's my own. I should have been better than the other guy." Wasn't it beautiful of him to say that?

Marcel's defeat had annoyed Edith. "I don't like this house any more; it's bad luck," she decided. She was very superstitious, and had her own peculiar beliefs about what was lucky and what was unlucky. Thursday brought her good luck. Sunday, bad luck. When she saw a flock of sheep, she'd say, "That's a sign of money. Close your fists to hang onto it!" Not much use in her case, I must say!

That's how we found ourselves in Boulogne, at 5 rue Gambetta, in a town house Edith paid nineteen million francs for. She didn't care how much it cost since the living room was big enough to be made into a gym for Marcel to train in. It was the one and only reason she bought it. "He'll train here at home and won't leave me." So we camped out in the house in the midst of all the workers. The decorator promised to finish up the job while we were in the U.S.

America had adopted Edith. She was to appear again at the Versailles during the month of October 1949. She left by herself and I stayed behind with Marcel, who was on tour all over France, giving exhibition bouts for boxers down on their luck. I followed him around; it was my job to keep track of him. "I'm counting on you, Momone," Edith had said. "Take care of him. I know he's not much of a skirt-chaser, but all men are sometimes. So keep tabs on him." It wasn't a very tough job in Marcel's case. They didn't come any better behaved.

Once the tour was over, we were to meet Edith in New York. The date we would leave was already set. We were to go by ship. Edith herself took planes the way she took taxis, but she was always afraid when other people traveled by air.

Twenty-four hours before Marcel was to leave, she phoned. "Darling, please come right away; I can't wait another minute to see you. Take a plane—a boat takes too long. Hurry."

"Fine," replied Marcel. "I'll be there tomorrow. Here's a kiss for you. I love you."

Those were his last words to her.

Why did Edith want Marcel to come on that particular day? I never knew. Was she bored? Was she afraid she'd do something silly? Afraid she'd cheat on him? Anything was possible with Edith.

I had two problems: finding two seats on a plane and getting my visa for the United States renewed because it had run out. I'd asked to have it renewed but they were slow about it and I didn't get it right away. It was that missing stamp on my passport that saved my life. Marcel and I went to so much trouble we finally scared up a seat for him. I went with him to the airport and said, "Good-bye; see you soon."

And then it was all over. When I woke up the next morning all the papers were full of Marcel Cerdan's death. They'd been able to identify him because he was wearing a watch on each wrist. I finally got my visa and left immediately. Edith needed me. When I landed in New York, M. and Mme Breton were waiting for me. They were very nice, and they were the ones who told me what had happened.

Loulou Barrier was in New York and never left Edith. It had been decided he'd be the one to pick Marcel up at the airport because the plane would arrive too early in the morning for her to go. It was October 28, 1949. When he got to the airport, Loulou found out that the plane from Paris to New York had crashed in the Azores and that Marcel was on the list of those who had been killed.

When Edith saw Loulou come back alone, she screamed, "Something's happened to Marcel! He's dead!" She'd expected Marcel to wake her up. No one had the right to do it but me or, in case I wasn't there, the man she loved. When she saw Loulou, she knew right away what had happened. Barrier couldn't speak. He couldn't get the words out. He looked at her, and his silence was the worst thing of all.

During the day telegrams began pouring in and people phoned from all over. Edith immediately cabled Jacques Bourgeat: WRITE ME RIGHT AWAY. NEED YOU. EDITH. And Jacquot, who was by then an old man, and not a very rich one, came. As for Mme Bigeard, she sent such a heartfelt telegram that Edith sent for her to come. Edith's sorrow shattered everybody. She couldn't see anything or hear anything. She cried constantly, not loudly, but without stop. When Loulou told her he had arranged everything so she wouldn't sing that night, she came to her senses and said, "I *am* singing to-night." She was so exhausted she had to take a stimulant. The Versailles was filled to the rafters. When she came on, looking tinier and more lost than ever in the spotlight, the whole audience got to their feet and applauded. And Edith said, "No, don't clap for me. The only person I'm singing for tonight is Marcel Cerdan."

She managed to hold up under the strain, looking pale and stricken, and she made it through to the end.

That night Loulou slept in her room. He didn't dare leave her by herself. When I arrived in the morning, she threw herself in my arms, shouting, "It's my fault, Momone. I killed him." It was unbearable.

Chapter 12

❧
❧ ❧

For Love, Edith Consults the Table

Edith thought it was her fault that Marcel had died such a terrible death. He had become the greatest love of her life—the only one. And it may be that because he died he *remained* her only love and wasn't returned to the ranks like all the others.

My poor Edith was in a frightful state. She wouldn't eat and went on a sort of hunger strike. She really wanted to die. She had to be drugged every night to be able to sing. She was like a crazed animal that had lost its master and was trying to find him again. In her sorrow and despair, the idea of table-tapping came to her. Marcel had been dead barely two days when Edith said:

"Listen, Momone, you've got to go get me a round table with three feet. We're going to use it to try and make contact with Marcel. I know he'll come. He's sure to hear me. Hurry."

So I went to a department store on Lexington Avenue, where I found a pedestal table on three feet. As I left the store I hugged it to my bosom, feeling it would be my salvation. I didn't know just how, but I was sure of it.

That night after the show at the Versailles, we came right home. The curtains were pulled shut, we turned out the lights and we put our hands on the table. We waited all night. Edith broke the silence suddenly by saying, "It's creaking, Momone; he's here. I can feel it. He's walking close by me."

But nothing happened. The feet of the table stuck to the floor as if glued there. We could tell dawn was breaking behind the curtains; it was getting lighter outside.

"You know, Edith, spirits never come in the daylight," I said.

"Really? But they do come at night, don't they?" Her voice was like a child's.

"Sure. It's been proved scientifically."

"It isn't just a lot of bunk. I felt him tonight. He was there—he brushed by me. Why didn't he speak?"

"It takes time. Maybe it's too soon—maybe spirits can't talk right away. We'll try again tonight."

I told her whatever came into my head. Anyway, she was so tense, and she believed so firmly, that she'd made me believe in it too, and I kept thinking, "He has to come."

The next night nothing happened either. Edith's face was drawn and I was miserable. She wouldn't eat a thing, and yet she was singing every night. It couldn't go on or she'd break down. She'd already fainted once between songs. Alone in front of the table I thought, "It's got to work, I've got to make it work." Edith lived for the moment she put her hands on the table. That night I said to her, "Don't worry; Marcel's going to come tonight, I can feel it. There's a new moon."

"He's mad at me, Momone. I should never have phoned him. He won't come; he's abandoned me."

Then I got fed up. "She's sure to go mad and so am I. This damn table's got to move," I thought to myself. And I got it to lift up just slightly. Edith clung to it, weeping for joy. "Marcel, is that you? . . . Stay! Come back! Marcel, my love . . . oh, it's you, it's you!" she stammered. Suddenly I realized how I could use the table—first to get Edith to eat, and then to calm her down.

"Eat," the table ordered. Since Edith didn't catch on, the table repeated, "Go eat."

Edith was astonished. "You think Marcel wants me to eat?" she asked.

"Of course, and right away."

Edith dashed to the kitchen, opened the refrigerator and began to eat to please Marcel. I could have wept. I looked at her the way you look at a sick dog willing to drink a little milk. It really did the trick!

Two weeks later we went back to Paris with Mme Bigeard and the table. We had strange times the first few months in Boulogne. Edith was in solid with the spirit world, the beyond and all the rest of it. Her dreams and her intuitions kept her going.

As was to be expected, she'd decided to give up the house. She didn't like it there. Marcel hadn't spent much time in it, but even that had been too long. We were still living there. What else could we do? The place wasn't easy to sell. She told Loulou to get rid of it. Easy to say, but nobody wanted the thing. She finally sold it three years later at a loss of over nine million francs.

Edith couldn't bear to see or touch the presents Marcel had given her. She finally distributed them among all those who'd been there the night of the aquarium trick. She was sure her little joke had brought him bad luck. She didn't keep anything for herself. Everything went—the earrings, the pin, all the jewelry Marcel had given her, and the souvenirs of his fight with La Motta, including Cerdan's trunks with the blood of her champion still on them.

"Here, Momone," she said. "I'm giving you the thing that means the most to me—the dress I was wearing when Marcel held me in his arms right after winning the world championship." I still have it.

Edith had only one thought in her mind, the table. We spent every evening huddled over it. There was no stopping the thing. Besides, it was still useful for me. I used it to keep her from drinking too much. Marcel had always hated it when she drank. When she'd been drinking, the table refused to say anything. Not a word. It was no use her begging: the table was angry.

It wouldn't have been so bad if we'd only used it at night! But even during the daytime it preyed on Edith's mind. She trusted it, but she was suspicious of it too. When she talked to Jacques Bourgeat about it, all he ventured was, "The world's full of phenomena we don't know the causes of." That didn't get her very far, so she fell back on me.

"Do *you* believe in it?"

"I believe everything I see."

"Still, I need proof. . . . I know! I'll ask Marcel to write me a song."

I don't know if you can turn pale inside, but I'm sure my guts blanched! Unfortunately, it wasn't Marcel who was going to write the song—it was me.

"Marcel couldn't write a song, Edith, you know that."

She looked daggers at me, and answered in a determined tone of voice, "Where he is, he can do anything."

This time I couldn't get out of it; I was lost. I mulled over lots of words in my mind all day long, but nothing came to me. I was as dry as the bottom of a pan hanging on the wall. That same night Edith addressed the table: "Marcel, write me a song." And the table answered, "Yes." From the very beginning of our sessions the table had always had an answer. It had to know everything. To Edith's way of thinking, nothing was impossible "on the other side." But the trouble was, I was on *this* side! I had to admit, though, that Edith blindly obeyed every order the table gave her. Marcel couldn't possibly mislead her.

I clutched the table and came up with the first two lines of a song:

> *Je vais te faire une chanson bleue*
> *Pour que tu aies des rêves d'enfant.*

> I'm going to write you a blue song
> So that you'll have the dreams of a child.

Luckily for me, the table's feet didn't talk very fast. I'd invent one or two new verses every session, and one night the table announced, "The song's finished."

We saw Marguerite Monnot every day, but Edith was too impatient to wait. She phoned Marguerite on the spot. "Come right over, Guite; I've got something for you."

It was nearer dawn than midnight, but Marguerite, who never knew whether it was day or night, came over, her hair uncombed and a coat over her nightgown.

"Listen, Guite," Edith said to her. "Listen carefully." And she read *"La Chanson bleue"* to her, as only she could do, already half singing it.

"Did you write that?"

"No, Marcel did."

"But when?"

"He just finished it, with the table."

"Don't say that! You give me gooseflesh. Be quiet!"

Guite had always refused to attend our séances, though she knew about them. She sat down and murmured, "It'll have only violins." Violins to her were the music of the angels. Marguerite could already hear the song, and Edith could too. I was so touched, I couldn't contain myself. I was staggered, and wondered if what I was experiencing was of this world or another. After all, was I really the one who was responsible? But when I saw those two women living that moment together, I had no regrets. And this wasn't the last time *"La Chanson bleue"* was to make me cry.

Each week for over a year Edith had a mass sung in memory of Marcel in the church at Auteuil. We all attended, of course; there was no way of getting out of it, nor did I want to. The mass was always sung by Edith's choruses. One day, just before her recital at the Salle Pleyel, they began to sing *"La Chanson bleue"* just as the mass was ending. We weren't just shattered—the word's not strong enough. Guite and I couldn't even swallow for fear of bursting into sobs. Edith turned toward the chorus with big tears rolling down her cheeks. "Marcel, can you hear them? It's for you . . ." she murmured.

I wanted Edith to throw the table out after *"La Chanson bleue."* If I could make it work, other people could too, and they might be bastards enough to use it for their own purposes. It was too much of a temptation with Edith. Paris wasn't like New York: we were never by ourselves now. The house in Boulogne was like the rue Anatole de la Forge, except not quite as ugly. It was kind of chaotic, and it housed lots of people trying to take advantage of Edith. She asked anybody who happened to be stranded there to take part in our séances. When Edith liked something, all her "friends" had to share her enthusiasm and think the way she did.

Although the table spoke a lot and Marcel was with her every night, Edith still had the notion she owed Marcel something. "You see, Momone, Marcel wrote me a song, and I haven't done anything for him! I'm sure he's waiting. He's too good to come right out and ask me, but until I've done something for him, he'll never be at peace."

Nor would we!

And then it just happened. That evening in the bathroom, she hummed a melody. Edith was really something; she often sang off-key. Michel Emer used to say, "She and Maurice Chevalier are the only ones who can sing any way they want and still land on their feet." She had a musician's ear though, and knew what people would like.

"What do you think of my little melody? And I have the title for it: '*L'Hymne à l'amour.*' I'm the only one who can do this song. It keeps running through my head, making my heart dance. It's for Marcel. Too bad I've only got the title! I don't know how the rest goes—I'm uninspired. I don't have a clue. . . ."

"Listen, Edith, I've got an idea. I've thought up a few verses:

> *Si un jour, la vie t'arrache à moi,*
> *Si tu meurs, que tu sois loin de moi,*
> *Peu m'importe si tu m'aimes*
> *Car moi je mourrai aussi.*
> *Nous aurons pour nous l'éternité*
> *Dans le bleu de toute l'immensité*
> *Dans le cieu plus de problèmes*
> *Dieu réunit ceux qui s'aiment.*

> If life snatches you away from me one day,
> If you die and are far away,
> It won't matter, if you love me,
> For I'll die too.
> We'll have eternity together
> In the immensity of blue,
> In heaven we'll have no more troubles,
> God rejoins those who love each other.

"Do you like it?"

"You just made it up, like that?" answered Edith.

I said yes, but I was bluffing. The verses had been running through my head, but I hadn't known what to do with them and I couldn't get any further. Edith jumped up to get a pencil and some paper, and went on with the song.

Edith had good ideas; she dreamed up nice images, but that was nothing new. As early as her first letters to Jacques Bourgeat she'd written: "Well, au revoir, my adorable little ray of sunshine . . ." But she was impatient; she had to come up with something immediately. It bored her to think up a story line and work out the verses. I was patient, so I helped her. Edith had learned a lot. And I'd followed her lead. We weren't really cultured, but we weren't ignorant any more either. We were even acquainted with guys like Baudelaire!

After we had more or less whipped a song into shape, Edith would phone Guite any hour of the day or night. "Hello, Guite? It's Edith. I've got to see you right away."

Guite never said no. She had no more sense of what time it was than we did. We'd get half dressed and, since it was almost always just after she'd set her hair that Edith got ideas, she'd wrap a scarf around her head and we'd be off.

When we got to Marguerite's, Edith would read what she'd dreamed up. Guite listened, her hands already on the piano. And one of those haunting melodies would emerge, the kind only she could compose. The night she got the music for "*L'Hymne à l'amour*" from Guite, Edith leaned on the table and told Marcel, "I've written a song for you; you're the first to hear it." And she sang it to him. Even if you didn't believe in it, you couldn't help being impressed.

Then she said to him, "I'm going to give a recital at the Salle Pleyel. Since I want everything to come from you, I want you to tell me what order to sing my songs in." You have to be in the business to understand what a responsibility that is. The success of an act—especially in a recital hall—partly depends on the order of the songs, the way they set each other off. The hardest part is finding where the new songs belong, songs that nobody's ever heard before. And I'd never tried that.

I couldn't sleep. And during the day I drew up my list, tore it apart and put it together again. Then, in the evening, I changed it again according to Edith's reactions. "Not bad, Marcel, you're a genius. . . . You think that's right? I'm afraid you're dead wrong. Personally, I'd do it this way. . . . You agree! You see I'm right!"

Once the list was decided, she got it into her head that he had to tell her about the lighting and the curtains too. There wasn't a dry spot on me that night in January 1950—I, who never perspire. You had to be damn sure of yourself to give a recital at the Salle Pleyel. This was the first time anybody had dared sing street songs in that temple of classical music.

Loulou had been going around for two days saying, "Just imagine, kids, there's not even an aisle seat left!" Boys delivering flowers and telegrams kept running in and out of Edith's dressing room. I had some change for tips, but in no time it was all gone.

"I'm cleaned out, Edith," I said.

"Oh, well, give 'em bills."

So I gave out bills as if they were métro tickets, and for a minute there I think I missed the streets . . . and all the poverty.

I left the wings before Edith went on. I wanted to see her as the curtain rose. The hall was stuffed with people. Their breathing formed a huge current of warm air, and their conversation was like the sound of the sea—a deep, majestic roar.

The houselights went out and there was silence. The red velvet curtain went up. Behind it hung a backdrop of another autumn color, to cut the depth of the stage. It was still too big for Edith. She was so tiny, they were afraid she wouldn't be heard. But her voice was so powerful that, all at once, it filled that huge hall like a concert organ. She sang *"Une Chanson à trois temps,"* standing absolutely still, rooted to the spot, her legs a little apart, her hands behind her back. She was nothing but a voice. She sang *"Ses Mains," "Le Petit Homme," "J'm'en fous pas mal," "Escale," "Un Monsieur me suit dans la rue," "L'Hymne à l'amour," "L'Accordéoniste."* I knew them all, yet I felt I'd never heard them before. She went on like that for over two hours.

At intermission I slipped through the crowd, which was packed into the place like the métro at rush hour. I heard things like: "Marvelous!" "Sensational!" "Never heard anything like it!" "The greatest!" The words filled my ears and my head, and I dashed to Edith's dressing room to tell her. I dumped them out like a cartful of flowers, and I think I was sobbing. She laughed and looked at me as if we were having one of our bathroom sessions.

"Calm down, Momone. You're not the one singing!"

Mistinguett said to her, "When you sing your first song, they say, 'Ah!'; at the second, 'Oh!'; by the third, they're very tempted to leave; by the fourth, they're in tears; and then you get to the twentieth without anyone noticing!" That meant something, coming from the great "Miss."

When the dressing room was empty, Edith looked at me and said, "You know, I've never had a triumph like this! But Marcel isn't here with me. Tonight only the table will talk to me of love." At that point I really burst into tears. I couldn't help it.

Singing was Edith's life; she gave it all she had, but it made her lonelier than anybody, with the kind of solitude known only to her race—the "monsters," the great performers—a loneliness that grabs you by the throat like a hand or attacks you right in the stomach, that you don't feel until the applause has died down.

"Momone, the audience is warm sitting out there in its dark hole. They gather you into their arms, they open their hearts to you, take you right inside. You're overflowing with their love, and they're overflowing with yours. They want you; you give yourself to them. You sing, you shout, you bellow your pleasure, you 'come' in your heart. Then the lights go out as the theater echoes with the sound of their footsteps as they leave. You're still warm in your dressing room. They're still in you. You're not quivering any more, but you're satisfied. Then you go out in the streets. . . . It's dark . . . your heart is suddenly chilled . . . you're alone.

"The ones waiting for you at the stage door aren't like the ones inside. They stretch out their hands—not to caress you now, but to grab you. Their eyes judge you. You can read what they say: 'Well, she isn't as good looking as she is onstage!' And their smiles have a bite. . . . Performers and their public should never meet.

Once the curtain comes down, the performer should fly away like a magician's dove."

I felt it too. The crowd clamored for her, cheering her. Then when we turned a corner and climbed into a taxi, Edith would take my hand. "Now we're going to have to spend the rest of the night all by ourselves." It was true. We'd go home alone and have dinner together, just the two of us. Things didn't always happen that way, but ever since Marcel had died, we'd had painful moments in Boulogne, times when nothing happened, empty stretches everyone knew about because it wasn't much fun at Piaf's any more. After the initial curiosity was over and the table tapping—which had amused some people and profited others—we often sat there like a couple of poor jerks in our fine town house.

I wasn't responsible for the last big message we'd got from the table: "A piece of news on February 28."

"Good news?" Edith asked.

"Yes."

That was as far as we went that evening. The next day the table started again: "A surprise on February 28."

"You already said that, Marcel."

"February 28."

"I've got the message. What else?"

Edith sat there huddled over the table, yelling at it, begging it. But it was no use: it was made of wood. February 28 was four months to the day since Marcel had died. Who was using the table at these séances? Who was taking advantage of this date and why? I found out later. It was Mme Bigeard, and she turned out to be right.

On the night of the twenty-seventh I couldn't sleep. I wanted to be the first to know so as to protect Edith. Somebody rang the doorbell at eight in the morning—a boy delivering a telegram. I opened it, as I usually did, because telegrams scared Edith and she'd never touch them except on opening nights.

COME. AM WAITING FOR YOU. MARINETTE. Was that what was supposed to happen on February 28? For months Edith had been wanting to see Marinette, to meet Cerdan's sons. She was sure it was impossible. Now Marcel's wife was asking her to come. I woke her up then and there and read her the telegram. I didn't even know if she was in any shape to understand it. But they were magic words. Edith leaped out of bed. Coats, toothbrushes, into the plane, and we were off to Casablanca.

Marinette welcomed us warmly. The two of them cried and kissed each other. The man who had separated them now brought them together. Twenty-four hours later, the three boys—Marcel, René and Paul—were calling her Aunt Zizi.

We brought Marinette, her sister Hélène and the three kids back to Boulogne with us. There was room for all of them. Marinette stayed with us for a while. I thought the way they'd got together was odd, but I wasn't all that astonished. I was used to things like that with Edith. She never behaved like other people. She followed wherever her heart led her. It gave the orders and she obeyed. Edith spent her whole life following it.

She wanted Marinette to be more beautiful than anyone. She had a very pretty dress made for her at Jacques Fath's and gave her a white fox cape to wear with it. Edith was happy. "See how beautiful she is, Momone."

It was true. But it was one of the few times I ever saw her indulgent toward another woman.

"Boy, Marcel must really be happy, Momone! I'm going to ask him tonight. . . ."

Marinette never dared attend our séances, and Edith preferred not to ask her to. She was keeping her Marcel all to herself.

We hauled that damn table around for three years. It had got rickety from tapping out so many messages. I don't know how many times we glued it together. We'd had a slipcover made for it, and of all our luggage, it was the first thing we took with us. In theaters Edith used to keep it handy in her dressing room. She'd even take it into the wings sometimes, especially on opening nights. It had turned into a good-luck charm. When Edith knocked on wood, it was always that table she touched.

Edith had believed in miracles since she was a little girl. She was right. To the very end, her life was nothing but a miracle. She loved stories with happy endings. She had the soul of a child, and when you told her a story, she'd open her eyes, cross her hands in her lap and listen to it, delighted. She'd say, "It can't be true! There's no such thing—but it's beautiful!"

The table was something like that. It was nice to have Marcel there every night, to ask him questions. She ended up only half believing in it, but she couldn't do without it. Almost every night for three years, whenever I was around, Edith never went to bed without hearing the words Marcel whispered to her. And that's what Edith meant by a miracle!

But then one day the table gave out on Edith. Marcel had really gone over to "the other side." He'd said to her, "Tonight's the last time. Maybe later . . ."

I didn't like Boulogne. We weren't comfortable there—not because there wasn't enough room: there was too much—even though we'd fallen in love with the house in the beginning and Edith had been happy when she bought it. She'd said:

"Just think, Momone! A Directoire-style house! Even the paving stones are antiques! And we have stables! What's more, it's the first time we're in our own place. It belongs to *me*. I can even blow it to hell if I want to! I'm not a bum any more. I've got a place to live, just like any bourgeois landowner!"

Her decorator had probably satisfied his own taste for luxury. The bedroom was princely, with walls covered in lavender-blue moiré and Directoire-style furniture in cherry wood. Quite simple —that's how Edith and I imagined the Château de Bagatelle in the Bois de Boulogne!

As a matter of fact, Edith guided people through *her* château as if she were conducting a tour. "My room is in silk moiré," she'd say, opening the door. "Beautiful, isn't it?" But her pride and joy was the bathroom, all done in pink and black mosaic. And there were two steps leading down to the tub.

"I don't give a damn about it for myself—I never take baths. But I've bought my goldfish a real swimming pool!" That's really what she'd done—put goldfish in it. She thought they looked nice against the black tile. Not for long though, because she decided that fish inside a house brought bad luck.

Edith's efforts went no further than the bedroom, the bathroom and the kitchen. The decorator had stopped, for lack of cash, while we were away. When we got back, Edith didn't feel up to going on with that or anything else. So in the great living room that was meant to be Marcel's gym there was nothing but a grand piano and two canvas lounge chairs.

The living room opened onto a dining room that was all in marble and unfurnished. It was so big you needed roller skates to get around in it. That was Edith's idea and she meant it.

"Listen, instead of these bourgeois felt pads people slide around on so they won't scratch their waxed floors, what if we gave our guests roller skates at the front door?" It was the sort of thing she might have done just to see the look on people's faces.

So her pals could have a place to sleep, Edith had bought studio couches at Lévitan's and put them around everywhere. And there were the concierge's quarters as you entered, which Edith had furnished very nicely, with a combination couch and bookcase, a table and armchairs. "Since I've become a homeowner, I need someone to let me in. That way I won't need keys. And I want the concierge to be comfortable," Edith had said. Luckily we never found one, because Edith took to living there. She felt at home. The bedroom with its quilted walls and the black and pink bathroom were for show. And for a long time the séance table occupied a choice place among the cheap walnut furniture in the concierge's quarters.

We didn't have a thing. No tableware, no glasses, no silver—just a few plates, some odd knives, forks and spoons, and mustard jars for glasses. We didn't give a damn. We ate family style in the kitchen, under the watchful eye of Chang, who was still with us and hid out in the pantry to have some peace. Much later, when Edith decided to entertain lots of people, she'd rent everything, from chairs to flunkies.

The bathroom continued to be our living room. I don't know whether or not it was the influence of the table, but Edith began to believe in reincarnation, so while I handed her bobby pins to set her hair, she'd talk about her previous life. This was Jacques Bourgeat's doing. That man knew all about everything. Whenever Edith wanted to know something, she'd phone him. This time she'd asked him, "Listen, Jacquot, do you believe in reincarnation?" He hadn't said yes or no. But since he hadn't told Edith it was stupid, she believed in it wholeheartedly. She was convinced she'd been Marie Antoinette and I'd been Mme de Lamballe in another life.

"I've really looked into it. I can't have been anybody but Marie Antoinette. We had exactly the same character. I'd have thrown cake down to them too, as much as they wanted. People blamed her for spending lots of money. So? What good is it being a queen if you have to count your pennies like a housewife? And that good-looking Fersen—I'm sure he had blue eyes, just like all the guys from the North. . . . And if I was Marie Antoinette, you couldn't have been anybody but Mme de Lamballe!" Edith was absolutely convinced. "No doubt about it," she'd say. "They're the only women who can be compared to us. Do you know of any others?"

All I knew was that poor Mme de Lamballe's head had been brought to her girl friend on the end of a pike. And that sent a shiver up my spine. I also told myself that Edith's and my ancestors didn't have shoes, blew their noses in their fingers and went around bare-assed singing that revolutionary song the *"Carmagnole."* Anyway, if we'd once been on the side of Louis XVI, alias Capet, I couldn't see why we hadn't stayed there. It was no use for Edith to say, "That's got nothing to do with it, Momone. You can be reincarnated as anyone. Jacquot explained it all to me; it's a question of your sins. If you've committed too many, you have to pay for them in your next life."

"Yeah? Oh, wow! We must have committed a hell of a lot of 'em while we were rolling in dough!"

I got a good laugh out of it though when Edith, as a revolutionary, sang *"Ça ira"* in Sacha Guitry's film about Versailles. Marie Antoinette, my ass! And Edith gave me an answer worthy of her: "If she'd sung it too, she'd have kept her head on her shoulders!"

All this made time pass, but Edith couldn't take being alone. So things went badly, like they always did when she didn't have a man who meant something to her.

For several weeks, in spite of the table, we really didn't know which end was up. There were nights when a sort of fury came over her and ate out her gut. We'd go and drag around Pigalle. She liked to go back to the same old places. She'd take a couple of rides on a merry-go-round and buy two gingerbread pigs, one "Edith," the other "Simone." And we'd end up at Lulu's, in Montmartre, as customers. We could always find some Joes there to take home with us. I can't remember their names—we'd forget by the next day—but there were a good ten or twelve of them in that month . . . maybe more.

When we didn't have a man, we'd go to the Lido, order champagne and invite the dancers to come sit at our table. The girls were flattered to be at Edith Piaf's table drinking with her, and she'd say to them, "Come home with us and make us french fries."

They'd laugh at the idea. They didn't believe her, but she was serious. She'd take the girls home, they'd make us french fries and we'd have lots to drink to wash them down. Then we'd hand the girls some dough so their evening wasn't wasted. Everyone had a good time. And we'd go off to bed. The next morning Edith would say to me, "I know I acted like a jackass, Momone, but I can't come home to this joint alone."

We felt so much at loose ends that Edith even went out singing in the streets again. "Come on, Momone," she'd say. "We'll put on our old rags. I feel lousy; I've got to work a street!" And she'd throw herself into the street the way others throw themselves into their mothers' arms. What was weird was that nobody ever recognized her. No one dreamed she could possibly be Edith Piaf. We heard comments like: "Listen, she's imitating Piaf," or "You can see it's not really her," or "What a difference between her and Piaf!" It made us laugh. But no Louis Leplée came along to hire us, even though she was pretty good, that street singer!

She was so fed up with everything that we stayed at the Claridge for a week. And I must say, the hotel deserved every cent they got from us. Even the table, which we'd lugged over to the Claridge, was powerless to hold her back. She made all the drunken promises, but she always found good reasons for drinking. One time I saw her looking at a bottle and said, "Remember your promise." "You're right," she answered, "but come to think of it, my promise was only for the bedroom, not the bathroom." And off she went to the bathroom to get plastered. Or else her promise was good only for the Claridge and not for the Champs Élysées. When she'd finally run out of excuses, she shouted, "But listen, Momone, I didn't promise not to drink in Belgium," and we took the train so she could get tight in Brussels.

That's why, nearly every morning around six or seven, we'd crawl in on all fours. There'd be a guy mopping up the lobby or the hallway—my mind was too fuzzy ever to remember the place exactly. Edith would give me the signal: "O.K., come on!" And we'd climb into his pail of water. I never understood how we both managed to fit in it, but it cooled our feet off. Edith would climb out first, and then me. She'd say in English, "I am a dog . . ." and I'd repeat, "I am a dog . . ." and since we were male dogs, we'd each gaily lift a leg. How we managed to stand up I'll never know. . . . All this in front of the elevator boy, the night porter, the receptionist, the chambermaids—the whole gang.

Finally we'd land in our rooms. And that bitch of an "Aunt Zizi" would decide this was the time to have a nervous breakdown. She needed people around her—anybody, anywhere, just people!

She'd grab the sheets and rip them to pieces. The first time she did it I was so frightened I almost sobered up, or at least enough to say to myself, "She's going to croak! She's losing her mind!" And I pushed all the buttons at once. I phoned down to the desk: "Mme Piaf's dying!" That put the fear of God into them: to go and die like that . . . in such a fine hotel! They came tearing in, and she had all the people she could want.

Someone called a doctor. He found her lying stretched out on the bed, deathly pale. She raised her eyelids a little and winked at me. The doctor gave her a bunch of prescriptions. The bellboy galloped off to the pharmacy. And once the doc had turned on his heel, Edith ordered champagne and invited all the hotel personnel to drink with her!

She'd had such a ball, she repeated the whole performance several times. Edith Piaf left lots of memories at the Claridge. . . .

What she did those nights may not always have been a very pretty sight, but I understood her.

Edith had never needed to be loved as much as she did then. Who could fill the emptiness left by Marcel?

PART TWO

❦

May 25, 1963

My Edith,

Now that I've escaped death, I'm not sure how (it's our special trick), I send you a kiss because you are one of the few people I think of with love each day.

JEAN COCTEAU

This note was written after Cocteau's first heart attack.

Chapter 13

※
※ ※
※

Just Passing Through Boulogne

Boulogne was another time when everything was temporary. There was nothing solid, nothing very good about our lives. I don't know why, but all the guys we met then were married. Maybe because they were the right age. Or else they only interested Edith because of the talent she saw in them, like Charles Aznavour and Robert Lamoureux.

Robert was one of those people she called "meteors." They streaked across Edith's sky with a bright glow, then fell—cold pieces of stone no one mentioned again.

That's the way Robert Lamoureux passed through our lives. He was merely a professional acquaintance. Then one day he showed up with his nice mug and his big frame on legs that were too long. The first time we saw him he had on a checked sports jacket even louder than the ones Yves had worn at the Moulin Rouge. I didn't know it was possible, even though with Edith I'd seen a little of everything!

Like a lot of others, he came to sell her songs. They all began like that. It was easy; you didn't need a letter of recommendation to see Edith. All you had to say was that you had a song under your arm. Edith liked him right away. "That guy's got talent," she said. "He'll make a career for himself. I'm going to help him succeed." And several months later she did.

Robert would have liked nothing better than to go on from a professional relationship to a more intimate one. It would have pleased me too, because he was a nice guy as well as good looking. He had a way of grinning at you from ear to ear that made you want to take a spin on a merry-go-round with him. He made you want to go off and celebrate.

Robert found Edith very much to his liking. If nothing happened, it wasn't because he hadn't, let's say, courted her. Robert poured it on, and he had plenty of charm. But it was his talent that impressed Edith. As far as the rest of it went, she just didn't feel like it. And her verdict was final.

It was the same with Charles Aznavour. Their relations were entirely professional, even though they both played around a lot.

One day Edith heard someone say, "I've discovered a fun place, a new one, Le Petit Club, on the rue de Ponthieu. There are lots of guys there who improvise and sing and play the piano. It's really nice."

"Let's go," said Edith. When something appealed to her, she couldn't wait five minutes. And it was true; it *was* a nice place, where everybody knew everybody else. There was Francis Blanche, thin as a rail, who soon became a good pal of Edith's and later wrote her a marvelous song, "*Le Prisonnier de la tour*"; Roger Pierre and Jean-Marc Thibault; Darry Cowl, a wonderful pianist (the hard part wasn't getting him to sit down at the keyboard but dragging him away from it); and the singing team Roche and Aznavour.

"What do you think of them?" Edith asked me.

"Nothing to get excited about."

"You're wrong. The little dark guy with the awful nose is a natural. He's got what it takes."

Aznavour hadn't talked to her ten minutes when she hit him with: "Your nose is no good for the stage; you've got to get it fixed."

"It's not a tire. I don't have a spare!"

"If you come to America with me, I'll get another one made for you."

The trip was six months away! Charles couldn't get over it and neither could I, even though I was really used to Edith. She'd known him less than an hour and was already talking about taking him to America. I had to get a closer look at this Aznavour guy— he must be worth the trouble. At first sight, he didn't have the build of Piaf's men, and he didn't have blue eyes. Then what was left? I soon found out.

"Hey, you write songs. That one you sang, *"Paris au mois de mai"*—is it really one of yours? You've got talent!" Edith told him. So that was it. She'd sensed he could write songs for her.

She immediately set him straight about his act with Roche. "It's not worth much; it's old-fashioned," she said. "Pierre Roche isn't bad, but he's not doing you any good. Your personality isn't coming through, yet his isn't really strong enough to cover you. You won't get far that way."

This bothered Aznavour, because he was very fond of Pierre, and Charles was always loyal to his friends.

"You've got to split up," Edith insisted.

"I can't. . . . Later, maybe. He's probably going to Canada soon. We'll see when he gets back."

"Come see me at the house after he's left."

Less than a week later Charles came to stay at Boulogne and soon was sleeping on a small couch a thirteen-year-old would have found too narrow. "You're like me—you're not big," commented Edith. That set the tone of their relationship. That's how it started, and it was only the beginning. Charles brought out the "Aunt Zizi" in her, and she didn't let him get away with a thing. He was given preferential treatment, like me. I was the handy sis and he was the handyman.

It didn't take long. He'd barely had time to realize he was living with us before he was driving the car, carrying suitcases and going out with Edith. From morning to night all you heard was: "Charles, do this. . . . Charles, do that. . . . Charles, did you make that phone call? . . . Charles, have you written any songs?"

"I've got two or three new ideas, Edith."

That kind of answer drove Edith nuts; she was just waiting for an excuse to explode.

"You begin hundreds of songs, but you never finish them. Since you don't know how, I forbid you to work on them! And watch out—if I see you writing, you'll have to give me the song right away!" That was how Edith's mind worked.

Charles had to hide to find some peace and quiet. To write, he'd sneak into corners where she couldn't see him. Since he was never satisfied with what he wrote, he dropped his little scraps of paper all over the place. I went around picking them up, and I still have some of them.

In any case, Charles did write for Edith, putting all his talent and heart into it. But they didn't work for her. It was the same with songs as with men: either they hit her between the eyes or they didn't. She sang only a few of his songs: *"Il pleut,"* *"Il y avait,"* *"Une Enfant"* and *"Plus bleu que tes yeux."*

One evening Charles brought her *"Je hais les dimanches."* It was one of her bad days. "Is that for me? You think I'm going to sing that? It's pure shit; you hear me?"

And she launched into a choice sample of the repertoire of insults that had stood her in good stead from Ménilmontant to Pigalle.

"Then you don't want it," Charles calmly replied. "I can do whatever I want with it?"

"You can shove it. . . ."

So Charles quietly took his song to Juliette Greco, who immediately put it into her repertoire. When Edith found out about it, she fell into one of her special brand of rages.

"Just come over here, Charles. So you're giving *my* songs to Greco now?"

"But, Edith, you told me you didn't want it!"

"*I* said that? What do you take me for, an ass? Did you tell me you were bringing it to Greco?"

"No."

"You think you can double-cross me! Me! You haven't heard the last of this. . . ."

Edith's bad faith was staggering.

Charles had got off on the wrong foot working with Edith. He said yes to her all the time; that was his mistake. He shouldn't have said yes to everything. You had to take it slow and easy, give in to her whims, go along with them, but stand up to her when it came to work. She might scream a lot, but she'd respect you. You had to know how to cheat, too, if you didn't want to get eaten alive. And that Charles couldn't do; he was too honest, too decent, too pure. He admired her so much that whenever she gave him a hard time he said, "Edith's the greatest; she can do anything she wants!"

When she talked to him about America, it was like dangling a carrot in front of a donkey's nose. "It'll do you good to go there. As far as show business goes, they're the best!" Charles raised his eyebrows and his eyes got big and round, like a dog with visions of roast beef, as he listened to Edith talk about her trips and her experiences.

He asked me behind her back, "Do you really think she's going to take me with her?" As if you ever knew with Edith! "Maybe, if you're good," I'd answer, and he'd laugh.

"But to help her make up her mind, there's no use telling her I'll do anything she wants—I already do. . . ."

If Charles had been "M. Piaf," everything would have been different. All his songs would have been works of genius. He'd have had to put up with her scenes but not her tyranny—at least not the same sort! I personally would have liked it to happen. I'd have had some peace with that one around. Edith rather liked him physically, and I told myself that if I pushed them together a little more, maybe it would happen.

One night when Edith and Charles had had a drink or two, some friends of theirs thought of undressing Aznavour and putting him in Edith's bed. While the guys worked on him, I fussed over the "young bride."

"Fix your hair. . . . Here, put on some perfume. . . . Wear your prettiest nightgown, the hemstitched one. . . ."

"What's wrong with you tonight, buzzing around me like that?"

"I want you to look beautiful."

"Who the hell for?"

"You never know. . . ."

"You think maybe some guy's going to drop down the chimney?"

I went into the bedroom with her. There was nobody there. The bed was empty. We'd failed! Charles had refused to go along with the idea. I think he loved Edith too much. Most of all, he was too decent.

Luckily for all of us, Edith's bed didn't stay empty for long.

Edith was appearing at the Baccara. One night a hefty guy, the muscle-rippling type, came to see her. And in a sort of Franco-American gibberish he explained that he'd written an English version of "*L'Hymne à l'amour*." It wasn't a stupid ploy; Edith was very much attached to that song.

The guy had a nice face, covered with pockmarks: he'd got a kisser full of them when he was a kid. But they made him look even more masculine. He had a great smile and a cool look in his eye. "There's a guy with a little luck going for him," I said to myself right away. The trouble was, we could only make out three words of his every ten. You may be able to do without conversation when you're in love, but in the beginning it helps!

"Listen," Edith said, switching to English, "your idea eez verry good."

"For you?"

"No, not for me."

"I'm very sorry."

"Don't be. It can be fixed. Call me."

Very much the "tough American," he raised two fingers to his head and said, "O.K. Tomorrow."

As soon as he left, Edith began to roar with laughter. I hadn't heard her laugh like that for months. It was the laugh Henri Contet once described so well:

. . . All of a sudden, an enormous laugh, magnificent, pure. It spurts out, flooding the room with joy. Edith Piaf comes over to me, clings to me, and laughs, laughs till she can no longer breathe, till she suffocates right there on the spot, and there's nothing to do. I see her extraordinary face very close to mine, with an expression that seems to change color. I see her eyes like the deep sea, her huge forehead, and that monumental laugh which possesses her and leaps out between her little animal teeth, as if happy to be bitten.

It was good to hear that laugh again. It got us out of the gray world we'd been living in. I could have kissed the guy.

"Well, with him, at least we won't get involved in conversations. What's his name, Momone?"

"I didn't catch it."

"Never mind. He'll be back."

The next morning a guy telephoned and I said to Edith:

"Somebody called Eddie Constantine would like to see you."

"I don't know him. What's he want?"

"To show you some songs."

"Tell him to come over."

Two minutes later we'd forgotten all about it. That afternoon the doorbell rang.

"Go see who it is, Charles," Edith shouted.

Charles ushered in the *"L'Hymne à l'amour"* American. It took us a moment to realize he was Eddie Constantine. He'd been afraid we wouldn't understand him because of his accent, so he'd had a pal call for him. That's how Eddie came into Edith's life.

Beneath all his gangster mannerisms he was very sentimental. He knew right away how to treat her: he had just the right line.

"The guy's softhearted, Momone. He told me he felt a 'passionate friendship' for me. Isn't that sweet?"

"And you managed to understand him?"

"I'm getting used to him. You know, *'L'Hymne à l'amour'* and the songs were just a way of getting to meet me. What do you see in him that's different?"

I couldn't see anything in him at all. But she liked me to admire her guys, to discover qualities in them other men didn't have. My brain cells started working right away, as busy as an anthill in the middle of summer. I wanted her to have a man again. It was time. And it was necessary. Physically he had what it took. As for the rest, you've got to take chances! So I gave her a hint as broad as a barn: "Edith, that guy's got a soul."

We hadn't had a guy with a soul yet! She was pleased. In any case, he had what Edith needed most: two arms to squeeze her tight. So he became the boss, because that's the way things had to be.

The handing over of power always took place quite simply.

Edith had a guy. He was in bed, like a pasha, and she'd announce to her personal maid or the housemaid, whichever it was we had then, "This is your new boss."

The guy would have to have lasted at least two weeks for that to happen. It was easy to tell when he was no longer temporary: he began wearing a chain and a medal (usually one with Saint Theresa of Lisieux on it) around his neck. If he wasn't Catholic, she'd give him a medal with his sign of the zodiac. Then there'd be the cufflinks, the watch and the cigarette lighter, all from Cartier's, on the night table. The suit lying on the chair would be of good quality, but in some color impossible to look at, much less wear! And there'd be a tie to match, meaning you could hardly fail to notice it.

Edith dressed her men to suit *her* taste. Theirs didn't interest her at all. She chose the cut, the fabric and the color of their suits. She was sure her men looked handsome when she dressed them. Sometimes it worked out, but other times it was frankly appalling.

Even so, they'd only have one or two of those fancy outfits in their closet. Their other clothes were always blue. It was her favorite color for her men, because of their eyes. It was just too bad for the ones with brown eyes: they got blue anyway!

Charles Aznavour still tells this story: "With Edith it wasn't hard to recognize her lover of the moment; he always wore a blue suit when he went out with her. One evening she invited several of her former lovers over. To please her, they were all dressed in blue —all eight of them! They looked like a bunch of chorus boys. Edith, who had an unfailing sense of humor, leaned over to me and said, 'How about that! I sure as hell haven't been twiddling my thumbs!' "

There was also the business about shoes. *They* at least were always terrific—in alligator. They made more than one guy suffer though. Edith had definite ideas when it came to shoes. "People with big feet are damn fools!" They all had to wear their alligator shoes one size too small—except for Cerdan and Montand, who refused. No doubt about it: she made her men suffer!

She was bossy, impossible and difficult to live with, but only in the little things. In all the rest, she was more or less the one who was had. She indulged herself in illusions about her men, but she wasn't always taken in. "What hurts, Momone, is that it is not *me* they love. Not old man Gassion's daughter. They wouldn't look at her twice. They aren't in love with me, they're in love with my *name!* And with what I can do for them!"

Meanwhile we had a new one. The whole house was turned upside down, and the atmosphere was madly gay. Boy, did I like that! Things between Eddie and me were never like they'd been with Yves or Contet, but he wasn't an unpleasant guy. He was nice. He always fought clean, and was decent in his own way.

The first time Eddie slept there, he did something that touched me. I found him in the bathroom washing out his nylon shirt. . . . He only had one! Luckily that didn't last long. Around our house we bought shirts by the dozen.

Eddie was an agreeable guy, but except for his fake tough guy's mug, he wasn't much to look at. He believed in Paris, but Paris hadn't yet believed in him. He was born in Los Angeles in October 1915, into a family of opera singers from Austria. His father, his grandfather, his cousin and his nephew all sang. He didn't have to beat his brains out to decide on a profession. His ambition was to sing classical music, and his bass voice had won him a prize at the Vienna Conservatory.

Bursting with confidence, he went back to California. Apparently there was no shortage of basses out there, because they told him, "Take it easy! Not everybody who wants to can sing here. Wait your turn." He certainly wasn't very high on the list, because he sold newspapers, delivered milk and was a parking lot attendant before he got a chance to sing on the radio—seventeen times a day, in a really poetic cigarette commercial. That did it for him. He soon was singing commercials for soft drinks, chewing gum, a funeral parlor company, as well as for Roosevelt's election campaign, and while he was at it, for Roosevelt's opponent, Dewey!

Singing commercials doesn't give you a chance to warble with much conviction. It's a little like the telephone time reports. It repeats and repeats; there are no surprises. So Eddie, who had ambition, left his wife, Helen (without being too heartbroken, it was nearly over between them), and his daughter, Tania, and came to Paris to try his luck. He'd told himself that an American in Paris after the war would go over big. He wouldn't need to have a reputation.

After beginning as an amateur on the Paris-Inter radio station, he was hired by Lucienne Boyer to sing at the Club de l'Opéra. He also appeared briefly at Léo Marjane's and Suzy Solidor's. It was a lot better than singing about the pleasures of chewing gum. He could at least get by because of his build, although he was hardly making a fortune.

Edith gave him his chance, as she'd done for many others. She had an astonishing flair for recognizing talent before anyone else did. She often amazed me. She didn't trust appearances. She could tell what people who approached her were going to achieve in five or six years, and that's what she'd think about when she took them under her wing.

Edith had always liked men who were real go-getters and had a lot on the ball. Eddie Constantine was no Yves Montand, but he wasn't a nobody either. So Edith began by making him learn French. He desperately needed to from every point of view, and most of all because their conversations were limited and Edith never liked repeating the same thing twice. With her, you had to catch on right away.

In spite of his pidgin French, Eddie had told Edith the story of his life. All her men had to. He didn't hide anything from her. She knew he was married but separated from his wife, and that he adored his daughter, Tania. He assured Edith it was all over between Helen and him, and swore he never thought about her. And, as Edith said to me:

"I'm glad he broke up with her long before he ever met me. That way I won't be accused of being a home-breaker! At least this one's free. Anyway, in America it's easy to get a divorce."

That was how she always let herself be dominated by men. She swallowed all their tall stories. They slid down her throat like a very sweet, sugary liqueur, with just the right amount of alcohol as a base.

One afternoon a boy named Leclerc came for an audition. Constantine was there, listening. Leclerc sang nothing but love songs. We were drowned in floods of love; we were swimming in sentiment: the crawl, the butterfly, or just floating. . . . He had a style for every taste!

Right in the middle of Leclerc's singing, Constantine got up, his eyes blurred with tears, and left the room. Edith dropped everything and ran out into the street after him. She was convinced Eddie had dashed off like a madman because he'd finally realized how much she loved him. The tears in his eyes had proved it!

"I caught up with him, Momone, and asked him, 'What's wrong, love?' And do you know what he answered? 'I'm thinking of Helen. . . .' "

She looked drained when she came back. "It's nothing; it only lasts two seconds and only takes two words. But those are long seconds, Momone! And afterward, you have to swallow them. . . ."

She'd had more than one blow like that, and they hurt. Actually, *that's* what we were paying for when she forced us to give in to her weird ideas. For example, she wouldn't let me eat butter. "You mustn't eat butter because it softens your brain and keeps you from becoming intelligent." She couldn't really have believed that, but it amused her. Most of all she liked people to obey her. I wasn't taken in though. The truth was she didn't like butter.

In a restaurant she might pick up the menu and in a domineering way order for everyone. Sometimes that's how she got even with people. A few days after the business with the love songs had made Eddie's tender heart weep for Helen, a bunch of us went to a restaurant. Edith ordered ten servings of ham with parsley. It was a new gastronomic discovery of hers, and every night without fail we had to stuff it down. This time Constantine ordered sausages. Since we were all horsing around, nobody noticed. But when Edith saw Eddie was quietly about to down something besides ham, she began to shout. "You really have to be an ass to eat sausages!" She yanked his plate away from him. "Here, taste this," she said to the others. Everybody took a small bite and said, "It's awful." When the plate got back to Constantine, it was empty . . . and he got nothing else to eat.

At Boulogne, we no longer had to go out to get dancers from the Lido for company. It was a real circus. There was always something going on, and everybody got into the act. Edith was getting ready for her fourth trip to the U.S. as well as a two-month tour through France. Pierre Roche hadn't returned from Canada yet, and before going to the U.S., she decided to take Charles on tour: "I want to see how good you are on a stage all by yourself. It'll do you good." Needless to say, Constantine was also in on the fun and games.

The rue Gambetta house had turned into a factory. Edith, Constantine and Aznavour—when they gave him time—were rehearsing. There were also the musicians, our pals Léo Ferré and his wife, Madeleine, Guite, Robert Lamoureux, who casually dropped in to pay his respects (he'd never stepped out of the picture completely, and he was right), and people I'd never seen before who all used the same set phrase: "Mme Piaf knows me; I'm a friend of hers." It made me laugh because Edith would tell me to throw them the hell out.

In the midst of all this, at any hour of the night, I'd make coffee and french fries, drag out bottles of wine and slice sandwiches. It was sort of fun, and would have been even more fun if I hadn't had my own troubles. Unfortunately, they couldn't go unnoticed for long: I was pregnant. Luckily Edith hadn't yet noticed. It wasn't any sin as far as I was concerned, but still I didn't dare confess to Edith. Then one morning I came right out and said, "Edith, I'm going to have a child."

She didn't get mad—it was worse. "Momone, you're kidding! You can't *do* that to me!" If I'd had a real mother, she'd have said the same thing. Naturally Edith told Constantine about it right away. And he was very sweet.

"But, Edith, that's marvelous. Really. Babies are a gift from heaven. It's happy news. It'll bring the place good luck. It's beautiful for a woman to have a little life in her belly. It's touching. . . ."

Edith didn't see it that way. As far as she was concerned, I'd betrayed her trust. Anyway, wouldn't I love this baby more than I loved her?

Eddie had a man's sort of patience and took his time. He found exactly the right thing to say to make her understand. It didn't take long. Two minutes before, she hadn't even wanted to see my future kid, and now she was ready to bawl me out for not having given birth to it already. Everything was changed. I was very grateful for what Constantine did for me that day. After all, he didn't give a damn about the whole business!

"It's as if your baby were mine, Momone," Edith said to me. "So don't do anything stupid, do you hear? Be careful. Babies grow strong and beautiful in their mothers' bellies. You mustn't look at anything ugly if you want yours to be beautiful. And I'm going to keep an eye on what you eat."

She didn't give me a minute's peace. When we went to the movies, she held my hand. And if she decided the show wasn't beautiful and was bad for the kid, she squeezed my hand. "Don't look, Momone. I forbid you to!"

It was like that with everything. "Drink beer—it's good for your milk." Actually, I wonder what I'd have fed a kid with. My whole breast would have disappeared in his mouth in one swallow.

Everybody knew I was expecting. Momone was pregnant, and they all knew they had to approve. During her Henri Contet period, Edith had made something of a spectacle about the baby she wanted, and still, every time she sized up a man, she wondered if he'd make a good stallion. It wasn't all an act though. It broke her heart to think her little girl had died in poverty, and that now when she had dough she couldn't have a child.

She didn't miss this great opportunity to consult her table as to whether it'd be a boy or a girl. And the good old table answered, "A boy—and he must be named Marcel."

Because of my condition, Charles Aznavour got a new job foisted on him: he was to be my nurse! "Stay with Momone, Charles. I'm turning her over to you. You're responsible for her and the baby."

When we went to cabarets, Charles pulled out my chair for me, held my purse, saw to it that I didn't drink. "No alcohol; it's bad for her," Edith had ordered. It wasn't much fun for poor

Charles to run around with this dame who was pregnant up to
her ears. Boy, did that guy sweat!

If Charles had the misfortune not to offer me his arm in the
street when Edith was around, she screamed, "Charles!" in that
famous booming voice of hers that inevitably made passersby turn
around and stare. Charles stoically endured his ordeal down to the
very last minute of my pregnancy. He was even more anxious than
I was to have it all over with.

A few days before the baby came, Edith got worried. "The
baby mustn't come while I'm gone. If you're sure of the date, you'll
be having the kid soon. It may come any minute. I'm going to tell
Charles to keep your suitcase with him all the time." Charles was
not only supposed to give me his arm; he was supposed to haul the
suitcase around as well as the dame! "Look proud," Edith told him.
"It's something to have a pregnant woman on your arm." I'll never
forget how kind Charles was.

The coming event didn't change our life at all. Edith dragged
me everywhere with her. One morning at seven we were gaily leaving a cabaret with the whole gang. Suddenly I stopped short on the
sidewalk. "This is it. The pains have started."

"Let's go," ordered Edith.

And off we went, with me leaning all my weight on Charles's
arm, and Edith, Eddie and our pals following. All of us arrived at
the hospital together. In spite of the labor pains, I was having great
fun. The nurse called Charles "monsieur" in a tone that implied a
great deal. He didn't dare say, "You're wrong, ma'am, I'm not the
father!" No maternity hospital had ever seen a patient enter like
that. It was like a wedding party that had been on one hell of a
spree. . . .

"We're the family," Edith regally announced to the nurse. The
poor girl had never seen a family like mine, that's for sure! Once
I'd been put to bed, the "family" came into the room and Edith
grandly declared, "We're not going to leave you, Momone, so
hurry up; I'm sleepy."

Hurry up! Nothing I would have liked better, because I was
beginning to feel a little woozy. "While we're waiting for the de-

livery, we'll have some champagne," announced Edith. What saved the clinic from being taken over by Edith and her gang was that they had no champagne. . . . Edith took off, leaving Charles there so he could phone her.

I was speedy. Three hours later, at ten in the morning, I gave birth to a fat boy, whom we named Marcel, and whose godmother was, of course, Edith. That damn table hadn't been wrong!

I had the baby just in time. Edith had got an engagement for Eddie, and she left with him and Aznavour to tour France. She wanted to have me along, but I couldn't go; I had to take care of my son. Still, whenever I could, I joined them for two or three days.

Poor Charles—what an ordeal that tour was for him! I wondered if the guy didn't have a vocation for martyrdom. . . .

Constantine still had a dreadful accent, and the way he went over in the provinces is best left unmentioned. That made Edith bloody mad. It was Charles who took a beating though. First of all, he was in charge of everything—Edith's baggage, the props, the staging. He also had to lead off the program. "You go first, Charles. We need you backstage during the show."

And poor Charles, who hadn't had time to rehearse and barely had time to get dressed, would crash onstage and do his little act for an audience that didn't give a damn. He had some really big flops, and it almost seemed as if Edith was glad about them. If one night things didn't go too badly for him, the next day Edith would order him to leave out the second and fourth verses of his song. "You won't sing them."

"But, Edith the song's worthless like that," Charles would protest.

"I know better than you. There's no use your staying onstage so long; they don't like you."

And Charles obediently cut the verses. Since the song was now meaningless, he went over like a lead balloon—at which point Edith would haughtily declare, "You see, I was right. Even that way the song's worthless."

Charles would give a sickly little laugh and say to me, "It doesn't matter. I'm learning my profession." And on he plugged.

He had his food, his lodgings and his laundry taken care of, and he was writing songs. The days of not knowing where his next sandwich was coming from were over. That's what he wanted. And he was laying the groundwork for his future.

One evening back in Paris, Charles walked in dressed all in black—a new suit. He thought he looked pretty chic and he was pleased. Edith immediately threw cold water on him. "So now you're copying me."

"But, Edith . . ."

"Shut up. That's the same suit I ordered for Eddie. I'm not going onstage flanked by two guys in black. It'd look like I'd hired a couple of extra hands from a funeral parlor! Go upstairs and get undressed." And he did.

Of course, she hadn't ordered a suit for Eddie. But she had a hunch that if Charles was dressed in black he might look a little like her, and that Edith wouldn't stand for. As a singer, he irritated her. "The Piaf style is fine for me. But it's not right for a man."

She was unfair. Charles's style never remotely resembled Edith's. All the others she trained, from Montand to Sarapo, picked up her gestures and intonations. But not Charles. Yet he was closer to her than all of them. That was what got her back up. She knew damn well there was only one singer who could move an audience the way she did, singing straight to their hearts and their guts: Charles.

I was very fond of Charles. He was a true friend, one of the very few men who was completely honest with Edith. We understood each other, maybe because we were born under the same sign—Gemini. In any case, it was a link between us.

We were scheduled to leave for America soon, and things were in a mad uproar. Eddie rode out Edith's storms, and Charles ran around all over the place. It made him laugh. "All I need is a jester's cap and bells on my feet to look like a one-man band!"

I personally liked all the confusion. These were happy days. Edith worked, sang, yelled and prodded Guite, Michel Emer, Henri Contet and Raymond Asso—all the composers she could get her hands on. She was taking English lessons, rehearsing the songs she'd had translated, and memorizing little introductory remarks. In be-

tween, she made appearances in some nightclub or vaudeville theater, and dragged me around to Jacques Heim and Jacques Fath.
This time she was in no danger of arriving bare-assed; she bought
twenty-seven dresses, with coats and all the rest of it to match, and
more than seventeen pairs of shoes. And she decided I should look
as grand as she did. "You mustn't look like a bum next to me. I'm
going to take you to Jacques Fath. Remember, Momone, when I
told you I'd buy your clothes from the great couturiers?" I hadn't
forgotten a thing, and I was pleased to cover my rump with those
fancy whore's duds! I could already picture myself strutting like a
duchess down the Champs Élysées. That was what I thought would
happen, but it didn't work out that way.

Even though I was a mother, I was still a girl to Edith. Obeying
her orders, I put a net over my hair and wore no makeup. "You're
like me—simplicity gives you class. You've got the face of a
virgin. . . ." Because I looked like her! And you couldn't do better
than her, could you?

At Fath and Heim everybody kowtowed to Mme Piaf, who
left them with millions of francs for dresses she never wore. More
than once I saw her buy three million francs' worth of dresses in
a half hour. When they were delivered, she rushed to try them on.
But since she was no longer in the atmosphere of a couturier's
salon, she'd decide she looked hideous. "I'm not a model. I can't
wear that!" So they hung in her closet. The next time it was the
same all over again. She who was so domineering, who had such
preconceived ideas, handed herself over to the couturiers. "Momone, these great dress designers know what they're doing. It's
their job."

I had proof of it. The minute we entered Fath's, the circus began. "Quick, Mme Piaf's fitting! Go and tell M. Fath!" And did
they bow and did they scrape!

"I don't want a fitting today. It's for my sister. She's going to
New York with me."

"Certainly, Mme Piaf. Call Mme Hortense."

It was like being in a whorehouse—all the cackling and chirping, and the sizing up. "I'm leaving her in your hands, Hortense,"

Edith said regally. "Do just what you'd do if I were here. I trust you."

She could trust them, all right! They chose for me. I didn't have the right to say a word. "This is *made* for you," they cooed, laughing inside, because they couldn't have been so giddy they didn't realize they were turning me into a trained dog.

Edith came for my last fitting. Once I was all rigged out, I had to twirl around gracefully like a model. The salesladies and Fath himself—who'd gone out of his way to be with us—said in chorus, "It's ravishing on you . . . with your complexion . . . your eyes. . . ."

I didn't believe a word of it. Edith pretended to be an expert, giving orders. She didn't dare say a word to them when the clothes were for her, but since they were for me it was different. "A little longer . . . a little shorter . . . a little higher; move that bow. . . ."

"You're so right, Mme Piaf," clucked the dames. I couldn't say anything, and I was paralyzed at the thought of walking out of their damn boutique, wearing all that in the street.

Though Edith didn't wear her dresses, she forced me to wear mine. She took me all around New York disguised like that. And Loulou, usually so kind and polite, thought it was a riot. "Don't think you were brought along for nothing. Your trip cost a lot. You're here to make us laugh."

I looked grisly. And I was never sure "Aunt Zizi" hadn't done it on purpose! You couldn't always know whether Edith was joking, making an ass of you or taking it all seriously. I felt like asking her, but I never dared.

Before we left for the U.S., Edith decided to give a few dinner parties.

"It makes a good impression, Momone. We have to—I'll be gone two months. This way they won't forget me." Anyone who came to our dinners would have had a hard time forgetting them!

The first guest she picked was Michèle Morgan, partly on account of Henri Vidal, with whom Edith had had a brief affair while they were filming *Montmartre-sur-Seine* together. It was before Vidal married Michèle.

We rented the whole works—table, chairs, silverware, dishes, tablecloth, flunkies—everything. "I'll start with Michèle Morgan, Momone, because she's an elegant woman and still so natural!"

Most of all, I think, Michèle was well brought up, luckily for us. Nobody had ever been to a dinner like this one! To begin with, the waiter plunked the lobster Thermidor right down the front of Michèle's low-cut dress, and she laughed uproariously. That really relaxed us, because the lobster bit was a little too much.

Everything, though, was wacky. We couldn't all have coffee because we didn't have enough cups of our own and we'd forgotten to rent some. So before Michèle Morgan arrived, Edith had decreed which of us would drink coffee and which of us wouldn't. Charles and I weren't supposed to have any. Since he was absent-minded, naturally when the coffee was served he said yes. At that point Edith's voice thundered, "Not for Charles. It keeps him awake."

That night I discovered that Michèle Morgan was an exceptional woman. After dinner Marcel's nurse phoned to say that my little boy was sick. Since he was out in the suburbs, quite a distance away, I phoned every hour to see how he was. And would you believe it? Michèle Morgan, whom I'd just met for the first time in my life, didn't run off to amuse herself with the others; she stayed with me the whole night, getting no sleep at all. But I was remorseful as well as worried; I knew my Edith, and I was afraid she'd make off with Henri Vidal. Although I was happy not to be alone, I was really upset about Michèle. She impressed me so much when she talked about her little boy, Mike, in a voice as gentle as a voice from heaven. When Edith came back at dawn with Henri Vidal, Michèle seemed to think it was so natural, I decided I'd been wrong to think evil thoughts.

After Michèle Morgan had left, Edith said, "You know, Momone, I respect that woman." And believe me, it took a lot to make Edith respect you!

There were only a few days left before we were to leave for the U.S., and nothing went the way we'd planned. To begin with, for the first time in my life I flatly refused to leave with Edith. She began yelling at me, but I was expecting that, and I stuck to my guns. "I'm not going to be so far away from my son for two months."

Constantine tried to patch things up. "She'll join us later."

"If she doesn't come with us now, she won't come at all."

Then Charles butted in. "Listen, Edith, she's right. Marcel's only a baby. But Eddie's got a good idea; Simone will join us later." It was the wrong thing to say.

"What are you butting in for?" Edith snapped. "You're not going! My first show's in Canada, and there's nothing there for you."

The storm really broke then and crackled in every direction. For the first time Charles stood up to Edith.

"That doesn't matter, Edith; I'll join you afterward."

Edith snorted. "When hell freezes!"

But she didn't know Charles. She hadn't been in Canada a week when she received a cable: DETAINED ELLIS ISLAND. SEND FIVE HUNDRED DOLLAR BOND. AZNAVOUR. Charles had kept his word and come to the States. He'd had rather a rough time of it. He'd come over on the deck of a boat, like an immigrant. And since he didn't have a contract or a single cent, the Immigration Service had said, "This way, Mac, to the soup kitchen." Edith was delighted. It was just the kind of thing she liked. "Little Charles isn't as assy as he looks. He managed to get here."

Naturally she paid his bond.

I'd played at being a big girl, but it couldn't last long. Marcel was being nursed and was well cared for. I was dying to join Edith. "That bitch," I said to myself. "She might just let me rot here."

When he left, Eddie assured me, "Don't worry. You'll come."

He'd had time to forget me, but he didn't. He had my ticket to New York sent to me. It was kind of him, but not as disinterested as one might think.

I hadn't been in New York three days when Eddie began to look like a man with a heart as heavy as a cannonball. He was grim.

"What the hell's wrong with you?" Edith asked.

"Nothing. But it's almost Christmas . . . and I'm not going to see my daughter, out in California."

"Why not?"

"My wife doesn't want me to."

The guy was no idiot; he knew how to handle things. Edith got bloody mad. She piled abuse on his wife and ordered him to go see his child.

The day he left, Eddie whistled while he shaved. As she put him in a taxi, Edith said to him somewhat dryly, "Don't forget to come back!" Fat chance of that!

The taxi hadn't even turned the corner when she shrugged her shoulders and said, "I think I've been had, Momone. . . ."

"Don't be silly; he's going to see his daughter."

Everything turned out all right. He phoned to say that Tania was overjoyed to see her daddy . . . blah, blah, blah. I thought he was laying it on pretty thick, and I could see Edith didn't believe everything he said. "He didn't mention his wife, Momone. . . . You think that's normal?"

"Why should he talk to you about his wife? Dames are all the same! What's important to him is his daughter."

There was no cause for complaint. He phoned regularly; and luckily we didn't have time to get bored waiting for him to come back.

Edith decided Charles should have his nose operated on. "Listen, there's not a goddamn thing for you to do here; you're no help to me at all. I want you to have your nose fixed; I promised you I'd get it done. It'll give you time to mull things over, give you a new outlook on life. With a new face, you'll think differently. And while you're in the hospital, write me an adaptation of 'Jezebel.'" It was one of Frankie Laine's songs that Edith liked a lot. Charles made it one of the big hits of the day.

Once again, there was no man around. But Edith had an idea, and his name was John Garfield. She could fall in love with a guy as easily as a teenager after seeing him in a movie or on the stage. One night she dragged me to the theater; they were doing *Peer Gynt*. "Listen, Momone, there's a guy in this I like. I've just caught a glimpse of him, but I've got to get a closer look."

So every night, before Edith went on at the Versailles, we'd go to see and hear John Garfield. The worst of it was that I didn't understand a word, and Edith didn't do much better. All I could make out was Edith, when she'd say, "Oh, Momone! What a handsome beast! God, is he handsome!" That text wasn't in *Peer Gynt*, but at least it was clear.

I don't know how many times we sat through that damn play. After ten I gave up counting. Charles was already up and around, with a bandage on his new nose, and still we went to that fucking theater!

In all seriousness, Edith said, "I'm studying him. See, that way I'll be sure to get him." And she did. She managed to spend a night in his arms. After it, she said, "We managed, but he gave us more trouble than any of them, didn't he, Momone?" I couldn't have agreed more.

The day after that happy night with John, Edith waited. Not a word that evening, or the next day, or the day after. She was furious. A month later, when we were about to leave New York, the phone rang and a man's voice said to her, "Hello, who's this?"

"Edith."

"This is John."

"Well! . . . You've got one hell of a nerve!"

"See you tonight."

And he hung up. But it didn't work. Eddie had long since come back, and John didn't interest Edith any more. So when he arrived that evening like the lord of the manor, he found me instead of Edith. He knew she was angry at him, but he never understood why. . . .

When Eddie got back from his domestic joys, I thought he acted like a guy who's double-crossed you—both pleased and embarrassed.

Since Edith was feeling a little guilty herself about John Garfield, she didn't ask too many questions. It was Charles and his new nose that supplied the main topic of conversation. "Are you happy with it?" Edith asked.

"Well, it's a change. When I catch a glimpse of myself in a mirror, it seems to be someone I know, but it takes me a second to recognize myself."

"What do you think of him, Momone?"

"He looks fine."

"What about you, Eddie?"

"He's a new man. He looks fine."

Charles was wondering if people in Paris would notice the change.

Before we left, there was a surprise in store for Edith. She met General Eisenhower. He came to hear her at the Versailles and, like Princess Elizabeth, he invited Edith to his table with Eddie, who was very proud to meet the man who was to become president of his country a few months later.

It all took place as if they were old pals. Edith was flattered, but not at all panicky. A general wasn't anywhere near as dazzling to her as a princess. Everyone was very relaxed, and the General asked Edith to sing his favorite song, "Autumn Leaves." She'd never sung it. I was afraid she'd louse it up, but it went very well. The General knew lots of French songs, and kept asking Edith if she knew this one or that one. He had a marvelous time and sang along with her. Americans aren't at all like the English; their thing is simplicity, but it can be just as classy.

All was going well as we got ready to leave. We were going to take Eddie and Charles back with us. There'd been no trouble about Charles's sidekick, Pierre Roche. He'd married a Canadian girl, who didn't want to leave her log cabin in Canada, so he and Charles separated, with no fuss. Edith was delighted; Charles was all hers at last. "You'll see, Charles. Leave it to me!"

And how! His situation with Edith was now hopeless. Since she was no longer afraid he'd leave her, she could do whatever she liked with him.

We'd barely landed in Paris when Edith decided to hop over to Casablanca to see Marinette and kiss the three boys—Marcel, René and Paul. She was very fond of them. She didn't stay long, because *La P'tite Lili* was hanging fire. There was a long story behind that musical comedy. For two years it had been a topic of conversation, and eventually it became a triumph of Edith's strong will.

There were a lot of nasty intrigues going on. Not one of the people involved wanted anything to do with the others. Mitty

Goldin, the all-powerful manager of the A.B.C., had commissioned Marcel Achard to write a musical comedy, *La P'tite Lili*. Achard told us the story, which was made to order for Edith. She wanted Raymond Rouleau to direct it. Rouleau declared once and for all that he'd damn well never set foot on a stage belonging to Mitty Goldin, and that, in any case, he'd never work with a book by Achard. Achard wanted Lila de Nobili to do the sets, but Mitty Goldin didn't want her. There was only one person everyone accepted without a murmur: Marguerite Monnot.

Friends met with friends, and each one loudly swore he'd never work with the others. Since they refused to meet each other, Edith played the role of a traveling salesman and visited each of her "customers" individually. Little progress was made, but Edith was determined that it would be produced, so it had to be produced.

"Momone, they give me a pain in the ass with their carryings on. I've decided to do *La P'tite Lili* at the A.B.C., directed by Raymond Rouleau, with sets by Lila de Nobili, and I'll do it! They're a bunch of loudmouths, all right, but I'm even louder."

Personally, I didn't believe she'd make it. I'd sat in on a few of their sessions, and they laid into each other so violently, I couldn't see how they'd ever get together. But I was wrong. Every bit of it was theatrics. They finally all agreed when Edith said, "I hold the bank and I call the shots!" God, what an experience!

It almost blew sky high again when it came to casting. Edith had decided that Eddie would play the part of Spencer, the gangster. Physically he'd do, but not psychologically. Mitty didn't want him. "He walks like a dancing bear, and his accent's dreadful." At that we all burst out laughing, because though Mitty had been in Paris thirty years, his accent sure didn't come from the heart of France!

It was Raymond Rouleau who finally won Mitty over by suggesting that some of Spencer's lines be cut. "Gangsters don't talk much; they act!"

Pierre Destailles was supposed to have the young male lead. But everyone had fooled around so long he wasn't available any more. So Edith suggested Robert Lamoureux for the part of Mario. On this everyone agreed; they didn't want him!

When Edith had decided a guy had talent, she never forgot him. Mitty and Raymond tore their hair out. "Two newcomers on the same bill—it'll ruin me!" wept Mitty, who hadn't even invested very heavily in the project. "I'll never make it!" moaned Rouleau. Not to mention the fact that Edith, as an actress, wasn't exactly a reincarnation of Sarah Bernhardt!

It all promised to be very gay, but the best was still to come. Achard hadn't even begun the script! For two years we'd been arguing about a book that wasn't written. The only things we were sure of were the title, *La P'tite Lili*, and the songs, which Achard had had lots of fun writing, and which made it possible for Marguerite to compose the music.

"The music and the songs are the main thing in a musical comedy. All the rest is padding," said Edith, who loathed learning the lines in a script. Marcel Achard was delighted to be understood so well. In fact, the only one who pulled a long face was Rouleau, who thought that, really, it *wasn't* enough!

The first day of rehearsal, Marcel, very much at ease, his twinkling, mischievous eyes contracted behind huge glasses that looked like diver's goggles, brought some sheets of paper, which he passed around.

"Here's the first scene, kids."

"But I need the whole play if I'm going to direct it," Rouleau cried.

"Don't worry," Marcel exclaimed. "I've got it all in my head."

Ten days later, Marcel Achard had given birth to a *P'tite Lili*— a strapping, healthy child. He wrote all night, and the following morning, fresh as a fish straight out of water, he'd turn up with the next scene. It was more exciting than a cliff-hanger. I didn't miss one rehearsal; and with good reason: Edith had got me a part in the play. I was one of the seamstresses, and in the first act I had to say to Edith, "Don't try and tell us you're a virgin!" Every time I said it, we laughed hysterically.

When Achard arrived each day with his little sheets of paper and Juliette, his wife—an extraordinary woman—everyone jumped on him.

"Am I the murderer?" asked Eddie.

"Am I the one who marries P'tite Lili?" asked Lamoureux.

And Marcel Achard, the joker, would answer, "Wait till the end, kids. . . . You'll find out then, just like the audience."

Rouleau took advantage of this and made Eddie's role, Spencer, a nonspeaking part. In spite of his accelerated lessons and all his good intentions, Eddie still had a dreadful accent. But it didn't faze Rouleau. "Say *terrible* again. You can't? Never mind, pal, we'll cut it!" And with a broad stroke of his pencil, he'd cross out the whole speech. This wasn't to Edith's liking. . . .

"Come now, don't worry about Spencer," said Raymond calmly. "The whole role depends on his biceps, his hat, his mug and his fists. The play will be better for it, and Constantine won't lose a thing by it."

Mitty had his own ideas. "No need for him to sing—it just slows down the action."

Edith blew up. They had a session in Goldin's office that made the seats in the A.B.C. shake. You could hear Edith's voice on the boulevard Poissonnière.

"You think I'm an idiot? You're a bunch of stupid bastards! All your bullshit makes me vomit. Just because Eddie doesn't know French very well, you're trying to cut his part down to nothing. He'll act and he'll sing or we stop the whole damn thing. I'm ready to pay for breaking the contract."

This is only a summary of her scene, which got longer and more violent. In the end they gave in. Rouleau shrugged his shoulders, and Mitty said, "I'll never set foot in this theater again. It's not mine any more!" For a week he stayed away and refused to speak to Edith.

Perhaps Edith would have given up the cause of Constantine that day if she'd known the surprise he had in store for her. We were in the middle of rehearsals one morning when Eddie took Edith's breakfast tray out of my hands. "Let me do it. I'll take it to her."

This was the first time he ever did, because Eddie was more the type to have breakfast brought to *him* in bed. But what he had to say to Edith couldn't wait. Or so he thought! He was no psychologist. If you woke Edith up with a piece of bad news, it was a good idea to show up with a shield.

"Edith, look, I've been thinking . . . It might be better . . . more proper . . . well, I'm having my wife come to Paris."

He'd no sooner got the words out of his mouth when Edith threw the whole tray—coffee, sugar and all—right in his kisser. Then she let him hear it in great Piaf style, just like in the good old days!

"Is that what your visit to your daughter was all about? You bastard! So you cheated on me with your wife. You jerk! You shit! . . ."

I won't repeat it all—it's best not to. In California, Eddie had seen his wife again, and they'd made up—for life. Edith tried not to let on, but it was a real blow. Only for the moment, however, because the next day she didn't think any more about it. She didn't have time to recruit a replacement. The premiere of *La P'tite Lili* was too close at hand to go sleeping around.

Therefore, when Eddie—once he'd left Boulogne, sure that he'd be forgiven—told Edith he wanted to introduce his Helen to her, she replied, "Of course! Bring her to the rehearsal tomorrow."

That day Edith got all dolled up. "I don't want to look like a hag next to his American wife!" To hear Eddie talk, Helen was one of those dream girls America produces. Edith, to my mind, was really brave and had a lot of style. It was a pretty decent thing for her to do. Even so, she had the jitters.

We arrived onstage, and I saw a magnificent girl standing near Eddie in the shadows—blond, elegant and looking like a high-class fashion model. It had to be her. Edith swept down on them as Constantine turned around. Right next to him was a little dame, plainer than plain, with a small hat on her head and her hair coiled over her ears. She was the one Eddie introduced to Edith. The other was Praline, one of the most beautiful girls in Paris. Edith laughed so hard that Constantine was blotted out, erased, liquidated—at least as a lover, because they remained good friends.

On the night of the premiere Edith was worried about him. She wasn't altogether wrong. Physically he was perfect: he had broad shoulders. But his lines came across a little moth-eaten, all full of holes. The audience made out whatever they could. But when Constantine sang, he had his little triumph. If I'd been his wife, I'm not sure I'd have been so happy. He was too good at holding Edith in his arms, too natural, as he sang to her:

> *Petite si jolie,*
> *Avec tes yeux d'enfant,*
> *Tu boul'verses ma vie*
> *Et me donn' des tourments.*
> *Je suis un égoïste.*

> *Voilà, jolie petite,*
> *Il ne faut pas pleurer,*
> *Le chagrin va si vite;*
> *Laisse-moi m'en aller.*

> Little one, so pretty,
> With your childlike eyes,
> You've turned my life upside down
> And torment me.
> But I'm selfish.

> Listen, little pretty one,
> You mustn't cry,
> Sadness fades so quickly;
> Let me go my way.

The audience demanded an encore. He'd made it. Knowing the whole story, I thought those words fitted Eddie like a glove.

The final song was a huge success for Edith. She loved it. The first day she heard it, she'd said to Achard, "That's the story of my life, Marcel, even though it's optimistic. If I ever write my autobiography, I'll start the book with it."

> *Demain il fera jour.*
> *C'est quand tout est perdu que tout commence;*
> *Demain il fera jour.*
> *Après l'amour un autre amour commence.*
> *Un petit gars viendra en sifflotant*

> *Demain,*
> *Il aura les bras chargés de printemps*
> *Demain,*
> *Les cloches sonneront dans votre ciel*
> *Demain,*
> *Tu verras briller la lune de miel*
> *Demain,*
> *Tu vas sourire encore,*
> *Aimer encor', souffrir encor', toujours,*
> > *Demain il fera jour*
> > *Demain.*

> > There'll be another dawn tomorrow.
> When all seems lost, life begins again;
> > There'll be another dawn tomorrow.
> After one love, another will begin.
> A little guy will come whistling along
> > Tomorrow,
> His arms filled with spring
> > Tomorrow,
> The bells will ring in your sky
> > Tomorrow,
> You'll see a lovers' moon shining
> > Tomorrow,
> You'll smile again,
> Love again, suffer again, over and over,
> > There'll be another dawn
> > Tomorrow.

The reviews were excellent. *La P'tite Lili* ran for seven months. And it would have run much longer if Edith hadn't had her first accident, the beginning of bad days to come.

There was an amusing side to the play. An audience who saw it one night could come back a week later and see an entirely different play. Edith could never remember a script—it bored her! A play that went on for three acts was too long. So when she couldn't remember her lines, she said whatever came into her head. As for Eddie, he had trouble remembering all the French words, so he translated them into American or shortened his lines. And

Robert Lamoureux, who was always a great comedian, answered with some quip or other. He had a job trying to follow the two of them, I must say!

It was like a commedia dell'arte, very lively. Everyone had a good time, and it was thanks to this musical comedy by Marcel Achard that Robert Lamoureux and Eddie Constantine got started. They could thank Edith for insisting they be in the cast, and Eddie, who was a good guy, did. In his memoirs, *Cet Homme n'est pas dangereux*, he wrote:

> Edith Piaf taught me—and a few others—everything we knew, everything about how a singer should act onstage. She gave me self-confidence, which I never had before. She made me want to fight, which I'd never wanted to do before. On the contrary, I'd just drifted along. She made me believe I was somebody, so that I'd become some-body. She had a kind of genius for bringing out and strengthening a personality. She told me over and over, "You've got class, Eddie. You'll be a star!" Coming from a top star like her, the statement electrified me.

What Constantine never knew was that Edith had also paid to give him confidence. When Mitty hired him, Eddie got five thousand francs, but Mitty only put up two thousand of it. Edith made up the difference. She did the same for benefit performances and tours. She loved to tell him, in all good faith, "Your fees are getting bigger. That's fine, *mon chou*, you're going up in the world. . . ."

That way of giving, of secretly helping someone she believed in—that, too, was Edith!

Chapter 14

The Bad Days Begin

For once, and for the first time, Edith was caught short. Eddie's successor wasn't far away, but he wasn't right there.

I liked André Pousse when he came to the house with Loulou. He had a good face, of the Belmondo soft-hearted hoodlum type, and an honest, firm handshake. He was thick-set, like a man of cement, but not without a heart inside. He had a nice smile, and the minute he opened his mouth to speak you knew he was Parisian.

He'd been a well-known cyclist, but unfortunately the legs give out long before the rest of the body in that profession. He wanted to try out the world of show business. And with Edith he was right on target; she was the ideal partner for him.

André had come to see Edith when she was in *La P'tite Lili.* He was her type—just the right build. Edith looked him up and down and burst out laughing. "I know you!"

"Yes. We met in New York in 1948. I was a champion cyclist and was racing at Madison Square Garden. I came to hear you at the Versailles with my teammate Francis Grauss. I needed a little whiff of Paree. It was really good hearing you! Were you a hit! The Yanks couldn't get enough. I was so pleased that a kid from Paris could set them off like that—knocking 'em dead. When I yelled, '*L'Accordéoniste*,' you laughed and said, 'There's a French-man in the house.' "

"That's right, and after the show the four of us—me, you, Loulou and your pal—went to a French restaurant to down a steak and french fries." With those "childhood memories," they were off to a good start. . . .

Charles and I calculated André's chances. They didn't seem too good. After the meeting in her dressing room, we didn't see Pousse again. And Edith never talked about him, which wasn't a good sign. As always, when she was in the trough of a wave, she was sleeping around. Charles and I would have been glad to see her stop waltzing with just anybody who came along in that dance of lost loves. Edith was exhausted by it, and so were we, trying to keep up with her. She lived life to the hilt, like one of those whirling dervishes who can't stop till they fall. She lived every day as if it were the last. She drained even the little things, the small pleasures, to the last drop, with total passion, without pause. She stuffed herself with everything she liked, right up to her ears. With all of us already nauseated, she went on with the ravenous enthusiasm of the first mouthful!

Marguerite Monnot had taught her to like classical music. One day Edith happened to hear Beethoven's *Ninth Symphony* on the radio. Guite was there, and Edith glowered at us. "Why didn't you make me listen to this before, Guite? Charles, did you know this existed?"

"Yes."

So *he* took the beating. "Well? Maybe you thought it was too beautiful for me? Go out and buy me the record right away."

She looked at us as if we'd betrayed her, and we all felt guilty— even me, who knew nothing about good music.

Naturally, we were clobbered with the *Ninth* for weeks. Edith said to anyone who came to the house, "I'm going to put on a terrific piece for you." And she'd play it over two or three times so he'd really understand it. Our ears hurt, but she listened to her record again and again with the same ecstasy.

It was the same with books. We all had to read the one she'd liked and talk to her about it for hours. We also had to reread her favorite passages to her. I still know some of them by heart, from

Via Mala, La Grande Meute, Sarn, The Old Man and the Sea, and *The Sound and the Fury. . . .*

One book had really made a big impression on her, a complicated thing on "relativity," about the love affairs of atoms and neutrons, of all things! It was harder than *Madame Bovary*, but Edith liked it.

"You see, Momone, all this gibberish is hard to understand. When you read it, you tell yourself you're a silly nothing on your little patch of earth. But at the same time, just because you're nothing and very tiny, you become very big. As big as the world. Understand?"

I said I did, but only to please her. I was more inclined to agree with her when she claimed, "Gide's really something, believe me!"

It would go on for days. Lucky for us she didn't read much! Her eyes tired quickly and her work took a lot of her time. She didn't just rehearse; she never stopped working. Whatever she was doing, wherever she was, in the street, at a restaurant, she was always looking and listening. Anything could give her ideas.

She never went to museums, but Jacques Bourgeat had managed to acquaint her with some famous paintings. Edith couldn't contain her enthusiasm. "Corot, Rembrandt—those two guys are damn good."

Edith had a passion for the movies. When she liked one, she took a whole row of seats and brought the gang. Charles and I got the worst of it. Long after the others had given up, she still dragged us with her. We saw *The Third Man* nineteen times. Charles remembered it as a nightmare.

Our only piece of luck was that she had taste. We didn't have to put up with duds. But no cheating was allowed; we had to be there at the beginning of the film. "The beginning prepares me for *my* part." She only went to see a movie for the parts that sent her into raptures. "At one point in *The Third Man*, Momone, Orson Welles raises his eyes . . . Don't miss it!" It was the next to the last shot in the film, worse luck, but there was no danger of missing it. Edith would hold my hand and squeeze it to make sure that I didn't miss a single crumb, a single tremor, that I throbbed along with her, that she wasn't alone. "Here it comes, Momone! Look at him. God, he's handsome!"

When there was a man in her life, we could breathe a little, while she busied herself with him.

I could sense that Charles wouldn't hang around much longer. He stayed with Edith only out of a deep feeling of friendship. His career was beginning to move, slowly but surely. He sang every night at Carrol's, although he wasn't paid much—two thousand francs an evening. But he was quite a hit there—which didn't stop Edith from giving him advice. "You're shy in front of an audience, Charles, even though you've got a lot on the ball. But you'll have a beard down to the floor before you make enough money to buy yourself a Rolls-Royce."

Maybe so, but meanwhile she was very happy he'd been saving some. One day the gas company came to turn off the gas. There wasn't a cent in the house. We searched our pockets and came up with almost nothing. The maid was fed up—Mme Piaf owed her too much. Edith borrowed thousands of francs from her at the end of every month. Then Charles bounded up the stairs to his own cozy little room on the third floor and came back down, proud as a pope, with three thousand-franc bills. He didn't talk about it, but he was quietly making his way.

Edith liked that. There hadn't been a man since Cerdan who'd opened his wallet for her. It was the gesture that counted; she didn't give a damn about the dough. So they'd cut off the gas and the electricity—big deal! She could always go sleep at the Claridge.

This may be hard to believe, especially when you know that Edith was then earning three to five hundred thousand francs a night. It's true though, and it was that way till the very end, when she got a million and a quarter old francs a night.

Loulou tore his hair in desperation. He arrived with a glum look on his face one day and collapsed in an armchair. "Listen, Edith, this can't go on. You're going to go broke." Edith just laughed. "I'm broke already—and I don't give a damn. So do like me—laugh!"

"I can't, Edith. What in the world do you do with your money?"

"I don't know," answered Edith. "Do *you* know, Momone?"

Imagine asking me! I was just like her. I think it was because we'd always managed to scrape up money, even when things had looked blackest. We'd always had enough to eat, drink and have fun with. We knew how it came and how it went; what we didn't know was how to hold on to it and, above all, why we should.

"Listen, Edith, someday you may need to have a little money put aside," said Loulou.

"What are you giving me? Are you kidding? I'll always sing, and the day I don't will be the day I croak. Don't forget that, Loulou. I'd like to do you a favor, but I can't save money. I'm not a housewife. I don't give a shit for the future—it'll take care of itself!"

Loulou tried to believe her, but he was afraid. Then he had a brilliant idea. "Listen, Edith, I'll set up two bank accounts for you. Every time you get money, deposit half of it in each account, but only use one of them for expenses. Pretend the other one doesn't exist."

Edith liked the idea. "You know, Momone, Loulou's scheme isn't so stupid. That way I'll finally have a little money on hand to spend whenever I feel like it."

Regarding the deposits, it worked beautifully. Mme Bigeard took care of them very well. Edith was radiant. Good old Bigeard kept an accurate account of the money that came in. "M. Barrier's system's fine. We must have three million in the bank already." Edith broke up—and with good reason: she'd made off with the whole thing. Instead of withdrawing money from one account, she'd been dipping into them both. "It's great, Momone. Now I write out two checks instead of one, and it seems like I've got twice as much dough!"

Money slipped through Edith's fingers like water, like sand. . . . She could never possibly keep track of what she spent in a day. There were always at least ten of us who ate together, in a restaurant, every night after the show at the A.B.C. Then, with the whole gang, we'd go from nightclub to nightclub, and in each place we'd drink a bottle of champagne apiece. If Edith was in good shape, she'd buy drinks for everyone in the club. It goes fast that way!

And then there were the gifts, her business expenses, her pals, her cars and all the rest of it. . . . That's what cost the most. And let's not forget the taxes; they were stiff!

Some friends suggested she buy a farm outside of Paris, because it was profitable, and she could go there weekends. "See, Momone, the air in Paris is poisonous. The country air will do me good. . . ."

O.K., buy a farm! Anyway, Edith surrounded by cows, pigs, rabbits and chickens—it'd be worth the trip. So Edith bought a farm for fifteen million francs at Le Hallier, near Dreux, and sank another good ten million into the place fixing it up. In five years she didn't spend three weekends there! And then she sold it for six million.

She hadn't seen Pousse for nearly a month. Just as I was thinking to myself, "Well, that's that!" she asked me in the bathroom:

"What do you think of Pousse, Momone?"

The answer was automatic. "That one's a real man!"

"He is, isn't he?" Edith murmured blissfully, ready to jump on love's merry-go-round again. "I'm going to invite him for a weekend."

This weekend bit was something new; she'd never done it before. Everything else took place as usual. When he came back from the country, Pousse went with Edith to Boulogne and stayed a year. Quite a weekend!

As he used to say, laughingly, "That's how you get into trouble. I told myself a night with Piaf might be fun, and I was hooked before I knew it. That's how you take a lease on love!"

From the start I liked Pousse. He was an honest guy who always spoke up for Edith's interests, not his own. Like Loulou, he wished Edith wouldn't throw her money around, and even scolded her for the gifts she gave him. "You're absolutely nuts," he told her. "I can't wear more than one suit at a time! If you'd at least wait for a holiday or a birthday—you know, for some reason to give people presents—but you give them any old time. . . ."

"Isn't pleasing you enough of a reason? Stop complaining. You can be sure a lot of the others never did."

"That's the point. I'm not like them. . . ."

"That's why I love you, you sweet idiot. . . ."

All that was very nice, but I could tell it wasn't the great love of the century. More important, Edith felt it too. André wasn't stupid; there was a brain underneath all those muscles, and he saw clearly when he said to me, "You know, Edith's always making believe. She has to have faith in love—she can't live without it. So she tells herself she's in love. But it's not often true. That's why she does all those crazy things!"

All those crazy things . . . He was right there, and it led to some serious fights. Edith wouldn't stop bugging him till he'd slap her around. Yet André was no brute; in fact, he was rather gentle. But there are some things it's not easy to get a man to swallow. And these were about the most gorgeous fights I'd ever witnessed.

Sometimes Edith and I might go out all afternoon with some other guy. When we got back, we'd really horse around. Not André; he'd yell, "You're not going to make an ass out of me!" He wasn't an intellectual, a complicated man you could soft-soap. He was a simple guy, and all he knew was that Edith cheated on him. So he'd fall into violent rages, and in the middle of the night he'd toss everything Edith had given him out the window. A friend of mine and I would go pick it all up by the light of the car headlights —jewelry, watch, clothes—everything André had laid his hands on. After the fight the two of them would calm down and go quietly back to bed, while I'd be on all fours down on the old paving stones picking up the stuff.

Edith constantly changed, and that upset André, who had trouble keeping up with her moods. One day the two of us came back with about fifty red balloons, all reading: "André Shoes, the Shoemaker Shoes."

"How did you get them?" Pousse asked.

"Go look in the car," answered Edith. It was full of bedroom slippers.

"See, Pousse, I never had a balloon when I was a kid. I used to see the other kids parading around with theirs. They were as plump and shiny clean as their red balloons, and there I was with my old man doing our sidewalk act; I was filthy and shabby—just a beggar to them. Today at André's they were giving away a balloon with each pair of slippers, so I bought enough to fill the house." She played with the balloons all evening, while Pousse watched her affectionately. The guy was tender-hearted, though he didn't know it.

Episodes like that helped to smooth down their love a little, so it didn't creak too much. She was attached to her Pousse, and had decided to take him on tour with Charles, who, as usual, had to do everything and anything. This time there was a slight change though; he stood up to Edith and managed to sing five songs that hadn't been too badly chopped up.

"See, I'm getting there," Charles told me, with his nice smile and his bright, mischievous eyes. "Ten more years and I'll be her costar!" The bad days were over for poor Charles; he was indeed getting ahead very fast. But in the meantime, he had to pack the car and drive it.

Edith left and I stayed behind in Boulogne. Pousse wanted to be alone with her, and I wasn't sorry to have a little peace. Edith and I phoned each other several times a day. On the twenty-fourth of July she called me earlier than usual. We chatted some, and then she said, "Momone, I've got a really good story to tell you; if it were any better, I'd be phoning you from heaven! This morning, I was dozing in the back of the Citroën while Charles was driving. Just outside Cerisiers, on a curve, we went off the road, flew through the air and landed in an apple tree! Pretty funny, huh?"

I had to wait till I caught my breath before I could laugh.

"Don't worry, Momone. Like I said, nothing's wrong with me. I'm not even bruised. You should have seen our faces, Charles's and mine! There we were, lying with our noses in the grass. We were so scared we'd find the rest of us scattered around in pieces, we didn't dare look at each other.... But you should see the car. There was nothing left of it! It looks like a piece of scrap iron hanging from the tree.... You know that as long as I've got little Saint Theresa on my side, nothing can happen to me."

I wasn't so sure. I'd had one hell of a shock. This was the first accident Edith had ever had. Now I jumped every time the damn phone rang. Three weeks later, she phoned me in a strange, faraway voice. "Imagine, Momone. I've just had a nice little plaster house put around my arm. Don't worry—everything's fine. But I'm coming home; I can't sing with my arm in a cast. . . .

"André was driving. He's not hurt. We were near Tarascon, and Charles and I were so sound asleep in the back seat we didn't notice a thing! We skidded on a curve, and that's that. See you tomorrow."

Boy, what a state I was in till she got back! I'd have worried even more if I'd known that those two accidents, practically one on top of the other, marked the end of Edith's luck.

When I saw her arrive in an ambulance, her face white and drawn, her eyes feverish, I realized she'd lied to me. It wasn't just her arm that was broken. She also had two caved-in ribs that kept her from breathing.

"I have to go to the hospital, Momone. Come with me." She was suffering horribly. Edith, who could really stand pain, moaned for hours. The only good moments of the day were when they gave her an injection. "I feel better, Momone. The injections help a lot. Thank God for that. I couldn't live without them!"

I was stupid enough to be glad she was in less pain. If I'd only known! Edith was acquiring a taste for drugs. She didn't tell me. She didn't talk about it. She was sure it wouldn't last, that once the pain disappeared she'd be able to do without morphine. But I began to worry, and I told her:

"Edith, you ought to wait a little. You just had a shot a while ago. . . . You'll get addicted."

"It hurts too much, Momone. Don't be crazy. No danger of *me* getting hooked on drugs; I remember my mother and how she croaked. I've done lots of damnfool things, Momone, and made promises I never kept, but fixes and shots, never!"

She hadn't been there two days when she said, "The food here is lousy, Momone. Ask Chang to make me my meals." So every day I brought her lunch and dinner from home. She wouldn't stand for anybody else bringing them.

One night she phoned me and said, "Bring me some books

along with my supper." When I got to the hospital, André Pousse was waiting for me in the corridor.

"Listen, Simone," he said, "things can't go on like this! *I* should be with Edith, not you." He bent my ear for a bit, explaining to me that I had my own life and should let Edith live hers without me. He looked so sincere I thought I ought to let him try his luck. Pousse was being logical; he might make it if he were by himself. Living with two women wasn't much fun for him. I always understood that some guys didn't go for that.

"O.K., it's fine with me," I said. "I'll take her her books and say good-bye."

"No, don't see Edith. If you say good-bye, she won't let you go. Let me help her by myself. If you love her, you must leave."

I thought that after all he might just be right, so I gave him the books and left. What bothered me was that every time a guy wanted me to hit the road, he fixed things so I'd seem to be sneaking out like a nasty bitch. I knew I'd see Edith again. This wasn't the first time a man had come between us. She'd always called me back. So I took André's advice and went off to see "whether the Tower of Pisa was still leaning." Poor Pousse; he'd have done better to let me stay around. He didn't last long after I left, not even a couple of weeks. . . .

Every day one of his pals, "Toto" Gérardin, a bicycle racer, came to see Edith at the hospital, supposedly to amuse her, but actually to quietly double-cross his chum. I heard about it, of course, and when Edith went back to Boulogne, since she'd chucked André, she asked me to come back.

It was a familiar song, a little too familiar! I wasn't alone any more: I had my own life, and a child. That didn't keep me from loving Edith, but it made me think. "Aunt Zizi" was terribly demanding: you had to be with her practically around the clock. You couldn't leave her for a second. She didn't take it very well—she called me every name in the book—but she finally accepted the fact that I couldn't live with her the whole time. I needed to breathe; I needed some freedom.

I was annoyed that André wasn't around any more. He was

reliable, and he would have kept her from sliding downhill. I didn't like her coming home so soon either. The business of the shots kept bugging me.

She still had her arm in a cast, but she was breathing more easily, though not well enough to be able to sing, and when Edith wasn't singing she was capable of doing any damnfool thing. As long as she had a nurse at home, it wasn't too bad. But she didn't keep her long.

"Why don't you have a nurse any more?" I asked her. "Who's going to give you your shots?"

"Don't worry, Momone; there are plenty of people around, and I can give myself the shots."

I didn't like that very much, but if she had morphine, it was because the doctor gave it to her. I couldn't know that the new faces prowling around her were generous types who made her pay through the nose for every tiny ampoule of morphine.

Toto came to see her every day, as he had at the hospital. He was slim and good looking, with a cold look in his eye, and the thighs and legs of a cyclist. He was more of a pretty boy than Pousse, but didn't have his nice, simple mug. Nor did he have much influence on Edith. He was a weakling. "You can't imagine how much that guy loves me, Momone."

He told her he couldn't live without her, that he'd never loved a woman before he met her. He made no bones about handing her a shameless line! He came to live at Boulogne.

Edith had the cast off by now and was feeling better. She seemed to want to get started again, and I told myself that maybe he could help her make it. But my illusions didn't last long.

There was a Mme Alice Gérardin, who wasn't standing for any nonsense. In December she accused Edith of being an accomplice of her husband, who'd taken a few little things belonging to her when he left home—a charming list, which the police sergeant read to Edith with a straight face, while Edith didn't know whether to rage or to laugh. "Champion's trophies of precious metal, bracelets, necklaces, pendants, rings, pins, a porcelain vase, a mink coat, forty pounds of gold bars, the contents of their joint family strongbox. . . ." Though there is no such thing as theft between husband and wife, Edith was accused of being an accomplice and of receiving stolen goods, no less! The head of the crime squad had a search warrant and, along with two detectives, went through every inch of the dump. I could see it all just as if I'd been there.

"Now listen carefully, Momone. The cops entered Mme Bigeard's room, searched all her closets and went through all her papers. She, who'd managed to stay out of trouble with the Gestapo, was now in a heap of it with our own fuzz! She was livid. They were beginning to piss me off, so I took them straight to the room where that poor fool Toto kept his suits. There were also a couple of bronze busts of my champion cyclist—he was so proud of them he'd had to bring them to me! The chief said to me, very seriously, 'We aren't looking for evidence of adultery, Madame, but for evidence of stolen goods.' So I let them run loose in all the rooms. They left empty-handed and not very pleased. It would have been a nice coup for the cops to have been able to bring down that Piaf they couldn't fifteen years ago, when she was called 'La Môme.' Pretty funny, isn't it?"

I must not have been in the right mood—it was hard for me to laugh.

Her affair with Toto dragged on a few weeks more. Alice Gérardin had hired a private detective to shadow Edith, who didn't enjoy it for long. Besides, ever since she'd sung in the streets, Edith could smell a cop fifty yards away.

She was alone once again. Poor Edith; how long the nights were in her fine town house! Charles wasn't there any more, and Mme Bigeard and Chang had left. This was a time in her life when new faces were to chase out the old.

Edith couldn't bear to be alone. It drove her bats. She was afraid of silence. "Momone, I swear at night I can hear the minutes dropping one by one, in this goddamn house. It's a hellish noise; it tears my heart out."

So she'd walk down the street and into the first bar she came across just to see people, and she'd drink.

Although I'd say, "Edith, now that you've got a vacuum around you, there's room for somebody new," she'd answer, "I'm fed up with waiting. There's no such thing as love; it's a lie I tell myself so I won't croak."

Edith, who loved life so much, now wanted to die.

One day, I had been with her since early morning. She was depressed. She started by talking to me about her mother, her father and then Cécelle. That I didn't like. It was a subject we never discussed; it just didn't seem proper.

"Tell me, how old would my kid, my Cécelle, be now? Remember how she used to look at me, how she laughed?" She kept babbling on about her. We had lunch. She didn't eat anything, and drank almost nothing, although that day you'd have thought she needed to. It hurt me to hear her talk about Cécelle like that. I'd always played any role she wanted me to, but I couldn't replace her little girl.

She'd told me Guite and Francis Blanche were going to stop by. I waited for them impatiently, and was very uncomfortable there alone with her. They finally arrived almost at the same time. They hadn't been there ten minutes when Edith suddenly beat it.

"What's wrong with her?" Francis asked me.

"I don't know. She got depressed."

"We mustn't leave her alone," said Marguerite.

That really struck us, coming from Marguerite, who never knew what was going on. We went to search for Edith and found her hiding in an empty room on the fourth floor. When she saw us, she slipped out on the balcony. "What are you spying on me for? I'm hot. I've come out here to get some air," she said.

The three of us looked at each other. We didn't like the idea of that balcony, but we didn't dare say anything to her. Suddenly she burst out:

"Stop bugging me! Get the hell out of here! I'm fed up with looking at you, you bunch of spies. You make me sick to my stomach!"

We didn't say a word. Francis murmured to me, "Has she been drinking?" "No, hardly a drop," I answered.

Edith was clutching the balcony railing and looking off into space. She didn't seem to be drunk; she wasn't woozy or dazed or anything. She was staring into space as if it held some sort of promise for her. There was something like hope in her eyes.

We stayed there waiting for her to get over it. But this fit of depression wasn't like the others. There was a sofa in the room, and we were all sitting on it. We sniffed the air like animals sensing danger. I was preparing myself for it, when suddenly Marguerite leaped up and screamed:

"She's mad! She's going to jump!"

Edith already had one leg over the railing, and half of her was hanging in space. Marguerite took her in her arms and was trying to hold her back. Francis went out to help. I was frozen with fear. I went out too, but Edith screamed:

"Leave me alone with Marguerite. Get the hell out."

We had to give in to her. Every time we'd come close, she'd struggle, and Marguerite had a hard time holding her back. So we left, and half an hour later Guite had finally brought her back to her room. Between the two of us, we managed to get her into bed.

I stayed with her all that night, talking to her about songs, talking shop, although I wasn't at all sure she was listening. Then she began to make plans, and I knew the crisis was over.

Before she went to sleep, she said to me, like a child:

"I'm sorry, Momone. . . . You know I wouldn't have done it."

When she said that, I knew she would have, but why? If I'd known the reason was morphine, I'd have stayed with her. But Edith had said, "See, it's all over now, I've stopped taking drugs; I'm not in pain any more, so I don't need them." I was stupid enough to believe her.

Chapter 15

Celebration of Love, with Jacques Pills

> *Car tout était miraculeux:*
> *L'églis' chantait rien que pour eux;*
> *Et mêm' le pauvre était heureux*
> *C'est l'amour qui f'sait sa tournée.*
> *Et de là-haut, à tout' volée,*
> *Les cloches criaient: Viv' la mariée!*
>
> For everything was miraculous:
> The church sang just for them;
> Even the poor man was happy
> Because love was making its rounds.
> And from on high, pealing loudly,
> The bells rang out: Long live the bride!

When Henri Contet wrote *"Mariage"* for Edith, he hadn't been mistaken—that was what marriage meant to her. Ever since I'd known her, she'd said to me, "Momone, marriage means a church, and bells . . . a celebration of love!"

But she hadn't talked about it for a long time, because she didn't believe it any more. Things often happened in Edith's life just when she thought that they never would again, that the end had come.

There she was, fighting it out with alcohol, drugs, fear . . . and lying to her friends—Guite, Michel Emer, Loulou, Charles, me and a few others—while on the *Île de France*, on the high seas, two men were talking about her: Eddie Lewis, the American agent who had replaced our friend Clifford Fischer when he died, and Jacques Pills.

They were in the bar. The ship was headed for France. Jacques was humming a song.

"What do you think of it, Eddie?"

"First rate. Did you write it?"

"Yes. Who do you think I ought to offer it to?"

"To Edith, of course!"

"I'm glad you said that. Actually I wrote it for her, but I haven't seen her for a long time. I don't know if I dare. . . ."

"Why not? When we're in Paris I'll fix it up."

Edith had first met Jacques Pills in 1939. They'd said hello and good-bye, nothing more. He was the great Jacques Pills, of Pills and Tabet, the most famous singing team of the day. Edith had just appeared at the A.B.C., but that was nothing compared to him. He was also Lucienne Boyer's husband. It was all pretty impressive and not at all within our reach.

In 1941, when Edith gave a performance in the unoccupied zone, we happened to see Jacques again—a little closer this time. He was handsome and elegant, with lots of class, and loaded with talent. A dream of a man.

At that time, we were on tour with Paul Meurisse and *Le Bel Indifférent*. And Henri Contet was next in line for her heart. Edith didn't lack for love, but she found Jacques very much to her liking.

"He's a real gentleman, Momone! *He* wasn't born in the gutter. . . ."

It was true. He was the son of an officer who had been stationed in Les Landes. Jacques had begun studying to be a pharmacist, but the prospect of some provincial drugstore and big glass jars filled with preserved tapeworms didn't excite him. He gave up everything to become a chorus boy at the Casino de Paris, and from there jumped into his act with Tabet. Then, after having a daughter, Jacqueline, with Lucienne, he'd divorced.

Lewis kept his word when he got to Paris. He phoned Edith and said:

"I've got a song you're going to like. It's by a boy with a lot of talent. He was thinking of you when he wrote it. It's very, very good."

"What's his name?"

"Jacques Pills."

"Come on over, quick!"

She hung up and rushed to the bathroom. A quick shot to get herself in shape—the "last one." That's how far gone she was.

"When I saw myself in the mirror, Momone, and remembered how I looked when Pills first met me in Nice, I began to bawl. My face was all swollen and lumpy, like an old drunk's, and my hair looked crappy. . . . I looked ten years older! I couldn't see them like that; I had to fix myself up. So I phoned and said, 'I'll come later, to your hotel. . . .' It was because of my sickness, you see, Momone. . . ."

She lied to me like that for a long time. It was only later I found out and understood.

She arrived late, laughing too loudly. The two men were waiting for her, calm, relaxed and smiling. "Jacques hadn't changed at all, Momone! He was handsome and seemed pleased to see me. We had two or three drinks, which set me up again, and then Jacques made his pitch. 'Listen, Edith, I've written a song for you. I did it while I was touring in South America, at Punta del Este, a pretty little town in Uruguay.'

" 'I didn't know you wrote songs. Do you write the music too?'

" 'No, Gilbert Bécaud, my accompanist, did the music. He's tremendously talented. Would you like to hear him? He's here.'

"Gilbert's a guy from the south of France, with Spanish eyes, and looks sharp as hell. He sat down at the piano and Jacques sang to me":

> Je t'ai dans la peau,
> Y'a rien à faire,
> Obstinément, tu es là,
> J'ai beau chercher à m'en défaire.
> Tu es toujours près de moi.
> Je t'ai dans la peau,
> Y'a rien à faire,

Tu es partout dans mon corps.
J'ai froid, j'ai chaud,
Après tout, je m'en fous
De c'qu'on peut penser,
J'peux pas m'empêcher de crier:
Tu es tout pour moi,
J'suis un intoxiqué.
Et je t'aime, je t'adore à en crever.
Je t'ai dans la peau,
Y'a rien à faire.

I've got you under my skin,
Nothing I can do,
You're there all the time,
There's no use trying to get rid of you.
You're always near me.
I've got you under my skin,
Nothing I can do,
You're everywhere in my body.
I'm cold, I'm hot,
After all, I don't give a damn
What anyone may think,
I can't help shouting:
"You're everything to me,"
I'm addicted.
And I love you, I adore you,
So much I could die.
I've got you under my skin.

"*Je t'ai dans la peau*" was better than a good beginning. It was love at first sight! Edith was off. She liked it all—the song and the man. She pictured herself making a new start. The nightmare with the hypodermic was over. Walking on the arm of this guy, she didn't need drugs any more.

An hour later, the two of them were having dinner at her house. She gave herself a quick little shot in the bathroom so they wouldn't notice anything, but that was really the last one. . . . And she believed it!

There wasn't a minute to lose. The next day and the next and the next, Jacques came back to work on the song. Jacques was in her heart, but under her skin she had drugs, and she was ashamed.

Except for the pushers—who began to blackmail her almost at once—no one yet knew she was on drugs. People thought she drank, that she hadn't recovered from her accident. They thought whatever they liked. . . .

Edith was sure she could beat the habit. For a few hours she fought against giving herself the first shot. Alone in her room, she struggled and struggled. Then she got down on all fours and crawled around looking for the hypodermic needle under the bed where she'd hidden it, and quick gave herself a shot.

Another time, she held out for a few hours with the help of her favorite saint, to whom she promised a forest of candles and a golden altar (which would have cost her less). But when Jacques saw her, she looked so unhinged he said to her:

"You're sick. You want me to call a doctor?"

"No, it's nothing; it'll pass. It's my rheumatism. I'll take my medicine." And she went off for another little dose.

With all her strength and with all her will, Edith wanted to take care of herself with no outside help. She was too ashamed. But I don't think anybody's ever managed to go it alone. One night she phoned me. "Come right away, Momone. I've got to see you."

I rushed there, and she threw herself in my arms like a kid. "If you only knew, if you only knew . . . The whole thing's too much for me, it almost hurts: I'm going to marry Jacques!"

The two of us looked at each other with big tears in our eyes.

"Boy, aren't we being stupid!"

It was true. But Edith and I were quick to show our feelings, and between the two of us we got carried away. If Edith was moved, so was I.

"Are you surprised I'm getting married?"

"Yes, a little."

I told her that to please her. But it was more the husband-to-be that surprised me. I didn't think he was up to the job. He didn't look tough enough. But after all, why not him? He had a lovely smile, and the winning ways of a professional gigolo. He was lots of fun, and Edith needed to laugh again, to have a man in the house to take over, to chase away the parasites and the bloodsuckers I noticed all over the place, who scurried off and hid in corners like mobs of cockroaches. I thought a husband would impress them more than a lover.

"Anyway, Momone, he's free," said Edith. "He got a divorce long before he knew me. I can't be accused of being a 'homebreaker' or a 'man-eater.' This time my lover's my fiancé. I'll have had one at least!"

The idea of getting married made her absolutely giddy. She told everybody about it, even people she hardly knew. Marriage was very important to Edith. She had the feeling it would change her social status, lift her up a notch. On the other hand, she didn't care a hang about having lovers; she was never embarrassed to talk about it. In fact, she was proud of it, and flaunted them all over the place.

Edith, who had experienced almost everything, had a convent girl's notions about marriage. To her a husband wasn't like any other man: he took care of you, protected you, helped you. And though you might cheat on him, you would never leave him! That was what she needed. She was convinced that marriage really transformed girls, and she wanted to experience it.

With a dazzled look on her face, she kept repeating:

"It's the first time I ever got married! By God, I really must love him. . . ."

What tormented Edith was the wedding dress. She wanted one. She didn't believe a wedding could be a wedding without the dress.

"But if I got married in white, it would be ridiculous, wouldn't it?" I thought that *would* be going a bit far! "And I can't have a veil either, can I? You see, there's something I'll always regret—not having made my first communion in a white dress with a crown and all the trimmings. Girls making their first communion look like little brides. How I used to envy them when I saw them!"

This woman, demolished by drink and beginning to be corroded by drugs, dreamed of a first communion dress like a ten-year-old kid. When I think of it now, knowing what I know, it's agonizing.

Then she got a bright idea. "Listen, I've figured it out. The Virgin's colors are blue and white, and there's no one purer than the Holy Virgin. . . . So I'll get married in pale blue. And I'll wear a hat with a little tulle veil in place of a long veil. That way, when they photograph me, I'll look like I'm all in white!"

She was so happy she was transformed. Actually, she didn't look very healthy, but she was less nervous. What I didn't know was that she'd found the solution—no more rationing of drugs. She wanted to be in good shape until the wedding, and after that she'd see. This was Edith's optimistic side: since she was in love and had a man, everything would turn out all right; it had to.

On July 29, 1952, in Paris, in the town hall of the sixteenth arrondissement, René Victor Eugène Ducos—known onstage as Jacques Pills—forty-six years of age, married Edith Giovanna Gassion, thirty-seven.

"You know, I didn't like that wedding at the town hall," Edith said later. "It was a rush job; we did it on the run. But I'm going to make up for it. We'll do it all over again in New York in grand style, in a church. I won't feel really married till we say our vows in front of a priest. You can't cheat with God. And to prove it, I'm not wearing my wedding ring. I didn't even want to see it before it was blessed."

She spent the month before she was to leave getting rid of the house in Boulogne. "I can't bear this house any more. Just going inside pains me. I've suffered too much here. It's stuffed to the rafters with bad memories. There are so few good ones. Some nights I was so lonely I felt like a dog howling because somebody'd died. I'd have gone mad if I'd stayed here.

"Loulou's found me a place at 67 boulevard Lannes, a ground-floor apartment with a private entrance, nine rooms and a little garden. It's fine. I'm going to furnish it. That way everything'll be brand-new when I get home with my husband!"

The joy it gave her to say "my husband." It was like a magic word, a talisman.

This was Edith's fifth trip to the U.S. In New York, on September 20, 1952, she had the wedding she'd dreamed of, at Saint Vincent de Paul's. That morning, in Edith's suite at the Waldorf-Astoria, Marlene Dietrich helped her to dress and handed her her bridal bouquet of white rosebuds with a pale blue voile bow. Edith was trembling with happiness. She was a little high, but not too noticeably. She'd already had her shot; she needed it to get through the ceremony. Loulou Barrier and Marlene were the attendants. Edith looked at them with an expression that always went straight to her friends' hearts. It spoke everything—her joy, her fears, her hopes. . . . And she said to them, "It can't be true . . . I'm dreaming."

But it was true. She entered the church on Loulou's arm. She was dressed from head to foot in pale blue. The bells rang, the organ played, it was beautiful, absolutely beautiful! Behind her was Jacques in a dark blue suit with a white carnation in his buttonhole. When she saw the flower, the thought suddenly flashed through her mind: "Carnations bring bad luck!" But she forgot all about it and walked on a little cloud. All at once, her simple heart had its reward: she was being married just as she'd dreamed she would when she was a kid. . . .

The priest came from an Italian family. His French was endearing. He gave little wings to the words. They were light as air. . . . "Edith Gassion, do you take René Ducos to be your lawfully wedded husband, in the sight of God and men, for better or for worse, until death do you part?"

The famous voice rang out loudly, echoing beneath the arches like a challenge to unhappiness. "I do."

The priest blessed the rings, and Edith put one of them on her husband's finger. Her hand was trembling . . . not only from emotion, but from alcohol and drugs. And she left the church to the sound of the "Wedding March." Outside the church, friends and strangers pelted them with handfuls of rice.

Nothing was too good for her wedding celebration. Two receptions had been planned—a cocktail party given by the Versailles, and a luncheon in the most famous restaurant in New York, Le

Pavillon. It was all very gay. The champagne was French. Edith, high on drugs, laughed a little too much. Then the guests left one by one, and Marlene hugged Edith one last time and wished her lots of happiness. The wedding ceremony that had united the couple was over. The life together that was to separate them was beginning.

A few hours after the wedding, Edith appeared at the Versailles and Jacques went on at La Vie en Rose, where he sang "*Ça gueule ça, madame,*" followed by a song he'd just written for her: "*Formidable.*"

For several weeks the "in" thing to do was to go hear Edith at the Versailles and "M. Piaf" at La Vie en Rose. When you looked up "PEALS, JACQUES," in the newspaper indices (that's the way his name was spelled in America), it said: "See PIAF, EDITH."

Their honeymoon trip was enough to make some people drool—Hollywood, San Francisco, Las Vegas, Miami. But for them it was all work.

The first night in Hollywood, Edith collapsed in front of her mirror. She couldn't powder her face; her makeup was all blotchy because her skin couldn't take it any more, and her hair was dull. The drug was taking its toll. Only her eyes were shining—too brightly. Edith fell into one of those mad fits of temper she usually saved for other people. There was a knock at the door and she shouted, "Come in!" It was the manager.

"Charlie Chaplin's in the audience, Edith! He's come to listen to you! He never goes to nightclubs, you know. You're a hit!"

"I was staggered, Momone," explained Edith. "Singing with Chaplin in the audience was really something! To me, he was the greatest! There are girls like us in his films, Momone. He knows what it's like to be poor in a big city, so I felt close to him. But since he was such a genius—God, was there a gulf between us!—I was scared stiff. I had such stage fright I almost couldn't open my mouth!

"I sang for him. I gave it everything I had. He must have felt it. He invited me to his table and told me things I've never forgotten—that he very seldom went to hear a singer, that he'd never been impressed by one, but that I expressed all the poverty of big cities as well as the lights and the poetry, that the tragedies I sang about were universal, with no frontiers, because they were about men and about love, and that I, Edith Piaf, had made him weep. . . .

"It took my breath away. God, I must have looked foolish sitting next to him, saying, 'Thank you. . . . Oh, I'm so happy!' I think I even blushed. I'd already heard enough compliments in my life to fill a library, but him—he was different. He talked to me about myself when he talked about my songs. And hearing him tell me what he saw in me was shattering. As I sat there face to face with him I acted so stupid that when I got home I told myself he must have thought I was an idiot."

The next day Chaplin phoned and invited her to Beverly Hills, where all the great Hollywood stars lived.

"Oh, Momone, if you could only see what a lovely house he has! I didn't dare touch a thing in it! It's like a set for an American movie in Technicolor—you'd think they repainted it every day!

"I got a better look at him there. He has very beautiful eyes, with thick lashes, and silvery hair, and a smile that goes right through you when he flashes it at you. His voice is gentle, calm. He hardly gestures at all. Everything he says is true and simple. He told me stories about the time when he was with Fred Karno's troupe. Then he played some tunes on the violin that he'd written himself. He's got talent; but it seemed to me his music wasn't like his films; it was a little too soft and sweet. When I left he promised to write me a song, with words and music just for me. Maybe he'll forget. But I won't forget that house. It must be nice to live like that. . . . But I'm sure I wouldn't know how—I don't have that kind of talent."

When Edith came back to Paris, to her new apartment on the boulevard Lannes, she made all sorts of promises. She even went up to our old Sacré-Coeur. She prayed to little Saint Theresa of Lisieux and begged her with all her heart to give her the strength to forget the drugs that made her whirl around backward like a drunken waltzer. Then she'd go home and collapse on the bed in her beautiful blue Louis XV–style bedroom. Why *that* Louis and not another? She had no idea. She didn't give a damn about decorating. Someone else had always done her houses to their own tastes. What she wanted was to be comfortable—and she was.

Her bedroom looked out on a courtyard. It was dark and quiet, just what she liked. In her living room—which was as big as a ball-room—there was nothing but a grand piano and all sorts of electrical equipment: radios, a tape recorder, a phonograph, a stereo system. . . . There were piles of records on the wall-to-wall carpeting that Loulou had given her, but no furniture. If you wanted to sit down, you dragged in armchairs from the sitting room, which was almost furnished, in no particular style, only comfortable stuff. If there were too many guests, you'd filch some chairs from the kitchen.

The kitchen was really great. It was straight out of a good-housekeeping magazine—and the whole gang ate in it even more often than they had at Boulogne. It's where Edith did her knitting and talked a lot of bull all night long. She entertained all her friends in the kitchen after midnight, véry seldom before. You were sure to find Jacques there, her pianist, Robert Chauvigny, her accordionist, Marc Bonel, with his dame, Danièle—who wasn't much yet but who was to become Edith's secretary—Michel Emer, Guite, Loulou and the temporary ones, the small fry that washed in and out with the tides.

A nightmare that lasted four years was just beginning for Edith. When she got back from the U.S. I was frightened when I saw her. This time it was serious. Where was my Edith who'd sung on street corners—perhaps a bit pale, like all Paris street urchins, and a bit on the skinny side, but in good health? . . .

"It's because I'm worn out, Momone, dead tired. Look, I've brought you a souvenir." And she gave me a rose from her bridal bouquet to bring me luck.

"Are you happy?"

"Oh, yes! Jacques is wonderful."

That's what she said, but I could see she didn't have a happy face. And she wasn't all there either. Where was she? I couldn't figure it out. I'd heard rumors. Some said, "The 'boss' is on drugs," but I didn't want to believe it. Edith was always healthy when it came to her pleasures—never anything artificial or complicated.

"Has your rheumatism come back again?" I asked. In 1949 she'd had a bad siege of crippling rheumatism that was soon over.

She latched onto this excuse right away, like a drowning man grabs at a life preserver. "Yes, that's it. The cortisone gets me down." She wasn't lying; the attacks *had* begun again. Edith was afraid of pain now and couldn't stand it any more. As soon as she felt it begin to gnaw, she filed its teeth with cortisone injections. The doctor had prescribed two a day, but she was taking four. Since she couldn't get it by prescription, she found bastards who'd sell it to her. She paid up to fifty thousand old francs for one ampoule of it, which was as expensive as drugs.

If she'd been just some poor slob, they would have left her to howl with pain. But Edith Piaf got what she wanted; she paid. Success and dough can kill you off quicker than poverty. There was also the morphine, which cost her a fortune—and this was only the beginning. The big-time drug pushers scraped poor Edith right down to the bone.

Since I wasn't living with her any more, I didn't quite realize what was going on. I knew her well, but that made me swallow what she told me all the more easily. Besides, she managed to make me take in anything she wanted. She'd look me straight in the eye, take my hand and say, "I miss you, you know. You're all I've got, Momone. You always guess what I want to say before I even open my mouth. . . ."

But it was clear I didn't. My eyes were blinded! That accident was to blame. She'd never have touched all that poison without it. Edith wasn't depraved; she didn't know what depravity was. Before this rotten period in her life, she drank to have a good time. When we got tight together, it wasn't just for another sensation; it was so we could joke around like a couple of jackasses.

She'd dress badly and throw a scarf over her head, go into a nightclub full of people, walk over to a table and announce, "I'm Edith Piaf!" That made them laugh, and nobody believed her. Then she'd turn to me and say, "These damn fools pay to see me, and when they can have me for nothing, they don't want me any more.

They'll see whether I'm Edith Piaf or not." And she'd begin to sing. She was very good at imitating herself. It'd turn into a real caricature. Everybody broke up, surer than ever it wasn't her. She'd leave laughing, very pleased with herself.

"When they get home, they'll say, 'There was a kind of crazy woman there, a real nut, who tried to make us think she was Edith Piaf. Poor sap—as if we could be fooled!' Well, they're the saps. . . ."

For Edith, it wasn't the men that counted; it was love. She had to believe in it; it was absolutely necessary. Without love she wouldn't have been able to live or to sing. That's why she was taken in so easily, and why she said to me more and more often now, "You'll see, it's hard not to be able to forget you're Edith Piaf, that you're exploited, that people don't give a damn about you, that even the guy in bed with you is thinking, 'It's EDITH PIAF,' in capital letters."

It got to be an obsession with her. It was all she ever talked about now. That worried me and I didn't like it; I had a feeling she was changing. Edith had never complicated her life with thoughts like that. She never gave a damn. She never even held grudges. When someone made fun of her, she often didn't realize it till a couple of days later.

"By God, Momone, that son of a bitch took me for some kind of a jerk!" she'd say.

Lots of times I saw her politely greet and even kiss people who had run her down or had played some rotten trick on her. Then once they were gone, she'd shout, "I was really had by that one! I forgot I was mad at him; he might have reminded me!" Then she'd laugh.

I watched her give money to people who'd been making a fool out of her. Then the next day in the bathroom she'd realize it and say:

"Why, he's made a damn fool of me. Well! If he turns up again, I won't give him a cent. He's had it. . . ." But by the next time, she had forgotten the whole thing and off they'd go with their dough. . . .

So I couldn't understand her getting bitter. I didn't like the way her eyes looked; they'd get as murky as dishwater. She didn't seem to see you when she looked at you. Or else they were too bright. She never got out of bed. She'd always liked to be in the sack, but not to that degree; it wasn't normal. She'd just lie there, spread out, limp as an old pile of rags. She'd stay there for days at a time, dirty, her hair uncombed, looking off into space.

It wasn't long before I realized what was happening. I phoned one morning and was told, "M. Barrier and madame's husband took her to a hospital in Meudon."

It had been clear to Jacques before they got married that Edith was on drugs. He thought at first it was only cortisone. She told him the same tall stories she told me. When he realized she was also taking morphine, she told him, "I'm in pain, but don't worry. There's no danger I'll get the habit."

Morphine was all that kept her going in the U.S. There was no question of her getting cured there. The publicity would have been disastrous, and she had to finish out her contracts. Edith would never have agreed not to keep her word. Once back in Paris, she cheated with herself. She swore not to give herself more than the two shots the doctor allowed her, which, according to her, therefore really didn't count. So she'd take two more. She was sure she was being good; only two shots, though she'd really given herself four. Trying to fight it, she waited as late in the day as possible. She'd be so bad by then that she didn't take time to boil the hypodermic needle or to rinse it in alcohol, but stuck it in her arm or in her thigh right through her dress and her stocking. When she reached that point, she was damn well done for.

Double contracts, for her and for Jacques, weren't working out very well, and since she didn't want to be away from him, she got an idea: she and her husband would play in *Le Bel Indifférent*. On the first part of the program they'd each sing in turn, and during the second part they'd do the play.

But in the state she was in, it wasn't possible, so she had agreed to go for a cure. One morning, clutching Loulou's and Jacques's arms, she entered the hospital. She was frightened but happy.

"You'd have thought I was going to jail, except that it was

cleaner. But there were bars on the windows, and the nurse they turned me over to looked like a prison guard. She could have won a wrestling match with Gorgeous George. I saw her through a sort of fog, the way I saw everything—including the guys who came to the house to bring me ampoules of morphine for fifty or sixty thousand francs. . . . The nurse searched me like a customs inspector who's convinced you're hiding a twenty-pound gold bar in your pants.

"It seems us drug addicts have lots of vices (that's what I was, and I knew it). After having scoured me in a tub, she put me in the sack and gave me my shot. The first day, what heaven!" Edith was allowed five shots. Then each day they cut down the amount until "zero" day came.

"I thought I'd go crazy. Terrible pains sliced through me like a knife opening me up, slashing at my muscles. I was jerking all over and was twisted up and knotted like the stump of an old grapevine; then suddenly I'd snap loose like a spring. All around me hovered vague creatures in white. Bits of their faces would appear and disappear. Their mouths gaped like fishes', but no words came out. I was tied down. I'd turned into an animal; I couldn't feel my body any more; I drooled and didn't even notice it. I didn't have a second's rest, and not for an instant was I clearheaded. They told me it only lasted twenty-four hours, but it seemed like a thousand years."

Twenty days later, the doctor told her the treatment was over, but that she wasn't entirely cured and might have a nervous breakdown. She didn't give a damn; she wanted to go home.

Both *Le Bel Indifférent* and singing were out of the question. She'd flop into an armchair and not move, or just sit on a corner of the sofa or lie on her bed, limp as a rag. She didn't want to eat or move or live any more. She'd see Jacques and Loulou come and go, but they didn't even know if she'd heard them. She refused to listen to music—any noise was painful to her. She'd sit staring at her hands as if she didn't recognize them.

One day she came to life and began to talk. It was no miracle; she was secretly on drugs again. The revival of *Le Bel Indifférent* was the worst flop of her career, and the worst financial disaster. Since no one wanted to put up the money, Edith said, "To hell with it; I'll back it myself."

We were all flabbergasted. She rented the Marigny theater and decided to direct the play herself and to stage the two singing acts, hers and Pills's. "It's wonderful, I'm alive again!" she said.

She was really sinking. . . .

She paid a high price for her mistake. The bill was killing. The sets cost a million old francs, and the musicians a hundred thousand francs a day. Conned by a "friend," she brought two mandolin players from Florence and paid them each three thousand francs a night. She doled out seven hundred thousand francs to the stagehands for overtime. And it was all like that. She'd send out a rehearsal call, then arrive several hours late, give herself shots to keep herself going, and work all night long.

Pills was nice. He was sure he loved Edith, but he wasn't up to it, either on stage or off. The Americans had called him "Mr. Charm," which about described him. So that his act wouldn't suffer beside hers, Edith had decided to take all the strong songs out of her repertoire and keep only the lightest, to give herself and the audience a rest. Mangled like that, her act wasn't worth beans. That blah, syrupy Piaf who didn't belt out her songs, who sounded like a dripping faucet, was a disappointment. If this was what Piaf had become, she was finished.

This was the only time Edith ever frightened me from a professional point of view. With a *Bel Indifférent* like that one, she could only fall flat on her face. And she did! Poor Edith; what a beating she took! Paul Meurisse's role was completely wrong for Jacques Pills. He was all smiles, all charm, and when he was obliged to stand there not saying a word and looking glum, he fell apart. He merely seemed bored, like a kid standing in the corner. And since the little ampoules of artificial happiness punched holes in Edith's memory, she made big cuts in the script. The opening night was painful, and the critics just barely polite. The singing bit didn't make them forget that *Le Bel Indifférent* was a flop; it made it all the more obvious. Edith paid to save face and to keep the show going a month.

Once this disaster was over, Edith and Pills were to go on tour. Lost in her private fog, floundering as if in a swamp, she clung to him. "Momone, I can't leave him; he's all I've got. If you only knew how nice he is, and how patient; he hasn't lost his temper once—and after what I've put him through. . . ."

I didn't say a word, but I would have liked him to blow his top and give her a good beating. There was no use counting on that: he'd spent his whole life being a charmer. It would have taken an iron fist to keep her in line! And Edith wasn't easy to handle, especially now that she was seriously going to pot.

She drank to keep off drugs. And during drinking bouts Jacques was more of a companion than a bodyguard. Anyway, he told himself that as long as she had a glass in her hand at least she wasn't sticking herself with a hypodermic needle.

They went on sensational binges together during their tour. One night in Lyons they went into a bar to have a beer at 12:30 A.M. and by eight in the morning they were stinko. Everybody else in the place was snoring. I don't know whether there's a god who looks out for drunks, but there's no doubt he drove the car that morning. Jacques and Edith had decided to go to Valence for breakfast. They got there, went into a café and ordered "two fried eggs and some white wine." They felt like masters of the world, with clear minds and bright eyes. Edith looked at Jacques admiringly: she'd finally found a guy who could stand up to her. She was thinking he was really as good as she was when Jacques asked, "Say, I wonder who brought us here?" with the smile of a charming drunk. He didn't realize that he'd been the one who'd driven!

At the casino in Royat where she was to appear, the mixture of drugs and alcohol finally frightened Edith. She couldn't find her way onstage and kept bumping into the scenery, yelling, "The bastards, they've closed off the entrance to the stage. They've filched the curtain; it's gone. . . ." You'd have thought she was blind. They had to push her onstage. Loulou was dripping with sweat and fear; it was awful.

"I thought I was singing, and all I was doing was mumbling words that didn't mean anything. I thought they sounded nice. People began to boo and yell at me the way they had during the

Leplée scandal; that sobered me up enough to more or less get through my act."

Then the drugs took over again.

"I don't know how I got through the tour. I'd arrive in my dressing room depressed, give myself a shot and sing. As I left the stage, Loulou would catch me in his arms; otherwise I'd have collapsed. I'd cling to him. I didn't want to give myself more than three shots, but I soon got up to four, then more. I was so disgusted when I looked at myself, I felt like puking. One night I said, 'No! I'm going to hold out, I'm going to cure myself . . .' and I didn't give myself a shot.

"I don't know how I got onstage. The spotlights were shining fire right in my mug, and I could see red stars dancing in them. I couldn't hear the musicians any more and waited for them to start playing before I launched forth. I felt a cruddy, sticky sweat pouring down my face, ruining my makeup. I stood there swaying on the boards. I grabbed the mike, clung to it and squeezed it hard. The mike and I were rolling like a mast in a storm. . . . I started singing. . . . Then I stopped short; I couldn't get any more out, not another word. In the distance I could hear the audience break into loud, vulgar laughter. Words came to me like bubbles, popping in my head and ears. Then I started bawling. . . . I yelled, 'Marcel,' and didn't know if I was calling my kid or Cerdan. . . . And I shouted to the audience, 'Forgive me! . . . It's not my fault. Forgive me!' "

They brought down the curtain. This was the first time Edith hadn't really sung at all—not even badly. They had to reimburse the audience. The next day the papers were kind enough to say that Mme Edith Piaf had been indisposed onstage, but it made a lousy impression.

Her condition was very serious. When she returned to Paris, Edith had to go back to the hospital at once. This was in 1954— not quite two years since the beautiful wedding ceremony. Jacques did what he could, but he wasn't there very often. He had his own career. Anyway, you have to have the vocation of a saint, not a singer, to be the husband of a derelict.

This time Edith didn't even last four days. She fled from the hospital before they took her off the stuff.

"My head felt like it was filled with slivers of broken mirror, their sharp points piercing my brain. There was a hammer pounding on my skull. They'd filched all my clothes. I didn't give a damn; I left in my bathrobe. I crawled by the guard's office on all fours, took a taxi and came home. I went straight to my hiding place. The whole cure would have to start over again. . . .

"Drugs are a carnival in hell. There're merry-go-rounds and roller coasters. You shoot up, you rocket down; you go up again, you come down again. . . . Everything's like everything else, always the same; monotonous; gray; dirty. But you don't even notice, you go right on. . . .

"When I stuck the needle into my flesh, I didn't gasp with pleasure—I gasped with relief. You're in a hurry to give yourself a shot, not because it makes you feel good but because it makes you stop feeling bad. Christ, are we stupid! The more you take, the more you suffer, and the more you have to take so you won't hurt so much inside. Your mind's been gone for a long time. It's like living in a fog."

That was the state Edith was in when she decided to leave for a ninety-day tour—three summer months, through all of France—with the Super-Circus. Nobody could stop her. She kept saying, "If I don't sing, I'll croak. . . ." What she didn't say was that she needed money to poison herself with. She spent every penny she earned on drugs. Loulou was desperate. "She can do it." And she did, but in what condition! She was a wreck.

Loulou kept waiting for her to collapse so he could take her to a hospital for the third time. He knew she'd never again go of her own free will. She didn't realize what a state she was in. Her arms and thighs were covered with swellings and scabs and sores. She had to be made up, dressed and pushed onstage. She had almost no idea what was going on any more. All she waited for was the moment when her supplier brought her the magic ampoule.

The tour was a nightmare for everybody. The people who'd gone with her trembled. The reporters, who'd been told she was sick, kept racing after her, hoping she'd collapse. You had to trick them in order to hide her from them and get her away after each performance. She was unconscious for hours at a time.

"It seems the Circus played a different city every day," Edith said later. "I don't know. I didn't see anything, and I don't remember anything. It's all blank. I can only remember bits and pieces . . . somebody pushing me into a car, then onto a hotel bed, and then out into the ring. . . . I'd give myself a shot just before going on . . . then I'd sing. And it went on like that day after day. . . . I didn't give a shit; nothing interested me. The Circus— damn good word for it!—stopped in Cholet. Loulou took me in his arms, wrapped me in a thick blanket and put me in a car. We drove to the hospital . . . and the doctor said to me, 'You again!' The whole thing started over. It was hell!"

The amazing thing was that Edith had sung. There were very few evenings she hadn't made sense. There were even some when she was again "the Great Piaf!"

This time, at the hospital, the cure began with ten shots a day. That's how drugged she was. When she got down to four, she went into wild rages. She'd get out of bed, smash everything around her, roar and yell, with her hair falling all over her face. Then she'd hurt herself, and they'd have to tie her down.

I phoned her every day, as I'd done the other times she was in, and went to the hospital to get news of her. The head nurse was a great girl; she obeyed the rules but she had a heart. She explained to me that this was what always happened, that it would soon be over, that I shouldn't worry, that Edith wasn't any worse off than the others. What tormented me was whether it would really stop, whether there'd ever be an end to it, whether Edith would ever be the same again.

"Of course," the nurse reassured me. "It's usually like this. There are always relapses. But there have been cures."

Edith wasn't allowed any visitors in her room. But the corridor outside her door was just as empty. I could see Loulou's big, thick shape pacing up and down sometimes. That's about all. I knew we couldn't do anything for her, that Edith didn't even know we were there, but such loneliness pained me.

The day came when she got no shot at all. I'd come to the hospital, not knowing it was such a bad time. As I got on the elevator, I heard a patient screaming somewhere upstairs. I thought I recognized Edith's voice. I didn't want it to be her. It was frightful—the cries of a dying animal. The voice knifed through my head and split my brain. I stood at the door of her room, rooted to the spot. Someone came out, and I saw a screaming thing strapped to the bed, the veins on its forehead ready to burst, howling without letup, gleaming with sweat. Around it were some dames and guys in white watching as one watches an object, looking at the bed where this animal that had once been a woman was foaming at the mouth and drooling. I couldn't even cry. "It's not her . . . it's not her . . ." I mumbled. The head nurse took me by the arm and said:

"Come on, don't stay here. It's upsetting to the family, but it's nothing. She'll be better tomorrow. You've picked the first day she's 'off' completely."

"But she's suffering so."

"Yes, abominably. But it's necessary. We have to do it."

She howled for twelve hours straight. And for days that animal cry rang in my head and ate out my heart.

Then she left the hospital. "Momone, I really yelled. I couldn't help it. But I wanted to get cured. This time I think I am. The doctor let me out. 'Watch it,' they said. 'You'll feel the need for drugs again at the end of the third, sixth, twelfth and eighteenth months.' "

So for eight months Edith lived on the boulevard Lannes in terror that *it* might come back. She was closed up in her room, in the dark, not wanting to see anybody. Which didn't keep all sorts of slugs from crawling around her. Pushers got by all the obstacles put in their way and offered her fixes. They handed her a line like: "Try 'snow,' Mme Piaf; it's not like morphine, it's not dangerous." When she refused, they threatened to tell the reporters she was on drugs. Even one of her own chauffeurs—there'd been a slew of them—came to blackmail her. He demanded a million francs to keep his mouth shut, and she gave it to him.

When Jacques was there, she was calmer. He made no bones about throwing everybody the hell out. He even punched one guy who, like all the others, wanted money. But he wasn't there very often, and Edith stayed alone with the help, who didn't give a damn about their work and wondered if there was still enough in it for them.

The cures, the drugs, the pushers and the blackmail all cost money, and Edith wasn't working. She sold the farm at Le Hallier, a few paintings she'd bought and a handful of jewelry she didn't really care a damn about. "I'm not the type to wear rocks and pearls," she said to me. "On me they always look like they'd been bought at the five-and-ten." But for her needs, ten million or so was a drop in the bucket. Loulou was in despair.

Then she stuck one foot out into the world. She could bear daylight again. The day I found out she'd opened the shutters in her bedroom, I sent her dozens of roses, the kind she liked best. She phoned me at once. Her voice was normal and almost gay.

"It's not all over for me yet, Momone," she said.

We all breathed again. It was about time! Loulou came up with a contract for the U.S., at the Versailles. "Do you think I can go, Loulou?" she asked.

"They're waiting for you. They don't know a thing. You've got to take it."

She was once more back in the arms of work. She'd made it! The only thing missing from the festivities was love. Edith had no desire for men. She was fond of Pills—maybe less so than of friends like Loulou, Charles Aznavour and Guite—but she knew her marriage was on the rocks.

"It's nobody's fault, Momone; it's the drugs! Jacques's a soft-hearted, affectionate guy. He was meant to laugh, not struggle with tragedy. Since he can't take part, he stands to one side, and I'm alone. You understand?" The gap between them widened. It was no longer a ditch; it was the Grand Canyon.

When she left for New York, Jacques went to London to rehearse for a musical comedy. And Edith came to life again in the U.S. America was good for her; she found the audience she needed. She thought the " 'Ricains" were reliable. When they fell in love it was serious; they were real men; they didn't fluctuate like broads, the way Frenchmen did. On the other hand, she hid everything from them. She wasn't part of the family there; so she behaved better.

She had as good a press as usual there. One critic wrote: "Edith Piaf, the little French Isolde, goes on bravely dying of love. She dies five hundred times during dinner, five hundred times after supper, and in the same admirable voice each time. . . . The strongest voice in the tiniest body!" Articles appeared about her every day and piled up on her bed. But that one she'd never forget; it had impressed her. When she got back, she told me about it. "The guy's right, Momone. I do die of love five hundred times an evening. What would he write if he really knew about my life! But when I'm not dying of love, when I don't love at all, then I *really* croak! You see, Momone, marriage doesn't get you anywhere!"

She didn't work in Paris; she waited. Edith didn't do anything for almost a year. She found it hard to get going again—maybe because it was her second wind, and it's not easy to fill your lungs with new air.

Suddenly everything changed. Loulou came up with a contract for her at Carnegie Hall in New York, at three thousand dollars a night. It was the first time a variety star ever sang in the largest and most elegant concert hall in the States.

She went to work feverishly again. The whole circus had started over on the boulevard Lannes. She threw herself passionately into rehearsing, as usual. She wore everyone out and accused them of being weaklings. She laughed, she was happy, she was in great shape.

In 1956, for the seventh time, Edith landed in New York. She was received like a queen. When she got off the plane, in the freezing cold, Loulou tried to get her to leave the airport. But Edith wrapped the mink coat Marcel had given her, which had escaped the general shipwreck, closer around her. The reporters yelled for a picture, then for another. "It's O.K., Loulou. I'm not sick any more. Let me give them what they want. I belong to these guys. . . ."

She was right. For several days people lined up in below-zero weather to hear her. Flowers kept arriving in her room at the Waldorf-Astoria, filling the corridor. Eddie Lewis, her agent, hovered around like a mad dog.

"You're in great shape, better than last time. How's your husband? Just think, I'm almost the one who married you off!" He didn't comprehend the worn-out look in Edith's eyes. She was branded, like anyone who's gone through hell. He only thought that that face and those eyes would make her an even bigger star.

That night Edith sang a song of Pierre Delanoë's, "*Les Grognards*," for the first time.

> *Ecoute, peuple de Paris,*
> *Ecoute, ces pas qui marchent dans la nuit,*
> *Regarde, peuple de Paris, ces ombres éternelles,*
> *Qui défilent en chantant sous ton ciel. . . .*

> Listen, people of Paris,
> Listen to the footsteps marching in the night,
> Look, people of Paris, look at those eternal shadows
> That file by, singing beneath your sky. . . .

It was shattering. You could see the Paris sky: you could see the French flag waving over the Arc de Triomphe and the Champs Élysées! Pierre Delanoë, who, like many others, had come over with Edith to hear her sing at Carnegie Hall, made a recording during the performance that is a unique document. At the end of "*Les Grognards*," the shouts, the applause and the whistles were as violent as a storm and lasted almost as long as the song.

It was wild. Edith sang twenty-seven songs. After the final curtain the audience got to their feet and stood for seven minutes, applauding that little woman all alone on the huge stage who had made them feel like shouting, like dying of love along with her.

"Loulou timed them. Seven minutes is long, you know. You have time to think. I listened to them . . . it was beautiful. It was so good it hurt! It was too much. You know what I mean, Momone? Well, during those few minutes while my heart was mad with joy

I felt I was married to the audience. It was all over with Jacques. It isn't his fault and it's not mine. He just came along at a bad time. . . . So I've asked him for a divorce. I'm not cut out for marriage. It lasted four years: that's not bad! But it's all over and done with now. Church bells won't ring for me again until my funeral. . . ."

Chapter 16

The Whirlwind of Drugs

To Edith, Carnegie Hall was more than a success, a triumph; it was *her* victory.

"I'm through with all that shit, Momone," she said. "My pals, the Americans, did me good, you know. Maybe they don't act distinguished, but at least when they love you, they don't beat around the bush. I can tell you, when I left for the U.S. I had the shakes; now I've got my courage back. I'm going to get ready for a new show at the Olympia."

"Be careful, Edith," I said. "Don't go too fast. Maybe you're still weak."

"Don't be a pain in the ass! I've got enough people around me who are. Do you know what Eisenhower told the doctors who told him to be careful? 'Better to live than to vegetate!' And I've got to make up for lost time—I'm too far behind."

The splendid nights on the boulevard Lannes began again. And there was no lack of a supporting cast. There were A. R. Chauvigny, Marc Bonel and Danièle; plus Robert Burlet, the chauffeur, and his wife, Hélène, who for a short time was Edith's general secretary; Christiane, the maid, and her mother, Suzanne, the cook. They were the background, they lived there; they were Mme Piaf's employees. Then there were all the old friends who came to see Edith and played the first and second leads: Loulou, Michel Emer, Guite, Contet, Charles. And there were others. . . .

Edith was no snob. She'd as soon have invited a bum she'd picked up at a métro entrance as she would André Luguet or Francis Blanche.

"They're all the same when they're bare-assed. So why shouldn't I have them at my table?"

In addition, there were those who just dropped in—her former patrons, who were always welcome when they came by to say hello—and those she'd temporarily adopted. The only thing we didn't have was a tenor, a lack we were soon to feel.

Those who had a taste of what nights on the boulevard Lannes were like came back again and again. There wasn't any place like it, and we couldn't do without it. We drank cheap wine or beer there, depending on the tastes of the "boss." We ate caviar by the ladleful. If someone merely said he liked it, Edith would buy pounds of it, although she didn't especially care for it—a teaspoonful was enough for her.

We listened to records, and talked mostly shop for hours at a time. It was warm, and we could stretch out and relax. The outside world probably existed, but nobody gave a damn; we were a self-sufficient group. When Edith was in good shape, she'd sing, trying out songs and working them over like a little horse, and that was great. The night might go on till eleven the next morning. When I was there—and I often was—Edith and I had a great old time. People were snoring all over the place, in chairs and in makeshift beds. "Look at them, Momone, not one left standing." I could hardly keep my eyes open, but I managed. I'd been trained! Anyway, Edith wouldn't have understood if I'd given up. A little soldier sees things through to the bitter end!

"Come on, let's have a bathroom chat, like in the good old days. . . ."

But it wasn't quite the same now. Edith played a part even with me. She was often in pain. The joints of her hands were beginning to get gnarled. Edith, who never cheated with life, was gambling with her body and wouldn't let it take the lead or deal the cards. Only she had the right to hold aces. When her tortured body protested too loudly, she refused to listen, and shut it up with drugs.

The hardest part was getting her to bed. "I'm not sleepy, Momone; I don't want to go to bed." She had no patience. Sleep had to hit her over the head like a club; she had to collapse. She didn't want to lie in bed waiting for sleep, so she stuffed herself with sleeping pills. But they didn't always work because she'd taken them for so long.

When I finally managed to get her in the sack, with plugs in her ears and her black mask over her eyes, I'd tiptoe out. It didn't work every time. Often, just as I touched the doorknob, I'd hear, "Momone . . ."

Edith spent her nights this way even when an opening was close at hand. The only difference was that she was working as well. We were right in the middle of her getting ready to appear at the Olympia again. Edith hadn't sung in Paris for almost two years. This 1956 opening was important to her.

Bruno Coquatrix, who didn't trust her because of all the rumors he'd heard, had hired her for a month, which wasn't so bad. Only big stars were hired for that long; the rest got two-week engagements.

The first night we were as nervous as hungry fleas on a new dog! If the show at the Olympia didn't go over in Paris, Edith's career would be in danger. The tours with Pills and the Super-Circus hadn't passed unnoticed. There had been some leakage of information: people were saying Piaf was finished, that she broke her contracts. They expected her to go down for the count. The wild beasts in the audience were ravenous. But after the fifth song they bleated like lambs. She sang, for the first time, "*Marie la Française*," "*Une Dame*," "*L'Homme à la moto*," "*Toi qui sais*," "*Les Amants d'un jour*" and "*Bravo pour le clown*."

I hadn't heard her onstage for quite a while. From the very first song that evening, I was captivated, moved, shaken. She'd never sung like that before. Her voice came from far away. When the sirocco blows, it's full of sand, it burns your lungs, it sweeps everything before it; it picks up the desert and throws it right in your mouth. Edith's voice had swept through the city and swirled around its squares. It had had a few drinks in the bistros. It had cried out its love for the slums, for the street corners, for chance encounters, for carnivals—and it hit you right between the eyes. It *was* the street; it came from the gut and slashed at your belly as it passed. The snobs, their little fingers crooked, were as struck by it as the proles, and they had no time to think. Actually, they didn't give a damn about the words. She could have sung "tralalala" or the phonebook listings—as Germaine Montero put it. She would have gripped your heart exactly the same way.

No one paid any attention to how her hair was done, or how she dressed, or even if she sang off-key. None of that mattered. If she made a mistake or stopped singing, people liked it even better; it made her more true to life. No tricks; nothing artificial. It all came from inside her, from her loving and her suffering. And those drugs which I cursed, which had almost killed her, had scraped her raw so she sang of love with a violence no one had ever heard before.

They couldn't bring down the curtain; she took twenty-two curtain calls and sang more than ten encores. My throat was dry and my hands hurt from clapping.

Bruno canceled the contracts that were next in line and renewed hers once, twice, three times. She stayed at the Olympia twelve weeks. The house was packed every day. Even tickets for the folding aisle seats were on the black market. She set attendance records, and the Olympia box office took in three million francs a day. Her record sales went up to three million; in four months she sold three hundred thousand, and the record of her recital at the Olympia sold twenty thousand the first two weeks. Her record company paid her thirty million old francs in royalties that year. Her fee, every night, was a million two hundred fifty thousand francs. Figures that made people say, "She hasn't suffered much! What a lot of money she must have socked away!" But she hadn't, not a penny.

Edith earned her dough with her life. The doctors warned her when she went back to the Olympia, "Every time you sing, you shorten your life a few minutes. . . ." They thought they'd frighten her, but all she said was, "I don't give a damn. I'll croak even sooner if I don't sing!" So she could bloody well throw away her money if she wanted to! As for saving, it was as impossible for her now as it had been in the past.

In *Ma Route et mes chansons*, Maurice Chevalier had written a warning: "Piaf, that little featherweight champion, drives herself relentlessly. She cannot save her strength any more than her earnings. She's a rebel and a genius, but she's racing toward abysses that I can see lying ahead. She is eager to embrace everything and she does, ignoring the age-old laws of caution every star must heed."

"Well," said Edith as she read it, "a lot of good it'll do him to be able to buy a gold coffin when he dies! When that day comes for me, I'll be satisfied with a pine box like the poor get buried in. Anyway, I want to die young. I think it's awful to get old, and sickness is ugly. . . ."

One of Edith's great admirers, the most important in her life—Claude Figus—turned up at the Olympia. He was nuts about Edith; he'd fallen madly in love with her when he was thirteen. And I mean really in love! No cure for addiction could ever have helped him. It was an old story. We'd met him one night around 1947, when Edith was appearing at the A.B.C. It was raining, and Edith was out of aspirin. Even though she never took aspirin, she had to have it on hand, so I trotted around looking for some. Just outside the stage door, I bumped into a kid rooted there in the rain like a stalk of asparagus with growing pains.

I walked past, and when I came back five minutes later, the stalk grabbed me by the sleeve.

"I saw you with Mme Piaf, mamselle. Couldn't you get me in to see her?"

So then I looked at him. He had gentle eyes, a brown curl falling down on his forehead, papier-mâché cheeks like kids in the slums, and was dressed cheaply but neatly. I liked him.

"Where you from?"

"Colombes."

"I'm from Ménilmontant. Look here, kid, you won't do. Take off!"

I was watching him out of the corner of my eye. He made me feel twenty years younger.

"Gee, you're great," he answered, falling in behind me.

"Oh, come on; I'm late."

I galloped on, but he took good long strides. I arrived backstage. Edith was about to go on.

"What's that you've got in tow? You robbing the cradle now?"

"Are you kidding? It's *you* he's after."

He looked at Edith as if she were Joan of Arc, just climbed down out of a stained-glass window to have a little chat with him.

"You can stay, but keep out of the way!"

He listened to her sing, so flattened against a piece of scenery the stagehands could have moved him out without even noticing.

The next day he managed to get into the wings by saying he was a pal of mine. He admired Edith so completely and so naïvely, she gave him a signed photograph.

"What's your name?"

"Claude Figus."

"How old are you?"

"Thirteen, Mme Piaf, but I love you."

Edith really laughed. "I know age doesn't keep you from feeling, but you'll have to wait at least ten years to marry me!"

Everywhere she sang, we ran across little Claude. First nights he paid for a seat in the peanut gallery and then came backstage. He was really a nice kid. Edith would say, "Let me touch your noggin, Claude; knocking on wood brings good luck!"

We got used to him trailing after us. We didn't even notice that he was growing up, that he was becoming a man. We had him underfoot for years, then one day he disappeared.

The opening night of Olympia '56—we dated them, like great wines—I was in the wings with Charles. We were watching people line up in front of Edith's dressing room, when I heard Coquatrix's voice: "Come on, clear out, you don't know anybody here."

"Yes, I do, sir. I know Mme Simone and M. Aznavour."

I looked at the boy who said it—a good-looking guy. Charles, who knew him as well as the rest of us and who'd always been very nice to him, said to me, "It's little Claude!"

"Why, you're a man now! Where have you been?"

"In the service."

"I know what you want—you want to see Edith. Come back tomorrow; things'll be calmer."

I realized by the way he said, "I'm sure she's forgotten me," that he still had a thing for her, but I didn't think any more of it.

"You know, you live on the same street I do," he said.

"Why didn't you come see me?"

He looked like a grown man, but you could tell he still had a kid's heart. The next day he came to see Edith. And since she needed someone around the house who adored her, she took him to the boulevard Lannes that very night and baptized him her secretary. He stayed with her almost eight years. He was a nice little guy, and very decent.

He still adored Edith. He was completely devoted to her. If she'd asked for the skin off his back to make a lampshade, he'd have offered her the skin in front as a bonus. She didn't have to humor him. He came at a good time for her; she could do as she pleased with this one. Poor little guy; he may have been taller than she was but he didn't have the necessary stature, and she gobbled him up.

For months drugs had taken the place of everything else in her life. Since they'd had her by the throat, suffocating her, she hadn't thought of anything else. But now the situation was different. She felt like being in love again. There was an emptiness inside her, and love couldn't grow in that climate, even though she needed it to live. Without love, she was going to throw herself into some damn thing or other, anything. I was sure of it.

There was the Olympia every night. But between the time she left the stage and the time she went on again, there were a lot of hours, a lot too many. So Edith drank. Not the way we used to do, for fun, but to knock herself out, to collapse into bed and finally sleep. She'd decided beer was less harmful to her than wine, and she got really loaded on it.

Claude didn't know it was as dangerous for her as drugs. She had him hide bottles of beer in her bedroom, in the bathroom, and just about everywhere, as if it were a good joke. He was the one who kept her supplied. She'd made him her accomplice.

Loulou and a few other old friends tried to help me in the fight against her drinking. But it wasn't possible if you didn't live with Edith. The minute you let her go to the bathroom alone, you'd had it: she'd already found the time and the means to do all the damn-fool things that came into her mind.

When Loulou tried to reason with her, she'd tell him to go fuck off; or she'd swear that it was all over, that she'd made a vow never to drink again. She was so full of booze that three beers were enough to get her tight. And Claude, that innocent kid, would say to me, "I swear to you she's not drinking much; I'm keeping an eye on her!"

Edith was about to leave for an eleven-month tour all through the States, the longest and most important tour of her career. They paid her very well there. She got the highest fee of any performer except Bing Crosby and Frank Sinatra. She was the best-paid star in the world, next to them. Once again, Loulou was in despair.

"What are we going to do? She'll be even less able to resist temptation in the U.S. than she is here. Almost a year—that's too long! Do something, Momone; she'll listen to you."

"I'd like to think that's true, but you know very well she hasn't listened to anybody for a long time now," I answered. "What do you expect? She's not in love. She's like a boat without a sailor; she's just adrift. We have to find her a man."

That's what she needed. The people who lived with her and were around her all the time didn't give a damn: they were her employees. They were afraid of losing jobs where madame didn't supervise anything and didn't see anything—not to mention the ceaseless flow of money.

Whenever Loulou had a search made, in every corner of the house—thoroughly—under the Louis XV bed, in the medicine chest, in the cupboards, the closets, the lavatories, the grand piano and anywhere else that a bottle could be hidden, including the garbage can—Edith, who realized she had nothing more to drink, would fly into a rage and break everything, or she would slip out into the night wearing her nightgown with a coat over it, a pair of old slippers on her feet, and go drink in a bar.

One morning Hélène, the chauffeur's wife, got a call from a

bartender. "It's six o'clock and we've got to close. Come get your boss, Edith Piaf. She doesn't want to leave; she keeps yelling, 'I belong to you.' We want to get some sleep. Bring her checkbook along too—she's run up quite a bill."

The chauffeur, his wife, Marc Bonel and Claude set out like commandos to recover their boss, who, according to her mood, might want to carry off the jukebox, the pinball machine or the curtains.

No, Edith's binges were no fun at all any more.

One night before leaving for the U.S., she'd decided to rehearse. In the middle of a song, she stopped dead.

"I forgot something in my bathroom."

"I'll get it for you, Edith," said Claude.

"That's right, come with me."

Ever since she'd been shut up in a hospital, Edith couldn't stand being alone. She had someone go everywhere with her, especially when she went to the toilet—a man or a woman, she didn't give a damn—and she'd leave the door ajar so she'd feel secure.

She came back after a while, her eyes shining. She started singing, and then she began to laugh. "I can't . . . the words keep knockin' into each other . . . they wanna all come out at the same time. 'Don't push,' I tell 'em. . . . They don't listen. . . . There's too many of 'em in my mouth. Got to go spit 'em out. . . ."

So off she went again. When she came back, she was pale, her nostrils were pinched and there was sweat on her forehead.

"Something wrong, Edith?" asked someone.

"Nah. It's jus' these words that keep me from talkin'. . . I'll be back. . . ."

A few seconds later, they heard a scream, followed by the noise of breaking glass. They all took off, with Claude in the lead, and found Edith standing on the bed having a fit of dt's, shouting and throwing beer bottles, empty or full, into a corner of the room, where they crashed against the wall. There were long trails of beer dripping all over, and the smell made them all want to vomit. Edith, her face completely distorted, was hiccuping, "Spiders . . . mice . . . kill them . . . kill them! They're coming at me, they're climbing! They're scratching me!" She was tearing off her clothes and scratching her face and arms, screaming.

"I couldn't bear it," Claude told me. "Simone, Simone! She's got so much talent; she's the greatest! How can she do things like this?" The poor kid had tears in his eyes.

The ambulance took her away that night. Two men were needed to hold her down. She was suffering abominably. The next day Edith was locked in the hospital. She got out a month later, exhausted but cured.

"Oh, Momone, that shitty cure is worse than anything. You wouldn't believe how I suffered! The bastards! It's like love—it always begins all right, but boy, does it end badly!

"The first day the nurse with the biceps—they've got some really hefty babes in there—came into my room and took my order for the day. While I was at it, I ordered a great assortment: white wine to begin with, beer for during the day, some good strong red wine with my meals, and a whiskey to top it off.

"During the day the old gal brought everything I'd ordered and watched to see that I swallowed it down properly. She needn't have bothered; she could trust me for that. At night I was really potted. I sang at the top of my lungs. I was having a ball, except that I was all alone.

"You know, those docs all have the same methods. They cut down your dose every day, like they do with drugs, but at the same time they pour some kind of medicine down you that makes you puke. So when you see the glass of booze coming and think you're going to down it, the mere smell of it makes you feel like vomiting. It's a perverse kind of torture. I didn't know where I was any more. I was like a sick dog, lying there clutching the bed. I hiccuped, I cried, I begged, 'That's enough . . . that's enough!' And I still had attacks. I saw nauseating animals, all sticky and hairy, with hundreds of legs! . . . That business about pink elephants—I swear it's not true. It's impossible to suffer that much.

"I'd never have believed our old sprees and great binges would end up in a stinking mess like that! The cure for an alcoholic is really disgusting. And still, Momone, anyone who's got the will to go through with it is O.K."

She had only ten days left to get ready for her tour, but she was in good shape when she left.

Eleven months is a long time when you're traveling from New York to Hollywood, from Las Vegas to Chicago, from Rio to Buenos Aires . . . especially if all you have to drink is milk and fruit juice! Edith had had a bellyful of it when she got home, but she was happy.

"You can't imagine how great the trip was—a little too long, but good. I had a funny surprise in Frisco. There was a French warship in the harbor, the *Jeanne d'Arc*. The captain invited me aboard. I never say no to a sailor, so I went with some friends and some American reporters.

"The captain's launch came to get me, and what do I see when I come aboard? All the sailors standing at attention like they do for an admiral. And that wasn't all. Along the gangway there was a squadron presenting arms for me, Edith Piaf! If you could've seen the expressions on the Yanks' faces! They thought we French really did things right.

"I was awfully sorry you weren't there; you'd have broken up seeing me inspect the French Navy. Just between you and me, the Navy owed me that. We've made more than one tar happy, haven't we, Momone?

"The kids there are absolutely terrific; their ideas warm your heart. On New Year's Day the students at Columbia University wanted me to sing them '*L'Accordéoniste*' in front of the Statue of Liberty. It was so cold out I must have been a little off-key, but it was wonderful to sing for them, and I got a raft of 'hip, hip, hurrays' that almost knocked the Statue of Liberty off its base!

"I could see why they were thirsty after that! It seems that's the effect I have on Americans. One reporter wrote: 'Edith Piaf is the best champagne salesman in the United States; the minute she sings in a nightclub, your throat gets dry with emotion.'

"Another funny thing happened. A guy in Paris sent me his best wishes in a big envelope. Since he didn't have my address, he marked it: 'Edith Piaf, U.S.A.' The guys at the post office wrote: 'The Paris postal employees send love and kisses' on the envelope. You can figure the number of places that letter hit before it got to

me! At each place the guys in the post office would write something: 'Us too'; 'The Chicago mailmen love you'; 'Los Angeles
agrees.' There wasn't a single inch of space left when I finally received it! They must have been afraid it'd get lost, because they
sent a guy to deliver it to me in person. And, instead of knocking
at my door, he whistled *'La Vie en rose.'* Wasn't that sweet?

"A year's a long time, though, to go without breathing the air
of the Paris streets or seeing my pals. And I was trapped in the tour
schedule like a fly in a spider web. There was no way out. But
aside from that, everything went well. The Americans would like
me to do it all over again. They were just terrific to me. I'm fond
of them, but I'm in no hurry!"

I watched Edith as she wandered around her living room, looking at it with a critical eye, as if someone had changed the walls on
her. I found her in good shape, not all bloated up any more, and
her hands were almost normal. But I knew I'd never rest easy
again, and would always be scared of its all starting over.

The trunks from the tour were brought in. Edith sat down on
one of them.

"They're pretty comfortable. I'm going to leave them here—
it's practical. We're always short of seats in this goddamn shack.
You know . . . I don't drink anything but water now till noon, then
a little glass of wine at lunch, and milk during the rest of the day—
I don't like it much—then no more than two or three glasses of
wine with dinner."

"Is it doing you good?"

"It hasn't hurt me any. But it's damn boring being sensible. Did
you see the pile of song manuscripts on the piano? There's going
to be plenty of work!" She picked through the manuscripts, read
some of them, strummed on the piano and called Guite.

"Guite, I'm home. What were you doing while I was away?
Irma la Douce? Are you happy? Good. Did you write anything
for me? You did? Well, get over here right away; you should
already be here! I can't live without you. God, did I miss you!"

I heard those words several times that day. And she meant it
each time. She'd missed all of us.

Before Marguerite could sit down at the piano, Edith handed

her a manuscript. "Read this. It's *Salle d'attente* by Michel Rivgauche. The guy's talented as hell. I've asked him to come over."

Before Marguerite had finished reading through it, Edith said:

"Listen to this record. I came across this music in South America, while I was touring Peru. It's a Spanish girl singing."

"Oh, Edith, it's really good!" Guite said. "Play it again."

"I need words for it. Who can write them for me?"

Michel Rivgauche wrote them for her, and the song became *"La Foule."*

> *Emportés par la foule*
> *Qui nous traîne,*
> *Nous entraîne, l'un vers l'autre,*
> *Nous ne formons qu'un seul corps.*

> Borne away by the crowd,
> Carrying us off,
> Bringing us closer to each other,
> We form a single body.

Michel was Edith's most recent find, a slim guy with a hairline mustache—like an Argentinian villain-seducer in the silent films—curving eyebrows and a mass of disheveled hair. He was a nice man, intelligent and very talented, and always a little out of things.

The boulevard Lannes apartment was a whirlwind. "The Great Piaf" was home again, preparing Olympia '58—one of her best performances.

Most of the new songs were by Pierre Delanoë and Michel Rivgauche. Though Michel conformed to Edith's way of working and became one of her nighttime pals, Delanoë never really got over his days as a civil servant. Night to him was meant for sleeping; or else one worked; but he didn't like to feel he was wasting time. He didn't know you had to go along with Edith, that she only worked when she felt like it, but that when she did, she left everyone else behind. Still, that didn't keep him from writing *"Les Grognards," "Le Diable de la Bastille"* and *"Toi tu ne l'entends pas"* for her.

The whole gang came back to Edith's. Claude didn't miss out on his boss's return. He was on hand, bustling about and devoted.

In a few weeks the recital at the Olympia was ready. The whole house was cheery. We old hands had got our Edith back. It was almost as good as when a new man came into her life. And one had: Félix Marten.

Before appearing at the Olympia, Edith had decided to break in her program with a tour of the provinces. Loulou had taken care of everything, as usual. Always extremely proper, and knowing his boss well, he'd warned her that there was someone new on her program—Félix Marten.

"I trust you," Edith had answered.

The night of the first stop, in Tours, Edith was in her dressing room with her usual attack of stage fright that got her in the gut. This was never a good time to pay her a polite visit. She was putting on her makeup when there was a knock at the door, and in came a rather good-looking boy, over six feet one with an insolent look on his face.

"Hello, Edith. I'm Félix Marten."

Edith may not have learned good manners when she was in diapers, but this guy didn't seem to have grasped the fact that she was the great Edith Piaf, and he introduced himself as if he were the son of God. Edith didn't like it one bit. She was going to fix him. But he'd no sooner introduced himself when he added:

"I'm happy to be working with you. Thanks."

"You're welcome. . . ."

Félix may not have had manners, but he had a way with him. Edith listened to him sing, once, twice, three times. Onstage he was a cynic, but she wondered if he didn't have a soft heart. He sang *"T'as une belle cravate," "Fais-moi un chèque," "Musique pour . . ."* There were no sweet nothings in *that* repertoire, either folksy or flowery. She listened and couldn't decide. She was sure, though, that he had something going for him, a real personality. The longer she looked at him, the broader his shoulders got, and she figured that hearing that guy say "I love you" would make your heart quiver plenty. A few days later, Edith phoned me. "Momone, it's happened—I'm engaged to love." We were off again. But this time I was the one who asked Edith:

"What do you see in him?"

"The guy's like a cocktail. He's got a little of Montand—he's six feet one and he was once a longshoreman. A little of Meurisse—the cold type who doesn't lose control. A little of Pousse—in his handsome, hoodlum way."

"Your guy's no man; he's a Harlequin!"

What she liked most about Félix Marten was the fact that she'd decided to make somebody out of him, to remodel him in her own way. She hadn't made a guy over for a long time. There was no time to lose, and she said to Loulou, "Phone Coquatrix and tell him I want Marten on the bill with me." So long as he had Piaf, Bruno trusted her judgment. He'd have taken on a deaf-mute to sing *Tosca* if she wanted him to. Besides, the less the others cost him, the happier he was—and Félix Marten's name wasn't really well enough known for him to demand a lot. So everything was all set. The only problem was that Edith had no more than a month and a half to create *her* Marten. She didn't like him the way he was. He had everything to learn before he could be a finished product of the Piaf factory. Edith didn't waste a minute. She phoned Marguerite, Henri Contet and her new discovery, Michel Rivgauche.

"Come over. I'll be in Nevers tomorrow, and I've got a new guy to show you. He's going to appear at the Olympia with me, and I want him to have a different repertoire."

All three met on the train for Nevers. She'd chosen the right people. Not one of them could say no to her. She set them to work that very evening. Two days later they came back to Paris dazed and empty-headed, ready for nothing but a twenty-four-hour sleep. But when Edith returned from her tour, she had her songs.

For about a month she merrily drove her team and trained her new guy. Félix wasn't exactly flexible. He had his own ideas, and they generally weren't Edith's. They had some knock-down, drag-out fights that reminded me a little of the ones she'd had when she was working with Yves and with the Compagnons.

"You'll sing about love."

"That's not for me."

"You'll do what I tell you. Love is the secret of success."

"I'm not a whore."

"That's right. Whores don't sing about love, they make it. . . ."

Still, Edith won out in the end, and Félix sang "*Je t'aime, mon amour.*"

Félix wasn't *really* the new boss, but he got a blue suit anyway. He entered the ranks of "Piaf's boys," as Charles Aznavour called them. He didn't have much time to get to know Edith, and I always wondered how they ever managed to have any privacy at all. . . .

When she came back from her tour, just before appearing at the Olympia, Edith somehow also managed to appear in a film, *Les Amants de demain.* "Look, Momone," she said, "if I don't make this film now, I won't have time to later."

What the rest of us didn't have time for was breathing. I was again dealing with the Edith of the great old days. I ran all over the place trying to see her. It wasn't always easy, because when she'd phone me and say, "Come to the house," I'd arrive and find she was already at the studio. I'd dash off to the studio and they'd tell me, "You just missed her. Mme Piaf's left for the Olympia." I'd race off again, and since she always wanted to see you right away, she'd yell at me, "What the hell were you up to? I wanted to see you today, not tomorrow!"

Les Amants de demain was an old story. Pierre Brasseur, one of her drinking partners, had had an idea for a scenario that Edith liked a lot. She'd talked it over with Marcel Blistène: then, as often happens in the movie world, the dough was left to rise. There must have been some good-quality yeast in it, because Edith got a phone call from Marcel right after she got back. "Are you free? We're going to start shooting *Les Amants de demain* in two months."

Michel Auclair, Armand Mestral, Mona Goya, Edith's old pal, whose last movie this was to be, Raymond Souplex and Francis Blanche were in the cast with her. Edith had fun with Francis. They both liked pranks and good jokes. There were no hitches during the shooting and it was soon over.

Pierre Brasseur not only did the scenario but wrote a song for Edith: "*Et pourtant.*" Their relationship was sort of funny. Things had started off several years earlier with a misunderstanding. Pierre would have liked to go to bed with Edith, at least once, and Edith had nothing against the idea. But it never came off, because the day he felt like suggesting it to her, she was with some other guy, so Pierre must have figured it was no dice for him.

Before shooting began on the film, he came right out and laughingly said to Edith, "You had your chance that night, if you'd wanted."

"Well," she answered, "you were wrong not to give me a wink, because I liked you too, and that guy meant nothing."

I was fond of Pierre, but I was just as glad he hadn't become one of Edith's men. Knowing their characters, I had trouble imagining them face to face. There already weren't many dishes left in the house, but what there were would certainly have ended up smashed to pieces. . . .

The two of them didn't quite agree on how they'd met. Pierre was sure he'd met Edith at Louis Leplée's, but Edith never let a chance go by to refresh his memory:

"That's not where you met me at all. It was in a dance hall, the Tourbillon. I wasn't Piaf yet and I sang songs through a megaphone with an orchestra."

Even if he couldn't remember exactly how he'd met her, she must have made an impression on him, because he'd always dreamed of writing songs for her. The idea bugged him so much that he finally phoned one day and said, "I've written a song. Last night I was reading Anouilh's *La Sauvage,* and one of the last lines gave me a goddamn shock, because it's made to order for you: 'There'll always be a lost dog somewhere to make me sad.' I think that's very beautiful, so I asked Anouilh if he'd let me use it for a song. He hesitated at first, but when I told him, 'It's for Piaf; she'll like it,' he answered, 'If it's for her then O.K.'"

And that's how the song *"Et pourtant"* came to be written.

At the end of the shooting, Marcel Blistène gave a cocktail party. Francis was playing the philosopher off in a corner, sucking on his pipe, but he was bored. He was waiting for his accomplice, Edith. When she got there, she was laughing.

"Listen, Francis. Guite taught me a funny thing today that'll be useful to us both. It seems you mustn't be nasty; it's bad for your health! That's why so many people are sick. No kidding. Don't laugh. . . . When you're jealous, when you're raging mad, or when you're aggressive, the adrenaline starts flowing, ruining your kidneys. So for me it's over. I won't be nasty any more!"

She'd no sooner finished the sentence than she caught sight of one of her best friends. . . . Edith opened her mouth. Francis looked at her. She bent over, put her hands to her back and said, "Oh, my kidneys!" She played that game all night. We never laughed so hard. When she wasn't holding her back, Francis was holding his. It was like old times.

The nights on the boulevard Lannes got shorter and shorter—they'd shrunk. Rehearsals speeded up. It was a circus. Everybody ran around madly. Claude kept up as best he could. Edith yelled and horsed around. We knew *that* score by heart!

Then there was Marten. There's not much to say about him. He blew in and out; he didn't last four months. Among those who'd been given the treatment—the watch, the cufflinks and so on—he was out of the picture in record time! Edith was bursting with ideas. She hadn't been in that good shape for a long time. I thought it was a resurrection, that it would last for years. But it was like the glory of Austerlitz—never to be seen again.

Meanwhile we were happy; we believed it would last. How could we help but believe it when all the signs were there? One night the whole gang was eating in the kitchen. There was even a woman there who thought she was at Maxim's. She kept her hat on all night. Michel Rivgauche, the new hit lyricist, was there as well as faithful old Guite. Everyone was talking about songs. Edith interrupted them all, saying, "I remember a song. . . ." Then she ground away at it: "I remember a song . . . say, that's good! With a tune something like . . ." and she hummed us a melody that had been running through her mind for several days.

Marten said he'd help her write the words.

"You see, you're coming around to love songs after all!" Edith teased. One of her composer pals, J. P. Moulin, was there. "Quick, to the piano!" ordered Edith.

And off she went, followed by the whole gang. Dinner was

forgotten. They worked all night. Félix, with his big body slumped down in an armchair, couldn't take any more and began to yawn. She immediately called him to order. "Hey! None of that! We work together around here and *then* sleep!"

"I didn't know," he answered.

Edith blew her top, but I was convulsed with laughter. The good old days were beginning again. By morning the song was finished. Félix Marten made a hit with it at the Olympia. Edith, energetic as a treeful of finches at dawn, said, in all her splendor, "Momone, make them some coffee; they're going to fall asleep!"

I looked at them. Their eyes were like huge hard-boiled eggs.

"By God, we'll have to wake them up just to get them to drink it!"

"What a bunch of weaklings! Come in the bathroom; let's talk. . . ."

This time Bruno Coquatrix took no chances with Edith. He signed her up for four months right off the bat. She broke all records once again, both for the length of time the show ran and for box office receipts. She was more than ever "the Great Piaf." And she was happy. But not quite: Félix Marten could barely keep her heart warm.

"That one'll last as long as my contract at the Olympia, Momone."

The words weren't very encouraging, but even so they were overoptimistic. After two months at the Olympia, Félix had had enough; he just couldn't stick it.

"I didn't know that's what Edith Piaf was like! *Vive la classe!*" While she said, "He's got broad shoulders, Momone, but he's not very tough."

I knew she was being unfair. Shoulders weren't all she needed; she had to be loved for herself with no hope of reward. She was often dishonest; her fits of rage weren't always funny; and she had a biting wit that she sometimes used cruelly, wounding her victims. She was tyrannical, jealous, and demanding. Yet you could ask her for anything and she'd always be ready to give it to you. Edith was all those things. She wasn't, and never had been, one of

Félix Marten's great loves. That was understandable. There were times when she was frankly impossible. She had glory and money now to back up her domineering ways. Too many ass-lickers kept telling her she was the greatest, the most beautiful, the best. When the neon façade was turned off, however, you could now see the damaged woman cracked by drugs and alcohol. Her heart pained her; it was scarred and bruised, covered with welts left by the blows it had received. Not one man ever spared her; they all left their marks.

To keep herself going Edith began to drink again. Not much, but enough so that her fits of rage were now nasty. So Marten lashed out at her. He thought he had it made: he was Edith's co-star, and after her he'd get lots of other contracts. He was no flunky; and besides, he was big enough to strike out on his own.

So they broke up. Edith's heart wasn't really touched; only scratched. But the claw marks hurt!

"He was the first one after all the emptiness, all the madness. I thought he was going to get me out of the hole, but instead he pushed my head right down in it without realizing."

It was a blow to Edith's pride and self-esteem. A man had ditched her. She'd fallen so low that a man could give her up, not give a damn about her! Every day, for two months, she was going to have to put up with Félix's dressing room right next to hers, with his self-satisfied little smile every time he passed her.

But it wasn't to last long. Waiting right at the door of the Olympia was Georges Moustaki. He was handsome and talented. And he was to be her last real disaster, the one that ushered in the end.

Georges Moustaki sang his own songs every night at the College Inn, in Montparnasse. He was no fool, old Georges. He played the big ace of hearts of admiration, which was still the best of all cards as far as Edith was concerned. Barely two days after she'd broken up with Marten, he knocked on her dressing room door.

"When he walked in, Momone, I knew that was it! It hadn't happened to me for a long time. He was slim, with caressing eyes and the grin of a kid at a carnival. Very nicely, and casually, he told me that he wrote songs and sang them in a nightclub in Montparnasse, and that he wanted me to come hear him because my opinion was important to him. You get the type." Didn't I though!

"I told him, O.K., I'll come tonight. You'd have done the same thing in my place."

"You bet! . . . So?"

"He's terrific, sensational! And what talent! You'd have really laughed if you'd seen how I left the Olympia. Robert [the chauffeur] was waiting for me with the car. I told him never mind, and got in Moustaki's car, a sort of washing machine on wheels, a real tub. 'Are you sure it runs?' I asked him. As a precaution, I gave Robert orders to follow us. After all, Georges's songs might have been as worn out as his jalopy!

"I can't tell you how I broke up at the thought that when we ran into Félix, he'd see I wasn't ready to enter a convent to weep over him, and that I hadn't had to look far to find someone else.

"But Moustaki really got me when he told me the truth: he'd been on the lookout for my breakup with Marten. He dropped by the Olympia every night to see how my love affairs were doing. Isn't that touching, Momone?"

I never could get over Edith's innocence, her naïveté, when it came to men.

Four days later, following a long established ritual, Edith introduced everyone at the boulevard Lannes apartment to the new boss: Georges Moustaki. He was given the whole works: the suits and all the trimmings; everything. For him, the first boss since Eddie Constantine, nothing was too good. The lighter wasn't gold but platinum—a little trifle that cost four hundred thousand francs. Three days later, Moustaki, a real bohemian, lost it. The next day Edith bought him another one.

Edith was sure she'd found a real partner in Georges. He was gay. He liked nights that were so long they ran over into the next day. He wasn't a snob; eating in the kitchen didn't bother him. He was ready to be friends with everybody. He lived his life any old way. He didn't give a damn about chaos. There was nothing of the puritan about him; to him the only good cause was living one hour after the other just as you pleased. He wasn't one who'd preach to Edith, "Go to bed . . . sleep. . . . don't drink. . . . Don't take drugs."

So with him, once again, Edith began a new life. And there's nothing moderate about a new life; it blazes!

For her Georges wrote one of his most beautiful songs, *"Milord."*

> *Allez! venez Milord,*
> *Vous asseoir à ma table;*
> *Il fait si froid dehors*
> *Ici, c'est confortable.*
> *Laissez-vous faire, Milord,*
> *Et prenez bien vos aises;*
> *Vos peines sur mon coeur.*
> *Je vous connais, Milord,*
> *Et vos pieds sur une chaise.*
> *Vous n' m'avez jamais vue,*
> *Je n' suis qu'un' fill' du port,*
> *Une ombre de la rue.*
> *Allez venez, Milord. . . .*

> Come, Milord,
> Sit down at my table;
> It's so cold outside
> And it's comfortable in here.
> Relax, Milord,
> And be at your ease;
> I've taken your troubles to heart.
> I know you, Milord,
> Put your feet up on a chair.
> You've never seen me,
> I'm just a girl from around the port,
> A shadow in the street.
> Come, Milord. . . .

Talent wasn't all he had going for him. With Georges, Edith recovered her taste for fighting with a man. More than once on tour with him she had to slap a lot of extra foundation on her face. The nights left their marks, and not always the marks of love. But it didn't matter—she'd always liked that. She sounded happy when she called me on the phone. "Georges and I had a brawl tonight. Boy, did we go at it. . . . I adore him!"

To Edith that wasn't ever a bad sign. When she made a guy sweat, it was because she was attached to him; and when he got irritated enough to give her a good thrashing, it was because he was attached to her. That was real "proof" of love.

She made Georges her guitarist, and decided to take him with her to New York on September 18, 1959, her ninth trip to America. Loulou had got her a contract for four seasons at the Waldorf-Astoria. She only managed one of them. Her visits to the States were over. She was never to go back.

For a change of air and a little rest when she got back from the tour she was on, Edith rented an estate at Condé-sur-Vesgre, in the Seine-et-Oise.

"I have to get some oxygen in my lungs before I leave for New York. It'll do everybody good."

What she needed most was to get away from melon with port and strawberries with wine, her latest discoveries, which could be better described as port with melon and wine with strawberries. . . .

Edith gave a lot of her time to Marcel Cerdan's sons after he died. But her favorite was young Marcel, probably because he looked like his father and wanted to be a boxer. She invited him to spend a month in the country. She'd brought the whole circus out there, which didn't keep her from being in Paris all the time. She never could stay in one place very long.

One morning she phoned me. "I've buzzed off to the country for a few days. You ought to come out too. Call Charles if he's there; he'll bring you—I haven't seen him for ages. That way you can get a better look at Georges and tell me if you like him. Since I'm coming back Saturday, you can come with us. Marcel's leaving for Casa, and I'm driving to Orly."

I should have said yes, but I said no. It may have saved my life a second time.

On September 7, Edith was in her third automobile accident.

Georges Moustaki was driving Edith's DS 19. She was in the front, next to him. Marcel Cerdan and a young girlfriend of his were in the back. It was raining. Georges saw a heavy truck moving out to pass, but too late. He slammed on the brakes and the car skidded. It flew off the road. Everybody dashed over and helped Edith get out. Blood was streaming down her face like a red veil. Cerdan, who'd been stunned, staggered out of the car. He was bleeding too. Georges, who hadn't been hurt at all, yelled, "It's Edith Piaf. Take care of her right away!" The guys who'd come to help were all truck drivers. To them Edith wasn't just Edith Piaf, the star; she was their kind of girl. They took her in their arms and wiped her face with their big paws. They smelled really like men and, despite all the commotion, Edith smiled at them and reassured them.

"I don't think anything's broke. What's wrong with my head?"

"There's a big gash, Mam' Piaf. With the head it's all or nothing; it bleeds a lot, but it's not serious. Don't move—the ambulance is on its way. Here, have a swig; it'll do you good."

After Edith was taken away, one of the guys said to the other, "Hey, look, your sweater's full of blood. You'll have to wash it."

"Are you kidding? Edith Piaf's blood? What a souvenir! I should have asked her to autograph my sweater. When I come back tomorrow, I'll drop in at the hospital to see how she's doing." And he did. When they asked him, "Who shall I say is here?" he answered, "Tell her it's one of the 'Grace of God' truck drivers."

She was taken immediately to the operating room at Rambouillet, where a surgeon sewed up the four-inch cut on her forehead, a gash on her upper lip, two severed tendons in her right hand. Her face was covered with wounds. On the whole, it wasn't too serious though, and I tried to tell myself she was lucky, but it was hard. Two days later, Edith said to me with a laugh:

"Guess where the accident happened, Momone! At a place called 'The Grace of God.' See how well I'm protected! Just take a look at the car and you'll understand.

"What a scare Marcel gave me! His face was covered with blood. For a moment he looked like a real boxer. What annoys me is having to postpone my trip to the U.S."

Even though she was in a good mood, I knew she was suffering. Her hand, which had been put in a cast because of the tendons, was bothering her.

When she got back to the apartment on the boulevard Lannes, she looked at us with her little poor-kid smile and said, "This time I'm done for. . . . I can't leave with a mug like this. The Americans would call me 'Miss Frankenstein'! Right, Momone?" An enormous swollen scar ran across her forehead, coursing up on each side toward her hairline. Her upper lip was deformed. It was hard to tell her she looked like the Mona Lisa! All I could think of to say was:

"Well, it's visible, but it's only superficial. . . ."

"What do you take me for? An ass? It's a lot more than visible! This thing with my lip keeps me from singing. It's like I had a cleft palate; I can't pronounce the words right. It's a nasty blow. . . . At the hospital they suggested facial massages. I'm going to do it."

The massage sessions were unforgettable. The guy massaged her skull right over the scar, then her forehead, then her whole face, pressing hard on the stitches. Edith got all red, and you could see the blood pounding under her skin. It wasn't a pretty sight, and it hurt her terribly.

"Should I stop for a minute?"

"Are you sure I'll be able to go to America and sing after all this torture?"

"Absolutely."

"Then go on. And don't worry—I can take it."

Edith got irritable. She didn't mind the pain, but she wanted it all to go fast. She'd grab the first person who came along and ask, "Do you see any progress? Is my face any better?" We'd answer as best we could. What really tortured her was the problem of pronunciation. It made her blow her top.

The only one who was spared was Moustaki. Edith, who was often unfair and disloyal, could also be extraordinarily tactful. When Georges said to her, "Edith, I did this to you . . . I'm so sorry!" she answered, "It's not your fault. I'd have had that accident no matter who'd been driving. It was in the stars. Stop bugging me with your remorse. . . . It's one thing to be sorry, but remorse, never!"

A month later in the U.S., she was greeted like a long-lost relative—flowers, speeches, cocktail parties, radio, television. Her press was marvelous. "The littlest of the big stars" was feted as only the Americans know how. It was like Edith herself: there were no limits.

For the first time in her life Edith felt intensely weary. Yet she loved that audience, that country. They were good for her. But the scenes with Georges went on. They didn't amuse her any more; they pained her. She was afraid she'd made another mistake. She stopped eating for a few days. She drank, but the alcohol burned through her. She writhed with pains that cut her in two.

On the twentieth of February, on the stage at the Waldorf, the room began to spin around like a crazy merry-go-round; then everything went black. Edith collapsed onstage. They carried her to the wings, where she began vomiting blood. She lost consciousness as they rushed her to the Columbia Presbyterian Hospital on 168th Street. The siren on the ambulance shrieked for her through that great city—her first love after Paris.

When she arrived, the doctors diagnosed a bleeding stomach ulcer. It was serious. When she came to, they got her ready for an operation. She had blood transfusions and as she watched the foreign blood flowing into her veins, she called Georges. They showed him to her room. When he came out he looked furious. Edith's musicians were there waiting.

"Is it serious?" they asked.

"They're going to operate," answered Moustaki.

In her room Edith was crying. She told me later, "I asked him to kiss me . . . to tell me he still loved me a little. And he answered, 'Later, Edith; we'll see.'"

Things happened fast at the hospital; there was no time to lose. Death crouched at the door of Edith's room for the first time. She was on the operating table for four hours, and was given three blood transfusions.

The Americans couldn't get over it. To them Edith was the

strongest little woman in the world. New York was worried; the hospital put out bulletins on her health, and people sent good wishes. There was a steady stream of cables, and flowers blocked the corridor outside her door. But Edith had never felt so alone. . . .

When I talked to her on the phone, she sounded less dejected than I thought she would. She didn't mention Georges, so I finally asked, "Is Georges around?" She exploded, "Don't ever mention that guy to me again, Momone! I want to blot him out. When I came to, he wasn't there. He'd gone to Miami. I felt as lost as I did at the Tenon Hospital when I had my little girl. He had the nerve to phone me to tell me it was sunny there. He knew I wasn't enough of an ass to think the only women down there were nuns! I couldn't say a word. After I hung up, I bawled—boy, did I bawl, Momone! Everybody around me was worried. The nurses kept telling me, 'You mustn't, Miss Piaf, it's bad for your morale.' Some morale, I can tell you—it was below zero! But don't worry. I feel better this morning: some guy I don't even know sent me a big bunch of violets. It did me good. He's an American. His name is Douglas Davies."

Chapter 17

"Non, je ne regrette rien!"

When Loulou came to see Edith at the hospital and found her propped up against her pillows, her hair combed and her face made up, he looked at her as if she were a ghost.

"What's wrong with you, opening your blinkers like that? Did you think I'd had it?"

She laughed, ready to yell at him, ready to bite, ready to live again. Loulou didn't know what to say. He just let his joy explode. "You're better! I can't believe it—you're better! God, I'm happy, Edith."

"You're repeating yourself! That's bad for the sound track! Cut!"

That was *his* Edith. He'd found her again.

"Not only better, I feel very well, and I need visitors. This place isn't good for morale. White's even sadder than black. I need colors and some real singing and shouting around here! You know anybody called Douglas Davies?"

Old Loulou caught on fast. He knew what was up, and didn't waste a second. "I'll go get him."

"I didn't ask you to bring him here. I asked who he was."

"A young painter."

"He must have talent to send a bunch of violets to a woman like me! I'd like to see his face. . . . For all I know, he may be cross-eyed!"

Loulou headed straight for the door.

"Don't take off like that—there's no fire. New York's not a village. How do you happen to know him? Is the kid all that famous?"

"Oh, no. Not yet . . ."

The light in Edith's eyes went out like a snuffed candle. Although she had real self-confidence, a few of its teeth had been knocked out.

"Did you tell him to send me that bouquet? If you did, you can throw it out, and yourself along with it!"

"No, Edith. I know the boy because he's been at the Waldorf every night you've sung there. And ever since you've been sick, he's taken a two-hour subway ride across the whole city to the hospital reception desk, just to ask how you are."

"Poor guy! Hasn't he heard about the telephone? Or doesn't he have a dime?"

"He prefers to come."

"If you're lying, I'll have a relapse. And if it's true, I'll be out of bed tomorrow. Run and get him—you should be on your way already! No, wait! Give me the mirror. Oh, shit! Is he going to be disappointed!"

"Maybe it's you who'll be disappointed."

"I'd rather not wait too long to find out. Step on it, Loulou. . . . Maybe it'll do me more good than a transfusion!"

It was considerably more effective.

Douglas Davies was twenty-three, with all the niceness and frankness of a typical American boy. He was tall and good looking. Most important of all, when he came into "Miss Edith's" room he went on seeing her as if she were still onstage, in all the magic of the spotlights. He didn't give a damn about her drawn, ravaged face, her skinny arms, her huge bare forehead, her sickly-looking skin. He only saw those blue-violet eyes looking at him, and that mouth smiling at him.

"Miss Edith, you're marvelous. Thank you very much!" he stammered.

Edith was in seventh heaven. Things were O.K. again. This

boy was love, smiling at her with twenty-three-year-old teeth! It was all beginning again!

She had somebody buy needles and yarn for her and began at once to knit one of those impossible sweaters only she knew how to knit. She hadn't knitted for a man since Marcel Cerdan. She was dead sure it'd be a great love affair this time—the signs couldn't be wrong!

When Jacques Pills, who was in the States, came to see her, she was so glowing he said right off:

"It can't be—you're in love! Do you know you're beautiful?"

"You know, Jacques, I was so far gone only love could save me."

Douglas came every day to practice his French with Edith. This "engagement" was a marvelous time for her. She had the right to be sentimental; to believe in miracles without anybody saying, "You're boring the hell out of me"; and to make plans. No one could call her a madwoman! She could say and do anything at all, because Douglas was lost in admiration. He'd never seen a woman like her. He wasn't wrong there!

Edith was convinced that the rotten luck and the bad days were over. . . . But not quite; she still had to wait a bit. On March 25, while she was convalescing and getting ready to leave on her "Dougie's" arm, she had a relapse. But this time she wasn't alone. Douglas walked alongside the stretcher that took Edith to the operating room for the second time.

She was so light (she weighed seventy-five pounds) and so tiny that a few days later a patient who'd seen Douglas in the hall with Edith asked him, "How's your daughter coming along?"

Dougie, her "American dream," stuck by her. When she came to, he was right there beside her.

About two months later, as she was leaving the hospital, leaning on Douglas's arm and on Loulou, Edith took a deep breath. "It was winter when I went in; now it's spring!" She looked at Dougie. "I'm happy—and everything in my heart's brand-new too. . . ."

You could hardly say that the people waiting in her room at the Waldorf were as optimistic. The musicians waiting for her looked anything but pleased. Even though their boss was out, there wasn't much spring in *their* mugs. While Edith was in the hospital —a little over three months—they'd had to work at all sorts of odd jobs. They hadn't had an easy time of it. In the States no one was panting after musicians. They had all they needed, with some to spare. So the guys had eaten hot dogs more often than foie gras.

Edith began to laugh when she saw them, "Well, well! Some welcome! You're the living ad for some gloomy play."

"Edith, the hospital cost over three million francs. And we have to pay for the hotel, and our return tickets. We're broke!"

Edith didn't give a damn about herself, but she did about the people who worked for her. She could barely stand up, but she said right away:

"You mustn't worry about that, Loulou, let the Waldorf know that I'm going to sing here for a week."

"No, Edith, you can't. It's madness!"

"Yes I will. It'll do me good. Anyway, I want to leave the Americans with good memories of me. I owe them at least that."

So she sang, looking more fragile and more pathetic than ever. But this time there was not only the despair of love in her voice; there was also the triumph. Dougie, who was in the audience, never took his eyes off her.

Edith wasn't wrong. She always knew what she had to do when it came to her work. Americans like courage. She had rave reviews. "Miss Courage . . ." "The brave little French girl . . ." "This woman has the strength of a lion . . ." "She's never sung better . . ." "Her voice is just as magical as ever" and so on.

Yet Edith took *"L'Accordéoniste"* off her program. The range was too hard on her and tired her. From then on, she sang it less and less often, and finally she dropped it altogether.

For a week that little black flame consuming itself shone brightly at the Waldorf-Astoria. She stuck it right to the end, and she not only got the money she needed, but had enough left over to be extravagant.

And extravagant she was. But this time it didn't involve any dough. "Come on," she said to Douglas. "I'm taking you back with me!" Exporting this pure "made in U.S.A." product was a serious mistake. It wasn't exportable; it was likely to spoil and lose its flavor.

When Edith got off the plane at Orly on June 21, 1960, the press was there in full force. She was proud of her American bear cub, and introduced him to everyone. Douglas tagged happily along after her, but you could see he wasn't with it; he never did get with it. He didn't know what it was like to be "M. Piaf," though he found out all too soon.

Douglas was a nobody to the inner circle of the boulevard Lannes. He never impressed them as the boss. He was an innocent. He was Daniel in the lions' den. They knew perfectly well that being called the boss didn't mean a thing. The boss didn't give the orders; Edith did. So they didn't give much of a damn about her guy! especially some kid straight off the plane from the U.S.! In any case, they'd realized long ago that Edith's lovers came and went, while they stayed. They gave him a friendly tap on the shoulder, called him Dougie and went about their business. He would have been less lonely in the desert!

I thought Douglas was awfully nice. He smelled like a cake of toilet soap. He seemed so clean and well scrubbed, inside and out. He was pleased to be in Paris; it was a kind of paradise for him, full of painters, galleries and museums. He was going to be able to work. Or at least that's what he thought life with Edith would be.

They had their first run-in when they got to her place.

"Dougie, darling, this is our room." He looked at the bed as if he'd seen a sea serpent lying on it.

"Don't you understand? This is *our* room."

"I'm sorry, Edith, it won't work. I'm not used to double beds. In the States everybody has his own bed."

Edith closed the door. She was purple with rage. No man had ever done *that* to her. He wasn't the first American in her life! Nobody had ever dared say no to her. . . .

"Do you realize what a blow it was, Momone? If I take up with a man it's so I can have him right there. If I have to walk across the whole apartment or ring for him like a flunky, I won't feel like slipping him between my sheets any more!"

That was just it. Douglas wasn't the type to curl up next to you in bed. And to him a man wasn't meant to be stuck to a woman all day. Where he came from, men lived their own lives. They went out to work, and when they came home they brought flowers, with their own little heart in the center.

The next day Douglas put his paintbox under his arm and, very relaxed, was about to take off. Edith's famous voice nailed him to the spot.

"Dougie, where do you think you're going?"

"I'm going to look at Paris, or maybe I'll paint, go to the Louvre. . . ."

"Are you nuts? You'll get lost. You don't know Paris. When you go out the chauffeur can take you in the car. But right now I need you. Stay with me, love. . . ."

He gave in with a nice smile, thinking it was only decent to stay with her the first day, and planned to go out the next. He didn't know that being Edith Piaf's lover meant he was no longer a free agent. That nice boy, stuffed with good American principles —respect for women and for freedom—couldn't fight her. She only let him open his paintbox once—to do her portrait.

"It's beautiful, eh, Momone? That's how he sees me!"

But this wasn't the Piaf you saw onstage; it was the image of the Piaf that the masses cherished in their hearts.

I realized at once that it wouldn't last, that reality would squash that boy's romantic dream. He couldn't help but be shocked by the boulevard Lannes, by the people around Edith, by the swarm of parasites that pounced on her sick body. It was all too far removed from anything he'd known.

Anyway, in spite of her courage and her will to live, Edith was seriously ill. She had barely a week to prepare for her summer tour. She jumped right into her work; she didn't take off the harness for a second; but she had trouble holding up without stimulants, drugs or alcohol. Her American doctor's orders were perhaps right, but not much fun: milk and broiled meat—that's about all she was allowed.

"This jockey's diet of theirs'll be the end of me. It's sure not enough for me to sing on."

She got another idea. "Say, Momone, have you heard about injections of embryonic cells? They're supposed to work miracles. . . . The Pope and Adenauer got them from a doc in Switzerland. I think I'll give them a try. They're exactly what I need." Naturally, she got the shots. A pity her faith in them wasn't enough to make them work.

The tour was about to begin. She was taking Dougie along, of course, and since he didn't like driving French cars, she bought a big Chevrolet just to please him. Michel Rivgauche was also included.

The night before they left, Edith was at the top of her form, the way she'd been in her peak periods, and Loulou said to me, "When I see her like that, I pinch myself. I keep wondering whether I had a nightmare in New York or if it was all really true!"

At midnight Edith refused to go to bed. She decided she'd sleep in the car the next day. "We'll show this American 'Paris by Night,'" she announced. "Poor baby, I haven't been able to pay much attention to him since I got back."

"That one's going to need a life preserver any minute!" commented Loulou. "You've got to rest . . . and think of your diet, Edith!"

"You give me a pain in the ass, Loulou. I'll drink milk. Stop bugging me. I haven't been so happy in ages!"

And the whole night they raced around, from Pigalle down to the Champs Élysées, Edith and all the hangers-on who had encouraged her. At dawn they all climbed into their cars to leave on the tour. Douglas drove the big Chevrolet for several hours. Edith opened one eye to look at him. He had the profile of Billy the Kid —a child's full, round cheeks, upturned nose, a funny little brown curl over his forehead, an innocent mouth and the beautiful hands of an artist. She closed her eyes again. How long would this one last? She didn't want to know. Before she left, she said to me, "I buy my happiness on the run now, like a head of lettuce or three lemons for twenty cents. I come by, I pay and I take the stuff with me. When I get home the lettuce is wilted, and the lemons give me a stomach ache. So? At least while I held them in my hands, while I carried them, I believed in them!"

For a second Douglas's attention lapsed; he shut his eyes going up a hill, and the big brand-new Chevrolet shot off the road right into some barrels of tar. Robert and his wife, Hélène, were following them in Edith's car. When they got to the scene, they found Edith unconscious and Douglas crying like a kid. Michel Rivgauche was groggy, the blood spurting out of a gash on his forehead.

Edith came to very quickly. She eyed all of them, one after the other, as if she were taking inventory, and said, "I don't have much luck, do I? Let's go!"

All told, she was in pretty bad shape: three broken ribs and bruises all over. A real stinking mess! They trussed her up tight with plaster strips. She demanded morphine. How could she sing without it? It wasn't for herself—it was to finish out her contract. Her salvation was killing her!

The doctor warned her she was playing with her life.

"Shit," she answered. "You have to play with something, and that's all I've got."

Then the insane tour began. It was hot. The plaster was real torture. With every breath she took, she was ready to scream. So that she could sing, she ripped off the plaster and had it replaced by elastic bandages. And she was determined that this time she wouldn't be had by drugs. The doctor gave her a shot just before she went on. After the tenth song, she came out into the wings for a second. She held out during the day, but, little by little, she began to drink again.

In Cannes Edith stayed on for a few days. The people toasting themselves on the beach got quite a treat when the Piaf-Davies couple walked by. Douglas had beautiful, well-trained muscles. In bathing trunks he really got the girls. She was Edith Piaf, so people forgave her (people always forgave her) her rompers, her shirt, the scarf on her head, and being white as a turnip. Her thighs were skinny and her knees too knobby, but she didn't give a damn; they could all go screw. She had a handsome twenty-three-year-old boy on her arm. . . . What no one realized was that under Edith's shirt was that fucking bandage, so tight she couldn't breathe. It was unbearable when she sat in the sun. But she stuck with Dougie and didn't leave him for a second. She loathed the sun and beaches swarming with people, but because she thought Douglas would be happy diving in the water, she went along with him. That way, she was sure she was doing the very best for him.

But Douglas wanted something else. Lots of artists—Picasso and others—lived near Cannes. All of contemporary painting was there within a couple of square miles. He'd dreamed of this back in the States. Now here he was in France, and he couldn't see anything he wanted to . . . just this little woman who'd torn up his nice, boyish heart one night in the artificial glow of the spotlights, singing with a sort of truth he'd never known, and which had shattered him. . . . He didn't know that this world by which he'd been seduced wasn't a tender world, that life in it was hard, that the rules were pitiless.

Edith fought illness with anything that came to hand. She'd been told garlic was good for rheumatism, so she ate it constantly. It made Douglas sick to his stomach. For the pain, Edith was taking cortisone again, which blew her up like a balloon. And she kept drinking to keep her spirits up. She was slowly committing suicide.

Douglas couldn't keep up with her. This woman who kept going with shots, who got irritated over trifles, who demanded that he stay with her every minute and blindly obey—she had worn him out. . . . He wasn't the only one! Even the toughest members of her entourage were down for the count. As for Edith, she was like a spring wound up tight; she went on uncoiling. She carried on with her usual energy, but she was close to collapse.

In Bordeaux, the next to last city on the tour, just before Biarritz, Douglas had a fight with Edith during the night. They threw a few bitter truths at each other like old garbage. Edith finally went to sleep after stuffing herself with sleeping pills, and Douglas took advantage of it to light out for the railroad station like a rabbit with greyhounds racing after him. He spent the rest of the night in the second-class waiting room like a bum, unshaven, with all his things under his arm.

When Edith woke up from her deep sleep, Dougie wasn't there. So "the Great Piaf" jumped into a taxi like a nut, her hair uncombed, wearing nothing but a coat over her nightgown.

"To the station. Hurry!"

"What train are you catching?"

"I don't know, just hurry!"

"I didn't want to lose him, Momone. I just couldn't—he was the last one. I looked like a madwoman in that station full of tourists, but I didn't give a damn. I had to catch him! The guy at the gate screamed, 'Where's your ticket?' and I answered, 'Shit!' Then I stopped in my tracks on the platform. The train was just pulling out, like in a bad movie. . . . God, I must have looked miserable on the platform of that goddamn station! It was all so stupid I stood there laughing and crying like a madwoman."

The end of that tour was really bad.

"But see, Momone," Edith said, "he didn't forget me. He phoned me from Paris and told me he'd be back. He promised me. . . . I loved that guy, Momone, and he's gone. If you only knew how sick my heart is!" Promises made to someone condemned to death, I thought to myself.

Maybe her heart was broken, but physically it was stronger than the rest of her. Her hands were giving her trouble; they were becoming deformed. And when she had one of her fits, she couldn't do her hair any more, couldn't hold a glass, and someone had to cut her meat for her. That was the state she was in when she left for Stockholm, where she was to appear at the Bernsbee, the largest vaudeville theater in the country. As she sang *"Tu me fais tourner la tête"* in front of five thousand people, Edith turned round and round and collapsed, like a little black rag, at the foot of the mike. The audience clapped, thinking it was part of her act. They lowered the curtain and carried her offstage.

For the first time, Edith was scared stiff.

"I don't want to die in Sweden. I want to go home."

"There's no plane."

"I want one. You can't let me croak here!"

She rented a twenty-four-seat DC-4 to get back to Paris. Her fear had just cost her a million five hundred thousand francs, which she couldn't afford. She wasn't working enough to earn all that luxury.

Bad luck dogged her. On September 22, she entered the American Hospital at Neuilly, where she was operated on for acute pancreatitis. When I asked a doctor friend what that meant, he told me that it was fatal unless operated on almost immediately, and that even then, only about thirty percent survive the operation. No one was allowed to visit Edith. Once again she fought against death all alone in the antiseptic emptiness of a hospital room.

I knew what has hidden behind the names of all those illnesses. I knew the truth. When they operated on Edith in New York, they had discovered she had cancer. Even then there was no escape. If she'd agreed to be sensible, she could have lived a few years longer, but her case was hopeless. Her life from then on was to be no more than a few ports of call between trips to the hospital. Yet she reached one of the peaks of her career a year later.

She was scheduled to record *"Milord"* when she got out of the hospital. We tried to pressure her into not doing it, but she insisted. She was released at eleven in the morning, and by 2 P.M. she was rehearsing. She was on her feet for eight hours, telling the technicians, "Just keep going. Don't let me stop; I'll never be able to start again."

Loulou got mad.

"That's enough, Edith. You've got to stop."

"Don't keep me from singing—it's all I've got left!" Words we were to hear again and again. . . .

This time, like all the others, she went too far. Loulou took advantage of it. He wrapped her up like a baby, shoved her into his car and drove her to his place in Richebourg. "Edith, you're not leaving here till you're well." But she didn't give a damn what he said. There was just one thing she wanted—to sleep and to forget. . . . There were only two people with her, a nurse and Claude Figus.

She was so used to having Claude underfoot she didn't even notice him any more. But to him she was still the greatest. He loved her enough to put up with anything. As long as she was there and wanted him with her, he was happy.

This time little Claude was lucky. There was nobody around to talk to Edith about love, to say the words she needed to hear. So one night when she was feeling better, Claude let himself go and blurted out absolutely everything; a lot had been locked in his heart since he was thirteen. Edith listened. Who could resist such frankness, so much love? She took him in her arms, and Claude earned one of those medals of love. That part of the treatment was all he ever got, but he didn't give a damn. His happiness lasted through Edith's convalescence.

For over a year, she learned to live again. Her rheumatism was so bad it crippled her to the point that she couldn't walk any more. Vimbert, a chiropractor, came every day. He patiently massaged her, straightened her spinal column and loosened the knots in her pain-wracked nerves and muscles, one by one. It was shattering to see how docile Edith was in the arms of this man who was teaching her to walk again, like a child. "Put your right foot forward. Fine. Now your left foot. Just three more steps, Edith. That's enough for today." He later went along with Edith on one of her tours; she couldn't live without his help.

When I saw her again on the boulevard Lannes, the place was about as cheerful as a tomb. You almost felt like tiptoeing around. There was no music—nothing. I'd never heard such silence. And Edith's face was so swollen you'd have thought she had a run-in with a swarm of bees.

"I look awful, don't I, Momone?"

"Your cheeks are a little full. But it suits you pretty well."

She shrugged, as if she didn't give a damn. "Meanwhile, can you see me on a stage with this mug?"

No; quite honestly, I couldn't. When Loulou had phoned to tell me she was coming back, he'd said:

"It's all right; she's made it. It won't be long now till she's well again. She's going to start over."

And so she did! He was wrong only about the direction she took. It wasn't long before she was headed back to the hospital in a hepatic coma. Ninety percent of the time, that means you're done for, but not Edith. She got over it, and the newspapers re-filed her obituary.

She was barely back at boulevard Lannes when she was asked

to go on tour again, from October 14 to December 13. All Loulou's protestations, and Figus's and my pleading, were pointless; she sent us packing.

"I've got two months to get ready for it! That's enough. Anyway, how do you suggest I eat? I have nothing more to sell. I'm flat broke. What can I do? I even phoned Michel [Michel Emer, always her last resort when she was on the rocks]. He went to SACEM for me. But they won't advance me a penny on my royalties. . . . Got it? So I'll sing!"

While she talked, I was thinking: "I guess no guy's going to come along to change her mind and help her out." But every time I thought that, somebody did come along. This time it was Charles Dumont.

Edith and I were to meet in the Bois de Boulogne. She wanted to take a walk. The minute I saw her, I noticed the change. Of course, it was a bad idea to look at her remembering what she'd been like two years before—it was too goddamn depressing—but there was a cheerful and buoyant spark in her eye.

"You're in love!"

"Does it show already? I'm not so sure myself yet."

"Tell me about it anyway. We can see later if it's for life!"

"Right this minute, you know, I don't want much. Everything gives me a swift pain. Michel Vaucaire phoned me. 'I'm sending over a guy who's just your type,' he said. 'You have to see him. His name's Charles Dumont. I want you to hear the song he's got. I wrote the words, he wrote the music. I can't say anything about the words, but the music's terrific.'

"I told him, sure, and made a date, thinking it was a hell of a bore. The day this guy was supposed to come, I'd forgotten all about him. I heard two timid rings at the door; and that got my back up. Claude came in and said, 'It's Charles Dumont, Edith. You said you'd see him today.'

"'He can go to hell!'

"I'd hardly got the words out of my mouth when he came in. Not my type at all—a tall guy, pretty hefty, and got up like an office clerk. He didn't dare look at me, but kept staring at his shoes.

If he'd been a vacuum cleaner salesman, it would have taken him a year to get one order . . . if ever, even with all the gods' help!"

Things were off to a bad start. Edith said to him curtly, "Since you've got a song, sit down at the piano." Poor Charles Dumont! Perspiration was dripping down his face but he didn't dare wipe it off, and it rolled down inside his collar.

Edith was pitiless. "Do you want a handkerchief?"

"No, I've got my own . . . thank you."

And he forced himself to play.

> *Non! Rien de rien . . .*
> *Non, je ne regrette rien!*
> *Ni le bien qu'on m'a fait,*
> *Ni le mal. Tout ça m'est bien égal!*
> *Non! Rien de rien . . .*
> *Non, je ne regrette rien!*
> *C'est payé, balayé, oublié,*
> *Je me fous du passé!*
>
> *Avec mes souvenirs*
> *J'ai allumé le feu.*
> *Mes chagrins, mes plaisirs,*
> *Je n'ai plus besoin d'eux!*
>
> *Car ma vie, car mes joies,*
> *Aujourd'hui*
> *Ça commence avec toi!*

> No, nothing at all . . .
> No, I don't regret a thing!
> Neither the good that's been done me
> Nor the bad. It's all the same to me!
> No, nothing at all . . .
> No, I don't regret a thing!
> It's all paid for, swept away, forgotten,
> I don't give a damn about the past!
>
> I've lighted a fire
> With my memories.
> I don't need
> My pains and pleasures any more!

> For my life and my joys
> Today
> Begin with you.

That did it. It was love at first sight.

"That's terrific! It's incredible; you're a sorcerer! It's me! It's what I feel, what I think! Even more—it's my last will and testament. . . ."

"Do you like it?" asked Dumont, trying desperately to get control of his shot nerves.

"It's beautiful!" Edith answered. "It'll be my biggest hit. I wish I were onstage right now singing it." And she sang it then and there. Dumont was deeply moved.

"When you sing it, it's shattering. . . ."

Everybody who clocked in that day was treated to the song. By the fifth time, she knew it by heart. And by the tenth time, she'd got it down so well that she hardly changed it at all when she sang it onstage.

Charles Dumont couldn't get over it. From the expression on Edith's face, he could see his luck blossoming, like a young plant, before his eyes. He was speechless with happiness. She told him to come back tomorrow to work.

"You know, Momone, he's been coming regularly for a week—like a little old clerk going to his office. At two-thirty on the dot he sits down at the piano and we sweat it out together. I like him; he's a real man. He seems so strong. I feel like leaning on his arm. He won't collapse; he'll hold up. Anyway, there's something about him that gets me—he adores his mother. That big guy, shy and sweet. He's got a heart."

She stopped and looked at me.

"I know what you're thinking. Dougie did too. But he was only a kid. He had a heart, all right, but no sense of reality. He saw me in pink and blue, American nursery style, half sister, half mother. There was no place for a real woman in his picture book."

I was always touched by Edith's good judgment. It was clear, left nothing in the dark and was so accurate it never needed retouching.

"Dougie's been calling me ever since Bordeaux. I even found out he's had an exhibition of his paintings in the States. He told me he'd be back when he'd 'grown up' a little. But I'm not the right age to take up with kids. I'm not young any more, and not old enough either. I really loved him, but he lived in an antiseptic world, and mine's swarming with germs. He hadn't been vaccinated enough to take it."

We talked a long time that day. Edith was in very good shape. "It's true, Momone—'I don't regret a thing.' But those drugs did frighten me, and still do. Every time they give me a shot of morphine now, I start trembling. I don't want to go through that whole thing again. I couldn't stand it. . . .

"Anyway, I met up with a feeling that knocked me on my ass: when I realize there are people who've seen me act worse than an animal, I could puke with shame. And when you make yourself vomit, it hurts!"

As I expected, Charles Dumont was unlike the others. He was patient, sweet and gentle, and never ordered her around. But he didn't obey her either. He was on her own level. That changed Edith and did her worlds of good.

Claude Figus had fallen back into the shadows. His devotion and the love he had ready made me sad. He didn't know what jealousy was. Edith looked better; that was all he asked. When the mood struck her, she paid some attention to him. He wasn't a bad guitar player, and she decided he had the makings of a singer. When she put him to work, Claude seemed to hold the keys to paradise in his hands, he was so blissful.

Charles Dumont didn't live in the boulevard Lannes apartment and that was bad for Edith, who was very lonely. But he did write about thirty songs for her. Some of them will remain "Piaf classics": *"Les Mots d'amour,"* *"La Belle Histoire d'amour"* (Edith wrote the words for that), *"La Ville inconnue,"* *"Les Amants,"* *"Mon Dieu"*:

> *Mon Dieu, mon Dieu, mon Dieu,*
> *Laissez-le-moi, encore un peu,*
> *Mon amoureux . . .*
> *Un jour, deux jours, huit jours . . .*

Laissez-le-moi, encore un peu,
À moi.

Dear God, dear God, dear God,
Let me keep him a little longer,
My love . . .
One day, two days, a week . . .
Let me keep him a little longer,
All mine.

She was in better spirits, but she hadn't really recovered physically yet. After the tour, she was supposed to continue at the
Olympia. Edith hadn't sung for almost a year. She was worried. A
fear stronger than stage fright had her by the throat, nearly par-
alyzing her. I was scared too, and with good reason: this tour
became known as her "suicide tour."

When she went on the first day, at Rheims, the audience gave
her an ovation that wouldn't stop. Her musicians started playing
the opening bars of the first song several times, but each time the
applause and the shouts started up again. Finally Edith sang, but
her throat was so dry she stopped in the middle. Everybody in the
wings had the jitters; it looked like a real disaster. But no—she
started again. And when she sang *"Je ne regrette rien,"* they
called her back three times. She'd made it!

But she counted on strength she just didn't have any more. The
next day she was so pooped she sang almost mechanically. The
audience realized it and was very cool, applauding just as mechanically.

Edith saw the long list of cities in front of her like a snake
waiting to coil itself around her neck and choke her. She had to
keep going, so she took stimulants. She still had the strength, though
this time they were for her own good, to refuse the shots offered
her. She gritted her teeth. "I'll hold out to the end."

The managers knew they were taking risks, that she might
collapse onstage. And for the first time in Edith's career, a few
cities—Nancy, Metz, Thionville—canceled their contracts with her.

At Maubeuge she came close to collapsing again. They had to

pull down the curtain and make an announcement to the howling audience: "Mme Piaf is temporarily indisposed. It's nothing serious. We ask you to be patient for a few minutes." Someone in the audience yelled, "Take her to the hospital! Take her to the Invalides!" Edith heard it and sat up. "Give me a shot—I'm going out there!" Drugs took over again.

The musicians and the stagehands objected. "No, don't; we have no right to do that. Helping her sing is like helping her kill herself!"

"If you won't play, I'll go on without you," said Edith. She'd already parted the curtains. The audience went back to their seats. She returned to the stage and got through it somehow. But at what a price! Singing had become a real martyrdom to her. Every inch of her body hurt and made her feel like screaming. She held out till the very last city, Dreux. The reporters were there like buzzards waiting for her to collapse; they knew it was inevitable. Edith knew it too, but had enough strength to shout, "Not tonight, you guys!"

When the curtain went up, there onstage was a little black figure, her face swollen by antibiotics—a circus puppet with the head of Edith Piaf. It was grotesque and tragic. She was both dying and delirious.

Loulou, Charles Dumont and the musicians all begged her to stop. The manager suggested they clear the house. Edith, who had swallowed half a bottle of stimulants, enough to kill a horse, shouted to them, "If you do that, I'll take a bottle of sleeping pills! Let me sing," she pleaded.

She leaned on the piano so she wouldn't fall. Icy sweat ran down her back. She sang and shouted to the shattered audience: "I love you, you're my life. . . ." Her words rang so true they gave her an ovation, urging her on like a boxer: "Come on, Edith . . . come on! You can do it!"

It was a ghastly bout—the struggle between this little dame and her illness. She wanted to give the audience what was left of her life; they understood and encouraged her. Backstage, everyone had tears in his eyes. But it was too much—she couldn't go on. At her eighth song, she was knocked out. Abruptly she fell to the floor and didn't get up.

No one asked for a refund. The audience filed out of the theater in silence. Each of them felt the pain and suffering of that woman who wanted to give them, to the very end, the best she had in her: her singing, her life.

In the black DS, Loulou and Charles Dumont watched over Edith, who was no more than a little heap of mink shivering with fever. They took her straight to the hospital in Meudon.

She was supposed to appear at the Olympia in sixteen days. Loulou Barrier and Bruno Coquatrix wondered whether they should cancel the contract. The doctors said, "She won't sing," but before she sank into the sleep cure that would finally allow her to rest and to forget, Edith forbade Loulou to cancel the Olympia engagement.

One of the doctors protested. "But madame, it's suicide!"

Edith looked at him and bellowed with all her remaining strength, "That suicide suits me. It's my own."

Six days later, she left Meudon and entered the Ambroise Paré Hospital in Neuilly. She was better. What she needed most was rest and quiet. She spent Christmas in the hospital, and left it on December 27, to rehearse for the Olympia.

On December 29, 1960, the curtain went up on Piaf about to perform in Olympia '61, the best Olympia of all.

Edith overcame everything—illness, drinking, drugs; they were forgotten, swept away. Her martyrdom had purified everything. She was still, and forever, "the Great Piaf." Even though she made a mistake in *"Mon Vieux Lucien"* and stopped short, she laughed, said, "Don't worry!" and started again.

That night Edith sang one of the toughest songs in her repertoire for the first time—*"Les Blouses blanches,"* by Marguerite Monnot and Michel Rivgauche. She began in a soft, distant voice:

> *Ça fera bientôt trois années*
> *Qu'elle est internée,*
> *Internée avec les fous,*
> *Avec les fous.*

Almost three years now
She's been shut up with the crazies,
With the crazies.

Then, as she became imbued with the frenzy of it, she began
to sway:

Et chaque fois il y a les blouses blanches . . .

And every time, the white coats are there . . .

In the song she sees the man she loves and begins dreaming:

Et reviennent les blouses blanches . . .

At the end Edith screamed:

J'suis pas folle, j'suis pas folle . . .

I'm not crazy, I'm not crazy . . .

The audience could no longer stand hearing her as she howled out
her madness. They wanted it to stop, to cut it off. That poor little
creature in black, swaying back and forth, shrieking; it was unbearable! Edith had never been as great as she was at that moment.

When she finally stopped singing, there was silence for several
seconds, and then *le tout Paris* applauded her as never before. The
women were weeping. Flowers fell at Edith's feet onstage as she
bowed. I was at the back of the theater; I had slipped out to the
ladies' room to weep in peace. It was too much; I couldn't take any
more. Someone wrote: "She shatters every idea you had about
her. . . ." "She's Piaf—until now an unknown phenomenon. . . ."
The critics couldn't find words noble enough or beautiful enough,
so they spoke of her in terms applied to the greatest concert and
opera singers, the Maria Callases.

On April 13 Edith left the Olympia for another tour. But she'd
gone too far, she'd pushed herself too much. After Brussels and a
few other cities, she gave up on May 25 and went into the American Hospital in Neuilly, where she was operated on for an intestinal constriction. Once more she made it, and Loulou took her to

his house in Richebourg to recuperate. The day after she got there, on June 9, she had severe pains and went back to the American Hospital, where they operated on her for an intestinal occlusion. Yet again she pulled through.

For several months she lived in slow motion. Charles Dumont never left her side, his dauntless affection perhaps supplying what she needed to help her recover. But the next man in line swept everything before him. And Edith was to live the last and most beautiful love story of all. As she confessed to me: "There have been a lot of men in my life, Momone, but I loved only one: Marcel Cerdan. Yet all my life I've waited for only one: Théo Sarapo. . . ."

Chapter 18

"*Ça sert à ça, l'amour!*"

A few months before she married Théo, Edith said to me, "When I talk about Théo, I feel like beginning, 'Once upon a time . . .'" She was right. It wasn't a story; it was a fairy tale. This love of hers was the most beautiful of them all, the purest.

When Edith chose to, she saw very clearly what went on inside herself and others. "You know, Momone, Marcel and I were very much in love, but he would have left me if he hadn't died. Not because he didn't love me, but because he was honorable, and so was I. He had a wife and three sons, and he would have gone back to them. If I hadn't met Théo, something would have been missing in my life."

Yet Théo Sarapo was the one people reviled the most. Edith was forty-seven, worn out, practically hacked to pieces, and she was famous. He was unknown, twenty-seven, as beautiful as Greek sunlight. Everyone said he was poor, but it wasn't true. His parents were quite well off. And Edith, who everyone thought was rich, was flat broke. No one could believe it, especially when they knew Loulou Barrier had signed a billion and a half old francs' worth of contracts for her. All the same, when she died, Edith left her husband forty-five million francs' worth of debts. To get by and have a little money of his own, Théo had to go and sing abroad; his fees in France were seized along with the ten million in royalties that SACEM still collects on Edith's songs.

Love and money don't often go together. But when the ground is cleared and the circumstances are understood, the story of Edith and Théo can begin, the way she wanted it: "Once upon a time . . ."

The winter of 1962 was a cold one for Edith. There was a chill in her heart and in her bones, and the days were long. "This isn't living. I'm not allowed to do anything; I can't eat or drink what I like or sing or walk. . . . Crying's bad for my morale. All I'm allowed to do is laugh, and I don't feel like it. Laughing and loving are two things no one can order you to do. So I just wait, and for what? I haven't the vaguest idea."

Charles Dumont, Loulou and Guite talked to her about new plans, to keep her going, but they were put off from month to month. Silence and emptiness surrounded her. There were no more good times at Piaf's—she'd run out of money. And going to see her became a good deed; it was considered an act of charity! Of all her friends, it was her men who were the most faithful. Yves phoned, and Pills and Henri Contet stopped by. Charles Aznavour did too, but he didn't have much free time. Raymond Asso didn't forget her either, although he'd grown bitter. When he phoned, it was to criticize, to find fault. Raymond was the only one who never forgave her for leaving him. Constantine was nice.

The old guard remained faithful. They all dropped in to say hello from time to time—both pals and friends: Pierre Brasseur, Robert Lamoureux, Suzanne Flon, Jean Cocteau, Jacques Bourgeat. . . . And her musicians and lyricists: Francis Lai, Noël Commaret, Robert Chauvigny, Michel Rivgauche, Pierre Delanoë, Michel Emer. . . . It sounds like a lot, but it amounted to no one.

On the days when Edith surfaced, there were still evenings and nights on the boulevard Lannes that were pale copies of the old days. The minute she felt better, Edith went too far. When Loulou told her to be careful, she answered, "But who am I supposed to behave myself *for?* Anyway, why? I never did! And I feel so much like living!"

On one of those nights when she just about managed to stand up, Claude Figus brought a pal to see her, a tall boy dressed in black with dark hair and eyes: Theophanis Lamboukas. He sat on the carpet in a corner, like a handsome thoroughbred animal, a kind of big black greyhound, and didn't open his mouth.

"How that guy got on my nerves, Momone! I don't like mutes. He should have left if he was so goddamn bored. I was making Claude work on his record, '*Quand l'amour est fini*' and '*La Robe bleue*,' and that other guy, Théo, sat there listening, not saying a word."

He was so quiet Edith finally forgot he was there in the corner. But he didn't forget her. How could anyone forget Piaf, even if he's only got a second's glimpse of her?

In February 1962, Edith went to the Ambroise Paré Hospital in Neuilly with double pneumonia. She'd run into a draft looking for a likely customer. "I feel right at home in a hospital now, Momone! I know how you should behave, what you should say and, most of all, how goddamn bored you get! So you bet I said yes when they told me someone called Theophanis Lamboukas was asking to see me. What pleased me most was that it wasn't anyone I knew. I was wrong though; it was the guy who'd sat in the corner on the rug. Claude's pal. He didn't bring me flowers, he brought me a little doll. . . . It really got me. He'd had to think about it and then do it. 'I'm a little old for dolls, you know,' I said.

"He laughed. He has a special smile that lights up like a flash. It makes you want to be pretty, even a little too pretty, and smile like he does, even more. . . . He looks like a big black tomcat and you feel like you want to do better than he does. And yet I felt very tiny, there in that hospital bed.

" 'You know, Edith—may I call you Edith?—this isn't just an ordinary doll. It's from Greece, my country.' "

They chatted like that, in a relaxed sort of way, about simple little things. Théo promised to come back the next day, and from the way he said it, she knew that he would and that she'd be waiting for him. . . .

The next day he brought her flowers. He said, "See you tomorrow." He brought her a present every time—nothing very expensive, but never just any old thing. You could tell he'd thought about it. Edith, who had squandered fortunes trying to please people, was now learning that it's the gesture that counts.

After a few days, Edith asked him, "Don't you have anything else to do, coming like this every day?"

"Yes, but I manage."

"I wanted so much for him to talk about himself!" said Edith. "But you'll be surprised to know that I didn't dare ask him questions. He seemed not to be hiding anything from me, but he was under triple lock and key, like a safe. That guy had a secret."

One afternoon he said to her casually, "Do you want me to do your hair?"

"Why? Are you a hairdresser?"

"He blushed, and I felt warm all over," said Edith. "That was his secret; he was a hairdresser. All of a sudden I wanted to be young and beautiful. . . . I felt a pain in my heart. Then I realized I was off on another round of waltzing. In the state I was in, though, the chances were I'd waltz alone. The wreck I'd become, walking arm in arm with that guy? Impossible. I turned away and told him no."

"Are you afraid I don't know how?" he asked.

It wasn't that. She was ashamed to have him touch the bit of thin mossy hair she had left on her skull.

"Théo's hands were made for silky hair, not for three sticks of straw."

He didn't listen to her and fixed her hair.

There were lots of next days. Edith would hold her breath, not daring to say, "See you tomorrow." Happiness musn't be talked about, you should keep it to yourself; it's fragile, anything can spoil it. And if he'd said no? Happiness is frightened of "no"s and clears the hell out!

Since Edith was feeling better, Théo stayed longer. He brought her books.

"Don't you read?" he asked.

"I'd like to, but it tires me."

So, patiently, he read to her.

"I felt like saying *tu* to him. *Tu* is like a caress. But I didn't dare. *Vous* suited us better. This was like an engagement. *Tu* is like a marriage."

Edith left the hospital, and nothing changed.

It took Théo a long time to confess that he wanted to sing.

"You don't know how happy I was, Momone. I could finally do something for him! I gave him a tryout on the spot. He's got everything it takes—a good physique, a voice, and sensitivity." Edith had found another reason to live—creating a new singer. She was the boss again.

"Your name, Theophanis Lamboukas—it's no good. Nobody will ever remember that. Anyway, it sounds too foreign; they'll think you're going to sing in Greek. Théo's good. But Théo what?" Then she came out with one of her rousing old laughs. "Sarapo! Your name will be Théo Sarapo, and it'll be me who gave it to you!" *Sarapo*—"I love you" in Greek. It was one of the few words Edith had picked up during her Athens affair with Takis Menelas, and she hadn't forgotten.

Edith hadn't given a damn about clothes for a long time. She had made an effort for Marcel Cerdan. Then she'd gone through her "couturier" moment when she went to the States, but it hadn't lasted very long. Now she traipsed around in a sweater and skirt the way we'd done when we were young; only occasionally did she wear slacks. Her dresses were fifteen years old. For months she lounged around in an old blue bathrobe a bum wouldn't have wanted.

In his soft, gentle voice Théo said, "We have to get you some clothes. Slacks would look very good on you." He was so loving, so tactful that he'd realized she didn't want to show her body or her legs. So, for him, she tried to be stylish again.

For the first time Edith didn't shout, "I love him! He loves me!" all over the place. She kept it to herself, nice and warm at the bottom of her heart. But it blazed and made her radiant. She beamed so much you forgot what she'd come to look like.

Yes, theirs was an extraordinary love—like in a novel, the kind you always tell yourself is too beautiful to be true. Théo didn't notice that Edith's hands were all knotted up or that she looked like she'd lived a hundred years.

They went to Biarritz together, that city where Edith had suffered so much three years before, just after she broke up with Douglas Davies. No ghosts were waiting for her in her room at the

Hotel du Palais. There would never be any ghosts in Edith's life again. Théo had chased them away.

Edith had always refused to sit in the sun or swim or to have any part of the outdoor life. But Théo didn't have to argue with her. She put on a bathing suit and went out to get a tan like all the other women. She exposed her body alongside theirs, but hers was the only one Théo saw. She didn't need to say to him, "Don't go," or "Come back soon." He never left her side.

"When I looked at that sun-child, handsomer than any of the others, Momone, I told myself that I was selfish, that I didn't know how to love him, that I didn't have the right to chain him to my wrist, that it couldn't last, that I'd done something crazy again. And, for the first time in my life, I felt like being thrifty and not wasteful or throwing away all those minutes, all those hours, all those weeks he'd already given me."

They came back to Paris, and Loulou began to talk to her about contracts again. The first one was for a September show at the Olympia.

"O.K.," said Edith, "but it's got to be with Théo!"

Théo was no professional. He'd just started singing. Loulou wanted to say no, but he said yes. Like the rest of us, he gave in when he saw the two of them together. The impossible became possible. Edith started to work again. Théo said to her, "The best lesson for me is hearing you sing."

At the end of April, Douglas, who was passing through Paris, came to see Edith. The boulevard Lannes had come to life again, though it wasn't the same as before. There were fewer bottles of red wine, fewer employees, and lots of young people, pals of Théo's.

"I want Théo to have friends around, boys like himself," said Edith.

She was happy to see Douglas again, but compared to Théo, he really seemed like a kid; he didn't carry much weight. And to her, no one ever would again. Dougie stayed with them for a few days. As a surprise for Edith, he painted Théo's portrait. "It's for you, Edith. You can hang it next to yours."

When he told Edith he was leaving, she said, "Already?"

"Oh, this was just a little visit. I'll be back...."

On June 3, 1962, Douglas Davies boarded his plane at Orly. A few minutes after taking off, the plane crashed to the ground. Her friends hid the papers from Edith and made sure the radio and television set wouldn't work. No one wanted to break the terrible news to her.

"What's eating all of you? You look like you're going to a funeral." They were tongue-tied. Some deaths can't be kept hidden. Edith found out and began to shriek.

"No, no! It can't be true! He died just the way Marcel did!"

The news hit her like a sledge hammer. She was depressed for days and only snapped out of it long enough to make Théo swear he'd never take a plane.

Once again Edith took to her bed. It was Michel Emer who got her out of it. Edith was penniless. She phoned Michel one day, the way she often did.

"Do you know why I'm calling?"

He had a pretty good idea.

"You've got to manage somehow to get me an advance on my royalties. Sickness is free, but getting well isn't."

"Don't worry, I'll see to it."

He marched straight to the SDRM (Society for the Rights to Reproduce Records of Lyricists, Composers and Music Publishers) and SACEM and got a tidy little sum. When he told Edith the good news, she asked:

"Don't you have a song for me?"

"You know very well I can't write a thing unless I see you."

"I look awful, you know, but come on over if you think you can stand it." Michel dashed over.

"Well, what about it?"

"Nothing. I can't unless I hear you sing."

Edith got up out of bed and sang her old songs and her new ones. It went on and on. Théo was happy. He'd never seen her like that. "Well, Michel, are you pleased?"

"Yes, I've recharged my batteries."

And the next day he brought Edith *"A quoi ça sert l'amour?"*

A quoi ça sert l'amour?

L'amour ne s'explique pas,
C'est une chose comme ça
Qui vient on ne sait d'où
Et vous prend tout à coup.

A quoi ça sert d'aimer?

What good is love?

Love can't be explained,
It's just something
That comes from somewhere or other
And suddenly hits you.

What good is loving?

One thing it's good for is getting engaged. On July 26, 1962, Théo very calmly asked Edith, "Will you be my wife?" He wasn't formal about it. He asked simply and gently, as if afraid he'd terrify her.

"Oh, Théo, I can't!"

"Why not?"

"I've been through so much. The past weighs on me heavy as a ten-ton truck. And I'm so much older than you. . . ."

"As far as I'm concerned, you were born the day I met you."

"But what about your parents? I'm certainly not the girl they've been dreaming of for their son!"

"We'll go and see them tomorrow. They're expecting us for lunch."

"I can't. I'm too frightened."

Edith didn't sleep all night.

"Yves was the only one who ever introduced me to his parents, Momone. But we weren't engaged; it wasn't because we were getting married! Remember reading those cheap novels: 'He introduced her to his parents'? Boy, did we think that sounded nice! It was the beginning of marriage and it was serious business. I haven't deserved such happiness, it's too beautiful. . . ."

All that preyed on her mind. She lay in bed thinking about it while Théo slept at the other end of the apartment. Edith had her own room now; she was a sick woman. Though she'd so loved having a man sleep next to her and considered it an insult if he refused, she couldn't bear it any more.

The lamp on her night table was lighted. She couldn't sleep. She liked the blue walls of her room; they calmed her. She began to daydream about all sorts of things. Her ghosts didn't insult her that night. They wore forgiving smiles. . . .

In the light of her lamp she could see her hands lying on the sheet. She thought of them for the first time in terms of the future. Were these the hands Sacha Guitry had had a plaster cast made of, to keep in his study next to Jean Cocteau's? The hands people had written so many poetic things about, comparing them to flowers and birds . . . to delicate things flying with wings? These two knotty stumps, with tendons and veins? She could barely open them any more for the simplest acts—for drinking or eating. She needed other hands, living hands to help her now. She thought, "I'm responsible for these hands. I ought to have foreseen today."

As if a sparrow could foresee anything!

Large, salty tears rolled down her cheeks burning her skin. That was the dowry she was bringing her fiancé, that boy so much too young for her! She couldn't do it; she had no right. What would she look like sitting next to him at the family table tomorrow? An invalid! It was one of the worst nights of Edith's life. She couldn't accept, but she couldn't say no either. . . .

"*Mon Dieu, laissez-le-moi encore un peu, mon amoureux*. . . ."

When Théo came to her room the next morning, she didn't say a word. She put her makeup on and he did her hair. She put on a blue silk dress. Every time she had her heart set on something she dressed in blue for good luck.

That day she was on time. She and Théo got into her white Mercedes, and she abandoned herself to her fate. She didn't feel like struggling any more; she just sat back and waited to see what would happen. Actually, more than a lot had happened to her in the past, and she'd always paid cash . . . sometimes even in advance. So . . .

She was cold in her old mink coat. Her right hand was in Théo's, and her other hand pressed her stuffed rabbit to her bosom for luck. That was Edith too—her hand held by a man full of life, a shabby mink coat and a stuffed good luck charm. . . .

At LaFrette, on the outskirts of Paris, Théo's parents had closed their beauty shop early. Dressed in their Sunday best, Papa and Mama Lamboukas and Théo's two sisters, Christine and Cathy, were sitting in the living room waiting for Edith Piaf, the fiancée of the boy of the house.

It wouldn't have been possible to carry it off with anyone else, but with Edith, everything became possible, because all people saw were those eyes of hers—like a lost child's. Edith and Théo's family liked each other from the start and they kissed. They thought Mme Piaf a nice, simple woman, and she thought them very likable. She had pictured the lunch as a nightmare, but it proceeded very well. Théo cut Edith's meat for her and quite naturally put her fork in her hand as he talked.

By the time dessert was served, they were all laughing. Edith discovered how happy a family, a real family, can be gathered around a table beneath a chandelier. She was about to have a father-in-law and a mother-in-law. Later she laughed and said, "What an unusual mother-in-law I've got. It's the first time in my life I've ever called a woman 'Mama.' " She was going to have two sisters-in-law as well.

"My heart was absolutely ringing with happiness, Momone, like bells. It had never made such a racket. It was all I could hear!"

Edith had an official engagement party—with just Loulou—at Saint-Jean-Cap-Ferrat, where she'd gone to rest up before the Olympia '62 show, in September. The date of the wedding was set for October 9.

There was a whirlwind of activity on the boulevard Lannes, though Edith had slowed down a bit. She slaved with Théo, correcting everything—his voice, his intonation, his gestures. She put her signed label on him, the way a great couturier does on a dress. She wanted him, too, to be perfect.

Edith's last gala performance was her most glorious. On September 25, 1962, two days before she was to open at the Olympia, she sang from the top of the Eiffel Tower for the premiere of the movie *The Longest Day*. Eisenhower, Churchill, Montgomery, Mountbatten, Bradley, the Shah and Begum of Iran, the King of Morocco, the Prince and Princess of Liège, Don Juan of Spain, Queen Sophia of Greece, Prince Rainier of Monaco, Elizabeth Taylor, Sophia Loren, Ava Gardner, Robert Wagner, Paul Anka, Audrey Hepburn, Mel Ferrer, Curt Jurgens and Richard Burton all had dinner in the gardens of the Palais de Chaillot, along with more than 2,700 spectators who had paid from 30 to 350 new francs a seat.

Edith Piaf, her shadow projected on an immense screen, sang *"Non, je ne regrette rien," "La Foule," "Milord," "Toi tu n'entends pas," "Le Droit d'aimer," "Emporte moi,"* and the last, *"A quoi ça sert l'amour?"* with Théo Sarapo.

I didn't pay a cent and I didn't wear an evening gown, but I'll never forget that night. I could see the Eiffel Tower from my kitchen window (the kitchen had always been Edith's and my favorite spot). So I opened my window on that day, that night unlike any other, and I heard Edith's voice thundering over Paris. It was beautiful yet frightening, like things that are too big for you.

At the Olympia opening, in September 1962, the snobs, the show people and all the others were again in the audience, sharpening their teeth, their claws and their tongues. They came to see Edith display—uncaged and without a net—her latest discovery and her husband-to-be: Théo Sarapo.

When she came on, the audience went wild. Thousands of bravos, whistles and screams: "Bravo . . . bravo . . . Edith . . . Edith!" and then suddenly the whole audience shrieked, "Hip, hip, hurray!" It was like a storm sweeping everything in front of it, then coming to rest at her feet. The public she loved and respected shouted out their love for her before she'd sung a note. For a minute and a half she couldn't begin. Then, with a single gesture of her tiny hand, she quieted them. The orchestra played the opening bars of her first song, and the whole theater became silent as a church. The audience took each word, each gesture to its heart. And throughout her concert, after every song, they gave her an ovation. It was their way of saying thank you.

The "Piaf miracle" had taken place once again. When she sang *"A quoi ça sert l'amour?"* as a duet with Théo, the audience accepted her marriage, and the bravos bore the two of them away in triumph. Edith had won.

Part of the miracle was that Edith managed to hold her hands open, flat against her black dress—that old gesture of hers that she had first made at Leplée's when she'd had stage fright and hadn't known what to do with them.

That night as she left the Olympia, huddled up next to Théo in her white Mercedes, Edith was happy. "You see, Théo, they're ours!"

Théo thought it was mostly her victory and that he'd been accepted in the bargain as a dividend. It had been a brutal shock for him going straight from rehearsals on the boulevard Lannes to the stage of the Olympia. He knew he wasn't a professional and that without her he was nothing. The car stopped in front of the Hotel George V. It was Edith's idea.

"Momone, I'm going to be married. I don't want to go back to that apartment every night. It brings back too many memories. I've suffered too much there and been defeated too many times. Once I'm married, it won't be the same. I can't wait. October ninth seems so far away to me! Important dates like that move further and further away the closer you get to them. . . ."

Singing every night exhausted her, but she didn't want to admit it. On October 4, during the night, she was tortured by excruciating pains in her wrists, her ankles and her legs. She chewed her sheets but didn't want to tell Théo. She went to her doctor and pleaded with him:

"I'm getting married on the ninth, doctor. I've got to hold out till then."

He gave her cortisone, and in two days the worst was over. But that wasn't the end of it. She caught cold and ran a temperature of 104 degrees. She couldn't breathe, but she sang anyway! On the ninth of October, Edith married Théo just as she'd planned at the town hall of the sixteenth arrondissement in Paris, the snobbiest of all.

"I had to laugh listening to all that blah blah blah from the mayor. . . . There I was, a kid from Belleville-Ménilmontant, getting married in that ritzy town hall, sitting in the same seat the people in the sixteenth put the edge of their butts on. All because I rented an apartment in that arrondissement! And when Théo said 'I do' and I did too, it was a bloody shock that got me right in the heart. . . . How happy I was!"

For the second time in her life, Edith heard church bells ringing for her and breathed in the smell of incense. The religious ceremony took place in the Greek Orthodox church, Théo's, surrounded with gold and chantings. And her "I do" was even more explosive than it had been in New York. She was happier than she'd ever been. If only it all could have ended there, as she came out of the church on her husband's arm. . . .

Life had never given Edith many presents, but, as she said to me:

"What a bill I'm going to have to pay! But I'd rather fork over what I owe right away. Then when I get to heaven I won't have any debts, I won't be faced with any more bills; I'll have paid in advance."

That night she sang at the Olympia with her husband. The audience went wild and kept calling for Théo. They wanted to see for themselves, to find out whether she was finally going to be happy. Then she went home, to find a surprise: Théo had furnished the empty rooms. They were cozy now; they didn't look temporary any more. Théo was happy. "See, it isn't your home any more. You've come back to a new home—ours!" That boy had made her happier than she'd ever believed possible.

Personally, I've always thought he was a pure, decent guy and that he loved Edith as nobody ever had before. All he could expect from her were sorrow and debts. Before their marriage, the doctors had informed Théo that there was no hope for her. He knew the truth, and married her anyway, which was proof of great love. The feeling he had for her went far beyond physical love. Thanks to him, Edith believed to the very end that she was still a desirable woman who was loved, when in fact she was no more than a poor dame whose body was wracked with pain that was sometimes unbearable. Up to the very last he gave her what she had lived for—love.

At the end of January 1963, Edith thought she was in good shape again. And that crippled woman, a little black shadow with an oversized head, began to live as intensely as before. She used up her last reserves of energy like a madwoman, never counting the cost. The only thing that kept her head above water was her will-power. Everyone around her was scared to death. All of us knew that the next big wave could carry her off, and that we'd have to watch her go under, unable to save her. She lived that month the way she'd always lived—passionately. At the same time, she was getting ready for an appearance at the Ancienne Belgique in Brussels, a return engagement at Bobino and a tour in Germany. She was sure she could carry it off.

Michel Emer, with René Rouzaud, wrote a very beautiful song for her, "*J'en ai tant vu, tant vu.*"

> *J'en ai trop cru, trop cru, trop cru,*
> *Des boniments de coins de rues,*
> *On m'en a tant dit, j'en ai tant entendu,*
> *Des "je t'adore," des "Pour la vie!"*
> *Tout ça pour quoi? Tout ça pour qui?*
> *Je croyais que j'avais tout vu,*
> *Tout fait, tout dit, tout entendu.*
> *Et je m' disais: "On ne m'aura plus!"*
>
> *C'est alors qu'il est venu!*

I've believed too much, too much, too much,
All that street-corner claptrap,
People have told me so many times, I've heard
 so many times,
"I adore you" and "For the rest of my life."
What was it all for? Who was it all for?
I thought I'd seen everything,
Done everything, said everything, heard everything.
And I said to myself: "I won't be fooled again!"

And then he came along!

The songs they wrote for her now seemed almost like last wills and testaments.

Some young songwriters—Francis Lai, Michèle Vendôme and Florence Véran—wrote her three songs straight off: *"Les Gens,"* *"L'Homme de Berlin"* and *"Margot coeur gros."*

"Momone, as long as the young people love you and write for you, it doesn't matter if you're sick; nothing's changed!"

Edith sang *"Margot coeur gros"* for the first time at the Ancienne Belgique.

> *Pour fair' pleurer Margot,*
> *Margot coeur tendr',*
> *Margot coeur gros,*
> *Il suffit d'un refrain,*
> *Air de guitar',*
> *Pleur d'Arlequin!*
>
> To make Margot cry,
> Tender-hearted Margot,
> Sad-hearted Margot,
> All we need is a refrain,
> A melody on the guitar,
> The tears of Harlequin!

The song was such a hit she phoned Michèle Vendôme that night before she went to sleep. "Your song's off to a great start. I'm happy for you. Come see me in Brussels!"

In February 1963, Edith appeared with Théo at Bobino. Once again she saw the red curtain open in front of her, felt the spotlights on her skin, breathed in the warm smell of her audience and heard their bravos. She introduced two new songs by Francis Lai and Michèle Vendôme. One of them was *"Les Gens."*

> *Comme ils baissaient les yeux, les gens,*
> *Quand tous deux, on s'est enlacés,*
> *Quand on s'est embrassés*
> *En se disant: Je t'aime . . .*
>
> The way people lowered their eyes
> When we put our arms around each other,

When we kissed
And told each other: "I love you" . . .

The other was *"L'Homme de Berlin."*

> *Je m' voyais déjà l'aimer pour la vie,*
> *J' recommençais tout, j'étais avec lui,*
> *Lui, l'homme de Berlin.*
> *Ne me parlez pas de hasard,*
> *De ciel, ni de fatalité,*
> *De prochains retours, ni d'espoir,*
> *De destin, ni d'éternité . . .*
> *Sous le ciel crasseux qui pleurait d'ennui,*
> *Sous la petite pluie qui tombait sur lui,*
> *Lui, l'homme de Berlin.*
> *J' l'ai pris pour l'amour, c'était un passant,*
> *Une éternité de quelques instants*
> *Lui, l'homme de Berlin!*

I could see I'd love him all my life,
I began all over again, I was with him,
The man from Berlin!
Don't talk to me of chance,
Or heaven, or fate,
Or coming back soon, or hope,
Or destiny, or eternity . . .
Beneath the filthy sky weeping with boredom,
Beneath the gentle rain that fell on him,
The man from Berlin.
I thought he was love, but he was a passerby,
An eternity in a moment,
The man from Berlin!

And it was on March 18, 1963, at the opera house in Lille, that Edith sang on a stage for the last time in her life.

Though she had had a relapse that worried everyone, she wanted to make a tape of *"L'Homme de Berlin"* and send it to Germany to be translated. She planned to sing it in German during her tour.

Everyone was against it. Singing calls for a strength she no longer had. This time her reserves had been exhausted. She didn't give a damn, and no one could keep her from working. On April 7, Edith sang *"L'Homme de Berlin"* with her accompanists Noël Commaret and Francis Lai.

From the tape a record was made, which was released five years after Edith's death. It is an extraordinarily moving document. Nothing was left of "the Great Piaf" but her aura. The voice on the record is worn out, and she pants for breath with every word. It's not sung and it's not spoken; the voice comes from very far away, it shatters you . . . and no one but Edith could have done it.

She asked Michèle Vendôme to come over, and after she'd listened to the tape, Edith said, "Vendôme, my poor girl, I'm sorry about your song. It deserved better than that!" Such honesty and generosity right at death's door—that, too, was Edith.

On the tenth of April, Edith came down with pulmonary edema. She was taken to the Ambroise Paré Hospital in Neuilly, and was in a coma for five days. She no sooner came out of it than she had a fit of true madness that lasted for two weeks, during which Théo never left her side. Although she didn't recognize him, he literally lived in her room, wiping the sweat off her forehead and unclenching her hands as they clutched at an imaginary microphone. In her madness Edith thought she was on stage and she sang night and day. Then she snapped out of it and the first thing she said to Théo was, "You didn't deserve that!"

Once again, Edith left the hospital. Théo had decided to take her to the Riviera to convalesce. Almost as if she knew she'd never come back, she did not want to leave the boulevard Lannes apartment. . . .

From 1951 to 1963, Edith Piaf had undergone four automobile accidents, one attempted suicide, four drug cures, one sleep treatment, two fits of delirium tremens, seven operations, three hepatic comas, one spell of madness, two bouts with bronchial pneumonia and one with pulmonary edema.

For almost two years, I had been living in Beauchamp, in the Oise. Everything separated me from Edith. Our lives had become two parallel railroad tracks. I too had spent time in the hospital, had been operated on and had almost died. I didn't weigh much more than she did—around 80 pounds. We walked alongside one another but rarely came together. Luckily there was the telephone.

Edith called me before she left for the Riviera. "Momone, I don't feel like going. . . . My territory is around Ménilmontant. I can get just as much rest here. Anyway, I don't want to miss going to America again! My little pals are waiting for me there; and I'm supposed to sing for Kennedy at the White House. I can't flub that! Imagine meeting that man! . . . He's got everything going for him, courage, brains—and with all that he's handsome too! He is great!"

We chatted like that for a while, and then Edith said:

"Come and see me when you're feeling better. In any case, even if I do go south, I'd like you to come live with me again when I get back."

Edith let Théo talk her into going. He'd rented the villa Serano for her at Cap-Ferrat for two months and at five million francs. It was a mistake. The sea air tired Edith; it was so invigorating that her nerves and lungs couldn't stand it. So Théo took her to the mountains close by, to "La Gatounière," in Mougins.

In June she went into another hepatic coma and had to have several blood transfusions. She had another relapse during the month of July, and on August 20 went into a third hepatic coma and was taken to the Méridien Hospital in Cannes. The doctors considered her case hopeless. For a week she was tenderly rocked to and fro by death as it waited for her to go to sleep forever in its arms.

Théo watched over her night and day. He hadn't left her once since the day he'd met her. Nothing disgusted him, and nothing could estrange him from her. He cared for her as if she were his mother, child and wife.

When she left the hospital, Théo took her to Plascassier, above Grasse. And in September that dying woman, who could barely walk, who was taken around in a wheelchair, was still listening to *"L'Homme de Berlin,"* and had decided to go back to work.

Physically Edith wasn't even a caricature of her former self. She weighed a little over seventy pounds, and her face was as bloated as a moonfish. The only thing left were the violet eyes and the look of the girl who had once been "La Môme Piaf."

Her mind and spirits were unchanged, but so was her character. She was as unbearable as ever. She refused to be sensible—to go on a diet or to sleep regular hours. She wanted to see a movie every night. Since she could no longer go to a theater, Théo had bought her a projector while they were still on the boulevard Lannes. He brought it with them to Plascassier, and every evening he showed her films. She still burst into laughter, and the famous "Piaf laugh" had not lost its ring. She never hesitated to spend what was left her of life.

I had a very hard blow, which fortunately never affected Edith, because it was hidden from her. On September 5, 1963, I read in the newspaper that Claude Figus had died at the age of twenty-nine. . . .

Like a well-brought-up helper, our little Claude had gone ahead to open the doors of death for his boss, the woman he had truly loved. The few sentences in the newspapers pained me: "Claude Figus has committed suicide. Two empty bottles of barbiturates were found next to his body in his hotel room. On several occasions he had announced his intention of ending his life, since all it had ever brought him was disappointment in love." Poor little guy! Yet his last record was just about to come out; he sang one of his own compositions on it, *"Les Jupons."*

"On Saturday evening," the paper reported, "he tore off the medal he always wore around his neck and gave it to friends, shouting, 'I won't be needing it any more. . . .' " It was the medal Edith had given him when he became what he laughingly called "the half boss." He didn't have the stature to be anything else, but it had made him happy for a while. . . . He'd believed it!

Next to the article about Claude was another headed: "In Her Retreat at Plascassier, Edith Piaf Is Still Unaware of Her Ex-Secretary's Tragic Death." The article read: " 'She mustn't hear us. She knows nothing about it yet; we've hidden it from her. We have to prepare her for it gently,' a spokesman said yesterday afternoon at the 'Enclos de la Rourre' at Plascassier, where Edith

Piaf is now living with her husband, Théo Sarapo." The article ended with: "We asked about Edith Piaf's health. 'Her condition is encouraging,' her nurse told us, 'and she has come here to convalesce.'"

How much longer would she hold out? She was still talking about the Olympia, Germany, the United States. . . .

Chapter 19

᎗
᎗ ᎗
᎗

I Can Die Now—I've Lived Twice!

I'll never forget that day. It was a Wednesday. The sky was a dirty gray, and Paris looked unwashed. My spirits had hit bottom. My skin hurt all over and felt too tight. The news I'd been getting about Edith worried me: "She can't come to the phone. . . ." "There's no great change. . . ." "She's about the same. . . ."

This was October 9, 1963. It was her wedding anniversary. I thought, "I'll call her; she'll be pleased." I phoned Plascassier and got Edith right away. A real piece of luck! I was so sure someone else would answer that at first I didn't even recognize her voice. We didn't talk long. I was so upset I barely noticed; it only struck me later. She said, "Come see me, Momone!" And I answered, "O.K., I'll come Monday." She wasn't pleased. She always wanted what she wanted when she wanted it. And she always said, "I've waited around too much in this goddamn life of mine to be patient." Her voice was clear, but weak. It didn't have the Piaf timbre.

"Monday's a long way off, Momone. . . . Can't you come sooner? Can't you manage to make it before that? . . ."

"No, Edith, I really can't come before Monday."

She didn't press me too hard. She seemed resigned. And Edith resigned meant things weren't going well, or rather, that they were going badly. She suddenly sounded pitiful, like an unhappy kid.

"All right. I'll expect you on Monday, without fail."

I hung up. My mind wasn't working, and I sensed there was something wrong, something I couldn't grasp, something I should have caught on to. Then it came to me: *Edith was calling me!* Not a second to lose—I had to go right away.

I phoned the travel agency. I didn't have a cent, but that had never stopped either of us when we'd made up our minds to do something. I'd been to the "Piaf school." So I asked the travel agency for a round-trip ticket to Nice. I borrowed thirty thousand francs from my grocery woman, who gave it to me without a qualm, and dashed to Orly, in slacks, taking with me nothing but my handbag.

As I sat in the plane, I had the feeling it wasn't making any headway, that it was motionless in the sky. Until I reached Edith, I had the impression I was two people. One Simone was watching a film in which another Simone was playing the part of Simone who was blind.

It was cold at the airport in Nice. There was a freezing wind making my blood congeal, and I couldn't believe it was the Riviera. When I saw myself standing there in the waiting room, no one with me, surrounded by all the mirrors and metal fixtures, I began to shiver. I had the feeling someone had put me in a refrigerator. My spirits dropped to a new low.

There was almost no one around. I'd taken the last flight. In the neon light everybody seemed to be made out of wax. It looked like Madame Tussaud's and gave me the jitters.

I wanted to talk to someone in the Air France bus to Nice. Edith and I had memories of this part of the country. I knew so well those little lights of the Baie des Anges winking in the darkness. All the memories I had started coming back to me. . . . My skull was stuffed with so many images it almost exploded, and I had more and more of a lump in my throat. Outside the dirty windows of the bus, the best years of our lives went past.

In Nice I found a taxi to take me to Grasse. Waiting till the next day, taking several buses and all the rest of it was out of the question. Edith had said, "Come!" I'd finally got the message, and I knew I couldn't waste a second. . . .

It was easy getting to Grasse, but nobody had any idea where Plascassier was perched. Just my luck: the taxi driver wasn't an amusing little Niçois, but a dried-up old man who wasn't talkative. He didn't know the region, which didn't keep him from taking me on a joy ride. He was having a look around, along with me. He finally stopped in a village. The town was deserted and all the shops were closed, except for a combination bistro-grocery. He had the nerve to say, "Go ask; there's a light on in there."

The owner's wife was a fat, oily, blabbering old hag. "Edith Piaf's house! She won't let you in at this hour of the night, you poor thing! She's very sick. We know her well. We're the ones who deliver M. Théo's groceries. To tell you the truth, I think the poor dear's about done for. You won't be able to see her tomorrow either. She won't even let reporters in. . . ."

"I'm her sister!" I shouted, and felt better.

"Oh, I see! Don't get angry. . . . I couldn't tell from your face. . . . Still . . . now that I've got a good look at you, there is a resemblance. . . . I'll call my husband. He'll go with you."

So off we started again. Since the husband was annoyed, the only words he spoke were to urge the driver to go faster. "You can't miss Plascassier. It's inside the Enclos de la Rourre park, on a sort of plateau."

It was getting colder and colder. The wind was vicious. Everything looked alike in the headlights. "We're lost!" I thought. When he'd had enough of the whole thing, the husband said to the taxi driver:

"It's there, down that road. . . ."

"I can't go any farther. The road's not built for cars. There's a house in there, you'll see. . . ."

I paid, and the two of them took off. They'd been wrong, of course. I sank into some goddamn muck. It had rained. Moonlight was splashing into the water, and I was splashing in the puddles. I was dead beat, but I was like a robot wound up tight. I'd have gone to the very end that night. I wasn't too sure what the end was, but it was something I had to get to. Finally I saw a squashed house

. . . at least that's the way it looked. There was a dim light on. I went up to it and looked through the windowpane.

Behind it was a scene straight out of a movie. I saw a kitchen. It looked nice and warm. Lots of good-smelling things were probably stewing in there. Around the table were the Bonels. I knew them very well. They'd been working for Edith for over ten years. The wife, Danièle, had become a sort of all-round secretary, as always happened with Edith, and Marc was Edith's accordionist. Like his wife, he too did a little bit of everything. There'd never been much love lost between us. I'd never thought they were bad, but they were a little like leeches. And they thought I cramped their style. It was true: the short time we'd lived together hadn't made us any fonder of each other. All the same, I must admit they were devoted to Edith in their own way. Our ways differed, that's all.

I knocked on the windowpane and they raised their heads. Then Danièle motioned to her husband to open the window. He took his time about it, and asked:

"What are you doing here?"

"I've come to see Edith."

He opened the door for me. They were in the process of cooking a rabbit. I hadn't eaten, and even if it was theirs, I felt like having some.

"We must inform M. Théo," they said formally.

Théo was with Edith. He came downstairs. When I saw him framed in the doorway I simply smiled at him, though I hadn't smiled for hours. He brought a breath of Edith with him as he entered the room. It was all around him; I felt it and recognized it. This was a guy you could depend on; he was good, and he loved Edith. I didn't know him. I hadn't been at their wedding; I'd been sick. I'd seen him at the Olympia and at Bobino, and Edith had told me a lot about him.

Théo was dressed all in black and was wearing a turtleneck sweater. He stood out against the white wall like a photograph. He had beautiful, quick-moving hands—the kind Edith liked—the usual medal around his neck, and chain around his wrist, and a wedding ring on his finger.

"If a guy's got *really* elegant hands, Momone, there can't be anything ugly inside him. Hands don't lie like faces. Especially when they speak. . . ."

All that ran through my mind in less than three seconds, but it stuck.

"You're Simone, her sister?"

And he smiled at me—a warm, tender, rather shy smile answering mine. It did us both good.

Even if she hadn't told me about him, I would have understood everything—how and why she loved him. The way he moved about like a big, slim tomcat, his hands, his smile—everything about him said that he was Edith's man, and above all that he was good, honest and sincere. "I don't think you can see Edith right now. She's going to sleep."

Behind him was a woman in white. It was Simone Margantin, the nurse. She didn't look either friendly or unfriendly. She seemed sleek and a little stiff. But I knew that Edith was fond of her, that this woman was very devoted to her and efficient. The last time Edith had been in a coma, she'd helped the doctors a great deal. And Théo trusted her completely.

She said, "Edith was much better today—truly resurrected. But she needs rest now. I don't think you'll be able to see her; I'm just about to give her her injection. You'll have to come back tomorrow."

I understood her. She was protecting her patient. It always got to be a real free-for-all, getting Edith to sleep. But I'd come to see her and I would see her. I'm not very tall or very substantial, but I had the impression I filled the whole room all by myself. She wanted me to leave! How? On foot?

I pointed out very sweetly:

"I've sent the taxi away. . . . But perhaps you have a tent? . . . I could camp under Edith's window; I wouldn't disturb her."

Then even more sweetly:

"You may not know it, but Edith called me this morning and told me to come."

Then Théo, in his own quiet way, implying, "Maybe you've

forgotten that *I'm* her husband," said, "If Edith wanted to see you, Simone, I'll go upstairs and tell her you're here."

While I waited in silence, old Bonel stirred her rabbit furiously enough to curdle the sauce.

When Théo came back down, he was absolutely joyous. "Come up right away. She's waiting for you."

They all looked astonished. They shouldn't have. It was only natural; it didn't amaze me. The hard part had been getting word to Edith that I was there.

I don't remember what the stairway was like. But I looked at the door of her room and at Théo's hand resting on the knob. He had something to tell me. Very softly, he asked:

"I take it you haven't seen her for a few months?"

"It was just before you got married. I was sick. We've mostly talked on the phone."

"She's changed a lot, Simone . . . but don't let on to her. . . ."

When he opened the door I saw what he meant. She was almost bald. Her face was too round, and all you could see were two very large eyes that devoured everything and a mouth that seemed to be caved in.

I smiled at her. Or rather, I tried to smile at her, as I always had when she'd say to me, "You're a good girl, you're a little soldier!"

"Oh, Momone, am I happy! I didn't expect you till Monday."

"Well, I've got something else I have to do Monday, so I came earlier," I said.

"I'm glad you did."

Théo had left the room. He was tactful too! The guy had every virtue there is!

"What do you think of him, Momone? He's great, isn't he?"

"He's better than that, Edith."

Was that why she'd had me come? I'd known all the others, and she wanted to know what I thought of this one.

"You understand me, don't you?"

"Of course!"

"I've changed, haven't I? No, don't bother denying it; it's not worth the trouble any more. It's hard, you know, to be a rag doll in the hands of other people, even if they're nice. The days and the nights are long, and I have time to think. I've done things that are worse than just damn foolish; I've ruined lots of things—my loves, my health. I don't deserve Théo, and I got him; so I think I've been forgiven. Right, Momone?"

Tears came to my eyes. It was horrible. Luckily she changed the subject. She smiled at me; she was happy. I was the only one she could talk to about her youth, about our old man, about her daughter, about P'tit Louis. . . . I was her witness.

"Do you remember . . ." Suddenly our whole life was in that room. Memories began swarming in, vivid and impatient, like a litter of little mice.

Edith no longer looked like a wretched invalid with no interest in anything. She was alive. She was no longer a dead woman who continued to breathe, barely kept alive by her heartbeats. She was Edith Piaf again, the same as always. Propped up against her pillows, almost in a sitting position, she had rosy cheeks, shining eyes, and she was laughing.

Only her poor deformed hands picking and scratching at the sheets reminded me that Edith was near the end. I didn't want to look at them.

"Oh, Momone, it does me good having you here. You know, my nurse has the same name as you. When I call her, I sometimes think you're still here, that you'll come. . . ."

I thought, "In two seconds she'll accuse me of having ditched her, the way she always does."

"I know this isn't the right time to talk about it, but I'll always wonder why you ran out on me."

It made me laugh, and Edith laughed too. How good it was to hear her laugh! It was no longer the laugh that had been too big for her. This one was just her size, weak and a little broken.

"No more than ten minutes!" the nurse had said. It had been much longer than that when Théo came in. He looked at Edith and then at me. His happiness did me good.

"I haven't seen Edith like this for a long time," he said.

He looked at us. He was trying to understand how it was between us. "Mind if I come in?" he asked.

"What an idea!" Edith answered. "You'd never be in the way. Anyway, if you bother us, we'll go into the bathroom—won't we, Momone?"

This time Théo didn't understand. He couldn't know. "But, Edith, you can't get out of bed!" he exclaimed.

Edith went on laughing.

"You couldn't understand, Théo. Explain it to him, Momone. Tell him about our life together."

He stretched himself out at the foot of the bed like a faithful dog. That's the way I'll always see him, a faithful dog, with loving eyes that refused to see reality, a reality I'd grasped at once: Edith was near the end. The curtain was about to come down. She'd got him so used to miracles he'd lost sight of reality. But it had struck me the moment I saw her. Edith could stay up all night if she felt like it. It wasn't all that important any more. . . .

And so Edith and I began to relive forgotten hours at a mad pace. We aired all the memories of our childhood and our youth in front of Théo with no restraint—there wasn't time to be restrained. Our stories came tumbling out in a heap. We were the only ones who could sort them, because Théo couldn't keep up. Everything poured out, faster and faster, round and round, like a carnival in Pigalle.

"Do you remember the little sailors, our pimps, the legionnaires, P'tit Louis, Papa Leplée? . . ."

"Do you remember . . . ?" All our sentences began that way. But that night Edith was completely honest. It didn't bother her any more to confess to me, "I lied to you that day . . ." or "I shouldn't have done that. . . ." She saw everything so clearly it frightened me.

There was a real whirlwind in my head. The past and the present were all mixed up, and the whole time my eyes never left Edith. Her sick woman's face was replaced for me alone—though perhaps also for Théo—by the glorious face of "the Great Piaf." She wanted to talk; she was all pink and wide awake. "You don't forget a night like this, kids!" she said. "I'll take this one to paradise with me."

As he listened to us, Théo discovered an unknown Edith. What struck me was that she talked only about her childhood, her youth and the present. That night Edith linked the beginning of her life to the end, securely and forever. . . . She wanted to explain to Théo what it had been like when she and I were young. He was putting eau de cologne on her face, combing her hair and washing her hands. He couldn't straighten out the gnarled fingers, crippled by rheumatism.

I felt like crying when I remembered those hands that used to live a song in the spotlight. I thought especially of one familiar gesture—her hands laid flat on her hips; almost on her belly, on the black of her dress, hands that seemed both to caress and to beg forgiveness. She'd repeated that gesture thousands and thousands of times, and she was trying to do it now on the bedsheet. Her hands were searching for the right place.

She was letting Théo take care of her. Little by little she was becoming a sick woman again. She looked at him, and I could see all the joy he gave her reflected in her eyes. "He's wonderful, isn't he, Momone?"

Yes, indeed. He certainly was. And this time I wasn't bluffing.

She wanted to talk shop, talk about her work, but I could feel her floating away. "I've had it this time, you know. I've decided to take care of myself. I'm working on my return engagement at the Olympia. That's serious business." For a few hours that night, as Théo and everyone else around agreed a bit later, Edith for the last time made us think she was going to pull through yet again.

Did she realize how sick she was? Was she sure everything was going to come out all right? I don't think so. She wanted to believe it just a little while longer, a few more hours . . . but her call to me, to her past, was of a kind that indicated finality.

She lowered her voice, and just the way as, at sixteen, she said, "I'd love to sing," she now said, "I'd love to sing some more. . . ."

The nurse gave her an injection. Edith still wanted to talk, to go on reliving her life, but it was all getting a little confused now.

In her old domineering way she declared, "You'll sleep downstairs in the living room. I'll see you tomorrow."

And with that, she took my hand. Her fingers closed on mine

like a sparrow's claw. A very strong, very warm current flowed between us. When Edith touched you, something happened. I'd have done anything to keep that current flowing. I didn't know there was nothing more to keep. . . .

She opened her eyes again. They already had a vacant stare. Then she said to me in a very loud voice, like a cry, "I can die now, I've lived twice!"

She paused for a moment, and then said:

"Be careful Momone. All the damnfool things you do in life you pay for. . . ."

I knew just what she meant. I knew it only too well. I kissed her and said good-bye. I knew what was happening. I didn't want to believe it, but I knew. It was all over. I wasn't mistaken. At dawn Edith went into a semi-coma and never came out of it.

At the door Théo said to me, "I'll leave you, Simone. It was fine; I'm glad you came. It was awfully nice of you to do that. I don't want to leave her now." And he went back to his wife.

I went down to the kitchen again with the Bonels and the small rabbit. They made coffee to stay awake. They didn't say, "You're thirsty; would you like a glass of water?" much less, "Stay here and sleep; your plane isn't till noon." They knew that. Danièle raised her head, looked at me through her glasses and said, "Are you leaving?"

Edith had ordered me to sleep downstairs in the living room, but the order hadn't got down to the kitchen. Yesterday, any order given by "Mme Edith" was carried out. This morning—it was 4 A.M.—Edith was no longer the boss. They realized I wouldn't bother Théo and wouldn't go back up to her bedside. . . . So one of them said, "There's . . . uh . . . what's his name, the chauffeur, who'll drive you to the airport."

It must have been five o'clock in the morning when we got there. The guy just left me, without even asking if I wanted some coffee or anything. The airport at that hour was a futuristic vision of end-of-the-world desolation. There wasn't a soul around. Finally I came across a nice employee who said he'd try to get me a seat on the seven-thirty plane.

So I took a taxi back to Nice and wandered around. Nice isn't a town that gets up at dawn. It yawns for a long time. It isn't easy to find a café open at that time of the morning to have a cup of coffee.

I had such a lump in my throat nothing would have gone down. The thought occurred to me that no one could like the sort of life we'd lived any more. . . . I went back to the Boîte à Vitesses, our Hotel Gioffredo, the passage Negrin. . . .

I returned to the airport and took the plane. I was exhausted.

When I got home, I went to bed but couldn't sleep. I tossed and turned, while all the past, all those images that haunted me, were jostling about in my head. It made a frightful racket. I collapsed.

I must have finally dozed off. The next morning the young boy downstairs came up. He seemed to have important news to announce. He looked so excited I couldn't tell if it was good news or bad. Finally he came out with: "Your sister's dead."

I knew it, but I didn't want to believe it. The boy went to get me the paper. It was true. Edith was dead. She'd gone to sleep and never waked up. It slammed me smack in the gut. If I hadn't gone to Plascassier, I'd never have seen her again. . . . Luckily she'd made me understand that Monday would be too late! and I'd dropped everything and gone. If I'd been small, I'd have weighed things and decided it wasn't sensible, and I'd have missed her last hours. . . .

Edith's body was brought back to the boulevard Lannes. She'd always said, "I want to die in Paris." She made her last trip in an ambulance. Théo took a big bouquet of mimosa from her room at Plascassier and placed it on her body. The bouquet is still in the boulevard Lannes apartment. It was put there six years ago, and it hasn't lost a single blossom or leaf; it has simply turned gray. There's no more sunshine in it. . . .

Nobody knew Edith had died in the south of France. It was more practical to say she'd died on the boulevard Lannes so people could pay their last respects. Even those who didn't like her or didn't give a damn about her came. Being there made a good impression: there were a lot of photographers on hand. . . . People

Edith had never even known came and went, solemn looks on their faces.

But the "little people" of Paris were there too, clinging to the iron gate in front of the house; they had begun their long vigil. Women with shopping bags and men in work clothes didn't hesitate to take an extra hour's subway ride on their way home from work to come say good-bye to Edith. All day long, a good part of the night and again early the next morning, the people she'd loved so much filed past. Women left simple little bunches of flowers, the only kind Edith liked. (She never used to take the baskets of flowers home from her dressing room; she gave them away.) Those simple women apologized to the maid: "Tell her husband I can't come to the funeral tomorrow. . . ." "This isn't much of a bouquet, but my heart's in it. . . ."

Those women, Edith's sisters, were thinking of Théo Sarapo, who'd collapsed in a corner of the beautiful apartment, crying like a baby over that fragile dead woman he'd only had a little more than a year to love. He kept saying, "I never believed it. . . . She'd got me too used to miracles!"

In Edith's bedroom were her old slippers and, on a chair, her little wool bed jacket, along with the brand-new leather coat Théo had just given her. (She'd liked it so much she never wore it.) The closets were full of her old dresses, and the famous black dress was hanging there, a little dead thing no one dared touch. Manuscripts and scores lay all over the piano. If Edith's lifeless body hadn't been lying motionless on the bed, it would have been easy to imagine she might come in and shout, "Why the hell are all of you standing around looking like it's somebody's funeral? You're really a bunch of weaklings!"

Théo's mother and his sisters—Edith's last family—were there with him.

On October 14, 1963, Paris wept for Edith Piaf. Forty thousand people crowded into the Père Lachaise cemetery. . . . Her funeral was like her life—crazy! It was a beautiful warm day. The black crepe was drowned in a sea of color. There were the guys from the Foreign Legion in uniform, soldiers who had never seen her but were all in love with her. Eleven cars of flowers followed the little body, lost in its big casket, and next to her lay the stuffed rabbit she'd had for good luck when she got engaged.

Everyone who'd had a part in her life was there, everyone who'd loved her and everyone she'd loved. . . . "Edith's men" no longer had on their blue uniforms—they were all in black.

The wives of the Parisians she'd loved so much, old grannies in shawls, wept for Edith. She, who'd never had a real mother, had thousands of them that day. There were men of all ages, even an old sailor in blue with a red rose in his hand, unashamed of the big tears flowing from his dimmed blue eyes. . . .

When the casket entered the row of graves where she was to be buried, the crowd went mad, rushing forward and breaking through the barricades. A great wave of people overwhelmed the police, pouring out over the graves, and finally stopped at the foot of the Gassion plot in section 97, row 3. Marlene Dietrich, in mourning, with a black silk scarf over her blond hair and looking very pale underneath her makeup, turned her head toward all those people and said, "How they loved her!"

The murmur of the crowd was like the sound of a raging sea —a long deep breath, vast and rumbling. Suddenly it stopped and there was silence. The detachment of legionnaires came to attention, the pennant of the Legion fluttered in the sunshine, and Father Leclerc said the Pater Noster.

Edith, who had loved God all her life, who sang to the glory of Jesus, who beseeched "Mr. Saint Peter," who adored little Saint Theresa of the Infant Jesus, who so often took refuge in a church, was not allowed to have a last mass said for her. Rome had declared that she had "lived in a state of public sin." But a bishop, Monsignor Martin, and Father Thomeur de Villaret took it upon themselves, as private individuals, to pray at her grave.

The grave gradually disappeared beneath the flowers, as all day long the crowd filed past.

The next day Jean Cocteau was also buried. He had died the same day as Edith, just as he was getting ready to read a funeral eulogy for his great friend Edith Piaf over the radio.

That evening Théo wanted to be alone. He went back all by himself to the disorderly apartment, with forgotten flowers smelling of the cemetery strewn all over it. On a table was a piece of wood carved in the shape of a leaf, bearing Edith's motto: "Love Conquers All!"

The papers carried front-page spreads on Edith, and for days afterward they offered their readers slices of her life. On her grave in the cemetery, towering over the flowers that by now were faded, was a huge bunch of purple wild flowers, tied with a tricolor ribbon, reading: "To their *môme Piaf*. The Legion."

Yes, Edith's grand finale was a success.

When I got home from the cemetery, I threw myself on the bed. I didn't cry; I had no more tears. The way I felt was beyond tears, beyond any sorrow I'd ever known. It wasn't only a sister I'd lost, but also a whole lifetime spent with her. She had always promised not to leave me alone. When she used to say to me, "I want to die young," I'd answer, "What about me?" "Oh, you'll come with me. . . ." It seemed logical to her, and I ended up believing it. Yet I was still here, and everything was spinning and. . . . It was enough to drive you crazy. . . .

To me Edith isn't dead. She's on tour. One day she'll come back and call me.

Very softly, and for me alone, I could hear her singing the poem Michel Emer had dedicated to her:

> *Une chanson à trois temps:*
> *Fut sa vie, et son cours.*
> *C'est beaucoup de chagrins,*
> *Et pourtant, c'est pas lourd.*
> *Toi, passant qui t'arrête,*
> *Fais pour elle une prière.*
> *On a beau être grand,*
> *On finira poussière.*
> *Pour laisser derrière soi*
> *Une chanson de toujours,*
> *Car l'histoire, on l'oublie,*
> *C'est un air qu'on retient,*

Une chanson à trois temps,
Voilà qui est parisien. . . .

A song in three-quarter time:
That was her life, and the way she lived it.
There were lots of sorrows,
Yet they didn't weigh heavily.
If you pass by, stop,
Say a prayer for her.
Even the very great
End as dust.
But she leaves behind
An eternal song,
For we forget the words,
It's the melody we remember,
A song in three-quarter time,
Voilà a Parisian. . . .

The author is grateful to the following music publishers who graciously gave their permission to quote extracts of Edith Piaf's songs.

All these songs were recorded on the Pathé-Marconi and Philips labels.

Editions PAUL BEUSCHER-ARPÈGE, 25 bd. Beaumarchais, Paris 4ᵉ:
"*Simple comme bonjour*" (R. Carlès, Louiguy).
"*Elle fréquentait la rue Pigalle*" (R. Asso, L. Maitrier).
"*Où sont-ils tous mes copains?*" (M. Monnot, Piaf).
"*De l'autr' côté d' la rue*" (M. Emer)
"*Le Brun et le blond*" (H. Contet, M. Monnot).
"*Elle a des yeux*" (M. Monnot, Piaf).
"*Mais qu'est-ce que j'ai?*" (M. Achard, M. Monnot).
"*Demain il fera jour*" (M. Achard, M. Monnot).
"*Petite si jolie*" (M. Achard, M. Monnot).
"*Mariage*" (H. Contet, M. Monnot).
"*Formidable*" (G. Bécaud, V. Vernardet).
"*A quoi ça sert l'amour?*" (M. Emer).
"*Et pourtant*" (M. Emer, P. Brasseur).
"*C'est merveilleux*" (H. Contet, M. Monnot).

Editions CHAPPELL, 4 rue d'Argenson, Paris 8ᵉ:
"*Margot coeur gros*" (M. Vendôme, F. Véran) (Copyright Chappell S.A.).

Editions SALABERT, 22 rue Chauchat, Paris 9ᵉ:
"*Milord*" (M. Monnot, Moustaki).

We should also like to thank, for their permission:

Les Editions Raoul Breton, 3 rue Rossini, Paris 9e:
"*La Petite Boutique*" (Roméo Carlès, O. Hodeige) (Copyright 1937–1965 by Ed. Vianelly).
"*Bal dans ma rue*" (M. Emer) (Copyright 1949 by Ed. Edimarton).
"*Monsieur Lenoble*" (M. Emer) (Copyright 1948 by France Music Co., N.Y. Ed. Breton).
"*L'Hymne à l'amour*" (M. Monnot, Piaf) (Copyright 1949 by Ed. Edimarton).
"*Je t'ai dans la peau*" (Gilbert Bécaud, Jacques Pills) (Copyright 1952 by France Music Co., N.Y. Ed. Vianelly).

Les Editions Fortin, 4 cité Chaptal, Paris 9e:
"*Les Mômes de la cloche*" (Decaye, V. Scotto).

Les Editions Musicales Hortensia, 46 rue de Douai, Paris 9e:
"*Bravo pour le clown*" (Louiguy, H. Contet).

Les Nouvelles Editions Meridian, 5 rue Lincoln, Paris 8e:
"*Les Gens*" (F. Lai, M. Vendôme).
"*Paris-Méditerranée*" (R. Asso, H. Cloarec).
"*Les Trois Cloches*" (Gilles).
"*Mon Dieu*" (C. Dumont, M. Vaucaire).
"*Les Blouses blanches*" (M. Monnot, M. Rivgauche).

Les Editions Métropolitaines, 3 rue Rossini, Paris 9e:
"*La Foule*" (A. Cabral, M. Rivgauche) (Copyright 1958 by Julio Korn-Buenos Aires-Publ. 1958 Les Ed. Métropolitaines).

Les Editions Patricia–S.E.M.I., 5 rue Lincoln, Paris 8e:
"*J'en ai tant vu*" (M. Emer, R. Rouzaud).
"*L'Homme de Berlin*" (F. Lai, M. Vendôme).

S.E.M.I., 5 rue Lincoln, Paris 8e:
"*L'Etranger*" (R. Malleron, M. Monnot).
"*Browning*" (R. Asso, Gilles).
"*Mon Légionnaire*" (R. Asso, M. Monnot).
"*Le Fanion de la Légion*" (R. Asso, M. Monnot).
"*Les Grognards*" (P. Delanoë, Giraud).
"*Non, je ne regrette rien*" (C. Dumont, M. Vaucaire).
"*L'Accordéoniste*" (M. Emer).

Index

72 73 74 75 10 9 8 7 6 5 4 3 2 1